Minority Stages

MUSIC AND PERFORMING ARTS OF ASIA AND THE PACIFIC

Series Editor: Frederick Lau

Javaphilia: American Love Affairs with Javanese Music and Dance

Henry Spiller

Hearing the Future: The Music and Magic of the Sanguma Band

Denis Crowdy

Vamping the Stage: Female Voices of Asian Modernities

Edited by Andrew N. Weintraub and Bart Barendregt

Broken Voices: Postcolonial Entanglements and the Preservation of Korea's Central Folksong Traditions

Roald Maliangkay

Making Waves: Traveling Musics in Hawai'i, Asia, and the Pacific

Edited by Frederick Lau and Christine R. Yano

Song King: Connecting People, Places, and Past in Contemporary China

Levi S. Gibbs

Minority Stages

SINO-INDONESIAN PERFORMANCE AND PUBLIC DISPLAY

JOSH STENBERG

University of Hawaiʻi Press
Honolulu

© 2019 University of Hawaiʻi Press
All rights reserved
Paperback edition 2021

Printed in the United States of America

26 25 24 23 22 21 6 5 4 3 2 1

Library of Congress Cataloging-in-Publication Data

Names: Stenberg, Josh, author.
Title: Minority stages : Sino-Indonesian performance and public display / Josh Stenberg.
Description: Honolulu : University of Hawaiʻi Press, [2019] | Includes bibliographical references and index.
Identifiers: LCCN 2018061662 | ISBN 9780824876715 (cloth : alk. paper)
Subjects: LCSH: Ethnic theater—Indonesia. | Chinese—Indonesia—Social life and customs. | Performing arts—Indonesia.
Classification: LCC PN2219.E84 S74 2019 | DDC 792.02/2—dc23
LC record available at https://lccn.loc.gov/2018061662

ISBN 978-0-8248-9245-6 (paperback)

University of Hawaiʻi Press books are printed on acid-free paper and meet the guidelines for permanence and durability of the Council on Library Resources.

Cover art: *(front)* Sino-Indonesian *barongsay* dancers greet a ship approaching Kemaro Island, Palembang, 2016. Photo by author. *(back)* Fat Cu Kung procession in Jakarta, 2012. Photo courtesy of Kristyna Cilkova.

CONTENTS

ACKNOWLEDGMENTS

THROUGHOUT the various stages of study and phases of research that have ultimately resulted in this book, I have been overwhelmed by the generosity of individuals and institutions in Indonesia. I am afraid that there can be no adequate accounting of all my debts of gratitude here, but I would like to mention the following: Mr. and Mrs. Zhou Xinghua; members of Yayasan Dana Sosial Priangan and Vihara Darma Ramsi; Toni Harsono, Sunny Gunawan, and the members of Fu He An; the late *wayang potehi* puppeteers Pak Sesomo and Thio Thiong Gie; Ardian Purwoseputro; Dwi Woro Retno Mastuti; the staff and students of STSI Bandung, and especially Pak Iip Sarip; Wanggi; Uli; Mrs. Li Huizhu; Ardian Cangianto; Sabria Mohammad Sabri; Pak Yensen and the Yensen Project; Rudi Heryawan and his family; Bu Yuni and her family; Ahwie, Acit and other *gezaixi* practitioners and patrons in Palembang; Bernadette Godeliva Fabiola Natasha; Lin Xuehua; Huang Bizhen; Sunny Kort; Ye Dongzhen; Xiaoxing; Songhua; Jin Meizi; Perhimpunan Penulis Tionghoa Indonesia; Soeria Disastra and other members of the Kota Kembang choir; Shalihong; Wu Guangzhong; Li Meiying; Cheng Gaoling; Chen Dexian; Valcyne Huang; Tang Jianyuan; Tang Aili; Tang Nantong; Lin Rongjin; Lim Ahok; Yang Fuxing; Armin E.S.; and Javier Yong-En Lee. At various stages of my fieldwork, I was accompanied by Elisabeth Kramer, who also provided a much-needed sofa on a half-dozen Jakarta research junkets; and by Ines Eben von Racknitz and Kristyna Cilkova; all of these friends helped me document these research trips. I am also grateful to Wayne Palmer for the advice and introductions he made during my first visit to Indonesia in 2011. Rangga Bhuana and Ratna Riantiarno provided crucial information and corrections as well as the Teater Koma photos. For other photos, I am indebted to Elisabeth Kramer, Kristyna Cilkova, the KITLV digital image library, the Rijksmuseum, Li Meiying, Bernadette Godeliva Fabiola Natasha, Lin Xuehua, Cheng Gaoling, and Indonesia's Ministry of Education and Culture and the General Directorate of Culture.

Fieldwork and archival research trips would not have been possible without the financial support of numerous institutions, including that of the Social Sciences and Humanities Research Council of Canada for doctoral and postdoctoral studies; the China Scholarship Council; the Darmasiswa program of Indonesia's Ministry of Education and Culture; the Association for Asian Studies; the Sydney Southeast Asia Centre and the Centre for China Studies, both at the University of Sydney; and Fulbright Taiwan.

For academic guidance, I am deeply indebted to my doctoral supervisor Yu Weimin and to the network of colleagues and classmates at Nanjing University, especially Jiang Chen. The teachers of the Jiangsu Kunju Theatre and the Fujian Province Liyuan Experimental Theatre have given me—over almost fifteen years—the knowledge basis and the personal relations to embark on Chinese theatre research. At the University of British Columbia, I owe a particular debt to Catherine Swatek and Siyuan Liu, both of whom acted as supervisors at different stages of my studies, and to Christopher Rea, Tim Cheek, and Alison Bailey. Without the patient language instruction of Tineke Hellwig and Manneke Budiman, I would never have found my way into Indonesian studies. And, if I may be permitted to stretch back fifteen years into the past, the encouragement of my undergraduate supervisor, Philip Kuhn, instilled self-confidence and an early taste for academic fieldwork. Helpful suggestions for this manuscript came from many colleagues in Indonesia, Mainland China, Taiwan, and the Western world, including Adrian Vickers, Charlotte Setijadi, Annie Katsura Rollins, Kim Hunter Gordon, Miguel Escobar Varela, Taomo Zhou, Jessica Kean, and Carol Chia. Bonnie S. McDougall's generous and conscientious proofreading greatly improved the manuscript. The technical assistance of Alvina Lock and Vivien Nara was invaluable.

For help in gaining access to tricky sources, I would especially like to thank Shi Xueqin, Xu Ke, and Zhang Changhong; Liang Peilin; and Yerry Wirawan and Jeremy E. Taylor, both of whom kindly shared primary sources from their own research. In Taiwan, I would like to thank the Taiyuan Asian Puppet Theatre Museum and its director Robin Ruizendaal, the latter also for his comments and suggestions on the manuscript. Tsai Hsin-hsin, the National Taiwan College of Performing Arts, Fulbright Taiwan, the National Library Museum, the G-Sharp Choir, and the Performing Arts Library of the National Theatre & Concert Hall made my stays and visits in Taiwan productive and enjoyable. Various chapters have benefited from feedback over the course of presentation in various fora and publications, including conferences at the University of Hong Kong and Institute of Southeast Asian Studies (Singapore) and invited talks at the National University of Singapore, University of British Columbia, and University of Nottingham Ningbo China. Some of the same material has been published in *Asian Theatre Journal*, *The Journal of Southeast Asian Studies*, and *Potehi: Glove Puppet Theatre in Southeast Asia and Taiwan,* and I am thankful to the editors of these publications both for their permissions and for the improvements I was able to make in response to editors' and reviewers' suggestions.

For their patience and suggestions for this book, I would like to thank those involved at the University of Hawai'i Press: series editor Frederick Lau, acquisitions editor Masako Ikeda, managing editor Cheryl Loe, copy editor Barbara Folsom, and editorial assistant Debra Tang. Thanks to proofreader Wendy Bolton for her many timely catches. Furthermore, I would like to thank the anonymous readers, whose comments and corrections proved invaluable.

Over the process of researching and writing in the last five years, I am grateful for the friendship (as well as, often, the housing and food) of many friends. Those whom I have not yet named include Hafliði Sævarsson, Beatriz García Martinez, Tom Renneberg, Aurélia Gomis, Flavio Silva, Julie Houde, Roberta Zavoretti, Yuliya Golubitskaya, Wang Jie, Eriko Toyoda, Vincent Chung, Eugenia Lo, Linda Olson and Levi Gao, Yanting Qiu and Jaylon Han, Alex Potapov, Oanh Nguyen, and Dang Vu.

I would like to thank my family, especially my parents, who have read and corrected this manuscript in parts or in its entirety more times than anyone could fairly expect, and who have somehow come to the conclusion that it is quite all right to spend one's time wandering and wondering about minority archipelagic performance. Above all, I thank Connor Sheng for his patience, support, and forbearance.

Needless to say, no amount of assistance has prevented me from committing the errors to be found in this work and that are mine alone.

NOTE ON STYLE

SINO-Indonesian personal names pose a difficulty in that individuals often have multiple names in various languages of China and Indonesia, which they use in differing contexts. In this work, the most cosmmon romanized version of a name has been provided for Sino-Indonesian individuals, with Chinese characters (if known) provided on first appearance. *Pinyin* transcription has been used for Mainland Chinese names and places as well as for Chinese terms, except for established dialect-derived terms such as "Hakka," "Hokkien," "Teochow," "Hokchia," and "Cantonese." It has also been used for Sino-Indonesians whose Indonesian names are not known to me.

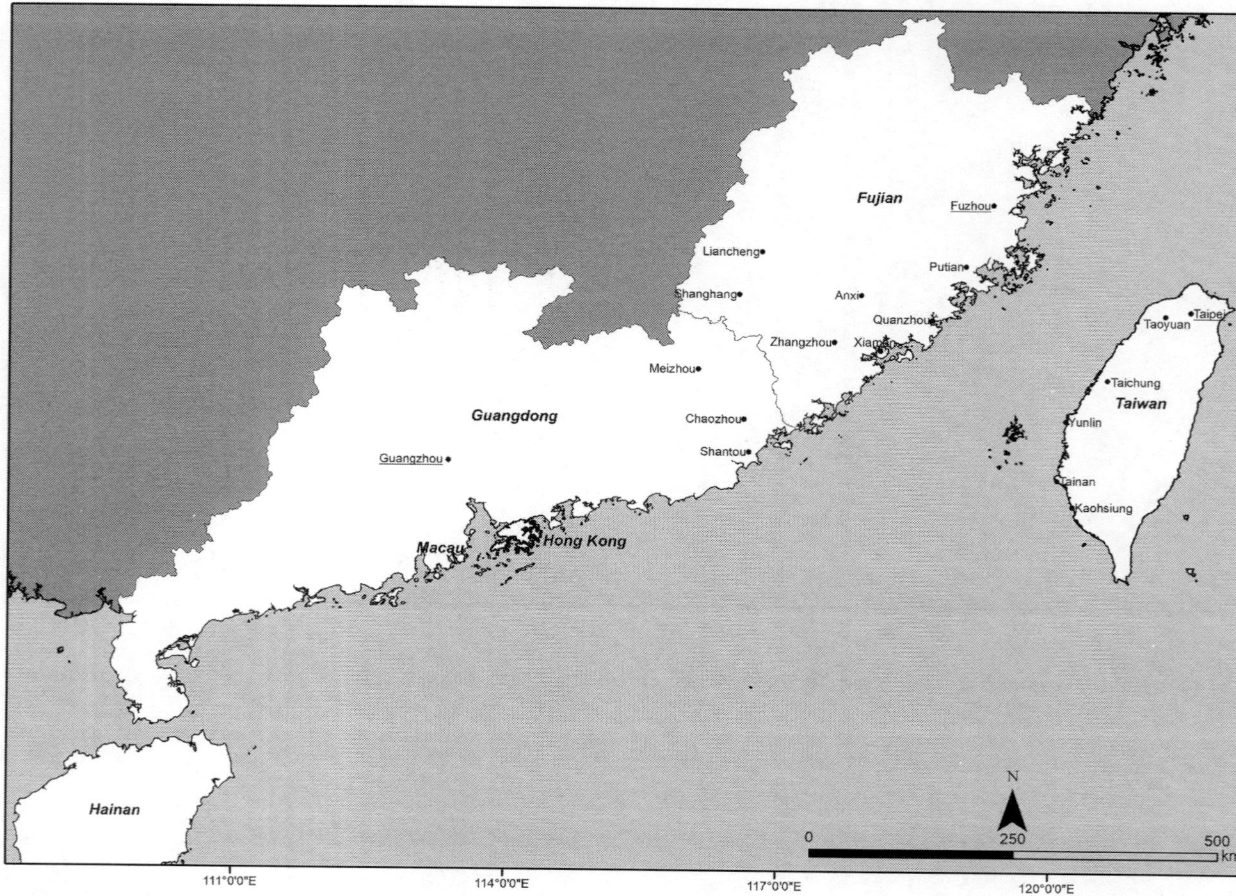

Map 1. Taiwan, Fujian, Guangdong, and Hainan. Map drawn by Alexandra Jones.

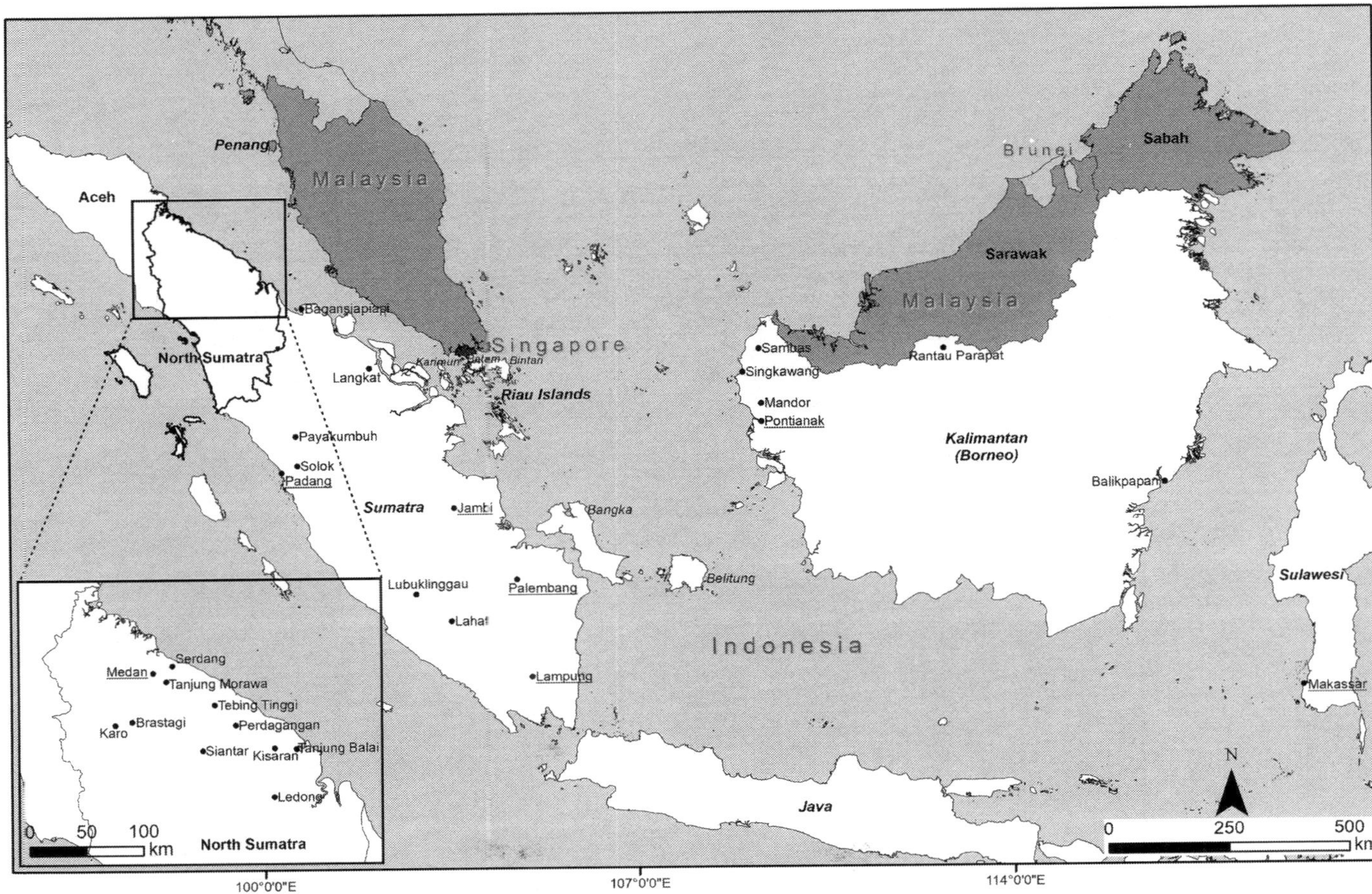

Map 2. Borneo and Sumatra. Map drawn by Alexandra Jones.

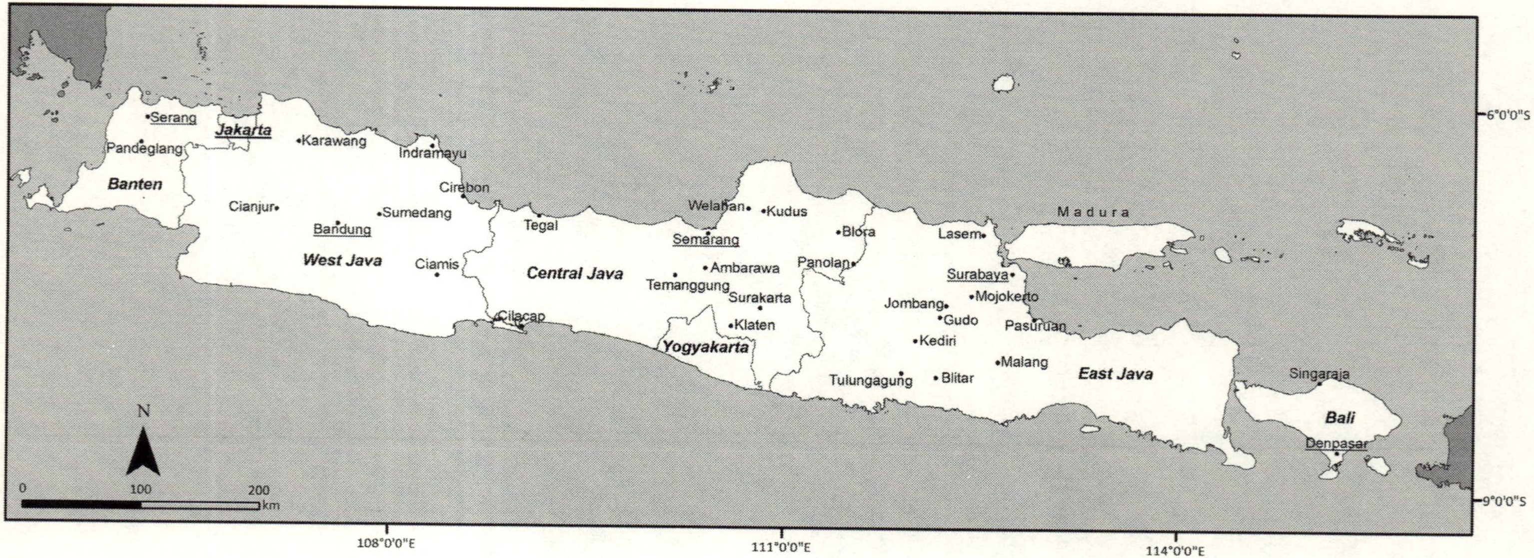

Map 3. Java. Map drawn by Alexandra Jones.

Minority Stages

Introduction

PERFORMANCE IN THE BACKGROUND

On November 16, 2016, at Liong Toh Kiong 龍渡宮 temple, Palembang, South Sumatra, the annual festival of three sainted worthies is being celebrated. The air is filled with murmurs and interjections in Palembang Hokkien and Palembang Malay, not to mention cinders from sacrificial paper money burning in three separate kilns. Young men, members or hired hands of the Theng 唐 Clan to whom the temple belongs, hurry by, bent under the weight of vats sloshing with food and shouting "Hot! Hot!" as warning to the impeding throng and the children underfoot. From 10:00 a.m. to 10:00 p.m., I will be asked at intervals not exceeding ten minutes whether I have eaten. Have I tried the pork? Perhaps I would like some sweet coffee? Tea? A smoke? Am I married? How many children? From Canada? Oh yes, Canada, Florida. . . . Have I met the man—he was here a moment ago—whose son lives in Idaho? Someone's sister's daughter is in Singapore, and she speaks English and Mandarin *perfectly.* Incidentally, have I tried the pork?

There are perhaps three or four hundred people in attendance. Even as the spirit mediums, flourishing their brushes, ink the spells onto sacrificial money for the faithful to take home and, in case of illness, burn, dissolve in water, and imbibe—even while the ritual to invite the euphemistic *hao xiongdi* 好兄弟 (good brothers, i.e., ghosts) to descend and partake of the feast is being conducted—all this time, for a daily total of about eight hours, the local Hokkien opera (*gezaixi* 歌仔戲) company has been performing, at times all but inaudible despite microphones, over the hubbub of the festivalgoers and the competing incantations of the Daoist *fashi* 法師 (ritual master), hired from Fujian by the religious association to which the temple belongs.[1] Against this background of material superabundance, it is incongruous though perhaps not entirely coincidental that the men and boys of the troupe are currently playing the scene from *Zhao Wuniang xunfu* 趙五娘尋夫 (Zhao Wuniang searches for her husband) in which the heroine's parents-in-law starve to death.[2] This narrative of want and danger goes on for hours, a satisfying counterpoint to the good fortune and (noisy) peace being celebrated by the festival.

One advantage to sticking out so badly is that I need not actively don my guise of inquisitive young sinophile researcher. Instead, conversation comes to me: a young actor, in his pink opera princess costume and eyeshadow, expresses his desire to find work in Taiwan; another older man asks me whether I have heard about the protests against the Chinese governor of Jakarta Ahok for alleged blasphemy (did I know that Ahok's wife is from Medan, and speaks Hokkien?); a third explains to me why women cannot be tolerated as performers, though views diverge when it comes to their presence backstage. A Lampung Chinese laborer, visiting for the festival, has learned that I am childless and kindly begins offering graphic technical advice from which I am delivered when the head of the temple undertakes to explain—gesturing at the censers—the compatibility of Pancasila, the five principles of the Indonesian state, with Daoism, which in his account is based on associating veneration of the Jade Emperor with Pancasila's requirement for Ketuhanan Yang Maha Esa (Belief in One Supreme God). And already the ritual fruit is being distributed—mandarins, longans, dragon-fruits; the gods have already partaken of them, and it is time for mortal consumption.

A journalist from *Radar Palembang,* a Sundanese transplant from Bandung, has been summoned by the temple to provide a sympathetic account of the festival and is instructed to interview me. Now members of the police make an appearance, to be fed, joked with, and rewarded for their efforts in keeping the festival safe. A high school student tries out her excellent English, telling me she has never met a westerner, and asking me what major to choose, which countries where she might study are not as racist. By the end of the night, I have lost my voice (on account of the smoke?); it is partially restored to me by a Theng widowed-matriarch-cum-shipping-magnate, who secretly extracts from the temple pantry a jug of sweet high-quality rice moonshine of her own making.

This was the pleasant way in which I passed the last day of my field research for this book. Reconsidering, for the hundredth and final time, how to begin my account, I settled on this descriptive sally, hoping to remind the reader, and myself, how the issues of identity and performance are always entangled and intertwined, embedded in the endless babble of experience, to be willfully transformed, one hopes, into the shapes and senses of reflection—with all the conscious and unconscious idiosyncracies that transformation will reveal. The threads that in this book I have tried to find and follow through space, genre, and time comprise only a few of many possible lines of inquiry; and laying out things in one way necessarily occludes other possibilities—some only glimpsed and relinquished, others wholly invisible to me.

The complexity of even a single festival day is a reminder to me of how both alarmist and celebratory approaches to Sino-Indonesian identity are liable to oversimplify. The openness, cohesion, and generosity of these interlocking Palembang organizations (temple, clan, ancestral place association, arts organization, religious congregation) are self-evident. However, despite outreach to media and officialdom, one can see, in this and many other cases, how Sino-Indonesian society might also appear to outsiders as insular or aloof, partly for the very same reasons of cohesion and (in some eyes and in some cases) ostentatious display. For instance, the prominence of pork and alcohol at these celebrations is, seemingly increasingly, an insuperable barrier to participation in the festivities for many, though by no means all, Muslims. And—casting our gaze a little wider—how confident can one be that the state and society of Palembang (or of Pontianak, Medan, or anywhere in Indonesia) will continue to allow celebrations such as these where pork, beer, and rice wine are openly consumed? During an event such as this festival, Chinese community activity seems to be driven by an organic and unstoppable energy; and it takes an effort to remember how new and how old it is, and also how it has ebbed and flowed and will doubtless continue to fluctuate.

Despite the definite progress towards Sino-Indonesian normalization during the present Reformasi period, the anxiety of Sino-Indonesian identity has not disappeared; it is not even visibly on a path to resolution. My research started just as Ahok, a Protestant Hakka from Belitung, was beginning his campaign as Jokowi's running mate in Jakarta. In hindsight, this may have been the high-water mark of Sino-Indonesian optimism. Since then, however, Ahok's blasphemy trial, conviction, and jailing, amid fears of increasing Islamization of Indonesia's secular state, have once again made a dent in Sino-Indonesian confidence and sense of belonging.[3] Longer-term, the rise of the People's Republic of China (PRC) and the close associations sought and maintained with it by some Sino-Indonesian associations are unlikely to assuage the long-standing Indonesian fears of divided Sino-Indonesian loyalties, especially as the potential for conflict between the countries reemerges.[4] On the other hand, some regard the rise of China principally in the light of its possibilities as a model for Indonesia, potentially improving Indonesian images of China and of Chinese Indonesians (Herlijanto 2017). Reformasi appears now as one new act in the Sino-Indonesian epic rather than as the uplifting conclusion to a centuries-old sociopolitical drama.

What Is Chinese about Sino-Indonesian Performance?

All action has a performative aspect, and in public actions this aspect predominates. Early work adopting a dramaturgical approach to social life was undertaken by Erving Goffman, who was interested in "the way in which the individual in ordinary work situations presents himself and his activity to others, the ways in which he guides and controls the impression they form of him, and the kinds of things he may and may not do while sustaining his performance before them" (1956, i). Although Goffman himself made use of this approach primarily to examine behavior in US work situations, this insight became instrumental for the development of performance studies, an approach that permits the simultaneous examination of both framed public display, such as theatre, and unframed social interactions in public.

More recently, Jeffrey C. Alexander has proposed that "Cultural performance is the social process by which actors, individually or in concert, display for others the meaning of their social situation. This meaning may or may not be one to which they themselves subjectively adhere; it is the meaning that they, as social actors, consciously or unconsciously wish to have others believe" (Alexander 2004, 529). Alexander's definition of "cultural performance" is broad, and I concur with the classification of theatrical events and public displays as "one of the many cultural manifestations that offer a way to consider how communities come together to investigate the social practices through which they operate" (Delgado et al. 2013, 2). This approach can be productive in that it allows for the joint analysis of a wide range of public displays, whether or not they were self-consciously devised as performance.

However—since a performative element in any behavior for which there is an audience, and in many for which there is not—this approach also contains the danger that, if applied indiscriminately, it can obscure the borders of performance to the extent that its object of analysis (in our case, Sino-Indonesian performance) disappears. For this project, it was not feasible to set parameters that encompassed performance only in its framed and narrow, formally theatrical, forms, not least because events that were both explicitly Chinese and explicitly theatre have now become far from common. Also, because many Sino-Indonesian communities interact with the broader society in other public ways, including rituals, processions, and community performance, it was obvious that the perception and self-perception of Chinese communities was mediated as much by such activities as by formal theatres. This study thus considers theatrical performance and other public displays as forming a corpus of Sino-Indonesian self-representations. It does not seek to draw less formal interaction—for instance, unframed social behavior between Chinese and non-Chinese Indonesians—into consideration, while acknowledging that such approaches do complement the present work.

Scholarship on Sino-Indonesian communities necessarily navigates tensions of identity. Some work, especially that written in Chinese and published in Mainland China, privileges a sinocentric view, with overseas populations envisaged in relation to an ancestral homeland. This reflects what has been called a "methodological nationalism" whereby "[d]iaspora studies often trace dispersed populations no matter where they have settled, focusing on the dynamics of interconnection, nostalgia and memory and identity within a particular population, relating them to a particular homeland" (Wimmer and Glick Schiller 2002, 324). An opposite tendency also exists: when the receiving country is the subject of study, diasporic connections or origins may be neglected in favor of an emphasis on its contribution to a core "native" culture.[5] In Indonesia, this has often taken a state-centered approach and has sometimes even dealt with the Sino-Indonesians, not as a cultural or ethnic entity, but as a bourgeois class.[6] Either approach, diasporic or state-centered, tends to strip Sino-Indonesians of agency and of diversity (both internal and vis-à-vis other Chinese populations; see also Dieleman et al. 2010, 4–8).

Similar tensions can be found throughout scholarship on Chinese performing arts outside Mainland China, with some stressing and some effacing "Chineseness." Mainland Chinese scholarship on *wayang potehi* and other forms of *budaixi*, for instance, has largely regarded Southeast Asian practice as unchangingly "Chinese," while also being inclined to regard it as of only marginal interest (and impractical to research) due to geographic and linguistic barriers. Conversely, Indonesian and Western Indonesianist scholars have been weak on the Chinese origins of this genre and the relations that should be traced with existing practices elsewhere (i.e., in Mainland China, Taiwan, Malaysia, and Singapore).

This study seeks to respect Chinese roots, Indonesian practice, and the position of such performance in a dynamic regional history. Critical studies of Asian or transnational performance have absorbed from ethnic studies the idea of the "flexible indeterminacy and contestability of Chineseness . . . remade and reshaped in different conditions of diaspora" (Ang 2013, 18), acknowledging that "'Chineseness' as an ethnic marker is no longer a theoretical given but a malleable category which fluctuates according to its immediate environment" (Lau 2005, 30). The uneven progress of cultural, linguistic, and genetic mixing means that the terms of "Chineseness" vary strongly by location within Indonesia as well as by generation. As Melani Budianta writes, the "process of self-identification as Chinese (or the acknowledgment that Chineseness is an issue that one has to deal with) differs from one generation to the other, from one individual to another" (2007, 171). This work takes the malleability and indeterminacy of "Chineseness" in Indonesia as a theoretical starting point and identifies Sino-Indonesian public performance and display as ways in which "Chineseness" is shaped locally and nationally. This, again, is why only works or communities that have an evident Chinese component in their performative *content* are dealt with here.

In Indonesia, as in other places, performance is and has long been a public negotiation of ethnic identity. For any given Chinese Indonesian performance type or troupe, the Chinese aspect provides only one window on diverse, fluid, and transnational practices. When considered in dialogue with one another and in historical perspective, however, the consideration of Chinese Indonesian performance forms can also suggest a coherent narrative of the evolution of group identity. As Chinese communities in Indonesia have reacted to sociopolitical forces, performance has been a key way in which to articulate identity.

The diversity within any single nation such as Indonesia or China is familiar and the socioeconomic networks of Chinese communities across Southeast Asia well known. But theatre and performance have been peripheral to academic investigation in these fields. Scholarship on Chinese performance studies tends to focus on Western-inspired forms and East–West (rather than intra-Asian) interactions. Performance, however, is a fruitful area for investigating spaces of hybridity and shifts in identity, and, as Indonesian performance studies have shown, also for analyzing the relationship between state and culture (e.g., Foulcher 1990; Jones 2013).

This book is organized by genre. Consideration of these genres as a group exerts pressure on several boundaries. One of these is the concept of "Chineseness" as it tends to appear within Chinese performance studies. Studies of Chinese performance, especially those in Chinese language (in which the lion's share of such scholarship occurs) have often been unreflective on this question and insensitive to the rich varieties of identity and expression available to Chinese performing overseas (or indeed in China's regions). The fact that "Chinese opera . . . is still regarded by both its practitioners and its Anglo-European audiences as the ultimate, quintessential representation of Chinese identity," partly as a result of the deliberate nationalist positioning of *jingju* (Peking opera) in the Republican period inside China and abroad (Huang 2009, 173), continues to obscure how much of Chinese "traditional" performance is contingent, situational, and contemporary rather than essential, eternal, ancient, or representative.

Another of my intentions is to expand the complexity of research approaches to Sino-Indonesian communities, organizations, and subjects, research on which has overwhelmingly adopted political and social perspectives. Focusing on theatre helps to recover the cultural history of the Chinese-Indonesian subject and to balance the profile of an identity that remains burdened, and sometimes persecuted, by the stereotype of being principally an economic actor.[7] The contemporary "image of the highly mobile and quintessentially flexible transnational Chinese capitalist" (Hertzman 2017, 8) is neither accurate nor helpful. Even within the broad field of culture, the Sino-Indonesian subject has been considered largely in terms of religion and literature; performance, which has featured in every Sino-Indonesian community, has barely featured.[8]

This book should prove useful also to those who are working on other areas of Indonesian performance and culture in that it charts the constant presence of Chinese narratives and performance practices in Indonesia as constituent elements of the nation's wealth of theatre and public display. As such, my project is in consonance with various sociopolitical tendencies in Indonesia that attempt to break down hard distinctions between *pribumi* (indigenous) and non-*pribumi* (putatively nonindigenous) citizens. I also avow a general sympathy for narratives of Chinese presence in the archipelago that situate them as integral and constitutive of Indonesia rather than as alien to it or essentially exploitative of it. Recent reports from Indonesia, firsthand and secondhand, raise the specter of renewed sinophobia; so a stress on the historical, integrated nature of Chinese cultural contributions to Indonesia is timely.

There is no question that Chinese elements have been a part of performance in the archipelago for hundreds of years. Historically, "[i]t is difficult to find any single line of trade where [Chinese merchants] have not played a part" in Southeast Asia (Tagliacozzo and Chang 2011, 2), and theatre is no exception. Records indicate the presence of forms of Chinese theatre in the Indies from at least the early seventeenth century. Chinese performance in the colonial period can be regarded as a regular and ubiquitous feature of community life, and, although certain genres naturally acculturated, there is no indication that the performances of Chinese communities were identified with a self-conscious effort to construct or retain a Chinese identity. In the late colonial era, the relatively privileged economic situation of some Chinese allowed members of the community to make substantial contributions to the development of commercial and amateur (often charitable) theatre while also continuing their own traditions of opera and puppet theatre. In the revolutionary middle of the twentieth century, Chinese-language spoken and musical theatre were mobilized in support of Chinese war relief, both sides of the Chinese Civil War (Nationalist and Communist) as well as (occasionally) the Indonesian National Revolution. In the Suharto era, Chinese performance was subdued and low-profile, but offered a space for a continued identity and, occasionally and locally, for resistance. In the present period of Reformasi, Sino-Indonesian performance of all kinds has been revived, largely in a self-conscious way, in order to present an image of "Chineseness" in Indonesia that is generally in favor of a constitutive perspective and does not conflict with Indonesian patriotism.

Different genres are accessible to different degrees, and through different methods. While the chapters on *xiqu* (Chinese opera) and *wayang* (Indonesian puppetry) attempt to chart a through-line by combining archival research with fieldwork, the later chapters present snapshots and case studies that allow the consideration of broader issues and can furnish materials and frameworks for further studies. Only those genres and works that have a substantive connection and investment in the performance of Chineseness will be considered here, not least because it seems most respectful to works and authors not to apply ethnic readings when they are not called for.

Throughout, the history of these communities testifies to the degree of contribution, assimilation, and acculturation of Indonesians of Chinese descent.

However, it is also hard to disagree, even now, with Mary Somers' assessment from over a half-century ago that in the academic study of ethnicity in Indonesia "it is relations between [*pribumi*] Indonesians and Chinese, the largest non-indigenous minority, that [have given] rise to greatest friction and attract most attention" (Somers 1964, 47). Despite the great easing of controls on Chinese-Indonesian cultural and community life during the Reformasi period, one has no choice but to conclude that, even today, "due to their ethnicity Chinese Indonesians are always vulnerable" and remain "convenient targets of harassment, exploitation, violence, and abuse" (Susanto 2010, 86). This may seem a rather drastic judgment, until one recalls that only twenty years ago anti-Chinese sentiment resulted in massacres and mass rapes in 1998 at the end of a ban on Chinese cultural expression that had lasted for an entire generation. Time and again, political instability has resulted in attacks against Sino-Indonesian individuals and properties. As this book was being written, events demonstrated that political actors in Indonesian politics are still liable to make use of ethnicity and ethnic minority in political power games, and that backlash against Chinese communities cannot be ruled out.

Early and Colonial History

The historical length, geographical breadth, and cultural depth of Chinese influence, and the facts of Indonesia's diversity and constructedness, show how unsound it is to conceive of Chinese as alien to the archipelago. Historical perspective should also, however, give us some notion as to why the legend of Chinese strangerhood has endured. These facts furnish the foundations for understanding the development of Sino-Indonesian performance in the context of the colonial Indies and postcolonial Indonesia. As French historian Denys Lombard noted, depending on whether one considers the Chinese presence on Java in the long or the short term, "this influence will appear either as profound and constitutive, or on the contrary as an epiphenomenon linked to the fate of a 'minority'" (Lombard 1990, 209). This is because Chinese influence "developed over several centuries in a receptive and favorable cultural context, before taking on a very different meaning in the last [nineteenth] century, following new developments in colonial policy" (209).

There have been ties between China and Southeast Asia from "the earliest times," before either region was constituted under any such name or concept (Wade 2009a, 1). Artifacts have been found that suggest there were cultural contacts two thousand years ago (Kartomi 2000, 277). In the fifth century CE, the Buddhist monk Faxian 法顯 visited a country called Yepoti 耶婆提, most likely situated in present-day Indonesia (Ptak 2007, 93–94). Shipwrecks bear testament to a lively trade in the eighth and ninth centuries, reaching a first peak in the tenth. By that century, the Fujian port of Quanzhou, to which so many Sino-Indonesians trace their ancestry, already maintained commercial contacts with Java and Sumatra (Schlottenhammer 1999, 279; Qin and Xiang 2011). Polities on Sumatra and Java had diplomatic relations with the Song dynasty from the beginning of their rule in 960, and there were substantial imports of cloves from the archipelago to China by the tenth century (Ptak 1993; Wade 2009b, 230). Records connected with the 1293 Mongol Yuan dynasty invasion of Java show Chinese groups residing in the archipelago, although Yuan attacks seem to have decimated trade between China and the archipelagic states. By this period, Chinese trade contact with Borneo had also been established (Heidhues 2003, 19; Chaffee 2008, 120; Wade 2009a, 7).

More intense Chinese migration to Indonesia began in the early Ming dynasty, and the famed eunuch admiral Zheng He 鄭和 made six visits to Java, finding, it seems, a flourishing Chinese Muslim community already present in the capital and port cities of the Java-based Majapahit Empire. Malay chronicles seem to corroborate this information, even if local Chinese beliefs—for instance, that Zheng He himself may have died in Semarang—must be regarded as unsubstantiated (Suryadinata 2005a).[9] Chinese tradesmen and religious figures are thought to have played an important role in the spread of Islam in the archipelago, and several Muslim saints (*wali*) are purported to have been of Chinese extraction (Kumar 1987; Kartomi 2000, 278). Sumatran kings also sent and received envoys in the early Ming, and Cantonese traders even ruled fifteenth-century Palembang for a time (Munoz 2006, 178–179, 184–185).

Substantial Chinese migration in the fifteenth century may justify the claim that this period gave rise to the "first Chinese diaspora in Southeast Asia" (Chang 1991). Javanese crops were being influenced by the Chinese export market, particularly pepper and safflower dye, and thirteenth-century Fujian texts include information on Javanese coinage (Christie 1999, 226–227, 238). In general, there is little evidence of animosity between Chinese populations and any native group before the beginnings of Western colonialism (Carey 1984), and some historians conjecture that the Chinese were mostly absorbed into the local populations over the course of the Ming ban on shipping in the late fifteenth century and early sixteenth century (Reid 1996, 37). Despite their importance in contemporary Sino-Indonesian self-perception, public commemoration, and discourse, however, these communities seem remote, and it is largely a romantic enterprise to attempt to establish substantive continuity between present populations and these antecedents.

The Dutch, arriving in the early seventeenth century, found Chinese groups scattered throughout Java and holding high positions at the Javanese courts (Kumar 1987, 609), and from that time on the record of Chinese presence in several parts of the Indies is unbroken.[10] Local Chinese provided the new Dutch East Indies

Company (VOC) administration with "large quantities of sorely needed skilled labor and financial knowhow" (Kartomi 2000, 280) and quickly began to serve as intermediaries between the Europeans and the indigenous population. Batavia, the colonial capital, was by some accounts predominantly a Chinese town until the massacre of 1740 at the hands of the VOC (Blussé 1981).[11] From the seventeenth century on, there is also a documented Chinese presence in the Moluccas, and Java-based Chinese began visiting Bali to purchase slaves.[12] Chinese migrants had arrived in Ambon by 1620, and eighteenth-century tombstones in West Java indicate a well-established Hokkien trading community there (Salmon and Lombard 1975; Knaap 1999, 111; Salmon and Sidharta 2000; Sutherland 2011, 176).

Assessment of the complex and shifting roles of the Chinese in the colonial period is a fraught endeavor. Often, the Indies Chinese emerge as the victims of colonial violence (Ricklefs 1983). This is most dramatically shown in the 1740 massacre in Batavia, in which perhaps two-thirds of the city's Chinese population was massacred by the Dutch, as well as the ensuing 1741–1743 Java War, where Chinese (sometimes joined by Javanese) fought the VOC. But a hundred years later, with Chinese merchants deeply involved in tax farming, moneylending, and opium farming, Chinese individuals usually appear in the historical record as colonial agents of the oppression and exploitation of the local populations, or, as one nineteenth-century European on Java put it, "our work tools" (H. MacGillavry, in Carey 1976, 67), and it was this reputation that would make them the targets of ethnic riots in early twentieth-century Java (Vickers 2005, 67–68). In 1897 an American traveler named Eliza Scidmore opined of the situation on Java that "The native hatred of the Chinese is an inheritance of those past centuries when the Dutch farmed out the revenue to Chinese, who gradually extended their boundaries, and by increasing exactions and by secret levies oppressed the people with a tyranny and rapacity the Dutch could not approach" (Scidmore 1984, 39).

Surely Scidmore underrates the colonial Dutch capacity for tyranny and rapacity, but her observation that the direct *pribumi* experience of Chinese revenue farming laid the foundations for an enduring ethnic animosity was borne out by later history.[13] Both chronological and regional distinctions are pertinent, and some areas do not conform comfortably to such a narrative: in West Kalimantan, for instance, the establishment of Chinese mining companies known to the Dutch as *kongsi* created almost entirely autonomous company-governments that controlled Chinese labor as well as indigenous populations (Heidhues 2003).

Moreover, Chinese in the archipelago have played a wide variety of economic roles. While the Chinese merchant (and later business) class was and is the most prominent group, the establishment of wealthy businessmen as the defining class of Sino-Indonesians in the public mind relies on a conflation of one group for the whole. The prominence of a few individuals and families continues to mark perceptions of the group today just as it did in 1948, when Baren, a Mainland Chinese

Communist, wrote: "in the eyes of the indigenous people, every Chinese does business, has a shop, has a tin mine, has a plantation—is rich. But in fact, having only seen a few big trees, they suppose that the whole area is a forest made up of great sky-scraping trees" (1986, 41). Mary Somers Heidhues, writing on postindependence official attitudes towards Chinese, writes that the early republic's rationale "err[ed] by regarding the ethnic Chinese as an undifferentiated (and apparently equally wealthy) group, although in fact Chinese... find themselves at the lower levels of the economic scale as well as at the top" (1992, xiv). Indeed, in several areas of Indonesia, Chinese work in agriculture or fishery up to the present day; and in all urban areas there are many Sino-Indonesians who operate stalls or small stores, work in factories, as domestic servants, or as drivers (see also Pepinsky 2009, 54). The prominent wealth of a small group of Chinese over the entire period of Indonesian modern history has too often obscured in the popular imagination the modest means of most and the poverty of many.

This conflation of class and ethnicity is due in large part to a race-based policy of the Dutch colonial system, which distinguished between Europeans, "foreign Orientals," and "Natives."[14] This defined the Chinese of Indonesia (along with Arabs and Indians, though their history in the Indies and Indonesia has been very different)[15] as essentially aliens, an identity that proved formative and remains an element in both external and self-conceptions of their role, even in the twenty-first-century Indonesian state. In the evocative words of contemporary essayist Goenawan Mohamad, "the colonizer took aim and threw his lasso into the jumble of people outside the government buildings, snaring them into groups of names and concepts," with the result that "Anything ambiguous, vague, unstable, and that represented exceptions to these 'groups' or 'ethnicities' was discarded" (Goenawan 2015, "Arrows"). Dutch rule resulted in the creation of a middleman Chinese community that "was required to serve the interests of the dominant class, which naturally overrode theirs" (Kartomi 2000, 272). Colonial officials assumed and perpetuated an image of Chinese as essentially mercantile. In the words of Sumatra-born Dutch colonial author Augusta de Wit: "the sum and substance of a Chinaman's life in Java [are] expressed in 'the making of bargains.' He could as soon leave off breathing as leave of[f] buying and selling; trading seems to be his natural function. And this, one fancies, is the great difference between his race and ours; and the true secret of their superiority as money-makers" (de Wit 52, 1912). This kind of racist caricature, reminiscent of European anti-Semitism in the same period, generated an enduring stereotype. Simultaneously the Dutch colonial government linked the Chinese "economically to Dutch interests [while keeping them] at arm's length in every other way" (Lev 1985, 62).[16]

The upshot, often identified as a part of a divide et impera strategy, was that, "by giving them unpopular jobs, such as tax farming, money-lending, and running pawnshops, the Dutch allowed a pariah image of the Indonesian-Chinese to emerge among the pribumi population" (Kartomi 2000, 273). Nor were Chinese people treated with respect by Dutch colonial officialdom, as "the bureaucrat in his office could and unhappily often did treat the Chinese shamefully [and] the police were on occasion even brutal" (Williams 1960, 41). At the same time, their unique position gave some Chinese individuals the opportunity to accumulate wealth, while also incentivizing a continued ethnic separation from the general population. Thus, even as the community was culturally, linguistically, and genetically mixed, there was always a socioeconomic motivation to retain a Chinese identity.

That mixing was very substantial and produced the Peranakan, the descendants of older Chinese populations, who were linguistically and culturally deeply assimilated. They were usually also of mixed blood, their Chinese ancestors having been mostly men who married indigenous women, but they retained a social and religious identity separate from local populations. Newer Chinese immigrants, arriving in the extended period of migration between the mid-nineteenth century and the outbreak of the Second World War, were known in Chinese as *sinkeh* 新客 or by the Javanese term *totok* (pure). *Totok*, who were usually defined as being China-born and Chinese-speaking, consisted of both men and women and regarded the Peranakan as being culturally estranged from their real heritage. To a substantial extent, these two Sino-Indonesian communities were once distinct. Much literature on Sino-Indonesians, even today, retains this distinction, but evidence from contemporary sociology suggests that the separation is fading; the usage rarely appeared unelicited in my own fieldwork. When asked, many of my Sino-Indonesian respondents reported mixed Peranakan/*totok* heritage; in any event, even someone on Java today with "purely" Chinese heritage is usually neither Chinese-born nor Chinese-speaking (the erstwhile criteria of *totok*). Furthermore, many Peranakan chose to drop the Chinese aspect of their identities during the thirty-two years of the New Order (Orde Baru) governance and today no longer identify as ethnic Chinese. This move and earlier assimilations mean that many Indonesians must have a part-Chinese ancestry that they do not, or only dimly, realize. Today, Indonesian regional distinctions (for instance, between Medan and Surabaya, or between Jakarta and Singkawang) within the Chinese Indonesian population seem far stronger than the Peranakan/*totok* divide.[17]

In the late nineteenth century, when Chinese nationalism was on the rise in the failing Qing dynasty and in overseas communities, many came to believe that Chinese communities in the Indies were insufficiently Chinese. Around the turn of the century, various movements, especially the Tiong Hoa Hwe Koan 中華會館 (THHK), established in 1900, sought to re-sinicize assimilated or hybrid Chinese communities with instruction in (usually Mandarin) language and Confucian values (Suryadinata 1978; Sai 2016). This corresponded to a general late

Qing push to enlist the support and loyalty of Overseas Chinese and a general sense that, "only by embracing modernity could [local Chinese] reach a 'civilized' status in colonial Indonesia" (Kwartanada 2013, 28). Schools, publishing enterprises, social associations—and theatre groups—were established and deployed for these purposes (Adam 1995, 72–75). Dutch authorities, nervous about the influence of such schools, responded by establishing Dutch-language education for Chinese children. Certain legal concessions were also granted in response to the claims of the community. In a short space of time, the Sino-Indonesians went from being a group that "lacked cohesion and were politically inarticulate" to one that "controlled the most active political force within the colony and made their wishes felt both there and in China" (Williams 1960, 19). But as Indonesian nationalism, developing simultaneously, emerged, "Chineseness became an important 'other' against which the new [Southeast Asian] national identities defined themselves" (Reid 1997, 55), even as the activities of Chinese publishers provided the medium by which an Indonesian nationalism could be articulated and disseminated (Adam 1995).

Japanese Occupation and Independence

The Japanese occupation (1942–1945) permanently changed the political situation for all Indies populations, including the Chinese. Hundreds of Chinese community leaders were interned, and only a single, closely controlled, Chinese association was permitted. Cultural policies, at least in Java, took a no less essentializing attitude than Dutch colonialism, resulting in the increased sinification of Peranakan communities, including in the fields of education (Kwartanada 2010a, 2010b). On Java, some Chinese traders showed some degree of support for Japanese initiatives and sought protection from the military police, while in other areas, such as West Kalimantan, the Chinese population was singled out by the Japanese as particularly rebellious, subjected to concerted violence, and in some cases massacred (Sato 1994, 40–42; Ooi 2011, 107–109). In several regions, Sino-Indonesians became the targets of ethnic violence by the *pribumi* at both the beginning and the end of Japanese occupation (Purdey 2006, 7–8; Vickers 2005, 91, 101; Heidhues 2012).

Some Chinese individuals fought actively on the side of the Indonesian revolutionaries (Hering 1982; Heidhues 1988), but this kind of engagement represented a minority orientation. The Chinese response to the Indonesian National Revolution as a whole cannot be easily generalized as, besides the minority of committed revolutionaries, some formed pro-Dutch militias, and a majority bided their time. By and large throughout the Indonesian National Revolution and the beginning of the republic, Chinese continued to suffer from their reputation of having been the middlemen of Dutch colonialism. The incidence of violence as the Japanese withdrew, particularly, "left many ethnic Chinese wary of an independent state" (Purdey 2006, 7–8; see also Twang 1998, 3–4; Somers 1964, 49–50).[18] Their concerns were not ill-founded, for independence would indeed bring "extreme political vulnerability" (Schwarz 1999, 104).

Systems of racial categorization and economic inequity were a bequest of Dutch colonial rule to the new state, and so it is unsurprising that policy in the Sukarno years (1949–1965) targeted rural Chinese businesses, which were characterized as being exploitative of *pribumi* Indonesians. At the same time, Indonesia retained cordial relations with the PRC and countenanced a Chinese cultural presence in a plural Indonesia.[19] Anti-Chinese sentiment continued to rise, and special taxes and bans directed at "aliens" increased Chinese suspicion of Sukarno's intentions (Skinner 1963, 114–115; Schwarz 1999, 104–105; Tong 2010, 123). A new directive (Regulation 10, known as PP10) in 1959 targeted rural Chinese business and resulted in "an exodus of the poorest Chinese traders from the countryside into the cities" as well as a wave of Sino-Indonesian "return migration" to the PRC unequalled before or since (Robison 2009, 86).

A few years later, shifts in the balance of domestic power between President Sukarno, the army, and the popular Communist Party of Indonesia (PKI) would change the course of Indonesian history. In October 1965, a putative PKI coup against army leadership led instead to "the army-orchestrated politicide of the PKI" (Roosa 2006, 224) and "a creeping coup d'état... disguised as an effort to prevent a coup" (4). Suharto, who led the anti-PKI move, was installed as president and swiftly engaged in a massive, nationwide campaign of violence and terror against purported Communists. In events ranking among "the worst bloodbaths of the twentieth century" (4), hundreds of thousands of people, mostly on Java and Bali, suspected of involvement in the coup, were killed. Although Chinese may not have been the principal targets as such, in certain regions some massacres took on an ethnic character, as Chinese-Indonesians were associated in the official and public minds with the PKI (Davidson and Kammen 2002; Purdey 2006, 14; Melvin 2018, 246–254; Melvin and Pohlman 2018).[20] Under the regime that followed, dubbed New Order by Suharto, Chinese culture was banned from public spaces by presidential decree. At the same time, as New Order wore on, a small number of Sino-Indonesian businessmen became closely associated with Suharto's crony politics, again to the detriment of Indonesians' perceptions of the Chinese.

Although anti-Chinese legislation and movements under New Order took various forms, one of its clearest formulations was the assimilation policy in which elements of "Chinese origin" were banned from public display. This did not, however, eradicate Chineseness from public consciousness, nor was it really intended to: on the contrary, it was in the interest of New Order to keep the Chinese population distinct but unacknowledged: "[b]y eradicating Chinese cultural symbols while preserving the essential distinction between Chinese and *pribumi* Indonesians, the regime perpetuated the stereotypes so necessary to maintain the New Order status quo" (Pepinsky 2009, 57–58). Such stereotypes included Chinese aloofness from society, failure to identify with Indonesia, loyalty to China and Chinese culture, and economic self-interestedness (Coppel 1983, 5). Official policy "pressured the Chinese minority to erase as many traces of Chineseness as possible" (Susanto 2010, 65), including Chinese personal names, the use of Chinese language, Chinese gatherings and holidays, and, of course, Chinese performance. But even when officially assimilated, the "suspicion (and official treatment) of such people left them marked as at best only semi-Indonesian" (Elson 2008, 254), not least because Sino-Indonesians had identity cards that "marked their difference as 'citizens of foreign descent' " (Budianta 2007, 169).[21] It is probable that the leaders of New Order saw the reproduction of Chinese identity in Indonesia "under erasure" as part of a necessary status quo (Heryanto 1998, 104).

But Indonesia is diverse by any measure, including the strength of state control. The relative density of Chinese communities and their distance from the political center produced varying results in the implementation of anti-Chinese policy. Fieldwork shows that pressure was not evenly applied: limits and suppression of expression and public displays of Chinese culture were more strongly felt on Java than on West Kalimantan or North Sumatra, where Chinese constituted a larger proportion of the population (Lyons and Ford 2013, 125; see also Pepinsky 2009, 54). In practice, even in Java, there were "many different reactions to assimilation from Chinese Indonesians in their daily lives" (Susanto 2010, 66), creating room for Chinese performance to continue in modified and adapted forms, in semipublic, or in remoter places. Meanwhile, some Sino-Indonesians "returned" to China where they were regarded as suspect (largely due to their Indonesian origin) and considered by the PRC "as a special group in need of continuous socialist education, transformation, and supervision" (Wang and Wong 2007, 189) before becoming, in 1966, subject to persecution during the Cultural Revolution (Godley and Coppel 1990, 190–191).[22]

Controls on Chinese language and culture began to relax somewhat, and diplomatic relations with the PRC were restored in 1990 (Heryanto 1998, 104–107). During the mid-to-late 1990s, Suharto's control over the country began to founder, leading in 1998 to a wave of riots in Indonesian cities. In May of that year, rioters, perhaps instigated by Indonesian military or pro-Suharto forces, targeted Chinese neighborhoods in cities such as Medan, Jakarta, and Solo (Purdey 2006). The result for many Sino-Indonesians was a crisis of identity: "quite assimilated ethnic Chinese began to ask themselves whether Indonesian 'pribumi' could really accept them" and "whether there was still a place for the Chinese ethnicity among the nations of Indonesia" (Liao [Suryadinata] 2002, 12). A week after the violence, Suharto resigned, and the present era of democratic reform, Reformasi, began.

The 1990s had already seen a diminution of anti-Chinese sentiment (Heryanto 1998, 96), but it was the dawning of Reformasi in 1998 that heralded a new state permissiveness towards the Chinese community and even paved the way for the official recognition of Chinese culture. The official terminology for Sino-Indonesians switched from the term *Cina,* deemed offensive, to the more neutral *Tionghoa.*[23] For a time, it seemed that Sino-Indonesians had never enjoyed such a secure position in the Indonesian polity, and to a substantial extent this still holds true today. Nevertheless, the aftereffects of the repression of Chinese culture continue to be felt, and, as some have noted, the "euphoria" (Budianta 2007, 169–170) associated with it has not quelled fears that prominent displays of Chinese culture and identity might also eventually produce a backlash. The crisis surrounding Ahok in 2016–2017 has, for some, augmented those fears.

Indonesia: Colonial Creation, Postcolonial Project

Indonesia's composition is determined not by any preexisting internal coherence but by colonial history. As historian Adrian Vickers wrote, "[b]efore 1945 there was no Indonesia, but rather a collection of islands spread across the Equator that the Dutch made into the Netherlands East Indies" (2005, 9). Since the independence of Timor-Leste in 2002, the borders of Indonesia closely approximate those of the Dutch East Indies territory after the last annexations (on Papua) in 1920.[24] Indonesia's international borders do not coincide with a linguistic entity[25] or an ethnic unity.[26] Indonesia inherited many regions that had only a slight experience of a government run from Java. Unsurprisingly, then, beginning in the early twentieth century, much effort has been expended in political and cultural spheres to construct a unified or coherent narrative, history, culture, and image of the nation (Hikmat Budiman 2013, 191). The New Order government and its successors have all continued the pursuit of a "unified national culture . . . to give this imagined community of nationhood a sense and a symbol of unity" (Arief Budiman 1990, 11).

Sino-Indonesian performance is part of the construction and negotiation of community identity and is concerned to a substantial extent with representing itself vis-à-vis the majority population and the state. Because identities are dialogic and contrastive, Sino-Indonesian performances are usually in some way concerned with contradicting or complicating the portrayal of local Chinese as strangers, outsiders, or aliens. In so doing, they are working against a long tradition in which they appear as a convenient outgroup against which to construct an Indonesian identity (Triandafyllidou 1998; Purdey 2006, 24). Under New Order, the Chinese were turned into what one observer called "the internal Other of the 'true' Indonesian" (Aguilar 2001, 505), a construct generated and constantly reaffirmed by state policy and organs.[27] Chinese culture was characterized as inherently foreign and inassimilable, and for that reason incompatible with the goals of the Indonesian state. Paradoxically, at the same time that Chinese culture was being suppressed and assimilation was being promulgated, official discrimination made real integration all but impossible and ensured that Chinese were "an easy target of racial and class hostility" (Hoon 2006a, 149). In the 1960 words of Pramoedya Ananta Toer, Indonesia's greatest novelist, "the Chinese have been turned into foreigners by new [postindependence] developments, political and judicial" that had come about because of "the rise of nationalism and its impact on minorities" (Pramoedya 2007, 91).

Chinese communities, residing for generations in the highly diverse societies that have now become Indonesia, also developed highly regional cultural forms and identities. Attitudes towards many aspects of Chineseness, from the level of interaction or assimilation with non-Chinese, to language use and religious observance, vary widely across islands and regions. For this reason, the Sino-Indonesian community must be conceived of not only as an element in the Indonesian ethnic patchwork but as itself inherently multiple, given that only historical accident has grouped together, for example, the Chinese Betawi of Jakarta with the Teochew and Hakka of West Kalimantan. Definitions of minority identity—even as they assert themselves against a majority— are often also "attempts at homogenization that ignores differences in class, region, gender, etc." (Tripathy and Padmanabhan 2014b, 9–10).[28] Investigating Sino-Indonesian performance invariably throws up questions on how varied Chinese minority communities decide to represent themselves to the larger society and the state, regionally as well as nationally.

The diversity of Indonesia has been deployed as a source of national pride and identity, exemplified by the country's national motto, Bhinneka Tunggal Ika, somewhat ironically expressed in Old Javanese rather than Indonesian and meaning "Unity in Diversity." However, nationalist ideology has also been used to "obscure the fragility below the surface" (Nagata 2003, 371), while the state has subjected the "diversity of groups . . . to an enforced homogenization, one calculated to limit and thus control the articulation of demands by prescribing the organizations entitled to represent these interest groups" (Acciaioli 1985, 150). The diversity of language, ethnicity, and culture in Indonesia can easily be perceived as threat, particularly given that in its short history Indonesia has experienced a secession (Timor-Leste), an unsuccessful separatist war (Aceh), and an ongoing independence movement in West Papua.

Proponents of rival identities make use of Indonesia's diversity for political ends: one of the most prominent Acehnese secessionists decried Indonesia as "not a natural geopolitical entity" (Kell 1995, 62), and the fear of this view has deeply informed ethnic politics and discourse. Outside of Java, it has been felt for decades that Java dominates both Indonesia's politics and its economics but also seeks to impose its culture elsewhere. Meanwhile, New Order Indonesia sought to promote itself to others as a "vibrant multicultural state," seeking to "style ethnic cultures in accordance with the taste of international tourism" (Hellman 2003, 14). Historiographically and artistically, it has become possible to revisit colonial history with an eye to "the contributions of ethnic Chinese to the articulation of an Indonesian culture distinct from that of Europe" (Winet 2010, 19).[29] New opportunities for integration and identification without assimilation form the basic strategy of most Sino-Indonesian organizations. Crucial to such attempts is to counter either/or thinking, a mainstay of ethnic essentialism in general and Chinese and Indonesian nationalisms in particular. It is my hope that my itinerary through various parts and periods of Sino-Indonesian performance will contribute to ways of thinking about ethnicity that give pride of place to the eclectic mixtures and fuzzy borders of subjective experience and identity.

CHAPTER 1

Delighting Verie Much in Playes and Singing

FOUR HUNDRED YEARS OF *XIQU* IN THE ARCHIPELAGO

By the early seventeenth century and likely earlier, the coasts of southern Fujian. and to a lesser extent those of Guangdong and Hainan, had become the point of departure and northern boundary for a web of interacting ethnic Chinese theatre practices that extended to many areas of Java, Sumatra, and Borneo, as well as to other parts of maritime and continental Southeast Asia. *Xiqu* troupes were established and regional networks and enterprises operated throughout the archipelago and the broader region, reaching their high point from the mid-nineteenth to the mid-twentieth century.

Xiqu travelled with Chinese migrants to receiving societies throughout the world. As a consequence, there is a *xiqu* history of North America, which is becoming relatively well known, and others in Latin America, Australasia, and Russia, which are far less familiar. Given the scale of Chinese migration to Southeast Asia, it is not surprising to find considerable past and present (if, on the whole, diminishing) *xiqu* performance throughout the region. Which genres specifically feature in a given place depends largely on the predominant area of Chinese emigration. In the maritime Southeast Asian region as a whole, there has historically been a predominance of Hokkien (Minnan; i.e., southern Fujian), Teochew (Chaozhou), Cantonese, Hakka (Kejia), Hainan, and Hokchiu (Fuzhou) forms of theatre, in approximately that order. Southeast Asian Chinese *xiqu* is therefore one of the primary and also among the longest-standing opportunities for the exploration of transnational topics in Asian performance, including the numerous cases of forms that have taken on non-Chinese characteristics.[1]

However, the Indies and Indonesia have not been prominent in *xiqu* scholarship in any language. In terms of Chinese-language accounts of Southeast Asia's *xiqu* history and contemporary practice, the more familiar territory and livelier contemporary scenes are in Malaysia, Singapore, and Thailand, relegating the archipelago largely to passing references (Lai 1993, 191, 195; Lai 1995, 50; Zhang 2007, 738–745; Zhou 2007, 52). Meanwhile, Western-language scholarship has touched on *xiqu* in the Dutch East Indies and in Indonesia largely in the course of studies on adjacent subjects—for example, Matthew Isaac Cohen in his research on early forms of commercial theatre; Margaret J. Kartomi in her work on Indonesian musicology; Claudine Salmon and Mary Somers Heidhues, sporadically, in their formidable bodies of work on Chinese-Indonesian history and culture. Nor has Indonesian-language scholarship, to my knowledge, provided any study of the history of local *xiqu*.[2] One result of this gap is the erasure of the influence of the *xiqu* on Indonesian modern theatre in its formative period, an influence now in the process of piecemeal historical recovery.[3] By mustering the available primary and secondary language sources in Chinese, Indonesian, and Western languages, a broad overview can be attempted, allowing for a consideration of how *xiqu* represented Chineseness in the colonial period and afterwards. This in turn allows further consideration of how *xiqu* interacted with other genres, especially in the late colonial period.

Evidence for an Early Indies *Xiqu* History

The first evidence for Indies *xiqu* in Western sources dates from the beginning of the seventeenth century,[4] when Edmund Scott, head of the British commercial establishment in the western Java port of Banten, reported:

> [the local Chinese] delight verie much in Playes and Singing: but they haue the worst voyces, that one shall heare any people haue: The which Playes or Interludes, they holde as Seruice to their GOD: In the beginning of which, they often vse to burne a Sacrifice, the Priestes many times kneeling downe, and kissing the ground three times one presently after an other. These Playes are made commonly when they thinke their *Iunckes* or Shipping are set foorth from *China;* likwise when they are ariued at *Bantan,* and also when they set out from *Bantan* towardes *China:* sometimes they begin at noone, and ende not till the next day morning, beeing most commonly in the open streete, hauing Staiges set vp for the purpose. (Scott 1606, N3; document image 51)

Scott's comments are remarkably early, and must be among the oldest English-language account of Chinese theatre anywhere.[5] Less than a decade later, in 1612, John Saris (who in the following year would captain the first British ship to visit Japan) and Sir Henry Middleton were treated by "Kewee, the chiefe China Merchant" in Banten to a show "by Scenicks of China, which was performed on a Stage with good pronunciation and gesture" (Purchas 1625, 354).

Cornelis de Bruyn, visiting Batavia in 1706, exactly a century after Scott, likewise saw behavior from actors that "gave me reason to believe, that the piece they were then performing had an intermixture of religious worship" (1737, 92) and found Chinese theatre "in most parts of the city" (92).[6] François Valentijn, twenty years later, also records performances of "a comic or tragic Chinese theatre as are shown very often in Batavia" preceding junk departures, describing the performers as "young men and women raised for the purpose." According to the same author, performances were subject to taxes and lasted for two or three hours in the afternoon, followed by performances from nine in the evening to three or four in the morning (Valentijn [1724–1726] 1858, 536). The evidently ritual nature of the performance as described in these two earliest accounts matches the enduring association of Hokkien theatre with temple-based and propitiatory activity.

The ritual importance of theatrical performance is also recorded in the Dutch East India Company *Plakaatboek* (Book of edicts). Company officials, apparently concerned about the influence of Chinese theatre (as well as courtesan performances of song and dance like *ronggeng* and *tandak*), described its performance as "dangerous and inimical to the colony and the good residents thereof" (van der Chijs 1889, 6:110).[7] In 1751, the company instituted taxes on such performances; the taxes were higher if women were among the performers. An appeal from the Chinese community the next year claimed that it had been "in all China a constant maxim, yea even a religious duty since time immemorial that whenever someone has grown wealthy through business or otherwise, by successful enterprises or also through good luck . . . [he] must show his gratitude by organizing a show of public theatre or so-called wayang in honor of the divinity or the saint who had brought him good luck, as was previously practiced in this place" (van der Chijs 1889, 6:276–277). Furthermore, the tax, the petitioners stated, was deplorable because "a good number of poor and needy people can survive by renting out the necessary actresses, costumes, etc. or have obtained from the spectators the means to survive, etc." (van der Chijs 1889, 6:110–113, 276–278; quotation on 277).[8]

In a non-European language, the first known reference to what may be an Indies *xiqu* performance occurs in a Middle Javanese text called *Nawaruci*, which mentions "awayang Cina." Some have taken this as evidence of the presence of Chinese puppetry on Java in the sixteenth or seventeenth centuries (Kuardhani 2012, 31), although the reference might equally indicate any kind of Chinese entertainment, including non-puppet forms such as *xiqu*. An intriguing, relatively early Malay-language reference occurs in a historical poem known as *Syair Kompeni Welanda Berperang dengan Cina* (Syair of the Dutch company fighting a Chinese uprising), which tells the story of the 1740 Batavia massacre of the Chinese population and the ensuing Java War (1741–1743); the poem was composed roughly twenty years later (Liaw 2013, 471). The text makes reference to *wajang tjina* being performed by the Chinese troupes in the leader's camp (Rusconi 1935, 47). Again, the precise nature of this *wajang* cannot be determined, but it was probably theatrical, and the dominant Chinese entertainment of the period would have been some form of *xiqu*.

Casual reports by Europeans, most often from Batavia, can be found throughout the eighteenth and nineteenth centuries, many of them cursory or repetitive. The profusion of accounts was sufficient for historian Leonard Blussé, annotating a sketch of a *xiqu* performance by Dutch artist Jan Brandes (1743–1808), to describe Chinese theatre as "part and parcel of the standard repertoire [for] Euro-

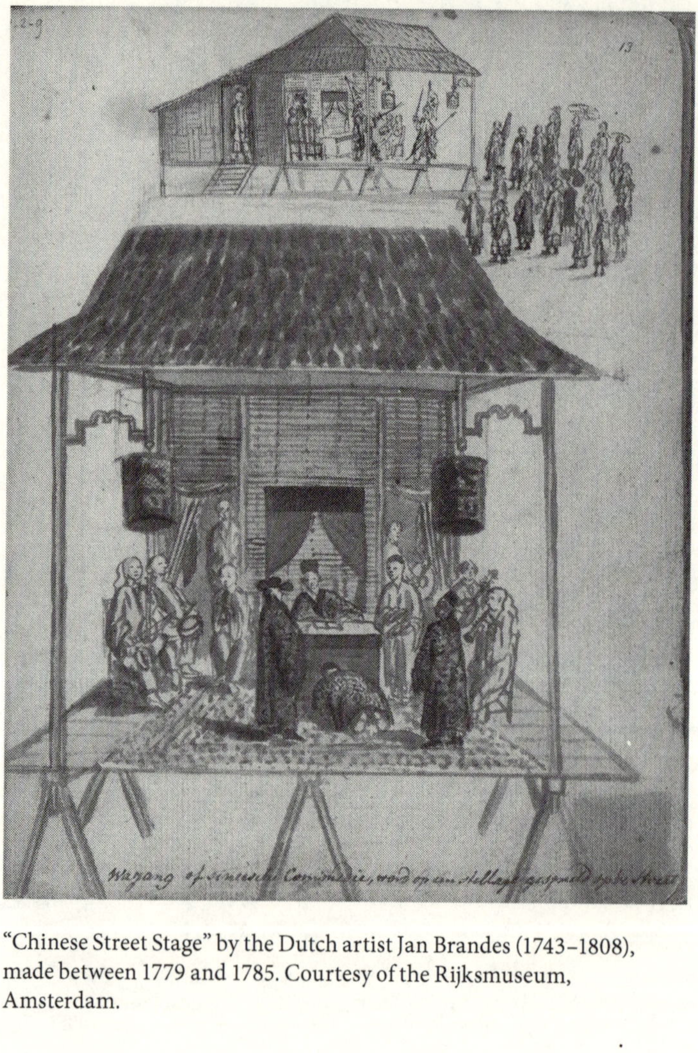

"Chinese Street Stage" by the Dutch artist Jan Brandes (1743–1808), made between 1779 and 1785. Courtesy of the Rijksmuseum, Amsterdam.

pean visitors to Batavia" (Blussé 2004, 207). The French explorer Bougainville, visiting Batavia in 1768, noted the daily "Chinese comedies" that were "performed on trestles at every crossroads in the Chinese quarter, [consisting of] little plays and pantomimes," entirely by "women playing the roles of men" (Bougainville 1982, 399). Others who noted the presence of *xiqu* in Batavia include Dutchmen such as de Bruyn and Jan Jacob Vogelaar (1792), the German Ernst Christoph Barchewitz (1752), and the Frenchman Charles François Tombe (1802–1806; Salmon and Lombard 1980, 263–264, 274, 276–277), not to mention the Swedish natural scientist Clas Fredrik Hornstedt, who in 1783 bribed his way backstage at a Chinese "comedy" and convinced a young actress to sell him the Malay-language script, apparently a translation from the Chinese (Kumar 1989, 252–253). William Thorn, an English military officer on Java from 1811 to 1814, reported that during the New Year "plays are exhibited on stages erected" in the Chinese quarter of Batavia, and "these pieces, which are called here 'Wyangs,' resemble our mountebank exhibitions." The performers, "who are female, trained up in the profession, . . . give the representations of battles between the Chinese and Tartars. The dialogue is all spoken, or sung, in the Chinese language" (Thorn 1815, 245–246).[9]

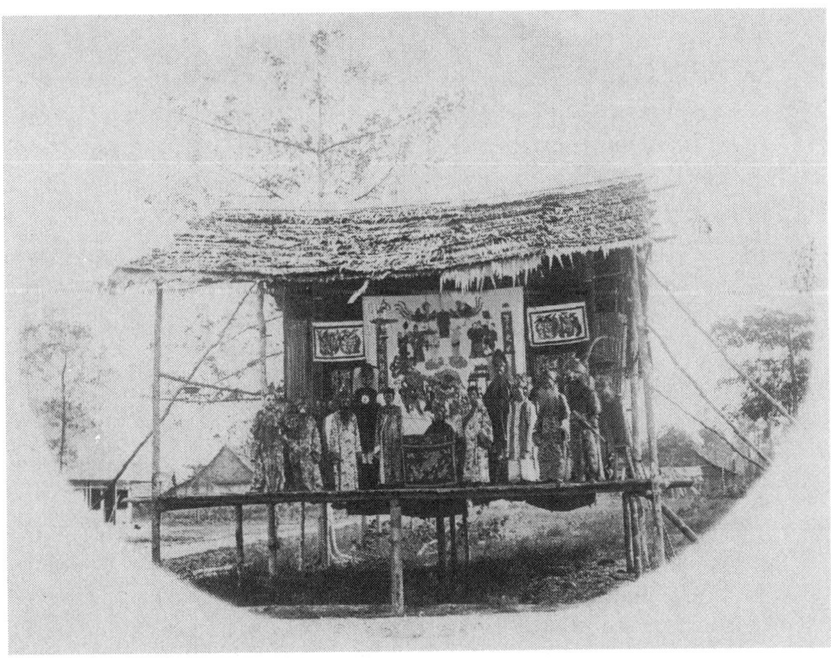

Xiqu stage, presumed in Batavia, ca. 1867. Courtesy of the KITLV digital image library.

One of the richest Western-language accounts of theatre in nineteenth-century Chinese Batavia is to be found in a text on the visit to Batavia of the USS *Potomac* in March and April 1832, fresh from the First Sumatran Expedition.[10] The author, Francis Warriner, "the schoolmaster responsible for the education of the seventeen midshipmen aboard the *Potomac*" (Goodrich-Hedrick and Hedrick 1972, 29), describes three separate encounters with Chinese "theatricals," all of them in some kind of ritual context. Despite Warriner's sniffy Puritanism and disdain for Chinese religion, his account contains valuable detail. Two of his encounters with theatre are associated with the "Festival of the Tombs" (i.e., Qing Ming 清明). The first of these certainly appears to be *xiqu* judging by its account of the orchestra, makeup, content, and vocal production.

> In front of this temple, theatrical scenery was exhibited, beautifully decorated, and extending over several feet of ground. Here various plays were acted. They consisted chiefly of representations of battles. During the encounter, the gongs, kettle-drums, cymbals, pipes, guitars, dulcimers, kept up the most deafening noise, reminding me of the description of the different instruments used in the days of Daniel and Belshazzar. The performers were the most grotesque personages that probably ever appeared upon a stage. Their faces were painted in the most fantastic and hideous manner. (Warriner 1835, 172–173)

Warriner goes on to describe the "rude song and whining recitative" performed by actors who "were engaged for a stipulated sum" in order to "appease the gods, in order to obtain from them special favors" (Warriner 1835, 173). His account is similar to that of a contemporary Dutchman, who complains that "a feel for music in the real sense of the word is unknown to the Chinese" (Sturler 1841, 135).

What Warriner saw in his other encounters with Chinese theatre is less certain. The second of the Qing Ming performances occurred at a famous tomb and was performed by "two little girls beautifully dressed, one of whom was handsome, the other perhaps was equally so, but her beauty was eclipsed by the large false mustachios she wore" (174). The orchestra consisted of "a couple of rusty old fellows beating a drum, which appeared as though it might have been a relic of the flood" (175). In the third performance, "the *dramatis personae* were, to all appearance, a man, a woman and a little girl, but I afterwards understood that they were all females of no very uncertain character" (Warriner 1835, 158). To Warriner the performances seemed "indecent in the extreme, yet they created much merriment for the Chinese by their efforts at drollery." The "farce" featured "singing in a moanful manner," and he "judged it to be some love affair" (158).

Despite the Chinese festival ritual context, it is not certain that all of what Warriner saw was indeed *xiqu*, and he makes no mention of the language used.

The instances of female clowning, female-to-male cross-dressing, and disreputability might suggest something like *ronggeng*, a dance form that has some Chinese roots and even today suggests "professional female singer-dancers whose duties are generally considered to include sexual services as well" (Spiller 2010, 82).[11] Warriner's account is valuable for recording the variety of performance in mid-century Chinese Batavia, including the presence of both female and mixed (or perhaps all-male) troupes, of comedy, romantic, and military features, of various kinds of orchestral accompaniment, the festival-related contracted employment of actors, and the likely coexistence and perhaps mixing of Chinese and non-Chinese forms.[12]

Chinese entertainments on Java seem to have been diverse in terms of gender, language, and ethnicity. Hornstedt's account of a Malay translation of Chinese theatre also suggests that hybridized Malay-Chinese theatricals were being performed as early as the 1780s, while Bougainville noted all-female cross-dressing troupes a half-century before Warriner. It seems that also by the late eighteenth century non-Chinese women were being trained as actresses in *xiqu* genres, with Wang Dahai 王大海, a Fujian literatus who lived in Batavia during the 1780s, noting that plays were performed all year long by "barbarian" 番 slave girls, doubtless Javanese or Balinese (van der Loon 1992, 32). Indeed, a Dutch mid-nineteenth-century source remarks about the Chinese that "at festivals they generally set up a kind of theatre *(wajang)* in which mostly various heroic deeds are presented, by actors and actresses, who (at least on Java) are servants or slaves, and mechanically learn their roles, without knowing Chinese" (Sturler 1841, 135; see also Cohen 2006, 8). A Dutch merchant, travelling to Canton in 1827, noted all-male *xiqu* troupes, the editors of the Indies newspaper in which it was published in 1840 remarking that "it is entirely the opposite in Batavia," presumably meaning that Chinese troupes in Batavia were mostly or entirely female (Meijer 1840, 215). Similarly, Viennese traveler Ida Pfeiffer reports the female-only *xiqu* company held by the Chinese major[13] Tan Eng Goan 陳永元 in 1850s Batavia, which she saw perform a military drama (Pfeiffer 1856, 189–190).[14]

However, A. W. P. Weitzel, in Batavia in 1858, reported both men and women performers (Weitzel 1860, 15), while at much the same time Aquasi Boachi[15] wrote of *xiqu* as a performance popular among new arrivals (*sinke/totok*) in which "only men can perform and only Chinese can be spoken" (Boachi 1856, 300), and Rees likewise noted all-male troupes in West Kalimantan (1858, 63). It seems probable that, while *xiqu* performances for Peranakan Chinese had acculturated in terms of theatre practices (in Malay and all-female), recent migrants from China performed *xiqu* that was not much acculturated (and was therefore in southern Chinese dialects and performed by men-only troupes). The flexibility of the terminology, and the unfamiliarity of the observers who wrote many of the surviving accounts, hinder the attempt to understand diversity and distinctions of the day. What seems certain, however, is that a variety of Chinese musical theatre practices, ranging from the highly adapted to forms recently arrived and unchanged, were familiar across the archipelago in the eighteenth and nineteenth centuries.

Commercial *Xiqu* and Touring

Troupes performing for wealthy individuals such as Tan Eng Goan began, it seems, to transform gradually into commercial enterprises. By the 1870s, Indies papers show that private *xiqu* clubs and public *xiqu* theatres had evolved, both indicating an increasing commercialization of the genre (Cohen 2016, 38–39). At the turn of the twentieth century, when *xiqu* was competing with the developing modern commercial theatre, Malay-language performances were evidently common, partly with a view to expanding the audience. Consider a 1900 Semarang newspaper report regarding a *xiqu* ("wajang Tjina") performance that had been given permission to replace a Stamboel company (in *gang* Gambiran, i.e., the Chinese quarter) stage: "the troupe consists of locally born Chinese [men] and women of this land who interpret the play in Malay, which will allow many people to get more out of it than from the usual wajang actors' gibberish" (*De Locomotief*, June 6, 1900). The fact that this was deemed noteworthy suggests that a shift was in progress; but also that a clear distinction was also being retained between this Malay-language *xiqu* (or *xiqu*-derived) form, and *stamboel.*

Genres competed and cross-pollinated, with several of the early Java-based commercial theatres sharing resources and narratives with *xiqu,* and some of the same ethnic Chinese entrepreneurs operating troupes in both genres (Cohen 2006, 8, 39–40, 56–57, 104, 231–232). Such shifts alert us to the fact that, as with later hybrid genres, *xiqu* as performed in China may not give us an adequate idea of what "wajang Tjina" or similar terms meant at the turn of the twentieth century in the Indies.

As a general rule, colonial accounts of Chinese theatre are the "stereotyped descriptions of Western authors who only tell us of their boredom and incomprehension" (Lombard 1990, 277). Consider this 1869 account from Batavia:

> A Chinese *waiang,* before its arrival from Singapore announced with great ado as "Chinese opera," remains at present for our public entertainment. The name "entertainment" is, however, badly-chosen; at least the shack built especially in Glodok is very little visited by Europeans, since the performances are of the kind that ladies judged them entirely "unpalatable." (*De Locomotief,* September 9, 1921)

Or this newspaper report from Semarang, a major center of *xiqu* in the late nineteenth century:

> Nocturnal noise. Inhabitants of the city, especially those who live near the Chinese district [*kamp*], complain about the cacophonous, piercing music [?] of the Chinese opera, which almost every evening until late at night makes their so necessary nightly rest next to impossible. (*De Locomotief*, November 11, 1881)

The question mark after "music" is in the original.

Although performances in Malay certainly suggest local troupes, by the mid-nineteenth century a complex international *xiqu* itinerary can also be discerned from Dutch and Chinese sources. A Dutch newspaper commented in 1860 that a visiting troupe was, "We are assured, the first time that a real Chinese wajang has come to Batavia" (Haan 1922, 1:507), and this does coincide fairly closely with the period when tours to the Indies appear in Chinese *xiqu* histories and gazetteers. Judging by these, touring was common from mid-century to mid-century, not stopping even during the wartime occupation of the Indies and Malaya.[16] Almost all itinerant troupes that came to the Indies also had stops elsewhere in Southeast Asia, most often in the Malay Peninsula, Sarawak, and the Philippines (ZGXQZ 1993, 47–55; 467; Chen et al. 1997, 41–43; Zhang 2007, 738–745; Lee 2009, 45).

Chinese accounts of such trips to the Indies start with the repeated visits of a Hokkien *gaojiaxi* 高甲戲 troupe called Fujinxing 福金興 (Fortunate and Golden Prosperity) between 1834 and 1844 (ZGXQZ 1993, 47; Chen et al. 1997, 41–43; Lai S. 2007, 497; Zhang 2007, 738–745). Outside the tours discussed below, gazetteers and histories mention several troupes that are recorded simply as visiting "Nanyang" (the South Seas), a Chinese term for much of Southeast Asia and including British Malaya and the Philippines as well as the Dutch East Indies (Chen et al. 1997, 41–43; Zhang 2007, 738–745).[17] Likely the tours captured by the historical record are merely a small fragment of the total picture.

It is around this time, due to the presence of Chinese sources, that one can begin to apply the apparatus of Chinese genre terminology. *Gaojiaxi*, a living southern Fujian form centered in the Quanzhou region, seems to have been the dominant form of Chinese theatre in maritime Southeast Asia until the 1930s. It is therefore also the likeliest candidate for the type of theatre seen by an envoy from Vietnam, Cao Bá Quát 高伯适, who wrote a poem about a 1844 *xiqu* performance in Batavia, "Contrast[ing] the valiant behavior of the protagonists in the drama with the Chinese spectators' total disinterest toward the tragedy that had recently transpired in their homeland (the Opium War)" (Kelley 1998).

Another record of *gaojiaxi* is found in 1848 (Wang 2011, 10), and by the 1870s and 1880s, *gaojiaxi* troupes were making frequent visits to the Indies from their homes in southern Fujian. The record of repertoire includes pieces from familiar narrative systems such as the *Sanguo Yanyi* 三國演義 (The Romance of the Three Kingdoms), *Shuihu zhuan* 水滸傳 (The Water Margin), *Xiyou ji* 西遊記 (Journey to the West), *Baishe zhuan* 白蛇傳 (The White Snake) and *Liang Shanbo yu Zhu Yingtai* 梁山伯與祝英台 (Liang Shanbo and Zhu Yingtai)[18] as well as pieces that are less well known today (ZGXQZ 1993, 47–55; Chen et al. 1997, 41–43; Zhang 2007, 738–745). In print, many of these narratives would make their way, often multiple times, into Malay, Javanese, and other archipelagic languages by the end of the century. There is also some indication that around this time Hainan troupes were already visiting or even settling in Bali (Salmon and Sidharta 2000, 106).

Wang Hanmin's listing of Fujian *xiqu* tours abroad (2011, 180–191) includes fifteen *gaojiaxi* troupes that visited the Indies (several of them evidently on more than one occasion and/or on trips lasting a number of years) from the mid-nineteenth until the mid-twentieth century, with the greatest concentration in the mid-to-late 1920s. The Indies were evidently integrated into many a theatrical career: a brief official biography of venerable *gaojiaxi* actor Dong Yifang 董義芳 (1902–1965), has him cutting his teeth as an adolescent in the Indies from 1917 to 1921; another troupe recruited children in 1915, trained them for four months, and then educated them as actors over three years of performance in Southeast Asia before returning them to their parents as free actors. The region seems thus to have been a major source of performance income for southern Fujian troupes, as well as an arena in which to acquire experience before returning to the Hokkien homeland (ZGXQZ 1993, 48, 471; FJSWSYJG; Wang 2011, 184).

Other visits from the Mainland in the first half of the twentieth century, as recorded in Fujian, Guangdong, and Hainan sources, include *waijiangxi* 外江戲, a West Fujian form[19] now forming part of the *hanju* 漢劇 genre (three troupes between 1910 and 1927);[20] and another living southern Fujian form, *xiao liyuan* 小梨園 (now absorbed into *liyuanxi* 梨園戲), which visited Surabaya in 1925. *Fuzhouxi* 福州戲, the antecedent to *minju* 閩劇, is represented by a single troupe (ca. 1931, performing in Surabaya and Semarang after stops in Malaya and Taiwan), as is *qiongzhouxi* 瓊州戲 from Hainan (1935), that is, the genre now generally known as *qiongju* 瓊劇. *Chaoju* 潮劇, which originates in the southeastern coastal area of Chaozhou/Shantou (i.e., Teochew/Swatow), also appears to have visited in the late colonial period, especially Medan and Surabaya (Zhou 1999, 178). The Laosai Yongfeng 老賽永豐 troupe, which ultimately settled in Penang, toured some part of the Indies, probably in the mid-century.[21] Nio Joe Lan 梁友蘭, a Batavian Chinese author, wrote in 1943 of the occasional visit of Cantonese troupes, presumably performing *yueju* 粵劇, though locals "don't go often . . . [as] most Chinese born here cannot speak Chinese anymore" (1943, 266).

Xiqu as a Pan-Indies Phenomenon

Although a documentary bias means that certain cities of Java are overrepresented, there are hints throughout the late colonial period of *xiqu* occurring throughout the archipelago. An 1858 letter shows it being performed in the festivities surrounding the coronation of the sultan of Lingga-Riau in the Riau Archipelago (van der Putten and Azhar 2007, 167). In 1902, Cantonese opera (often referred to as *wayang makau*) was being performed alongside Malay opera (*komedi melayu*, probably a form of *bangsawan*) for Chinese ritual performances in Padang (Cohen 2003, 215).[22] Reports from Dutch newspapers also show that performances occurred in Surabaya, where pieces might "take four or five days

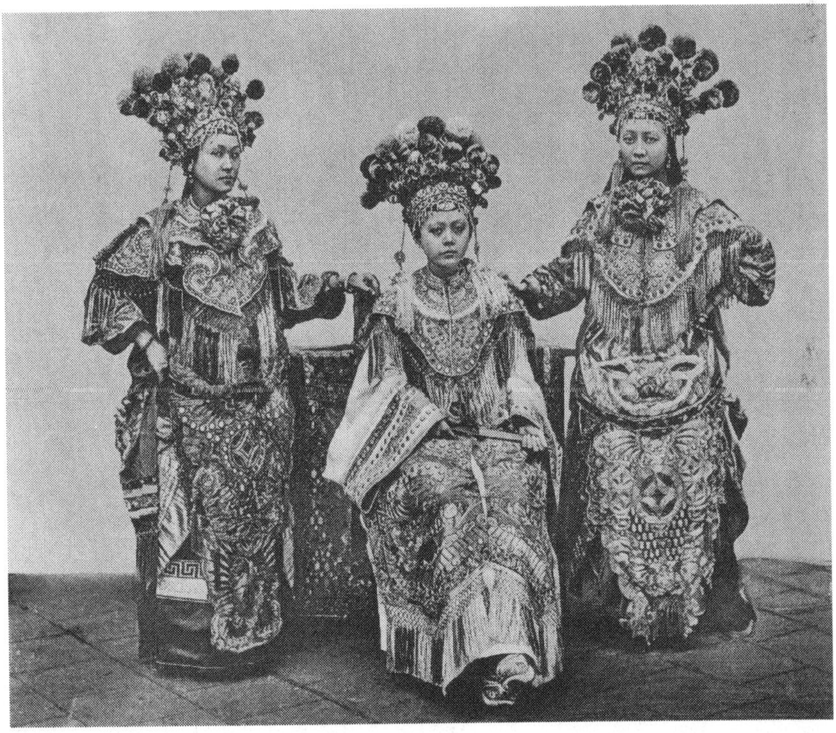

Lithograph of *xiqu* actors in East Java ca. 1910. Courtesy of the KITLV digital image library.

before they are at an end" (*De Locomotief,* November 16, 1885) and in Makassar (*Soerabaijasch Handelsblad,* August 22, 1929). Cantonese opera seems to have been active in Malang into the 1950s (Budianta 2012, 264).

The heavily Chinese areas of West Kalimantan also hosted frequent *xiqu* performances, with perhaps the earliest mention occurring in Rees' 1858 account of Hakka-dominated *kongsi* life in Montrado. Rees' passage, despite the contempt typical of nineteenth-century Western-language accounts, paints a picture of *xiqu* much as it would have been anywhere in southern China: temporary stages were set up across from temples on festival days, with orchestras on the side of the stage. The description of plots as "partly taken from the history and legends of the Heavenly Empire, partly drawn from the realm of fantasy" seems a reasonable account of *xiqu* narrative sources (1856, 61–63).[23] Mary Somers Heidhues' history of West Kalimantan's Chinese community also mentions *wayang* performance, in the context of that period very probably some kind of *xiqu,* in Pontianak in 1884 and in Mandor in 1885, both as part of festivities (Heidhues 2003, 107, 113). The references may well have resembled the *xiqu* shows on a little square in Pontianak as described here by a Dutch official. A series of performances formed a

> single drama of amazing length, with which neither the Chinese, who understood it, nor the Inlanders [*pribumi*], who understood not a syllable thereof, lost patience for even a moment. The attractive and rich costumes of the actors and their dashing performance formed a strong contrast to the primitive and poor condition of the high-uplifted stage, with its bamboo supports and roof of leaves. No wings were provided, so that the staging was in no way concealed, while the musicians sat right on stage among the performing actors. The sounds produced by the orchestra were reminiscent of a busy copper- or tinsmiths' workshop, with a screeching and scratching and squeaking accompaniment of fiddles and bagpipes and clarinets and of shrill triangle clanging. Just as among the Chinese shops the nose is very sorely tested, thus by such performances is the ear. (Buys 1892, 47)

He goes on to remark that it was fortunate for Indies Europeans that their districts were generally located far away from the Chinese areas.

A documentary gap intervenes, but vibrant *xiqu* practice must have continued in that region for at least half a century: according to Matthew Isaac Cohen, in the early twentieth century *xiqu* troupes, "[i]mported from China via Singapore, attracted large audiences night after night in tent shows" all along the west coast of Dutch colonial Borneo (Cohen 2006, 317), and a generation later, a visitor to the same city reported that people were brought in by motorboats for "cinemas, Malay and Chinese 'opera'" (*NDNI,* February 25, 1926). In the 1930s, there were still *chaoju* activities (alongside drum and instrumental works) at the Teochew Society (Chaozhou gonghui) in Singkawang (West Kalimantan; Hui 2011, 250–251), and visits of touring Hakka troupes persisted until the 1960s (Kartomi 2000, 304). Older Pontianak community members have retained a memory that *chaoju* was performed in Pontianak in the colonial era; Singapore elder performers recall visiting *chaoju* groups there and Jakarta in the 1920s and 1930s (Yeo How Jiang, pers. comm., October 28, 2016).[24]

In Bangka, too, *xiqu* performance seems to have been quite lively. The musicologist Margaret J. Kartomi reports Hokkien and Hakka opera on that island until the mid-twentieth century (Kartomi 2000, 306; 2012, 401n4). Almost a hundred years earlier, in the 1860s, the painter Jan Toorop (the child of a Dutch father and a British-Chinese mother) had spent his childhood years there. His words (as quoted by Kwee Kek Beng 郭克明) describe his wanderings through the Chinese quarter: "They were performing theatre on the street! Beautiful! I've never seen anything like it again. The beauty of the gestures! That inner rich civilization! Our clothing is so deplorable! And our stage sets! The Chinese know about: the grand sweep [*de grote lijn*]" (Kwee 1936, 86).

As to Medan, *xiqu* was witnessed there in 1922 by the greatest Dutch author of the period, Louis Couperus. He reported enjoying *xiqu* (*Wajang-Tjina*) despite the "ear-splitting, heart-rending discords" and although after a few hours "our Western nerves and admiration could not be held in suspense." He noted the spare stage furnishings and compared *xiqu* favorably to the commercial Malay-language theatre *stamboul,* which he also saw (Couperus 1924, 70). A newspaper report from 1928 suggests that at least some performers in Medan were still being recruited from China; the article concerns an actor who had decided to convert to Islam and stay in the Indies, and whose employer objected that he would have to forfeit the deposit he had paid for his entry at Medan's port of Belawan (*De Sumatra Post,* February 3, 1928).

A generation later, *chaoju* was still being performed in Medan's Huaqiao zonghui 華僑總會 (Chinese General Society) and later in the Chaozhou Huiguan 潮州會館 (Teochew Society), where it was attended by members of various Chinese communities (Tsai 2008, 248; 2013, 83; Linbai 2011).[25] Local respondents in recent interviews remembered there being, during the Sukarno years, two or three active *chaoju* troupes in Medan alone, largely serving temple fairs.[26] Indonesian tours were also an important source of income for Singaporean troupes in the prewar period up to the 1960s, likely visiting Java as well as Sumatra and Riau, in *chaoju, yueju,* and even *jingju* (i.e., Peking opera) genres[27] (*Lianhe wanbao,* July 30, 1983; National Archives 1988, 49; *Straits Times,* December 25, 2000). It seems probable that, with enough time and effort, evidence of *xiqu* practice could probably be turned up in nearly every part of Indonesia between 1850 and 1965.

Xiqu as a Nationalist Project

Though much of *xiqu* performance was rural and much of the audience illiterate, the new late-colonial Chinese intellectuals could also incorporate *xiqu* into projects aiming to boost cultural nationalism among late colonial Indies Chinese. In 1936, Kwee Kek Beng wrote (in Dutch) that "along with Chinese literature, theatre forms one of the invisible ties that still connect Overseas Chinese with the old homeland, on which the great heroes and sages, whose deeds they follow with rapt attention, fought and lived. Statues are not erected to China's great men, but they live on through theatre and literature in the hearts and minds of the people and thereby enjoy virtual immortality" (Kwee 1936, 85).

Yet because local Chinese could not usually speak any Chinese language, the shows were "Chinese plays in Chinese costumes with Chinese music and according to Chinese stage technique" but with the "actors and actresses doing their utmost" in Malay. Kwee singles out two performers from twenty years before his 1936 article, a Peranakan woman called T(h)eng Poei Nio[28] of the company Swie Ban Lian, and a *pribumi* woman called Samirah who, "in her enactment of Chinese roles was in no way the inferior of her Indo Chinese [i.e., Peranakan] rival" (Kwee 1936, 85). He goes on to note that the theatre was declining under the pressure of cinema and other entertainments, despite efforts at revival. He would repeat the comments fifteen years later, dating the golden age of Indies theatre to the first decade of the twentieth century (Kwee 1951).

A 1941 report of performances in Batavia shows institutional support for *xiqu* and an attempt to frame it as "classical" Chinese culture. As with many other Chinese community performances, the event was connected to charity drives,[29] in this case to benefit the Chinese Red Cross, which was providing relief to China at a time when the Second Sino-Japanese War was in progress but the Indies were at peace; the Chinese consul-general Robert Tschou-Kwong Kah 葛祖爌 was in attendance.[30] The show was organized by the China Instituut[31] and the Ta Hsioh Hsioh Sing Hui 大學學生會 (Chinese Students Association) in order to introduce the classical Chinese opera to the European and [ethnic Chinese] Western-oriented public (*Bataviaasch Nieuwsblad,* January 29 and February 10, 1941). Performers came from Jambi and Palembang, perhaps suggesting that by this time Sumatra had a livelier *xiqu* scene than Java. The show consisted of a version of the Wang Baochuan 王寶釧 story ("Lady Pearl Stream") and an episode from the *Three Kingdoms* in which Guan Yu 關羽 captures Cao Cao 曹操 but is honor-bound to release him.[32]

Such performances ran parallel to, and were probably influenced by, the effort of Republican Chinese intellectuals to represent *xiqu*—usually *jingju*—as the epitome of a classical culture. This tendency was typified by the tours of Mei

Lanfang to the United States (1930) and Europe and to the Soviet Union (1935), both of which were reported in Indies papers (e.g., *De Sumatra Post*, February 28, 1930; *NDNI*, February 15, 1935) and of which Chinese communities seem to have been generally aware.[33] The same impulse to claim *xiqu* for classical culture may have lain behind local efforts to translate Chinese plays into Dutch or Malay, a project that Kwee linked to efforts during the same period in Beijing to render dramatic works into German (Kwee 1951, 20).[34] For one Cantonese photographer, a transplant arriving from Singapore in 1928, the idea of *xiqu* must have carried a certain international ethnic prestige, for he decorated his Semarang studio with "[e]legant portraits of wealthy Singaporeans and Chinese opera stars . . . testaments to both his skill and his cosmopolitanism" (Strassler 2008, 416). The new project to re-sinicize Chinese-Indonesians and the equally new Mainland Chinese project to make *xiqu* a symbol of national pride and culture seem to have briefly come together, at least for some people and some events.

Mixed Audiences, Hybrid Genres, Checkered Reputations

It would be an error to imagine that performances occurred in some kind of ethnic Chinese isolation. Even before commercial theatre attracted the multiethnic audiences that are sometimes linked to the stirring of urban modernity, records make it clear that Europeans and *pribumi* were routine members of various *xiqu* audiences (see also Thorn 1815, 245; Zhang 2007, 78). One mid-century Dutchman reported that Batavia Eurasians were especially fond of Chinese entertainments (Abeyasekere 1983, 25). Newspaper reports throughout the nineteenth century, such as this one from Semarang in 1895, show audiences to have been thoroughly mixed: "The Chinese *waiang* played yesterday in gang Pinggir. There were hundreds of spectators, [so many that] you could have walked on their heads. The Bandar [store manager] of the local opium lease had on this occasion arranged some festivities to watch, to which a number of Europeans, Chinese and distinguished *inlanders* [*pribumi*] were invited" (*De Locomotief*, October 14, 1895, 189, 14:10).

Similarly, in Thio Tjin Boen's 張振文 1902 novel *Cerita Oey Se* (Story of Oey Se), the *wayang makau* (Cantonese opera) is hired for his daughter's wedding, which is attended by European officials and high-ranking Javanese. The performance series lasts a whole month, at ruinous expense for the Chinese protagonist, and is evidence of his breakneck pursuit of wealth and status (Thio 2002, 227). The colonial newspaper record shows that Chinese, European, and *pribumi* genres might appear side by side at lavish Chinese weddings (Abeyesekere 1983, 26).

At other times, *xiqu* venues feature in the colonial papers as sites of trouble. An 1874 article reports a scuffle involving a Javanese man who had stopped to watch “wajang chinees” in the Chinese quarter of Semarang and grown angry with a Chinese man for repeatedly illuminating the curtains behind which a Javanese woman in a *glinding* (carriage) was concealed, presumably in an effort to see her figure (*De Locomotief,* June 1, 1874). Though hosting performances of *xiqu* was prestigious, the actors themselves, as in China (and many other places), were often held in low regard (Cohen 2006, 56–57). Dutch-language newspaper reports involving kidnappings and pickpockets in the milieu of the Chinese theatre confirm that theatre was looked upon with suspicion.

If the audiences for all *xiqu* performances were mixed, the performance practices also continued to show evidence of hybridity. In the last decade of the nineteenth century, the innovations of theatre financier Yap Goan Thay 葉元泰 (a key figure in the development of a vernacular and commercial theatre as well) included the removal of gongs as too noisy and the addition of Malay-speaking clowns to certain performances of his Pasuruan-based *xiqu* troupe (Cohen 2001, 330). Thio Thiong Gie 張忠義 a senior puppeteer of the *wayang potehi* genre, a hybrid Hokkien-Indonesian glove-puppet form, reported that as a youth in Semarang in the 1950s he had performed “Hokkien opera” (Thio, pers. comm., January 23, 2013).[35] Crossover between puppet and human *xiqu* genres seems also to have occurred in West Kalimantan. Such practices result in an unclear relationship to the relatively rigid genre boundaries of *xiqu* as defined after the establishment of the PRC and projected backwards on Chinese *xiqu* history. The fluidity between genres may suggest local adaptation and a wide variety of less formally framed performance, as well as the small number of trained performers. The popularity of puppetry on Java may also have encouraged such crossings.

Other forms of Chinese musical theatre existed in prewar Batavia, with no obvious counterparts elsewhere. One such was called *wayang sin pe* or *sinpee* 新琵, performed only by children and devoted to “enacting Chinese dramas for the many residents of Chinese descent,” even though “none of [the child actors spoke] Chinese ordinarily” (Nio 1935, 198–199). Unsurprisingly, martial stories were popular in this genre, especially those belonging to the narrative world of the Tang dynasty hero Xue Rengui 薛仁貴 (in Indonesia, usually Sie Djin Kwie; Phoa 1949, 37).[36] *Wayang sin pe*’s musical system may have been similar to other Peranakan (i.e., acculturated and mixed Chinese-Indonesian) forms (Phoa 1949, 37; Yampolsky 2013a, 355, 360), featuring prominent use of the *gambang,* a xylophone-like instrument that is also part of the *gamelan* orchestra. The name *sin pe,* however, is apparently drawn from another instrument in the orchestra, the lute-like *pipa* (Nio 1935, 198; Yampolsky 2013a, 355), while its notation seems to have been a form of *gongche* (Phoa 1949, 37), the predominant notation system in China from the eighteenth century (Lam 1997, 36) until the twentieth.

For martial scenes, such as “Wu Song Slays a Tiger,” a familiar highlight drawn from the Water Margin narrative system and common to many *xiqu* genres (including several from Fujian), "Chinese tamborines [*sic*] and cymbals [were] used" (Nio 1935, 200). On the other hand, the *gambang*, long a favorite of Peranakan communities, was such a central element that one *sin pe* society, a branch of a larger cultural organization called Ngo Hong Lauw 五鳳樓 (Five Phoenixes Tower) described its aims as "the study of the *gambang* through the introduction of melodies and the promotion of harmony among the Chinese," although the melodies are described in the same article as being "purely Chinese," and costumes appear to have been based on (or perhaps borrowed from) *xiqu* (Nio 1935, 198–199), and most performances were held for Chinese institutions or families on the occasion of major Chinese holidays (Nio 1935, 199–200). The project of performing old Chinese narratives in Chinese (probably Hokkien, as *sin pe* reflects that pronunciation) is illustrative of how Chinese performance, including *xiqu*, could be in its intention part of an effort to retain a specific Chinese cultural identity yet in its form an expression of Chinese-Indonesian hybridity.

A vaguer account by economist Ong Eng Die 王恩帝 (the Indonesian finance minister from 1953 to 1955), suggests a great deal of hybridity among *xiqu* and related performance: "beside the original Chinese theatre associations, Malay-speaking associations have emerged with actors born in Indonesia, who perform Chinese plays in Chinese costumes, with Chinese music and according to Chinese stage technique. The difference is that the text is given in Malay" (Ong 1943, 216). Ong may be describing performances such as those by the newspaperman L. Soema Ciu Sing, whose "Chinese Opera" troupe "gave frequent performance throughout the occupation," donating the proceeds to Jakarta schools and victims of the war, both Peranakan and non-Chinese. While probably best categorized as *sandiwara* and performed in Indonesian for both *pribumi* and Peranakan audiences, the stories, music, and costumes were clearly influenced by *xiqu* (Kartomi 2000, 296; Kwartanada 2010b, 400).

Other genres are even more vaguely remembered. At the beginning of the twentieth century, one could "find a street narrator on one of the busiest parts of the lower city of Batavia, reciting popular folktales for which he received payment from the listeners" (Nio 1947, 15). Mid-century Chinese associations performed classical Chinese stories in "tableau or pantomime form" (Nio 1943, 266). My respondents in Bandung born in the 1930s and 1940s had childhood memories of market-based Chinese performances of acrobatics, narrated stereoscopes, stilt-walking, and storytelling, especially around Chinese festival times. One Bandung respondent mentioned Shandong storytellers, corresponding to Jaap Kunst's mention of "itinerant Chinese Shantung peddlers" playing small drums called *klontong* (1973, 1:218–219). These largely undocumented performance types, dimly recollected, suggest that in the mid-twentieth century there was still a wide spectrum of Chinese-language performance practices in Sino-Indonesian communities that likely had developed hybrid, local, and/or novel characteristics.

Unfortunately, the passage of time and the small-scale and unscripted form of the performance make that history largely unrecoverable, and it is difficult to form any conclusions when confronted with information such as the fact that children in Batavia once performed "on a boat made of bamboo and paper" in a genre of uncertain etymology known as "T'ang Hua Ko," singing the "Song of the Beggars" (Nio 1935, 200), or that in 1711 Valentijn saw Chinese children in Ambon performing a "song drama danced on hobby-horses" (van der Loon 1992, 29). Whether or not such genres ought to be classified as *xiqu* is something of a moot point, given the present paucity of information.

Decline in the Late Colonial Period and Early Republic

Although clearly widely performed until the late colonial era, it would seem that *xiqu* was declining due to assimilation and loss of language as well as the competition of cinema (Kwee 1936, 85; 1951a, 21) even before its suppression under New Order. As early as 1922, an account from Batavia considered that the frequency of performance and the splendor of costume had declined, and that in general "the Chinese stage has ceded to the cheaper convolutions and screeching of native [*inlandsche*] ronggeng." The development marked, in a view of that author, a decline in Chinese piety, as *xiqu* performances had ritual purposes (Haan 1922, 1:507). This view was seconded thirty years later by Kwee Kek Beng, who found that the decreasing frequency of performance was "not only an artistic loss" (Kwee 1951, 21).

Elderly fieldwork respondents from Java and Kalimantan, born in the 1930s and 1940s, generally reported that human *xiqu* was something their own parents, but not they themselves, had listened to or watched. Nor does the cultural memory generally take a very specific form. The genre distinctions tend, when ethnic Chinese are speaking Indonesian, to be phrased in such vague terms as "Hokkien opera" (presumably *gaojiaxi* and *gezaixi*). Dutch-language colonial accounts are no more exact, referring to "Chineesche opera," while in Malay- and Indonesian-language sources, a variety of often ambiguous terms are and were used, including "wayang orang [i.e., human-actor *wayang*] Cina," "wayang Cina," and sometimes "opera Cina." Varieties of Chinese theatre became more thoroughly and rigidly defined on the Mainland after the establishment of the People's Republic; it may thus be anachronistic to try and fit the current terminology of *xiqu* genres too closely onto these historical forms.

The living memory in North Sumatra is more vivid, with the *chaoju* and *yueju* scenes already mentioned. As part of a wide range of performing arts running the gamut from Indonesian dances through the minorities of China, the largely PRC-leaning voluntary organizations also produced a considerable amount of *xiqu* in the years before the Suharto period. Connections with Mainland China and leftist groups in other parts of Southeast Asia were considerable in this period, and at least two Medan performers eventually made careers in PRC theatre.[37] Visitors to China brought back ideas for improving theatre productions, and at least one Fujian theatre director, Xu Ke 許可, came to work in Medan. There he directed not only the great Hokkien opera classic *Chen San and Wuniang* 陳三五娘,[38] which was shown throughout the North Sumatra region to packed houses, but also Zhejiang *yueju* 越劇.[39] Simple costumes and props were made locally; more complicated items were brought from China (Han 2007b, 67). Similar community *xiqu* productions occurred in Jakarta, on some occasions attended by PRC diplomats (including ambassador Huang Zhen 黃鎮) and Jakarta municipal politicians ("Fujian liyuanxi Chen San Wuniang"; "Qin Xianglian" Huang Kunzhang 1991, 30; Taylor 2018, 180n97).[40]

In Sumatran Chinese communities particularly, with their close ties to Penang and Singapore, the appearances of touring troupes seem to have been very common: one diary of a migrant arriving on Sumatran shores in 1947 bound for Siantar, records him watching *chaoju* en route, in the town of Tebing Tinggi, on his third night in Indonesia (Huang Zhenkun 2010). According to Chinese-language Medan author Jin Meizi 金梅子, in the early 1960s a *chaoju* troupe's performance (also in Tebing Tinggi) was interrupted and the costumes burned, likely by leftists who perceived an association between the troupe and the KMT (Jin Meizi, pers. comm., November 7, 2016). In both Medan and Siantar, the popularity of *chaoju* performance, perhaps under the influence of Hong Kong–produced *chaoju* movies,[41] persisted into the 1960s (Linbai 2011; Fu 2012).

If *gaojiaxi* seems to have begun the touring history, it was largely replaced mid-century throughout the Hokkien world by *gezaixi*. One record from 1932 reports a mixed-gender *gezaixi* troupe Fenghuang ban 鳳凰班 (The Phoenix Troupe), then known as *taiwanxi* 台灣戲 (Taiwanese opera) visiting Singapore on the way to and from a performance in Medan (Lai Suchun 2007, 498). Afterwards, this genre seems not to have found popularity in Indonesia, with the exception of the heavily Hokkien Sumatra town of Bagansiapiapi.[42] There, Hokkien was almost universally spoken, but relatively few people were literate, a fact that might have made theatre (as well as the instrumental genre *nanyin* 南音)[43] particularly popular and influential. *Gezaixi* troupes were invited from Taiwan and Singapore for temple festivals until 1965, especially from 1945 to 1955, during which time there was a commercial theatre building, the Guangrong Theatre 光榮戲院. The most famous local troupe apparently was known as Sin Sai Hong 新賽鳳, bearing the same name as one of Singapore's most famous *gezaixi* troupes.[44] Regular daily performances diminished into an occasional festival temple performance before the beginning of New Order (Chen Dexian, pers. comm., November 7, 2016). Some *chaoju* shows, including *The Accused*

Father 告親夫, *The Riverview Pavilion* 望江亭, and *The Phoenix Hairpin* 釵頭鳳, were reworked into *gezaixi* in the early 1960s for use in a Bagansiapiapi Chinese school, where some of the Sin Sai Hong veterans also taught performance. Apparently, such *gezaixi* adaptations were also on the verge of being staged in Medan when the events of September 1965 intervened (Chen Dexian, pers. comm., November 11, 2016).

The decline in *xiqu* was in part due to the arrival of new mass media, but *xiqu* was also to some degree incorporated in these. As the audiovisual culture of the East Indies developed, *xiqu* also became an element of mass media: radio programs in 1937–1942 list "Chinese opera" being played regularly on the Malay-language channels V.O.R.O. and Nirom. In 1937, a Nirom broadcast of a Chinese troupe called Hiap Kioen Hie "had to be cancelled, because the script had not been sent to the government 14 days beforehand for approval" (Yampolsky 2013a, 183). Hiap Kioen Hie appears in radio listings throughout the late 1930s on the V.O.R.O. channel, described variously as "Chinese opera," or "radio play" by a "music and opera society" (*Bataviaasch Nieuwsblaad,* March 3, 1937; December 9, 1938; and February 25, 1939), although on the few occasions where Hiap Kioen Hie's repertoire is listed, titles suggest more a Malay-language musical theatre than a *xiqu* performance; on one occasion the troupe's show was even referred to as "Chineesch-Maleeisch tooneel," that is, a "Chinese-Malay play" (*Bataviaasch Nieuwsblaad,* March 3, 1937).[45] Other programs, however, such as *patim* (i.e., *bayin,* 八音 "eight sounds") or "Amoy music" (perhaps *nanyin/nanguan,* i.e., southern Fujian small ensembles, most often with a singer) may have included some vocal or even theatrical music, and in any event *xiqu* music was available to Chinese consumers through imported Mainland or Malay Peninsula recordings (Yampolsky 2013a, 39, 117, 253).

Furthermore, movie listings from 1934 to 1935 for Siantar in North Sumatra indicate that *xiqu* films were being shown (e.g., *De Sumatra Post,* June 28, 1935), and some opera films were among the Hokkien dialect films shown in Indonesia in the 1950s (Taylor 2011, 9, 135).[46] The probable effect of such films was felt in the choice of repertoire in both *chaoju* and *yueju,* at least in Sumatra. By the mid-1960s, however, the great period of traditional Chinese *xiqu* on the silver screen was coming to an end, and so was the freedom of the Chinese community to present itself on the public stage of Indonesia.

New Order and Contemporary Human *Xiqu* in Indonesia

Despite the many and repeated claims of its imminent demise inside and outside China, and in the face of political suppression and changing technologies, *xiqu* has proven resilient time and time again. In Indonesia, genres of *xiqu* altered as migration patterns changed and local adaptations increased. Official contacts between Indonesia and the PRC flourished during the 1950s, and so commercial tours were replaced with diplomatic delegations. A break of almost thirty years would follow before the modest revival of *xiqu* in Indonesia over the last three decades.

In 1955, a visiting delegation from the PRC included *Jingju* performers (*Shenghuo bao*, June 25, 1955; *Het nieuwsblad voor Sumatra*, August 3, 1955), although the first dedicated postindependence *xiqu* tour may have occurred in 1959. On that occasion, *minju* performers including Zheng Yizou 鄭奕奏 (1903–1993), sometimes known as "Fujian's Mei Lanfang," were invited by Chinese organizations in Jakarta, Bandung, and Solo to teach for six months (ZGXQZ 1993, 27, 55). Zheng's students in Bandung and Solo founded amateur associations, which continued after Zheng's departure (Lai 1993, 228). Little if anything is known of these groups' further performance, but Fujian *xiqu* artists were also included in a June 1961 Chinese cultural delegation to Indonesia (Wang 2011, 196), at a time when local troupes were vanishing in all but a few Indonesian locations. All of these visits likely depended on official support, and the 1955 and 1961 visits were completely official in nature and must be understood in the context of the PRC's cultural diplomacy of the period. With the establishment of New Order and its repression of expressions of Chinese culture, however, the age of widespread *xiqu* performance came to an end.[47]

Theatrical exchanges were not again possible until the late 1980s, not least because diplomatic relations only resumed in 1990. On one occasion, in April 1989, a visit from a Taiwanese *jingju* troupe was cancelled for reasons related to the restrictions on Chinese culture and a more general tightening of control on the cultural sector (Harsono 1989, 15; Tan 1991, 118; Asmara 1995, 172).[48] In the last Suharto years, theatrical exchanges resumed, for instance with the visit to Jakarta in 1994 and 1995, respectively, of the Hebei Beijing Opera and forty-six *minju* and song-and-dance performers from state troupes in Fuzhou and Quanzhou (Heryanto 1989, 107; Wang 2011, 229).[49] In recent years, diplomatic, community, and temple invitations have now attracted nearly all of the major Fujian companies, in both *xiqu* and puppetry. However, Indonesia still attracts fewer *xiqu* visits than one might expect based on its size and Chinese population: Wang (2011, 81) counts six *xiqu* visits from Fujian between 2000 and 2009, putting Indonesia in that period well below Malaysia (36), Singapore (19), and even Brunei (9).

Sometimes, as with two performances I attended in Bandung in 2012, *xiqu* is part of a more general program of Chinese cultural offerings sponsored by Chinese community associations. While interesting as part of the PRC's and ROC's efforts to engage with Chinese Indonesians, the productions I saw featured a largely stereotyped version of *xiqu* heritage, including *bianlian* (mask-changing),[50] *jingju* singing or a selection of *gezaixi* excerpts, performed by visiting troupes from the Mainland or Taiwan (*Yinni Xingzhou ribao,* September 26 and December 21, 2012).[51] On both occasions, the influential Bandung Hakka hometown association, the Yayasan Harapan Kasih 客屬聯誼會 (Hakka Friendship Association),[52] provided the venue. The presentations, provided with Indonesian translation, were designed to appeal to a largely Sino-Indonesian audience that had no prior knowledge of *xiqu.* Even speakers of Mandarin in Bandung, most of whom were over sixty and attended the pre–New Order Chinese schools, reported to me that they only knew *xiqu* performance from PRC state television's programming.

A similar type of show, providing *gaojiaxi* and *potehi* highlights from Mainland Hokkien troupes on the invitation of a Hokkien association, has also recently been performed in Surabaya (*Guoji ribao,* July 25, 2011), and the North Sumatra branch of the Chinese-Indonesian association INTI invited Mainland *chaoju* star Ding Peihong 丁佩紅 for Chinese New Year in 2014 (*Haobao,* January 21, 2014). Sometimes only brief excerpts are presented—making use of the symbolism of *xiqu* as a shorthand for Chinese identity. For instance, in 2013 the director of the Fujian Province Liyuan Experimental Troupe 福建省梨園戲實驗劇團, Zeng Jingping 曾靜萍,[53] performed alone in Surabaya for ten minutes to taped music at the invitation of the Chinese consulate and alongside a number of other Fujian artists.[54] Indonesian invitations are often not a matter of full performance but of using *xiqu* as a token show of "Chineseness."

The older traditions of performing *xiqu* in the Indies and Indonesia are thus unfamiliar to most Sino-Indonesians today, including those of the older generation. PRC- and ROC-sponsored performances, along with the incorporation of *xiqu* into Confucius Institute instruction, appear to have been designed as attempts to engage the interest and perhaps ethnic loyalties of Sino-Indonesians. Chinese voluntary associations are also active in attempts to revitalize Sino-Indonesian interest in Chinese culture, including theatre, in the forms now performed in the Mainland.

There are, however, a few ways in which amateur local *xiqu* and transnational commercial touring *xiqu* have reemerged, in some cases directly out of pre–New Order institutions. Among the more prominent are the various Guangdong *yueju* organizations that descend from the amateur group Cunyi Tuan 存益團 in pre–New Order Medan. According to one such performer, Li Meirong 李美蓉, there had been *yueju* in Medan since at least the 1930s, when all-male troupes performed at the Tongle 同樂 teahouse. The Medan scene was galvanized in the late 1950s by the appearance of two professional troupes from Hong Kong, the Jinlong Yueju Tuan 金龍粵劇團 (Golden Dragon *Yueju* Troupe) and the Taiping Yueju Tuan 太平粵劇團 (Peaceful *Yueju* Troupe), who showed on Medan stages for two or three months.[55] Local Chinese amateurs bought the costumes off these troupes on their departure and in 1958 began to organize a *yueju* group under the auspices of Cunyi.[56]

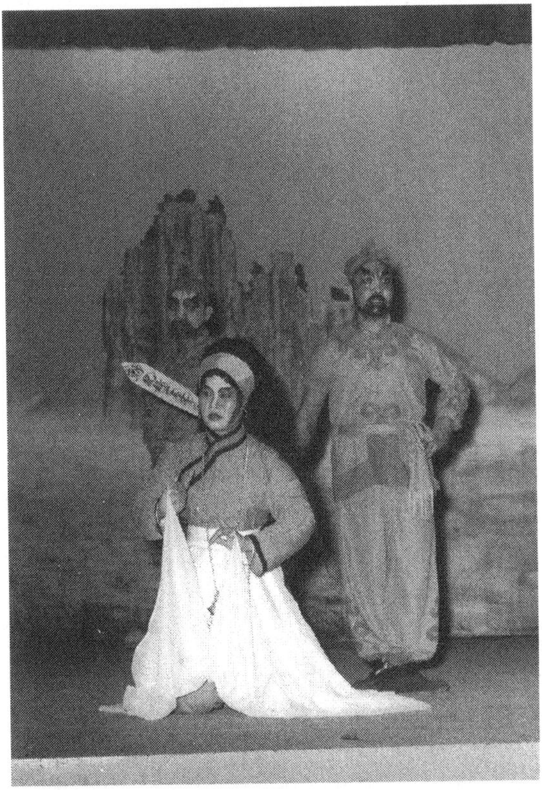

Li Meiying as Dou E 竇娥 in a *yueju* production of *Snow in Midsummer* by Medan's Cunyi tuan. Medan, early 1960s. Photo courtesy of Li Meiying.

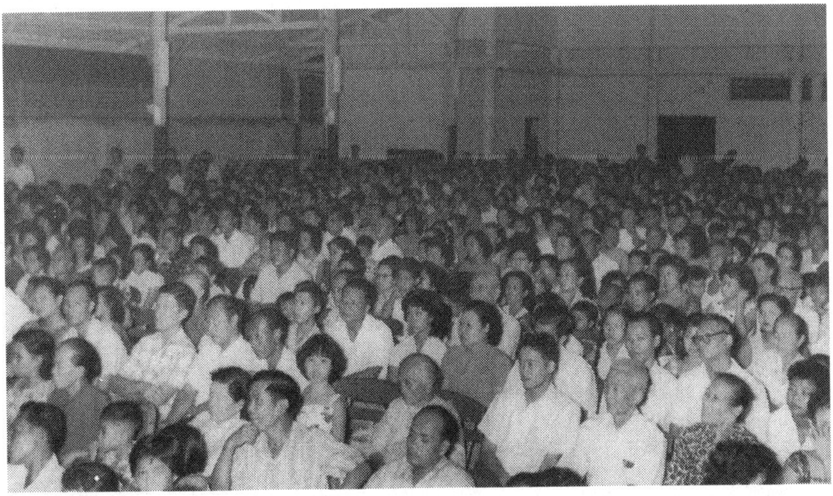

Cantonese opera audience at the Chinese General Hall in Medan, early 1960s. Photo courtesy of Li Meiying.

Larger, formal performances, like those in which Li participated, began in 1960. Like *chaoju* before the construction of the Teochew Society building, these performances were held between 1960 and 1965 at the General Chinese Association 華僑總會 in Medan and also toured the smaller cities of North Sumatra. Performances were ticketed, with revenue going to local schools and charities. Chinese subtitles meant that members of other Chinese linguistic communities attended; Li remembers shows as often being sold out, with the same show continuing for a month without a change in programming. At its height, the troupe involved over a hundred people, up to half of them actors. They sent away to Guangzhou and Hong Kong for scripts and scores (Li Meirong, pers. comm., November 5, 2016; *Guoji ribao*, March 22, 2013). The influence of *xiqu* cinema is discernible, for instance in the choice to stage three *yueju* plays in 1961, all of them the subjects of recent Hong Kong *yueju* films: *Escape from Banishment* 附薦何文秀 (1960), *Guan Hanqing* 關漢卿 (1960), and *Princess Flower* 帝女花 (1959; Liao 2007, 288).[57] According to Li, this influence was felt not least because the PRC consulate in Medan would invite troupe members to watch showings.[58]

After 1965, these performances came to an end until the last years of New Order. At that point various invitations came to perform scenes, largely in Jakarta, where many troupe members had moved. One post-show picture, taken at the Cantonese association 廣肇會館 (Guangzhou-Zhaoqing Association/Yayasan Suaka Insan), shows performers in full *xiqu* costume as early as 1994. Seventy-year-old Salim Tan 陳新廉, a onetime member of Cunyi, was also affiliated with the Jakarta Cantonese association, where he performed from at least 2007.[59] Tan's is one of the few published accounts of the personal experience of *xiqu* suppression: having left Sumatra for Jakarta to work in construction, he passed his leisure time "reading opera books and singing to myself" (Zhang 2012).[60]

Similarly, between the early 2000s and 2013, Medan-based performers such as Li Meirong were invited to perform scenes at Chinese New Year–themed events, on television, and in hotels, and on one occasion at the local public university, the Universitas Sumatra Utara (USU). They have also represented Indonesia (one of sixteen countries or territories attending) at the 2016 Yangcheng *Yueju* Festival 羊城粵劇節 in Guangzhou and continue to gather to sing together, even if full costume performances no longer take place (*Harian Analisa*, January 15, 2006; Liao 2007, 285; *Yinni xingzhou ribao*, July 25 and September 25, 2007; Zhang 2012; *The Jakarta Post*, January 19, 2012; *Indopos*, February 11, 2013; Li Meirong, pers. comm., November 5 and 9, 2016).

If this amateur revival in Medan and Jakarta had all but disappeared by 2015, contacts at a temple level have once again resulted in a parallel pattern of contemporary *xiqu* performance in Indonesia, concentrated in northern Sumatra. In 2012, a Zhangzhou *chaoju* troupe performed for three months in temples in and around Medan from July to September (Lin Rongjin, pers. comm., October 28,

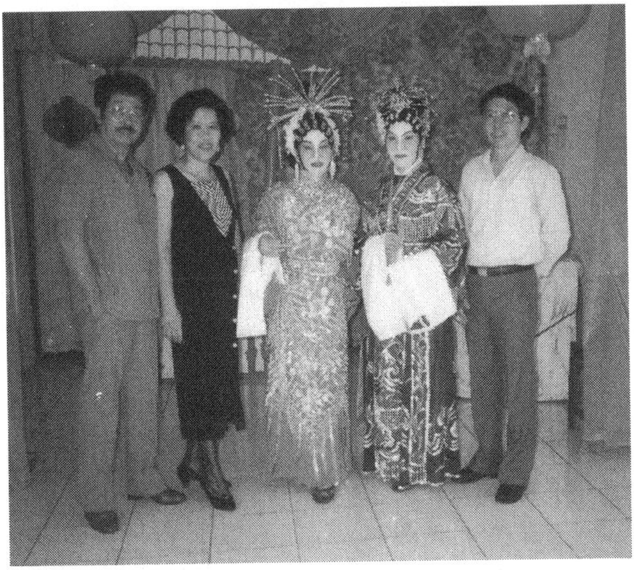

A 1994 *yueju* performance at a Jakarta local-place association. Photo courtesy of Li Meiying.

2016); in October of the previous year a *chaoju* troupe from Yunxiao 云霄 County, also in Zhangzhou, had visited Tebing Tinggi for two weeks at the invitation of the local Chinese associations, in honor of the birth of the Guanyin; a report on the performance noted that much of the audience had travelled from Siantar or Medan to see it (Fu 2012). The most sustained commitment has been from the six-month tours, beginning in 2010 and still current in 2017, by a company from Zhangzhou called Lihua Xiangju Company 麗華薌劇團. This group is engaged by a Medan Hokkien middleman who takes care of visas and accommodations, and also handles the requests from temples to book performances, usually for festivals. The area of Lihua's activity ranges from Medan in the north, where they perform largely in suburban temples, to Serdang and Ledong in the south of the province (Linbai 2011; *Guoji ribao,* October 15, 2012; Lim Ahok, pers. comm., November 8, 2016).

On a smaller scale, *xiqu* troupes from other areas of Southeast Asia also continue to visit Indonesia, through both temple and institutional contacts: Thai-based *chaoju* troupes have been visiting Sumatra for at least twenty years (Lai 1993, 180; *Guoji ribao,* October 4, 2012).[61] Various Singaporean troupes have visited, on several occasions through the efforts of the Jakarta-born head of Singapore's Chinese Opera Institute Dr. Chua Soo Pong 蔡曙鹏. The most prominent Singaporean *xiqu* production to visit Indonesia has been the 1991 *chaoju* version of *Ramayana,* which in 2003 performed in four cities at the invitation the Indonesian Ministry of Foreign Affairs. Selections from the same script were performed by another *chaoju* troupe, the Thau Yong Amateur Musical Association

陶融儒樂社, at the 2013 International Ramayana Festival and the Majapahit International Festival, in conjunction with Ramayana versions from other countries.[62] Chua's inspiration to transform the *Ramayana* for use on the *xiqu* stage was, as he himself noted, derived from memories of performances of *wayang kulit* he had seen as a child in Indonesia (Cai 2011a, 60–62; "Xinchuan" 2004).[63]

Closer to home, Singaporean troupes have also frequently visited the Riau Islands that are reachable by ferry, including Batam, Bintan, and Karimun. Both the amateur Macpherson Teochew Opera Group 麥波申潮劇團 (2003) and the Opera Institute have performed at the Xuantian Shangdi 玄天上帝 temple in Tanjungpinang, on Bintan.[64] Participants in the 2003 show reported audiences of up to two thousand for each of three nights; over sixty troupe members and two hundred other Singapore residents were also reported to have made the trip. At least one of the performers was herself Indonesia-born and expressed satisfaction at thus "returning home" to perform (*Lianhe zaobao*, October 5, 2003; Javier Lee, pers. comm., October 28, 2016). A 2005 visit to Tanjung Balai on Karimun by the Opera Institute's *chaoju* troupe for three days of temple performance was hailed as the first *xiqu* show there in forty-two years (*Lianhe wanbao*, May 9, 2005). Invitations from the region have not been restricted to *chaoju;* the Opera Institute's *qiongju* troupe has also performed there at the invitation of the local Hainan association (*Guoji ribao*, September 5, 2011).

The most remarkable case of present-day *xiqu* transmission in Indonesia, however, is in the South Sumatra capital of Palembang. Two amateur troupes are active there, known respectively as the Sam Khau Bun Gei Siah 三教文藝社 (Tridharma Arts Society) and the So Lam Kok Gie Siah 蘇南國藝社 (South Sumatra National Arts Society), both of which perform *gezaixi*[65] in the temples of heavily Chinese areas (the former urban, the latter semirural). Their story of survival encapsulates the resilience and flexibility of the performance of Sino-Indonesian identity more generally.

There were reportedly several Palembang Hokkien theatre troupes in the 1940s and 1950s, all serving temple festivals.[66] Both currently active troupes trace their descent from two troupes founded in the 1950s and called Huaqiao Troupe 華僑劇社 (Chinese Theatre Society; est. ca. 1953) and Xiongfeng Troupe 雄風劇社 (Powerful Wind Theatre Society; est. in the later 1950s).[67] According to veteran performer and director Yang Fuxing 楊福興, the former was established by actors coming from Bagansiapiapi. In about 1961, teachers from China were invited to train actors, and larger theatrical activities took place until 1965.

Along with all other Chinese performance, activities were stopped in 1965, but—unlike anywhere else in Indonesia—temple-based performances were again undertaken by both troupes between (according to troupe estimates) 1972 and 1980 and again between 1982 and 1998, interrupted by a brief suppression. By this second period, Huaqiao had disappeared, whereas Xiongfeng continued and was joined by the newly founded Yayasan Kok Gie Siah 耶耶山國藝社 (Theatre Society Foundation). Despite official bans on Chinese culture, performances could occur by arranging permissions from local contacts with the police and/or by performing in more remote temples.[68] Around 1990, the troupes merged to form Tridharma Arts, at the same time changing the name to reflect the group's entry into the Tridharma religious association. However, in response to the tense ethnic climate of 1998, troupe activities again ceased until 2000 with the advent of the Gus Dur presidency. Since then, performances have continued without interruption, with South Sumatra Arts splitting from Tridharma Arts in 2007.

Since 2007 the voluntary head of Tridharma Arts has been local businessman Tan Tiau Guan 陳朝源, usually known as Acit and sometimes by his Indonesian name, Hasan Solihin. Acit, a successful businessman and the son of an actor, described his commitment to the theatre as a result of a command given by the deity Generalissimo Tian 田都元帥, adding that I should "write that [his support] is a matter of conscience, a way of paying debts." (Acit, pers. comm., November 16, 2016). The troupe has on some occasions invited teachers from Fujian to teach *gezaixi,* and Acit himself has made frequent trips to Xiamen and Suzhou to buy costumes and props. Copies of two hundred texts, which provide scene summaries rather than dialogues, have been in use since the early 1960s, when they were brought from China. Indonesian versions of scene summaries hang in the wings for easy reference, and the actors elaborate the lyrics and dialogue during rehearsals, although much of it is improvised.[69] Much of the repertoire consists of shows that they have adapted from Taiwanese and Fujian *gezaixi* troupe recordings. For instance, several young actors expressed a particular liking for the productions of the prominent Taiwanese troupe Ming Hwa Yuan 明華園.[70]

Tridharma rehearsals occur three times a week at a Guanyin temple in Taksam, Kelenteng Dewi Kwan Im 觀音廟.[71] Performances occur in ten to fifteen temples a year, mostly in the neighborhood. The most prominent *xiqu* event of the year, however, is during Cap Go Meh at the Hok Ceng Bio 福正廟 temple on the river island of Kemaro. For temple festivals, the temple gods are consulted, by means of spirit possession, about the nature of the entertainment and the number of nights.[72] The troupe has also toured to other Chinese temples, including to other South Sumatra communities such as Lubuklinggau and Lahat as well as trips to North Sumatra (Tebing Tinggi, Medan) and Jambi, but the overwhelming majority of shows are in Palembang temples.[73] As most temple engagements consist of two shows a day for three or four days, the total number of Tridharma Arts shows in a year reaches fifty to seventy.

Tridharma Arts boasts thirty-five members, at least half of them under twenty. The actors and the temples consist overwhelmingly of people of Anxi 安溪 origin, and Acit is also an executive of the local Anxi Society 安溪公會.[74] Some performers are veterans of earlier performance periods; others are youngsters who grew

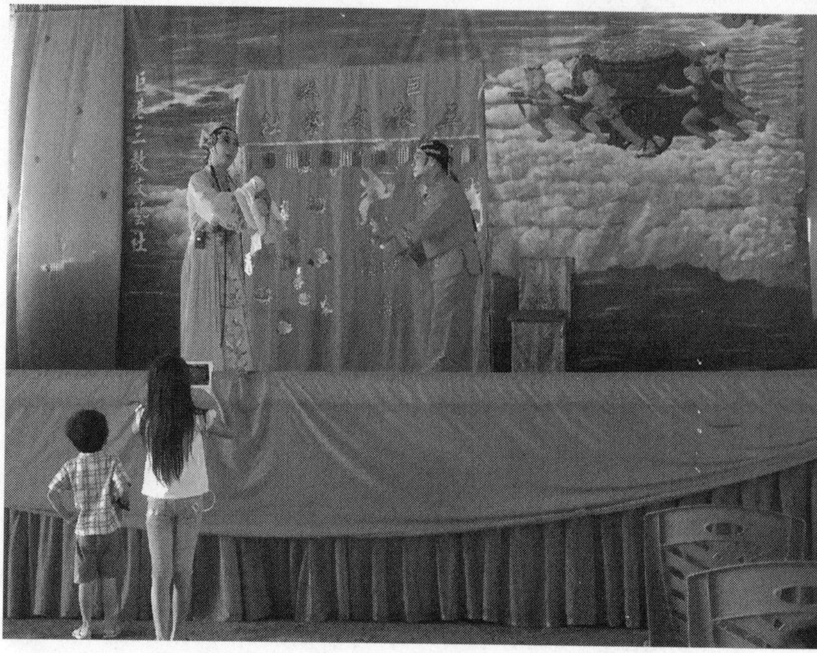

Children watching a *gezaixi* performance in Palembang by Tridharma Arts during a temple festival, Palembang 2016. Photo by author.

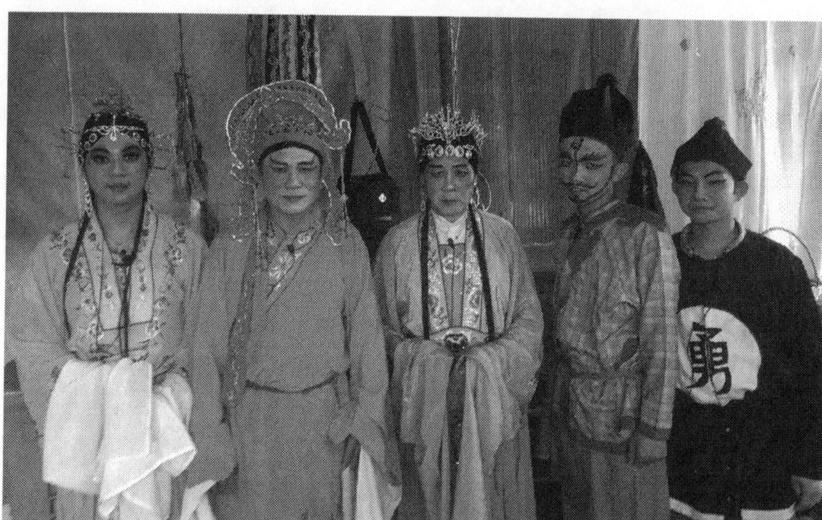

Two generations of Tridharma Arts: Iwan, Johan, Cui Toh, Andre, and Suwandi. Photo by author.

up watching the theatre in local temples. Financially, the troupe is supported by a combination of donations from local temples and, to quote Acit, "rich people" among the Palembang Chinese, as well as an important contribution from Acit himself. The other troupe, based in the less wealthy area of Karya Baru, has greater difficulty meeting its costs and was consequently dormant at the time of my 2016 visit.[75]

The troupe is distinguished by its ritual character, and it is clear that at all levels—including, most prominently, the name, which is a translation of Tridharma—religious belief is motivational. Tridharma Arts has no female members, a remarkable and perhaps unique circumstance in contemporary *xiqu*.[76] Performances are exclusively confined to the birthdays of deities in Tridharma temples or to Cap Go Meh, and they are situated in the context of temple fairs, with rituals (including spirit possession), sacrificial money, and incense burning, free food, coffee, and tea. Indeed, when I asked troupe members how it had been possible to perform in the New Order 1970s, they responded that they had simply performed in response to the demand, revealed through divination, of various temple gods. The presence of the Hokkien theatre god Generalissimo Tian, whose altar is behind the stage, is also an indication of the theatre's ritual basis. It seems probable that, much as with other Chinese forms that I discuss in later chapters, it was possible to make local arrangements to continue performance practices so long as it was firmly identified with ritual.

Unlike other Sino-Indonesian practices, *gezaixi* in Palembang has not adapted linguistically,[77] nor has it shown any move towards non-Chinese performers or much hybridity of language, costume, music, or narrative material. Neither audience nor performers are, on average, particularly elderly. The ritual impetus was present also in other Sino-Indonesian communities, but did not lead to an ongoing *xiqu* practice. The explanation for this Palembang exception can be sought in the high residential proportion of Chinese in certain areas of town,[78] the relatively good local ethnic relations, the general use of Hokkien, the ties to strong Hokkien communities in Medan and perhaps Penang and Singapore, the recent increase in theatre ties with Mainland China and Taiwan, the support of local community leaders and temples, and, above all, of a small group of committed amateurs and patrons.

Delighting No More?

Chinese-language scholarship tends to derive twentieth-century *xiqu* in the Indies from late nineteenth-century visits of Chinese troupes, while also suggesting that these performances account for the popularity of some of these narratives in non-theatrical contexts (Zhang 2007, 738–741). On the other hand, Western and

Indonesian scholarship has seldom, if ever, made any reference to the visits of these troupes. Given the piecemeal nature of the evidence, the best model is to suggest that between the mid-nineteenth and the mid-twentieth centuries there were both local *xiqu* troupes and visiting troupes from Fujian, Guangdong, Hainan, and elsewhere in Southeast Asia, especially British Malaya (including Singapore). Chinese records, confirmed by the 1869 Dutch report of a troupe "arriving from Singapore" (*De Locomotief*, September 21, 1869) also suggest a lively maritime circuit of commercial theatre throughout Southeast Asia; and in 1935 a Chinese Batavian still wrote of "travelling opera troupes from China" performing "Chinese songs and plays in [Batavia] as well as in every other town of the South Seas which they visit" (Nio 1935, 198). While tours would have provided direct stimulus for the transfer of new genres or pieces or for the creation of amateur societies, *xiqu* seems also to have maintained an unbroken local presence in the Indies from the seventeenth century.

In the present day, most performances are by rural PRC, non-state-sponsored *chaoju* and *gezaixi* troupes, largely from Fujian but also from other parts of China and Southeast Asia, which are regularly being invited to perform for the Hokkien-speaking Chinese communities in Sumatra. Given the ritual purpose of much Hokkien theatre, it is probable that these invitations are motivated by the wish to observe temple festivals with theatre performances. The Palembang troupes provide the one thriving practice of Sino-Indonesian *xiqu*, while the elderly survivals of pre–New Order continue to sing informally in Medan and perhaps Jakarta. In the absence of local troupes elsewhere in the country, and with the relative affluence of many temples and the emergence of low-cost regional air travel, invitations to Mainland troupes has become feasible. Meanwhile, PRC and ROC governments sponsor *xiqu* troupe visits as part of soft-power cultural diplomacy directed to Sino-Indonesian society.

A focus on *xiqu* in the Indies helps integrate older diasporic performance practices into a transnational theatre history, which neither subordinates that experience to Chinese "origins" nor suppresses its place in the developing commercial theatre world of the Indies. A focus on the exchange of intra-Asian performance practices such as *xiqu* challenges West–East migration and/or cosmopolitanism as the founding axes of transnationalism. Taken as a whole, the range of Sino-Indonesian theatre practices disturbs narratives of Chinese essentialism and questions the boundaries of *xiqu* wherever strong linguistic, musical, and narrative shifts occur. At the same time, *xiqu* was and is only one part of the Chinese transnational theatre exchange in Southeast Asia.

Colonial visitors to Batavia often remarked on the prevalence of *xiqu;* and a fair view of the early history of Indonesian theatre requires an acknowledgment of its presence. There is convincing evidence that *xiqu* was a major source of entertainment for both Chinese and non-Chinese residents of the Indies and early postindependence Indonesia. The fact that it is now returning to more common and public practice in a few regions highlights its organic role in Chinese societies and temples and their transnational networks, as well as having an intriguing role in the soft-power diplomacy of the PRC and ROC. As will also become clearer in chapter 3, the emerging Indies commercial theatre at the turn of the twentieth century owes a debt to *xiqu*. Doubtless further research will explore this connection and deepen the integration of *xiqu* into Indies and Indonesian theatre historiography.

CHAPTER 2

Glove, String, and Shadow

SINO-INDONESIAN FORMS OF *WAYANG*

WAYANG is an expansive term.[1] Derived from the Javanese for "shadow," it is "the general word applied to many kinds of traditional theatre in Java, Bali, Lombok and some other parts of Indonesia and Southeast Asia, both puppet theatre and actor's theatre" and can apply to "(*wayang*) performance, (*wayang*) puppet, or (*wayang*) character" (Mrázek 2005a, xiii). The term has been used for "a wide variety of forms and related entertainments," a number of which are associated with Chinese communities (Cohen 2007, 571). From the late colonial period, the term can be contrasted with emergent forms of "modern" theatre such as *bangsawan* and *sandiwara*, although actors in these forms, too, are known as "children of the *wayang*" (571).

The term *wayang*, especially during the colonial period, was applied colloquially to Chinese entertainments of all kinds—as seen in the reference to *xiqu* performances as *wajang tjina* or *wajang makau*. This usage to describe *xiqu* remains common in Singapore or Malaysia (National Archives 1988),[2] but is no longer generally found in contemporary Indonesia (perhaps partly because *xiqu* has something of an interrupted history there).[3] In its Indonesian usage today, the term incorporates genres performed by dancers (*wayang wong/orang*), by puppets (of leather, *wayang kulit;* and wood, *wayang golek*), and by narrators using story scrolls (*wayang beber*); is performed in languages including Javanese, Balinese, Sundanese, and Sasak; and embraces forms whose origins vanish into precolonial history and others that are recent inventions, as well as genres that are explicitly religious alongside those that are patently political.[4]

Most *wayang* genres along with a number of other Javanese arts have demonstrable and long-standing historical links to Chinese practitioners, audiences, and/or patrons (Kartomi 2000; Pausacker 2005, 194). Boachi noted as early as 1856 the popularity of *wayang kulit, wayang golek, wayang orang,* and *topeng* among Chinese populations (299–301), and Javanese *wayang* features in colonial Sino-Malay literature.[5] It is and was common to include Javanese *wayang* performances at Chinese festivals, and often at Chinese temples (Tjan 1947/1948, 56; Pausacker 2005, 187), and historically at least one all-Chinese *wayang orang* troupe is known (Budianta 2012, 268). Chinese *wayang* practitioners in various genres are still prominent today,[6] and in contemporary *wayang* new Chinese influences, such as that of the Chinese-language movie industry, have made themselves felt (Petersen 1991, 133).

One Sino-Indonesian puppet genre, *wayang potehi*, has borne the name of *wayang* for well over a century and probably longer, while, more recently, contemporary scholars and institutions have extended the term to West Kalimantan's Hakka marionettes. This chapter is structured according to genre, first examining the best-known Sino-Indonesian form of theatre, *wayang potehi*, before moving on to the three other known genres of Sino-Indonesian puppetry. The fates of the different genres in contemporary Indonesia are largely linked to their ability to present themselves as expressions of a hybrid Sino-Indonesian identity.

Origins of *Potehi* in Mainland China and Transmission to the Indies

Wayang potehi can be directly traced to the southern Fujian (Hokkien) glove puppet theatre practice, *potehi*.[7] Since Chinese immigration to Java originated largely from southern Fujian, it is not surprising that the local puppet form arrived with these migrants at least a generation before Hakka populations brought their marionette genre to West Kalimantan.

The history of southern Fujian puppetry, including *potehi*, presents considerable difficulties. As with many other folk arts, the scarcity of documentation limits historical certitude. Accounts of the Chinese origins of *potehi*, not least those written in Indonesia, usually provide a vague, ancient heritage for the art, measured in thousands of years, based seemingly on English sources about Chinese puppetry in general. A brief account of the genre's origin in China is called for.

While Chinese puppetry is much older, specific evidence for puppetry in southern Fujian becomes strong only in the twelfth century, and the first conclusive reference to *potehi* itself is found only in the nineteenth. Song dynasty records of Fujian show puppetry troupes exceeding one hundred members. In 1192, while in Zhangzhou, the great neo-Confucian philosopher Zhu Xi 朱熹 appears to have forbidden puppetry out of concern for the morals of the local people, and his local disciple Chen Chun 陳淳 (1159–1223) elaborated on the immoral aspects of theatre, explicitly including puppets. In nearby Putian, numerous references in the work of poet Liu Kezhuang 劉克莊 (1187–1269) suggest elaborate puppetry performances, including full costumes, high stages, and full narratives. Some Ming dynasty records mention puppets in the course of general censure of theatre as an unwholesome activity. Four Ming and Qing versions of the local *nanxi* 南戲 (southern drama) script *Lijing ji* 荔鏡記 (The lychee mirror) all make reference to puppets—most likely shadow puppets—being performed during the Lantern Festival. This practice is corroborated by a record from 1612, which also notes paper puppets during that festival in Zhangzhou (Wang 2006; Xie 2009, 17–59, 221–222; Tseng 2010; Ye 2010; Ma 2012).

So far, there is little reason to assume that any of these forms of puppetry closely resembled *potehi;* many sources clearly do not refer to glove puppets, while others give no further information and could indicate any of the several types of puppetry—marionettes, shadow puppets, or glove puppets. Accounts amounting to *potehi* creation tales are recorded in Quanzhou, Zhangzhou, and Taiwan, all of which date the genre from the Jiajing (1521–1567) or Wanli (1572–1620) reigns, while the movement of *potehi* from southern Fujian to Taiwan and Guangdong is usually thought to have taken place during the late Ming dynasty (i.e., early to mid-seventeenth century). None of these accounts themselves, however, can be dated earlier than the nineteenth century. *Yangzhou huafang lu* 揚州畫舫錄 (The Pleasure Boats of Yangzhou) contains an account of *jiandanxi* 肩擔戲 (shoulder-load theatre) glove puppets in the late eighteenth century (Xie 2009, 22), but since Yangzhou is far from Fujian, this at best suggests a precursor or a parallel tradition. The first solid regional evidence is the local gazetteer for Jinjiang in southern Fujian for the Jiaqing reign (1796–1820), which makes mention of *potehi* by name; there is no certain evidence of it on Taiwan before 1874 (Wang 2006, 226; Xie 2009, 222; Ma 2012, 34).[8] Thus, while the evidence for *potehi* becomes more plausible in the sixteenth century, even such a surmise must draw on evidence from accounts written three centuries later. In any event, there is no doubt that it was a popular entertainment in nineteenth-century Fujian, when the greatest migration occurred.

By the early twentieth century, *potehi* had been transmitted to various places in Southeast Asia. Tentative evidence from Singapore suggests that *potehi* troupes were active in the late nineteenth century (Chia 2016, 67).[9] Tan Sooi-Beng's work has, on occasions thirty-five years apart, examined the Penang branch of this tradition (Tan 1981; 2016). Tan's work records puppets reaching Penang in the 1920s or 1930s, suggesting that transmission there may have taken place later than into the Indies or to Singapore. Recent research of the Taiyuan Asian Puppet Museum has produced evidence of a practice in Yangon lasting from at least the mid-twentieth century to the 1990s (Ruizendaal and Ma 2016). *Potehi,* interpreted according to Spanish orthography as *puteje,* was presented in the late nineteenth and early twentieth century in the Philippines (Ghulam-Sarwar Yousof 1994,

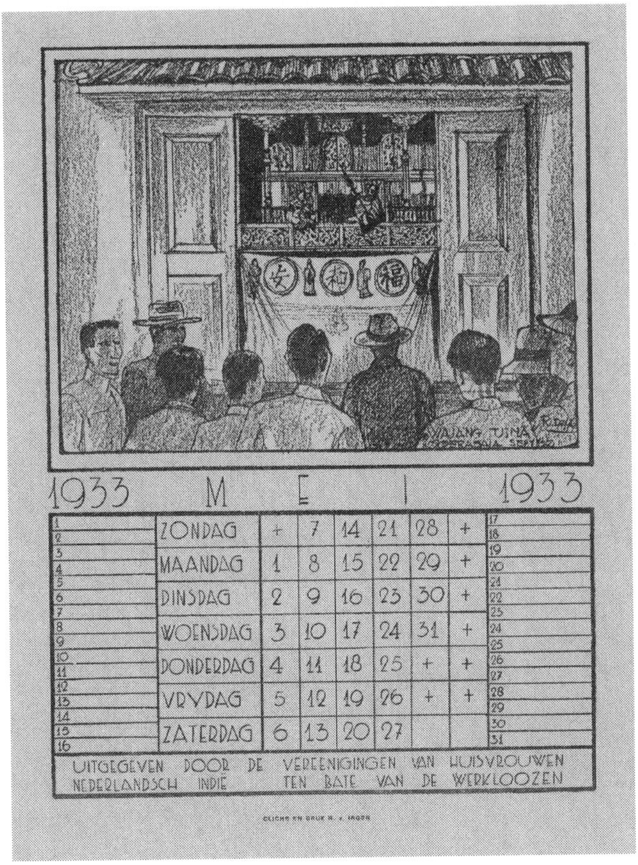

"Wajang Tjina" (i.e., Potehi) in Surabaya, from a Dutch-language Indies calendar for 1933, by H. van Ingen and B. W. J. Deppe. The characters read "Fu He An." Courtesy of the KITLV digital image library.

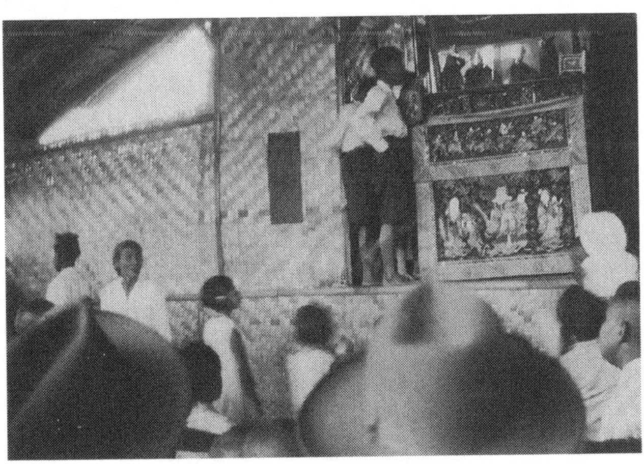

Potehi in Bandung, 1931. From the travels of J. P. van Winter. Image courtesy of the KITLV digital image library.

219), and Quanzhou *potehi* troupes would continue to visit the Philippines. For instance, famed puppeteer Li Rongzong 李榮宗 toured Manila in 1947, and his son Li Tianbao 李天寶 performed there for extended periods of time in the early 1950s; at least two more visits from Fujian troupes occurred in the 1980s (Lin Jinzhi 1989, 42–43). It is not improbable that future research may establish broader transmission of *potehi* there and in other sites of Hokkien migration, such as Bangkok, Songkhla, or central Vietnam.[10] While researchers have only recently begun to join forces to move from national towards a more regional account of the genre, it is becoming clear that Southeast Asia's Hokkien migrants of the late nineteenth century arrived in new lands bearing glove puppets.

Potehi in the Eighteenth- and Nineteenth-century Dutch East Indies

As with the history of most theatre genres, it makes little sense to attempt to pinpoint a single origin or arrival. Several existing puppeteer lineages can trace their origins to masters arriving from China, and the most appropriate model is to assume repeated entries of *potehi* practices and materials in various areas of the colonial Indies. As with the origins of *potehi* in China, evidence that has been adduced to demonstrate the great antiquity of *potehi* in the archipelago is inconclusive.[11]

The earliest credible evidence for *potehi* performance in the Indies concerns the invitation of a Batavian *potehi* troupe in 1772 to Semarang.[12] According to the author Liem Thian Joe 林天佑, the opening of new buildings in Tay Kak Sie 大覺寺 temple in *gang* Lombok was celebrated in that year with a performance series lasting two months (Liem 1933, 50). Since the temple complex still hosts *potehi* today, if the account is accurate it situates 240 years of *potehi* performance in the same location. Liem writes also of "the first temple in Semarang" (Sioe Hok Bio 壽福廟) being built in 1753, writing that for the opening "there was a small celebration that evening. There was no *wajang pow-tee-hee* performance, because at that time Semarang had no *pow-tee-hee* troupe" (23–24). The fact that Liem specially notes the absence of *potehi* suggests the extent to which it must have been an ordinary component of temple festivities in his own time, and at least notionally places *potehi*'s arrival on Java between 1753 and 1772. Since Liem's history draws substantially on documents of the Semarang Kongkoan (公館 Chinese council), which he salvaged when it closed in 1931, the claim might have some documentary credibility; the documentary text itself, however, is absent. (If accepted, the reference would also furnish earlier evidence for *potehi* than is available from reliable sources in the Hokkien home region).

It is clear that by the mid-nineteenth century *potehi* figured as part of the program for major Chinese and civic festivals in Batavia and in several other Indies regions in lineups otherwise also including *wayang wong*, dancing, and *xiqu*. Most performers were invited from China, and permission had to be obtained for troupes' three- to six-month sojourns (Chen 2009, 70). Some of the troupes may have been coming from closer at hand: in that period, for instance, a royal wedding in the Surakarta region featured Chinese puppets from Singapore, most likely *potehi* (Sumarsam 1995, 86).

Accounts continue throughout the late colonial period. It is clear that *potehi* was ritually important, as well as being included in both *pribumi* and Dutch festivities.[13] Van Groenendael cites an 1869 month-long performance in Kediri to exorcise smallpox (1993, 7; see also Poensen 1873, 163). Chinese puppets—almost certainly *potehi*—were present at the quintessential Dutch Sinterklaas festival in Semarang in 1877 alongside the Dutch puppet Jan Klaassen. One journalist in Panolan by Blora, wrote an extended and quite favorable comparison between the two traditions (*De Locomotief*, December 7, 1877; May 23, 1902). In Ambarawa, near Semarang, *wayang potehi* is reported in 1899 alongside *wayang orang*, *tandak*, and *wayang kulit* on the occasion of the ghost festival (called *rebutan* or *cioko* in Indonesia; *De Locomotief*, August 19, 1899). Colonial articles often indicate that the audiences at markets and festivals were ethnically mixed; for instance, the 1899 Ambarawa article reports dozens of Javanese viewers coming early in the morning and staying until the evening. *Wayang potehi* also attracted the attention of several colonial-era Dutch-language researchers on Javanese theatre; some of them considered it probable that *wayang golek* derived directly from *potehi* (Hazeu 1897, 92–93).[14]

Present-day Sino-Javanese *dalang*[15] lineages in *potehi* mostly originate at the turn of the last century. For example, Surabaya *dalang* Ki Mudjiono describes his teacher Gan Co Co as "third generation," which suggests a turn-of-the-century arrival of the genre there. *Potehi* performance in Surabaya is reputed to be "as old as the temple," an institution that is tentatively dated to 1899 (Xiao 2010, 245, 252; *Kabar Independen*, August 5, 2012). The Gudo troupe, near Jombang in East Java, estimates the beginnings of their tradition to 1915–1920, when the present patron Toni Harsono's grandfather arrived from Fujian (Purwoseputro 2014, 42). The Kediri *dalang* Ki Bejo learned the genre from Tan Ang Ang 陳紅紅, the pupil of a *dalang* who arrived in Semarang in the 1880s (van Groenendael 1993, 17); another Semarang group seems to have arrived in the 1920s (Tan 1963, 152). The puppet theatre in that city was prominent enough at the turn of the century even to spawn a short-lived spin-off company called *Komedie Boneka Stamboel* (Stamboel Puppet Theatre), which used *potehi* puppets but emulated the costumes, narratives, and music of the Stamboel theatre (Cohen 2006, 277).[16]

In the first half of the twentieth century, *potehi* is recorded in a broader swathe of the Indies than is presently the case. The puppets were found, for instance, in

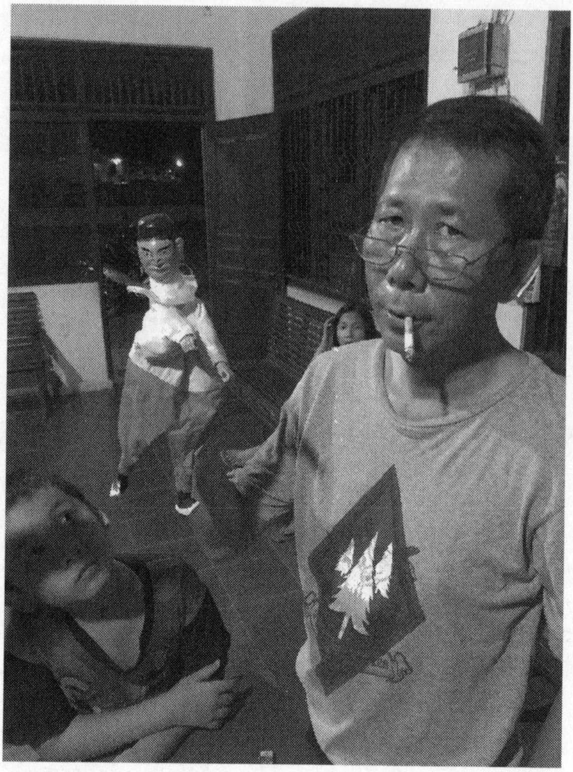

Palembang arts patron Acit with a locally made *potehi*, 2016. Photo by author.

Sumatra, recorded in Padang in the 1870s and 1901, in Solok (West Sumatra) in 1891, in Medan in 1925 and 1933 (van Hasselt 1882, 1:131; "Chinese poppenkast" 1891; *De Sumatra Post,* September 6,1901; September 25, 1925; and February 25, 1933).[17] Reports from a 1936 assessment of Chinese arts on Java suggested that both *potehi* and *xiqu* as well as Chinese dance and musical performances could "all be seen fairly regularly in the larger places on Chinese feast days" (Pigeaud 2003, 308). According to respondents from Bagansiapiapi, there were also a few visits from Singaporean or Penang troupes in the 1950s or early 1960s (Chen Dexian, pers. comm., November 7, 2016). At least one of the Hokkien opera troupes in Palembang once included *potehi* performance, with puppets locally made in the late 1940s. Twenty-four puppets and a half-dozen costumes are still in the possession of the local *gezaixi* troupe, one of whose members, Ong Kok Kie 王國基, also performed *potehi* from the age of thirteen.[18] The Sino-Indonesian author and journalist Huang Bizhen 黄碧珍 remembers that in her childhood in Balikpapan (East Kalimantan) in the late 1950s and early 1960s, puppetry was also performed there (pers. comm., September 28, 2017), and there are reports of it from Makassar in the 1930s (Wirawan 2013, 197–198). On balance, it seems appropriate to posit widespread performances of *potehi* in the Hokkien communities of Sumatra, Java, and Kalimantan, narrowing geographically to East and Central Java over the second half of the twentieth century. Today, the patronage of *potehi* troupes by affluent Chinese in East Java is once again extending the range of performance, both geographically and as regards venue type.

Despite disruption by war and revolution, *potehi* performance did not go into precipitate decline mid-century. Accounts from Surabaya report *potehi* performance in the Sukarno period occurring "as usual" (Maskurin and Alrianingrum 2014, 177), and ethnologies from Semarang and Sukabumi show that *potehi* continued to be one of several genres invited to perform at temples for Chinese festivals in the first fifteen years of independence (Willmott 1961, 219; Tan 1963, 152). A 1954 Dutch-language Jakarta newspaper advertised for Pehtjun 扒船 (i.e., Duanwu 端午) festivities in Tangerang, including Indonesian-language *potehi* from Semarang.[19] Along with other accounts of the mid-century, this ad suggests that a linguistic move slowly occurred from Hokkien to Malay/Indonesian; some troupes selected the appropriate performance language depending on the audience (Purwoseputro 2014, 42–44).[20] Since the performers came from Semarang, it may be that by this time *potehi* had already retreated from Sumatra and West Java. By the estimation of Thio Thiong Gie, who became a *dalang* in the early 1950s, there were in that period no more than ten *dalang* in Indonesia, all of them in Central or East Java.[21] At the same time, additional stimulus may also still have been coming from China, as the Zhangzhou *potehi* troupe toured eight cities in Indonesia in 1963 (Wang 2009, 111). This was likely the last of several pre–New Order trips for Mainland Chinese *potehi* troupes.

Potehi under New Order

One way to begin considering the question of *potehi* under New Order is by means of a biographical sketch of the only *dalang* who seems to have performed before, during, and after the Suharto period.[22] This was Thio Thiong Gie (1933–2014), who by the time of his death was one of the best-known, and one of the few ethnic Chinese, *dalang*. Born in Demak, Thio moved with his family in 1942 to Semarang after his father's store was looted during anti-Chinese riots. Thereafter, he lived in the historic Chinese quarter; our 2013 interview was conducted around the corner from where Liem situates the 1772 *potehi* performance.

As a young boy, Thio watched Quanzhou *potehi* masters performing in Semarang. At the age of twenty-five, he found some scripts for *Ciyun zouguo* 慈雲走國 (Prince Ciyun leaves the country), amid some junk paper his father had bought. Hearing the young Thio recount the Ciyun narrative with gusto, a friend of his father's suggested that he consider performing *potehi*. Soon, he was invited to perform *Prince Ciyun* at Cianjur, where he was contacted by the Blitar *dalang* Tan Ang Ang, who gave him various books of Chinese stories. Using these books, Thio proceeded to develop his career as *dalang* in Blitar, where he soon attracted large audiences of adults and children, particularly around festival time. Thio began to step in for Gudo performer Tok Hong Kie (father of Toni Harsono, of whom more later) in Blitar when he was unable to perform, reporting that "within a week, I learnt to be a *potehi dalang* autodidactically" (Kuardhani 2011, 35). At the height of his career in the early sixties, Thio performed two or three engagements a year, usually around the temple holidays. Many of the engagements were of considerable length: on Mojokerto on one occasion he was engaged for four or five months, in Sukabumi for two months and seven days. The farthest away he ever performed was in Lampung and Palembang (both on Sumatra, at the time several days' journey from Semarang).

According to Thio, his performances as *potehi dalang* adopted what he described as a *xiqu* tonality, drawing on his experience as a young man on the Hokkien-language *xiqu* stage. However, he also made use of a great variety of broad musical influences. For instance, he used the melody of "Siji ge" 四季歌 (The song of the four seasons), a song adapted from a Suzhou folk song by He Lüting 賀綠汀, one of China's most prominent twentieth-century composers,[23] giving the song Indonesian lyrics for use in his *potehi* performances. Conversely, he also translated lyrics from Javanese- and Indonesian-language songs for use as Hokkien *potehi* incantatory phrases.[24] Another *dalang* makes use of "Bengawan Solo" (Solo River), perhaps the most emblematic of Indonesian songs, as well as songs popularized by Taiwanese pop diva Teresa Teng 鄧麗君 and Chinese-language cinema (Tsai 2015, 87–88). Thio described the quality of "craziness" (*gila*) as imperative for a *dalang*, defining it as an openness to all sorts of influence.

Since Thio could become a *dalang* without formal study and musical influences could be added at will, it is probable that by the 1950s the genre was already loosely defined—far more loosely than could occur on the Mainland, where theatre was at that time undergoing reform and standardization. This looseness, in turn, suggests that at a performance and repertoire level divergence between *potehi* performance in China and in Indonesia was already substantial. Meanwhile, Taiwanese *potehi* was "moving away from the traditional southern Fujian glove puppet style into a distinctive Taiwanese style," beginning to feature larger stages, puppets, and "technical innovations, such as recorded music and light and sound effects" (Ruizendaal 2016, 17). Penang *potehi,* for its part, had adopted the popular musical system of *gezaixi* (Tan 2016, 32). The remarkable divergence of *potehi* in its various regional practices suggests that this type of puppetry is particularly open to innovation, far more so, for instance, than Hokkien marionettes.[25] It also suggests the contingency of tradition, as it is discursively available to such diverse practitioners.

Narratively, however, Java has proven the most conservative of *potehi* branches. Despite recent adaptations, the repertoire remains heavily weighted towards popular Qing fiction, especially the Xue Rengui narratives and other martial stories set in the the Tang. Several of the same narratives once featured prominently in Quanzhou marionette repertoire, and *puxianxi* troupes (a *xiqu* form originating in Putian) shows similar repertoire in Malaya between 1920 and 1930. Xue Rengui narratives are recorded also as Chinese shadow-puppet narratives, including in Taiwan. A continuity between puppetry and literary transmission is also apparent: the same stories were much translated and adapted in the late nineteenth and early twentieth century, and enjoyed great popularity in the Indies, first in Javanese and later in Malay versions, and eventually in a number of other archipelagic languages (Salmon 1981, 501; 2013b, 238–239, 241; 2013c, 268; Ruizendaal 2006, 151–152; Lai Bojiang 2007, 137; Wang 2011, 14, 19).

By the mid-century, *potehi* could evidently serve to bridge linguistic gaps within the Chinese communities. One Sino-Indonesian intellectual noted (in a Dutch-language article) in 1948 that *potehi* performances had one relative advantage over *xiqu*: "due to their greater frequency of performance, they can have more influence on the Chinese, even on those who can't speak any Chinese anymore, yet who can follow the plot being performed, because they have already read or heard the story told in Malay" (Nio 1948, 27).

Potehi language dynamics would continue to change under New Order. In Thio's own performance, the change occurred in the 1970s and 1980s, and approving authors cited the change about the same time as evidence of acculturation (Soelarto and Albiladiyah 1980/1981, 6).Thio considered the shift largely in terms of audience interest, but he did also report harassment from authorities aimed at removing superficial Chinese elements: Hokkien incantations and lotus-flower imagery for instance (Purwoseputro 2014, 50–52).[26] In Surabaya, in the same period, the language shift was accomplished over one teacher–student relationship: "Gan Co-Co was an old Chinese man, he could only speak a few simple words of Indonesian. Because he saw that the young Mulyanto was enjoying the potehi show, he brought him into the [back] stage and showed him how the performers manipulated the puppets" (Xiao 2010, 253).

At the same time, new puppets were beginning to be made on Java, especially in Tulungagung and Surabaya, supplementing those that had been brought from China. The involvement of *pribumi* Indonesians in *potehi* (due, in the first instance, to the absence of young Chinese willing to undertake the profession) thus appears just as the genre was becoming linguistically, performatively, and materially more independent from Chinese sources.

Despite New Order's anti-Chinese climate and legislation, *potehi* did not disappear. Scholarly, journalistic, and interview sources record the widespread presence of *potehi* throughout the period. Margaret J. Kartomi saw *potehi* in Malang in 1974, and van Groenendael, conducting her research between September 1984 and June 1986, saw *potehi* at various sites, describing the genre as then "very popular" in East Java (van Groenendael 1993, 11; Kartomi 2000, 298–303).[27] Sino-Indonesian activist and academic Dede Oetomo, writing on *potehi* in his hometown of Pasurunan, reported that, although "cancelled periodically as a result of a wave of anti-Chinese feeling or a spell of rioting aimed at Chinese business" (1987, 52) the practice had been resumed there since the 1970s. Claudine Salmon and her husband Denys Lombard saw *potehi* performances at Jakarta temples (Salmon and Lombard 1980, 74; Lombard 1990, 277), as did, in 1993, a German musicologist (Claus-Bachmann 2006). Research in Surabaya suggests that temple performance continued throughout New Order "without interruption" (Xiao 2010, 252–254; Maskurin and Alrianingrum 2014, 178–179), though the local *dalang* Sukar Mudjiono, who learned his art from a Hokkien speaker in that period, reports considerable difficulty in getting permission to perform outside the city during the New Order years (*The Jakarta Post,* February 11, 2010; Tsai 2015, 73).[28]

New Order restrictions seem to have had unintended consequences: Ki Bejo of Kediri thought that restrictions had shifted the center of Chinese performance from Central Java to East Java, where policy was less stringently enforced (van Groenendael 1993, 18). Respondents in Gudo told me that the ascension and birthday of the temple god Guangze Zunwang 廣澤尊王,[29] with its biannual month-long puppet performances, was an even greater festival in the Suharto years, as none of the other temples of East Java dedicated to that god could celebrate the festival, and hence all the devotees came to Gudo. Indeed, the biographical account of the chief *dalang* there, the late Ki Sesomo, shows that he began performing as a musician in 1964 and became a *dalang* in 1968, arriving in Gudo specifically to perform *potehi* in 1971 (Purwoseputro 2014, 52). New Order not only failed to interrupt *potehi* careers—it fostered the emergence of non-Chinese performers and the switch from Hokkien to Indonesian.

It seems appropriate to regard the effect of anti-Chinese measures as deleterious to the performance of *potehi,* but in practice regulations were unevenly applied and observed—the fate of the genre was subject to the New Order inconsistency one scholar has called "diversity in compliance" (Susanto 2010). Besides a possible geographic shift, a net result was a move towards the maintenance of performance in temples and the disappearance of the genre from broader festivities outside the immediate community. Chinese temples, as places of religious worship of a recognized religion (genuinely or nominally a form of Buddhism) were permissible even when Chinese culture and language were formally banned (Koji 2012, 389–398); *potehi* seems to have survived partly due to its plausible (and genuine, if not exclusive) association with religious practice.

The balance of evidence suggests stronger suppression towards the beginning of New Order, widespread but often clandestine performance in the late 1970s and 1980s, with performance frequency progressively growing towards the end of the period as anti-Chinese policies were relaxed. During New Order, the linguistic shift to Indonesian became all but complete (with Hokkien fragments retained for the incantatory *suluk* as well as for interjections, wishes of good fortune, stock phrases, and ritual elements).[30]

Symbolism, Promotion, and Identity

Potehi patrons are at pains to invoke symbolic patronage that can serve to show that prominent Indonesian individuals and institutions support the genre (and, by extension, are friendly to Sino-Indonesians). For instance, pictures of a member of the Surakarta royal family are featured at the Gudo temple in the workshop area where the puppets are made. *Potehi* puppet in hand, the royal also offers his good wishes in the front matter to the published biography of local patron Toni Harsono, comparing *potehi* with the most emblematic of *wayang* genres, writing that, "like *wayang kulit Purwo Jawa, wayang potehi* very much deserves to be protected, as a cultural heirloom of great value," and going on to praise Harsono for preserving the patrimony of his ancestors (KGPH TA Sinuhun Tedjowulan 2012, 6–7).[31] The renowned part-Chinese Yogyakarta dancer Didik Nini Thowok also wrote a preface to the same book, in which he recalls watching *potehi* versions of Xue Rengui and Three Kingdoms stories with his grandfather in his native Central Java town of Temanggung (Didik Nini Thowok 2012, 8–9).[32] Scholarship on his work notes that he was a fan of *potehi* from a young age and "performed a home-made children's version of it for his Javanese and Chinese friends at his home—with dinner plates used for sound effects, and puppet heads carved by a friend" (Mrázek 2005b, 266). As a recognized giant in the Javanese arts with acknowledged Chinese heritage, Didik Nini Thowok can symbolize the same kind of relation of community to culture as *potehi* claims—local Chinese as a component of Javanese culture. In another recent *potehi* book, dedicated to "Tolerance, Acculturation and Indonesian Nationalism," the foreword is written by an icon of Chinese integration with the Indonesian state, then Minister of Tourism and Creative Economy Mari Elka Pangestu 馮慧蘭 (Mastuti 2014, x–xi).

Association with political figures can also operate through the puppets themselves. In some Mojokerto performances, I have seen former presidents Gus Dur[33] and Megawati, then-Jakarta-governor Joko Widodo and his then-right-hand-man Ahok represented as *potehi* puppets. In December 2012, during a well-attended show in a Mojokerto-area village, the Gus Dur puppet appeared at a break in the Monkey King story and encouraged the young (non-Chinese) visitors to become *potehi* fans, highlighting the fact that as an Indonesian art, the genre belonged to everyone present. Efforts to invoke political figures in puppet form to further the acceptance of *potehi* and encourage a positive view of Sino-Indonesian culture and community may or may not be effective; but this would certainly seem to be the intent. Symbolic associations such as these allow prestige and legitimacy to accrue to *potehi,* just as the growing space for exhibitions of Sino-Indonesian culture has brought the puppets into more upscale venues, such as shopping malls and art galleries. Locations where *potehi* has recently been performed include Hotel Majapahit Surabaya, Hotel Grand City Surabaya, Trans Studio Bandung, the Chinese Cultural Center and a Javanese Protestant church (Gereja Pugeran) in Yogyakarta. Recent performance trips by troupes and patrons to Japan and Taiwan have also enhanced the genre's prestige.

Exhibits and performances are one manner of raising the profile of *potehi;* both scholarly and popular publications serve the same purpose. By sponsoring publications and the travel of *potehi* scholars, patrons are helping to create a network of scholars and specialists on the cultural aspects of Chinese Indonesian life. Indonesian texts on the genre often take an overtly celebratory tone. Hirwan Kuardhani writes that "[t]hrough performances of Chinese Peranakan Wayang *potehi,* other ethnicities such as the Javanese, Sundanese, Balinese and Minangkabau can interact with and understand the patron of the performance in terms of Chinese ethnicity," making the claim that *potehi* is "loaded with moral messages and guidance for noble behavior" (Kuardhani 2012, 105). Purwoseputro writes that the Javanese ethnicity of most performers shows "that *Wayang Potehi* is no longer an art that is exclusive to the Chinese-Indonesian community, especially the Hokkien subgroup and followers of [Chinese religions], but belongs to the wider public" (2014, 19).

Fifty years ago, theatre scholar James R. Brandon made the claim that *potehi* was the only *wayang* to be performed in the national language, Indonesian (Brandon 1967, 49). Though this is likely less and less accurate, the observation does yield a certain inspiring irony.[34] The tendency in Indonesian texts and public pronouncements to stress the genre's Indonesian characteristics (usually with a focus on the language shift to Indonesian), however, is growing. Affirmations that the "specialty of *potehi* in Java is a manifestation of the adaptive and assimilative attitude of the Chinese people who had already arrived in the region of Java hundreds of years ago" (Kuardhani 2012, 105–106), or that the genre is "no longer an exclusive Chinese art, but one imbued with Indonesian values" (Kwartanada 2014), are now common. Mastuti points out that it is a shame that "the Sino-Javanese acculturation had not been sufficiently appreciated by the people" (Mastuti 2004, 13) and explicitly connects it with *wayang*'s then new status as a UNESCO Masterpiece of Oral and Intangible Heritage of Humanity (2004, 15). Pangestu connects *potehi* explicitly to Indonesia's motto *Bhinneka Tunggal Ika* (Unity in Diversity), considering that *potehi* "can serve as a means to develop mutual understanding and tolerance between ethnic groups" (Mastuti 2014, x). Evidently, the hybridity of the genre has prompted many to adopt it as a symbol of Sino-Indonesian integration.

New Performance Models

In the search for legitimacy as an Indonesian form, *potehi* promoters and patrons have sought various new contexts for performance. The exhibitions in galleries and museums are now culminating in the establishment of museums for *wayang potehi* in Gudo (opened 2017) and another in Mojokerto, the Museum Wayang Yensen Project 2017, in which *wayang potehi* plays a central role. The narrative form and sociological context of *wayang potehi* have also begun to undergo noticeable changes. For instance, beginning in December 2012, Mojokerto's Roadshow Wayang Potehi toured eighteen villages near the city of Mojokerto in East Java, deliberately targeting non-Chinese audiences.[35] The poster for the roadshow features stickers proclaiming *wayang potehi* 100 percent Indonesian, and is described as being sponsored by "the Yensen Project for the city of Mojokerto," with performances consisting of the *Journey to the West* and *Xue Rengui's Campaign to the West*. These one-evening performances replace the traditional *wayang potehi* practice of performing one narrative over several weeks for a particular temple festival.

This project is led by and named after Pak Yensen, a Mojokerto Hokkien plastics manufacturer who has watched *potehi* in Mojokerto's central *klenteng* since his childhood.[36] The roadshow project, by bringing *potehi* into villages and integrating it into a program of Javanese festivities, was designed to demonstrate that there was no contradiction or distance between local *pribumi* culture and Sino-Indonesian culture (here separated from temple context and implicitly secular). Attendance was sweetened by the offer of five tricycles as "door prizes" (though, as these were performances on tarps at village crossroads, there were no doors). Of the roadshow, one observer has written that it is "a tactical conservation measure." Whether consciously or unconsciously, taking *potehi* out of the temple grounds recalls the pre–New Order festival context, allowing people to realize that *potehi* is acculturated and "really a genre particular to the folk culture and art of Java" (Kuardhani 2012, 108).

Just as colonial *potehi* was once presented alongside *wayang wong* and social dances, puppetry performances are for the Yensen Project one element of an ecumenical program featuring many other genres. Taken as a whole, the project seeks to promote the integration of Chinese culture into the concept of the Indonesian nation, and thus it produces DVDs of *potehi* performances, has established a *barongsay* group, recorded patriotic Indonesian-Chinese music ("I am a daughter of

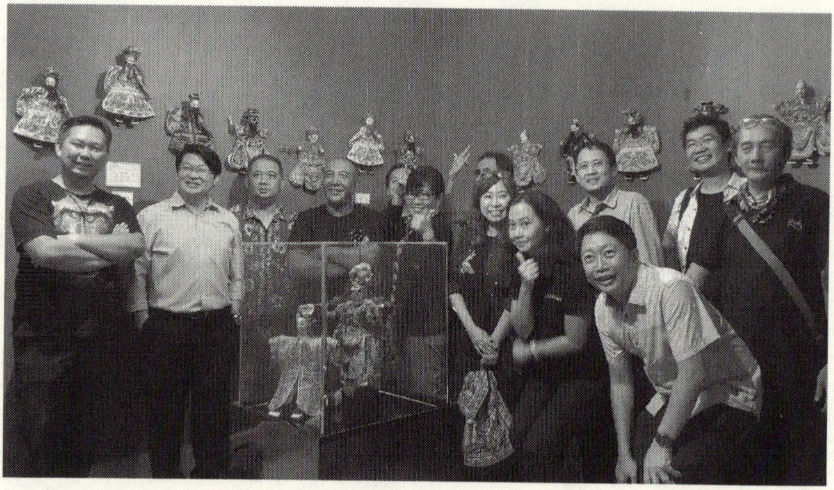

Wayang potehi patrons and enthusiasts pose at a Surabaya art gallery, 2016. Photo courtesy of Bernadette Godeliva Fabiola Natasha.

the Chinese people, and my nation is Indonesia" [Aku putri Tionghoa, dan bangsaku Indonesia]), funded the roadshow, and acquired puppets, stages, and accoutrements for the museum.

Potehi patrons invest a great deal in their collections, stages, performance troupes, and support of recordings and research, all of which contribute to the public representation of the genre and consequently of the community. It is certain that the troupes they support do not turn a profit (except perhaps on the karmic ledger, since temple performances are meant to bring their sponsors good fortune). Given the close cooperation between the roadshow and the city of Mojokerto as well as the presence of dignitaries at the roadshow performances, the dynamics of local politics certainly make themselves felt.

A further project has taken the Indonesian patriotic rhetoric of *wayang potehi* to its natural conclusion. Dwi Woro Retno Mastuti at Universitas Indonesia has devoted herself to the study of *wayang potehi,* especially in Gudo, for over a decade. Herself ethnic Javanese, she has in recent years founded a fifteen-member student group, the Rumah Cinwa (Cinta Wayang [Love *Wayang*], although the interpretation Cina is also intended) for the practice of *wayang potehi.* This troupe has already been invited to perform at temples and schools (*Kompasiana,* November 20, 2015). Since neither students, instructor, nor audience have overt Chinese connections, this project shows *wayang potehi* in a fully integrated form, even as it retains Chinese narrative and aesthetic material.

This development is the result of concerted direction and support from various actors: patrons, state officials, academics, museums, and so on. To some degree, the following genres, for which far fewer materials are available, must serve as a foil for *potehi*—these are genres that were not similarly adopted, did not adapt, and therefore have all but entirely disappeared.

Singkawang's Hakka Marionettes

In the words of the official song of Indonesia's principal Hakka organization Yinni Keshu Lianyihui 印尼客屬聯誼會 (Indonesian Hakka Friendship Society), "Wherever the sun shines, there are Hakka people / Wherever the ocean flows, there is Hakka love" (Yinni Subei Keshu Lianyihui 2011, 20). As the song suggests, there are Hakka populations all over Indonesia (and for that matter, the world). Of all Indonesian cities, none is more profoundly marked by Hakka emigration than Singkawang, in West Kalimantan. The Chinese presence in that province is most famously associated with the Lanfang Republic, a kind of mining state in West Borneo that had something resembling autonomy for over a century, ending in the late nineteenth century. The Hakka descendants of the Lanfang Republic's population are now one of the principal ethnic groups of Singkawang and its hinterland, and their culture can be easily distinguished both from the Teochew in Pontianak (the province's capital) and the Hakka communities elsewhere in the archipelago. Ethnic relations with other local groups, and how that is worked out in performance and public display, will be dealt with more extensively in chapter 6, but for now we will consider the community's *wayang gantung* marionettes.

Their existence allows Singkawang Hakka to boast, it would seem, of the only marionette (as opposed to shadow or glove puppetry) practice in Indonesia. The practice has also retained its original language, being performed in Hakka rather than in Indonesian. Known locally in Hakka as *chiao theu* 樵頭[37]and in Indonesian as *wayang gantung*,[38] the Singkawang variety can be situated, like *potehi*, in an international family. The tradition from which the Singkawang practice originates is still alive in Mainland China, found today in the Hakka areas of western Fujian, especially Shanghang 上杭[39] and nearby places such as Longyan 龍巖 County and Liancheng 連城,[40] where it is attested since the Ming dynasty (Lai 2014). With the waves of Hakka emigration overseas throughout the Qing dynasty, marionettes appeared in Taiwan[41] and in what is now West Kalimantan. Hakka marionettes have also been known (at least until recently) in the New Territories of Hong Kong (Kagan 1978, 74). In other areas of Hakka settlement in the Indies archipelago, however, there is no conclusive evidence of Hakka marionettes as a present or historical practice.

Until recently there has been no formal documentation of the practice in Singkawang, and records on the area's earlier cultural history are few. The fact that no practitioners are literate in Chinese complicates matters. According to the reports of old marionettists and community respondents, a man from eastern Guangdong called Ajo or Ajong arrived in Singkawang in 1929 or some time in the preceding two decades. However, according to one practitioner, Tai Siuk Jan 戴淑圆 (b. 1949), Ajo was better known as a *guzheng* (zither) instrumentalist than as a puppeteer. In her account, the puppeteer's name was Li Tung Jin, and he brought Hakka-language theatre in both *xiqu* and marionette form from Mainland China to Hakka Borneo. The puppet troupes that subsequently emerged were all headed by his students or their offspring (Wulandari 2009, 45–46).

These are inadequate materials from which to establish the history of a theatre genre. Most likely, as in the case of *wayang potehi,* there was more than a single moment of transmission, and the various waves of migration brought their own puppetry practices, possibly from different parts of the Hakka homeland. It seems best to try to approach the genre's history from the perspective of its single surviving troupe, Shin Thian Chai 新天彩, and only principal puppeteer, Chin Nen Sin 陳能成 (b. 1949). Tjin Nen Sin, who is Tai's husband, now divides his time between Singkawang and Jakarta. The youngest of nine children, he grew up in Lirang, near Singkawang. In the late 1950s, when Chin was a child, his father Chin Jat Ching 陳義清 invited teachers from Sambas and Pontianak to Singkawang. Their names were Chai Piang Shiu and Ho Lin Fu, and they taught the children marionette manipulation in the evenings as well as puppet carving. Tjin proved the most adept of his siblings and began to perform locally, forming one of several troupes at the time. In early adolescence he left school and worked otherwise as a rubber tapper.

The Suharto era did not end Tjin's performance practice, though restrictions meant that performances were given only in semi-secret family or temple-based venues. In the 1980s, marionette performance suffered a severe setback, as the anti-Chinese laws and the increasing prevalence of television combined to diminish performance opportunities. Seeing the handwriting on the wall, the other troupes sold all their puppets to people from Singapore. Tjin, however, persevered. Of the thirty-nine puppets that are now in Tjin's possession, some were made in China and were inherited from older marionettists, and some are his own carvings. In 2008, Tjin left his agricultural work to his children and moved into the urban area of Singkawang.[42] Besides puppets, he also earns a living making funeral and devotional items as well as musical instruments and running an orchestra, Pat Jim Pan 八音班, that performs independently and also accompanies funeral processions (see also Kartomi 2000, 305).[43]

As with *wayang kulit* on Java, *wayang gantung* was instrumentalized for family-planning purposes in Singkawang,[44] where such policies were deeply unpopular given the community's relatively poor and rural profile. Performances in the 1990s such as those seen by musicologist Margaret Kartomi were only fifteen to thirteen minutes long and mostly contained propaganda in favor of the two-child policy.[45] There was no musical accompaniment, Hakka speaking or singing, or incorporation of Chinese narratives: audio was provided by an Indonesian-language tape. Besides family-planning *wayang*, it seems there were also Pancasila performances, though neither type has enduringly marked the genre. At the time of Kartomi's visit, the troupe was known as Wayang Tri Dharma, a name likely motivated by the Indonesian official concern for permitting Chinese theatre only when it appeared as a religious, rather than a cultural, product.[46]

When I visited Singkawang in 2013, there had not been a performance in over a year, and it seemed that the genre might disappear. Without state support and with the increasing penetration of television and the Internet into West Kalimantan, *wayang gantung* had become unprofitable. The usual performance fee, three million rupiah, struck many temple officials as unaffordable since they can invite popular singers or variety shows at the same price or more cheaply.[47] Cost was also the reason several local respondents cited for the nonparticipation of the genre in Cap Go Meh (Lantern Festival) celebrations, in contrast to previous years.[48]

However, in the intervening years, invitations from Java-based Sino-Indonesian institutions seem to have lent the genre new viability, leading to new recognition at home in West Kalimantan. This culminated in the conferral of an award (one of several Provincial Figures for the Year 2014) on Tjin by the vice-governor of West Kalimantan during 2015 celebrations of the provincial government's anniversary (*Antara Kalbar*, January 29, 2015), specifically citing the several invitations to perform on Java. In the current period of Reformasi, efforts of government control have been replaced by a more benign modicum of institutional involvement. This can be seen as running in parallel with the local government's incorporation of festivals and the positioning of Chinese culture as a tourist draw and a constituent of local multiculturalism.[49]

Both Chinese organizations and local government have created initiatives to help *wayang gantung* survive. The PERMASIS (Perkumpulan Masyarakat Singkawang dan Sekitarnya / The Community Association of Singkawang and Surroundings) has in the past invited the group to perform and has also produced DVDs of their performance, and the Taiwanese chamber of commerce in Singkawang has also been known to sponsor performances. However, Tjin's longstanding hope that his Lirang home could be turned into a puppet museum or transmission center was dashed by a destructive 2008 fire.

Indonesian scholars, too, have begun to show a modest interest—again echoing a trend more vigorously found on Java. A spate of articles has tried to integrate the genre more formally into the *wayang* family of arts, or to highlight it as a distinctive feature of West Kalimantan culture. As with the paucity of performance opportunities, it is the lack of sponsorship structures analogous to those used to popularize *wayang potehi* that has made *wayang gantung* an all but extinct art, while *wayang potehi* troupes now tour nationally and internationally as a symbol of Indonesian, or Sino-Indonesian, culture.

As with *potehi*, performances have decreased in length as attention spans diminish and demands on time increase. Until the 1960s, performances might be spread over several days and accompanied by *barongsay* or storytelling practices. The troupes toured throughout the West Kalimantan Hakka area, typically performing twice a day (afternoon and evening) for engagements lasting up to a week (a schedule resembling *wayang potehi* practices up to the present day). In more distant localities, such as Sambas, performances might last up to a month. Nowadays, the rare performances last only one or two nights.

The marionettes seem to be connected to, or perhaps have inspired, a *xiqu* practice. Eighty-four at the time of our 2013 interview, Huang Yuntian 黃雲添, a onetime collaborator of Tjin's, recounted that *wayang gantung* had formerly performed alongside (and with the same artists) as extinct non-puppet *xiqu* practices. Several theatres had performed Hakka-language *xiqu* during the Dutch colonial period, and Huang himself had performed with a group called the Sanxing Kexi Tuan 三星客戲團 (Three Star Hakka troupe), which existed approximately from 1962 to 1967.[50] At the same time, Huang also performed puppetry with Tian Baoshun 天寶順, a puppetry theatre led by an arrival from Mainland China named Zhang Zixiang 張子祥. Doing double duty with puppetry and human Hakka theatre allowed Huang to earn enough to get out of agricultural work. Moreover, these troupes often also performed Hakka *pat jim* orchestral music in concert, just as Tjin's troupe still does. According to Huang, since human theatre was more lucrative, the troupe would borrow *wayang gantung* stories and adapt them for use as human theatre.[51] Such practices did not survive the violence of the mid-to-late 1960s.

Wayang gantung repertoire seems to be less closely linked to the Qing-fiction narratives that are found in *potehi* (or *wayang kulit cina-jawa*, of which more in the next section). It seems, for instance, that there are no Xue Rengui stories; this is likely because, distant from the printing cultures of Java, the influence of Sino-Malay literature on Borneo was negligible. Most of the repertoire is drawn from *Three Kingdoms, The Water Margin,* and *Journey to the West* stories, as well as *Baxian guo hai* 八仙過海 (The Eight Immortals cross the sea). There are also improvised and comical pieces, and "Tangshan songs"[52] may be incorporated. Tjin, like *potehi* performers, does not use scripts; unlike them, he does not even use notes.

The genre has undergone little or no indigenization or hybridization, in substantial contrast to *potehi*. Nevertheless, developments suggest that it may be increasingly incorporated into larger Indonesian ideas of *wayang*, perhaps especially since Kalimantan has little or no other narrative theatre (Chinese or otherwise). In the context of the general (but problematic) symbolic association of *wayang* with Indonesia,[53] the impulse to incorporate a Chinese theatre from West Kalimantan into national narratives is growing both for institutions on Java (including Chinese ones) and in local government. The genre provides a striking instance where cultural adaptation has been relatively slight, and where the recent incorporation of Chinese practices into Indonesian official conceptions of performance has proceeded more slowly and less smoothly than in Java. This is because the local population has also not been culturally or linguistically integrated to anything near the same degree as Javanese Sino-Indonesians, but also because this poorer community has had limited access to the kinds of systems of patronage that are available on Java and that have profoundly altered the situation for *wayang potehi* and for the next genre to be discussed, *wayang kulit Cina-Jawa*.

Wayang Kulit Cina-Jawa

This leather-shadow puppetry genre from Yogyakarta is known by several names, of which the least ambiguous is used here.[54] This genre was invented and substantially promoted and practiced by the Yogyakarta Peranakan *dalang* Gan Thwan Sing (1885–1966).[55] Though the genre used Chinese narratives, it borrowed its performance conventions largely from *wayang kulit*.[56] Closely identified with its creator and dormant for many years after his death, it has recently drawn greater attention and even been revived. Though the puppets and other material aspects are extant, revivals rely substantially on guesswork as far as performance practice is concerned (Prasetya 2014b, 126).

Most of what is known about *wayang kulit Cina-Jawa* is due to two substantial collections of puppets and forty scripts. The Yogyakarta Sonobudoyo Museum acquired some of the puppets from Gan directly (Seltmann 1976, 55), while another set, for the story *Sie Jin Kui Ceng See* 薛仁貴征西 (Xue Rengui's campaign to the West), was held until recently in the German town of Überlingen, as part of Walter Angst's monumental *wayang* collection.[57] Angst died in 2014, and Sino-Indonesian efforts to have the *wayang kulit Cina-Jawa* puppets repatriated to Indonesia proved unsuccessful. Instead, his brother and inheritor, Sir Henry Angest, donated the entire collection to the Yale University Art Gallery, where it has been housed since 2017 (Cohen 2018). The Cina-Jawa *wayang* puppets in his collection, numbering 345 items, formerly belonged to Fredrik Seltmann, of Stuttgart.[58] As for Gan's (Javanese-language) scripts, thirty-nine of them were acquired from Seltmann by the Berlin State Library, where they remain publicly accessible.[59]

Source materials for this genre are few. A 1976 article by Seltmann first brought the artifacts to scholarly attention, attempting to situate the genre within the larger context of Sino-Indonesian puppetry. The richest source, however, is a 1980/1981 government publication entitled *Wayang Cina-Jawa di Yogyakarta*, based on interviews with Gan's son and Yogyakarta cultural figures, many of them Gan's contemporaries. More recent work by Indonesian and Taiwanese scholars have filled in some of the gaps and stimulated renewed interest in this performance history and the artifacts that remain from it.

All sources provide the same basic biography: Gan Thwan Sing was born in Jatinom (northeast of Yogyakarta) in Central Java, the son of the Chinese immigrant Gan Ing Kwat. It is reported that as a child he lived with his grandfather, who instructed him in Chinese traditions, including language, writing, and legendary stories. He became enormously attached to the all-night performances of the *wayang kulit* tradition and "knew intimately all aspects of the Javanese shadow puppets" (Seltmann 1976, 54), eventually moving to Yogyakarta in 1900. There he reportedly became a *sandiwara* (spoken-theatre) artist in an amateur Peranakan Yogyakarta troupe. While working as an actor, he engaged in the study of Yogyakarta *kulit* puppetry styles, including from musical, material, and puppeteering perspectives.[60]

It was thus natural that Gan's own invention, emerging in 1925, should be the fusion of traditional *wayang kulit* narrative and performance and musical char-

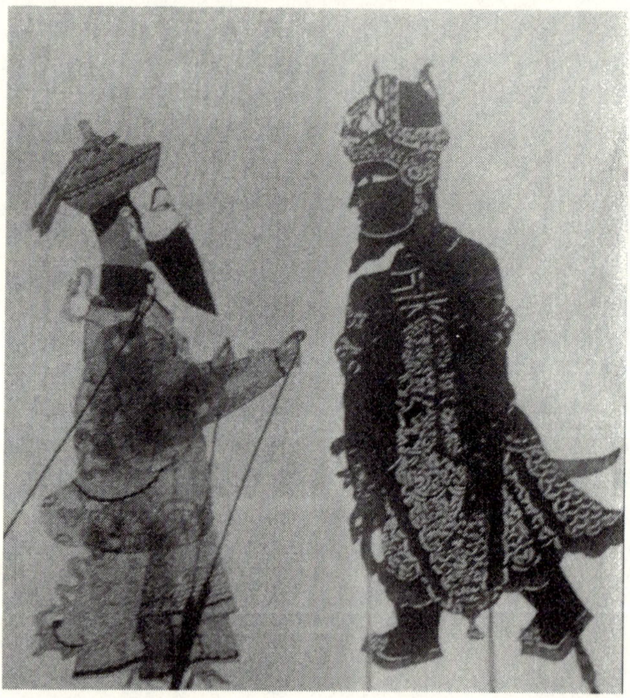

Photo of *wayang kulit Cina Jawa* ca. 1920–1925 by J. L. Moens. Image courtesy of the KITLV digital image library.

acteristics (including use of the *gamelan*) with Chinese legends, largely the same type of popular Qing narratives that feature in *potehi*.[61] If the means of production and the performance context present similarities with *wayang kulit,* a major difference is that the colors used in the costumes reflect Chinese theatre conventions rather than Javanese ones (Mastuti 2004, 6). Later, Gan made clown figures derived from *wayang kulit,* presumably to suit the tastes of Javanese audiences accustomed to that genre. He also made time in performance for an interlude of humorous banter in Javanese and colloquial Malay, interspersed with a few Hokkien phrases or terms (Soelarto and Albiladiyah 1980/1981, 35–36)—a practice perhaps not so dissimilar from the improvisation in contemporary *potehi* practices. As befits a materially and performatively hybrid genre, it attracted mixed audiences as well as both Chinese and Javanese noble disciples; at least initial sponsorship came from a local Chinese businessman (Soelarto and Albiladiyah 1980/1981, 9; Pausacker 2005, 195). Although Gan wore Western clothes when performing rather than usual *dalang* dress, the performance contained ritual elements and lasted, like a *wayang kulit* performance, from evening until the early morning (Ontoro 2014, 21–23). Unfortunately, Gan's students predeceased him, and Gan's last performance was in 1960, by which time he was too ill to teach. His son did not have the same gift as a *dalang,* and the form died out.

Gan's manuscripts, memory aids for his own performance use, are written in Javanese script.[62] One of the principal characteristics of the texts is a close similarity to *wayang kulit* models (Seltmann 1976, 54; Soelarto and Albiladiyah 1980/1981, 10–11; see also Pigeaud 1975, 253).[63] The names of the characters, the state, heaven, and others were given in Hokkien, while royal and bureaucratic positions were given Javanese equivalents. The scripts have earned themselves a modest place in Javanese letters. Dwi Woro Mastuti considers his oeuvre to be in the "literary language used by such Javanese poets such as Yasadipura or R. Ng. Ranggawarsita," using "straightforward, concise, and short sentences" (Mastuti 2004, 12). Theodoor Pigeaud, one of the leading Dutch Javanists of the twentieth century, described the scripts as "unique" and comments that the "author or translator was a man of culture, he had a large choice of words and he was familiar with the Javanese *dalang's* idiom. He took pains to reproduce the sounds of the Chinese characters as accurate[ly] as possible with the Javanese characters at his disposal" (1975, 252). On the other hand, Pigeaud also considered that "the overwhelming mass of Chinese characters makes it difficult to follow the story" and that the text was written "awkwardly and slovenly" (252), although it may bear repeating that the manuscript was for performer reference, not publication.

The material aspects present certain intriguing questions. It is not certain whether Chinese shadow puppets reached Java, or whether Gan was familiar with them.[64] A 1954 Dutch newspaper account of the period linked the puppets to a "Chinese form of [*wayang kulit*] developed about 70 years earlier [in the 1880s] by a Chinese *kapitein*, Liem Kie Tjwan, who came under the influence of Javanese [*wayang kulit purwo*] and then adapted it for the Chinese taste." The article further remarks that it was sponsored by a local Chinese and was attracting substantial interest due to its rarity (*De Locomotief*, January 14, 1954). Material evidence suggests that Chinese shadow puppetry may have also influenced Gan's creation of the genre: *wayang kulit Cina-Jawa* are relatively small, and their heads are detachable. Since detachability is also typical of Chinese shadow puppets (Chen 2007, 7), these features offer circumstantial evidence that Gan was influenced by Chinese models. Local experts speculate that later puppets by Gan were modelled more closely on *kulit* to improve performance effect (Tsai 2017, 54).

The genre is interesting also from the perspective of the transference of Chinese stories to the Indies. Like *potehi*, press, and comic books, *wayang kulit Cina-Jawa* made substantial use of the martial narratives about the Tang dynasty that had been particularly popular in the Qing. Claudine Salmon noted the similarity between one of Gan's scripts[65] and a section of *Wuhu Pingxi* 五虎平西 (Five tigers pacify the West; Salmon 2013b, 244–245). This was a story popular in China around the turn of the eighteenth century and that had been translated into Javanese in 1862 (Salmon 2013b, 241; Zimmer 2002, 168). Di family stories, much like Xue Rengui, were ultimately derived from cycles that were popular as fiction from the mid-Qing, and also appear in both northern Chinese and Taiwanese shadow puppetry repertoire (Chen 2007, 111–112). The other narratives Gan used are no less implicated in webs of Qing fiction,[66] even when there are no known translations into Javanese, or when the narrative is not known from Chinese shadow puppetry practice records—Gan might have known them, for instance, through Malay translations (Salmon 1981, 2013c). The other Berlin scripts include *Journey to the West* stories, stories about Zhao Kuangyin,[67] a story called *Dongyou ji* 東遊記 (Journey to the East),[68] and *Fan Tang yanyi* 反唐演義 (The revolt against the Tang Dynasty).[69] The narrative world of *wayang kulit Cina-Jawa* was evidently intimately connected to Hokkien shadow-puppet repertoire,[70] the Sino-Malay press and translation efforts, not to mention *wayang kulit*. By the 1950s, when Gan was active, the Xue Rengui stories were also being run in local newspapers as fiction and as comic strips.

Wayang kulit Cina-Jawa disappeared before the Suharto-era suppression of Chinese culture, and as such cannot be considered a casualty of New Order. Thirty-five years ago, in the middle of the New Order period, it was already a respectable subject for research in Yoygakarta, as demonstrated both by the publication of a monograph on the genre by the Directorate General of Culture in 1980/1981 (Soelarto and Albiladiyah), and its inclusion of the genre in the 1983 exhibition of puppets alongside other *wayang* puppets at the epicenter of official culture, Taman Ismail Marzuki in Jakarta (*Kompas*, August 5, 1983). In the Reformasi cultural climate, naturally, interest has greatly increased.

The form's hybridity is now especially welcome to Indonesian authorities. *Wayang kulit Cina-Jawa* could have no existence outside of the Javanese cultural context, being linguistically and musically bound to Javanese, not Chinese, sources. Because the last performance was over fifty years ago, it may be described as extinct, though nothing prevents the revival and use of *wayang* puppets, narratives, and/or scripts. Thus, a kind of rebirth occurred in a 2014 exhibit at the Museum Sonobudoyo entitled "Wacinwa: Silang Budaya Cina-Jawa" (Wacinwa: A Sino-Javanese interculture). With the help of actors and researchers, the curators attempted to identify all the *wayang kulit Cina-Jawa* puppets and scripts in their collection and mounted an exhibition also featuring Sie Djin Kwie–based comics,[71] Gan's scripts and tapes of a *ketoprak* adaptation of Sie Djin Kwie,[72] and photographs of the Gan family. The year 2015 saw a slew of related performances, with some of its support coming from the Yensen Project, one of East Java's principal *potehi* sponsors (Tsai Tsung-te 2017, 62–63).

As with *potehi*, academics and official authorities are now concerned with integrating *wayang kulit Cina-Jawa* into the Indonesian multicultural image. In a preface to the museum exhibit, the head of culture in Yogyakarta expressed himself reservedly, stating that the exhibit is "an attempt to reopen the past memories related to the interaction existing between Chinese and Javanese as represented through art" (Yudaningrat 2014, 5), but the head of the museum expressed herself more enthusiastically: "Chinese and Javanese are two ethnic[itie]s which never stop interacting" and "fill and absorb each other" (Riharyani 2014, 6). In the terms of two publications of recent years (Mastuti 2011; Riharnyani 2015, 90), the genre, like *wayang potehi*, can be used to illustrate how the local Chinese have "become Javanese" and, by extension, Indonesian.

Other Forms of Sino-Indonesian *Wayang*

As with *xiqu*, there are some bits and bobs of evidence for other genres; little more can be done at this stage than to mention them in passing. Malaysian theatre specialist Tan Sooi-Beng visited Medan in 2003 and was taken to a Teochew rod-puppet performance at a temple in Kota Bangun, a predominantly Hokkien rural suburb. Her recollection of the performance (and the photo she took) make it seem quite similar to the Penang *potehi* practices she has written about (Tan Sooi-Beng 1981). At the time of her visit, the performers were between the ages of seventy and ninety. The art form was referred to as *wayang klitik*, presumably by analogy with the Javanese wooden shadow puppets of that name. Tan, who kindly shared her field notes with me, was at the time pursuing other lines of research and has not since returned to this subject.

During a visit to Kota Bangun in November 2016, I was able to establish, through interviews with local inhabitants, only the rough contours of this now-vanished performance: the puppets had apparently been brought from Penang, and the performance group was sometimes as large as twenty people. Local respondents thought that performances had occurred in the 1960s or 1970s in the area surrounding the area temple, Kuan Theng Bio 高亭廟, usually as part of the observation of the ghost-month observations; it had been popular among older people. The youngest member of the group, Ahuat 阿發, had moved away some years earlier, although local respondents remembered him being a relative of Chang A Eng (perhaps Zhang Aying 張阿英, died ca. 2014), who appears in Tan's notes as a puppeteer. They remembered no name for the troupe itself and were under the impression that the genre had been transmitted locally, that is, without recent arrivals from Penang or Chaozhou (Ahok, Ajek, Guan Tianxing, et al., pers. comm., November 8 and 10, 2016). Kartomi had also noted a Chinese form by a similar name, *wayang klithik Cina,* that was being performed in Malay with "scores of small three-dimensional wooden puppets" in certain Chinese temples of Central Java (2000, 298), coexisting with *potehi* and using a similar orchestra. As with Sino-Indonesian *xiqu,* it seems very likely that various puppetry practices have disappeared without documentation.

In his 1988 overview, *Wayang, kebudayaan Indonesia dan Pancasila* (Wayang, Indonesian culture and Pancasila), Pandam Guritno established a typology of *wayang,* involving twenty-eight distinct traditions from the islands of Java, Bali, Lombok, and Sumatra, and performed in various regional languages such as Sundanese, Betawi, Palembang Malay, and Sasak (Guritno 1988, 14). This attitude—inclusive towards various *pribumi* forms but drawing the line at genres of Chinese origin—was until recently reasonably typical of the Indonesian conception of *wayang* and the pre-Reformasi reception of the *potehi* form.

Given the internal diversity of the concept of *wayang,* however, and the renegotiations of Chinese identity in the Reformasi era, it is not surprising to find a growing practice of inclusion of Chinese puppetry forms in the category of *wayang,* not only in the efforts of patrons or scholars, but also, for instance, in the display of *wayang potehi* puppets (as well as reproductions of *wayang kulit Cina-Jawa,* a Sino-Javanese *wayang kulit* genre) in the Wayang Museum in Jakarta. By 2016, the *Almanak Wayang Indonesia* included individual entries for all three of the major Sino-Indonesian *wayang* forms discussed in this chapter.

While there is no need to seek an exact equivalence between Sino-Indonesian *wayang* and genres such as *wayang kulit* and *wayang golek,* there seems ample reason to expect continuing recognition and further integration of the forms as a special *wayang* genre representative of Sino-Javanese culture, particularly as patrons devote resources to the popularization of the form. The positioning of these genres is thus judicious as well as strategic, namely, to present the culture of the Chinese minority as an integral element of an Indonesian whole.

From the perspective of Chinese performance studies, these genres may be a peripheral phenomenon—perhaps even a case testing the limits of terms such as "Chinese." A theatre with often little or no singing, not performed in a Chinese language, using scripts that are derived from the *dalang*'s reception and transformation of novels and stories in translation, bears little resemblance to anything known in China. The particularity of such genres also points to the dangers of sclerotic thinking when it comes to the genres of Chinese performance, as the process of defining and imposing genres, so powerful in China and Taiwan, does not neatly reflect practices of these genres in diaspora. How ought one to think of *wayang potehi*'s relation to Fujian or Taiwan (or Malaysian, or Singaporean) *potehi; wayang kulit Cina-Jawa*'s relation to Chinese shadow puppetry; and *wayang gantung*'s relation to the practices of Western Fujian Hakka marionettes?

The boundaries of Chinese performance genres are to a substantial extent determined by the vocabulary and cultural policy of a given political regime, capable of shifting radically along one axis while retaining great traditionality on another. Clearly, it is insufficient to regard such practices, as they sometimes are in Chinese studies contexts (when noticed at all), as simple derivatives or extensions of "motherland" practice, even if it would be disingenuous to deny their ability to underline cultural heritage and transnational continuities. There is no need to disclaim their roots in coastal China, which have furnished the material and/or narrative framework for the genres. There can be no tidy separation of Chinese and Indonesian elements, and those considering the matter from either perspective would be wise to view the inevitable and necessary hybridity of the Sino-Indonesian subject and its cultural products as a rich resource for both cultures.

CHAPTER 3

Five Ancestors, Twice Over

CHINESE-LANGUAGE SPOKEN THEATRE IN INDONESIA

THE space for the articulation of a nationalistic Chinese community spirit in the Indies had grown during the late colonial period, associated with a strident and self-conscious aspiration to modernity. Having undergone a process of re-sinification in the first few decades of the twentieth century, the Sino-Indonesian community experienced an increase in leftist sentiment over the 1940s. The establishment of the People's Republic of China was greeted in many Sino-Indonesian quarters with great enthusiasm. In the 1950s, PRC representatives distributed Indonesian-, Chinese-, and English-language materials in efforts to reach both ethnic Chinese communities and Indonesian individuals and government officials (Hong Liu 2010). Pro-Beijing tendencies almost certainly represented a majority of Chinese Indonesian associations by 1957 (Suryadinata 2004, 75). As that political orientation developed and strengthened, the tenor and uses of theatre also shifted, and contacts with the PRC arts world—theatre, cinema, music, and dance—increased. In the turbulent 1940s, Chinese-language theatrical activities, predominately pro-Beijing in orientation, flourished.

The first two chapters have attempted to show how Sino-Indonesian practitioners of *xiqu* and *wayang* have responded over time to shifting socioeconomic positions of their minority. This chapter considers how mid-twentieth-century ethnic Chinese intellectuals in the Indies and Indonesia sought to use another genre—Chinese-language spoken theatre (*huaju* 話劇)—as a way of negotiating their identities as two new states, the People's Republic of China and the Republic of Indonesia, emerged from World War II and the more local wars that, in both regions, prolonged the period of hostilities. With the materials presently available such an account is necessarily piecemeal. The focus here is therefore on a particular case study, although it may be hoped that as Sino-Indonesian archives become more broadly available, deeper study will become feasible. This theatre was also not indigenous in the same way as other cases examined in this book—its materials and inspiration derived from Chinese leftism before and after establishment of the PRC, and sometimes operatives from China were directly involved in Indonesian theatre. Some of the work thus stands at a certain remove from Sino-Indonesian identity, even if the fact that performers and audiences were local Chinese means that a legitimate place can be claimed for them in the annals of Sino-Indonesian theatre.

Unfortunately, few Chinese-language scripts from Indonesia of any kind survive; as with *xiqu*, one must attempt to connect the dots between the accounts of spoken theatre fortuitously mentioned in the course of community or school events. The preponderance of material is on a couple of scripts, and so this chapter falls into two unequal halves: the first, an attempt to chart the activities of spoken and related Chinese theatres in Chinese communities; and the second, an attempt to track the shift in Sino-Indonesian identities by examining these two spoken theatre pieces that deal with the same narrative. In contrast to both *xiqu* and *wayang*, this is at present a wholly historical endeavor—the practice of spoken theatre has been revived in the Reformasi period only in very minor ways.[1]

The history of Chinese-language spoken theatre in the Indies and Indonesia, in contrast to those of Singapore and Malaysia, is neither well-known nor especially distinguished. From the perspective of literary history, other genres of Chinese-language works, including fiction, poetry, and memoirs, have been more substantial, and more significant authors can be identified from the colonial period and early Republic.[2] Since Reformasi, the activities of Sino-Indonesian authors and literary associations have reemerged and now exercise a significant social function in the Sino-Indonesian community and its transnational networks. There is, however, little or no dramatic work among these contemporary authors (Winkelmann 2008; Stenberg 2017). Chinese-language spoken theatre is thus a history quite abruptly cut short in 1965 and accessible, when at all, through the materials of its performance history rather than dramatic texts.

Even that history is limited by a considerable paucity of documentation. The greater part of documentation currently available deals with Jakarta and North Sumatra. In the latter region, troupes were more active and local voluntary associations have published a handful of texts that bear on local theatre history. Chinese-language spoken theatre in the late colonial period and early Republic was probably most pervasive there, where Chinese communities largely spoke and still speak Hokkien. On Java, Chinese-language spoken theatre was more limited, focusing on Mandarin-language schools and voluntary associations. Performance troupes often bore patriotic names (e.g., Guofeng 國風, National Wind), resembling their contemporaries in Mainland China. Scripts, including Mainland comedies and translations of classic European theatre, were imported from China and performed in schools (Jugang zhonghua xuexiao 1938, 190–191, 194).[3]

Troupes were composed largely of young people, mostly students. By the time the Sino-Japanese War began in 1937, Chinese-language spoken theatre (like other voluntary organization activities, and indeed like the dramatic performances of Java-based *xiqu* as well as Malay-language Chinese theatre groups) arranged for patriotic fund-raisers, sometimes coordinated with patriotic holiday celebrations, to aid Mainland China or local Chinese charities.[4] Though Chinese-language spoken theatre in Java largely stopped during the Japanese occupation, North Sumatran troupes were able to continue staging "patriotic" performances, though at considerable personal danger. After the war, performances resumed also on Java.

The late 1940s and 1950s were a high-water mark for Chinese-language community theatre. Amateur groups staged works by some of the major Mainland Chinese dramatists of the twentieth century, including Cao Yu 曹禺 and Guo Moruo 郭沫若, as well as stage adaptations of the short fiction of Lu Xun 魯迅 (Zhang Tao 2008, 100).[5] New works in PRC drama were quickly taken up in Indonesia: *Funü daibiao* 婦女代表 (The female representative), a one-act play by Sun Yu 孫芋, was published in the principal Mainland dramatic publication *Script* 劇本 in 1953 and produced already the next year by a Bandung school (ibid.). Similarly, the script for a 1956 children's show, *Malan hua* 馬蘭花 (The iris), was brought back by Sumatra Chinese from a Mainland trip and successfully staged soon thereafter by a Medan troupe (Han 2007a, 63–64). Dance troupes also drew on performances members had seen in China to reimagine their sets and costumes, facilitated through connections among Medan *guiqiao* 歸僑 (Overseas Chinese in Mainland China; Lao Pan 2007, 279–280).

There were a few locally written scripts, such as a 1949 satirical piece for *International Woman's Day,* called *Zhiye funü* 職業婦女 (The professional woman) that was staged by the Ba funü xiehui 吧婦女協會 (Batavia Women's Association), with the revenue going in part to help women's associations in Mainland China (*Xinbao,* March 5, 1949).[6] In the same month, Samarinda local youth groups also performed a patriotic play, *Zhonghua wansui* 中華萬歲 (Long live China), and a satirical morality piece, *Qian shi wo de zuzong* 錢是我的祖宗 (Money is my ancestor), on the occasion of Youth Day (March 29). On that occasion, ticket sales benefited local Chinese charities (*Xinbao,* March 20, 1949).

It is clear from promotional materials and programs that on most occasions spoken theatre was only a part of a larger program of entertainment. It is most accurate to imagine a kind of variety show, in which patriotic, political, or folk songs, dancing, and sketches might also be included alongside spoken theatre. Harmonica bands, brass ensembles, choirs, and *die luohan* 疊羅漢 (human pyramid) acrobatics abounded. A general exhortation to adopt "modern" social practices is likely represented by such titles as *Tiao nüxu* 挑女婿 (Choosing a son-in-law) and *Shijin bumei* 拾金不昧 (Returning found money), both produced in the North Sumatra town of Binjai (Huang Jianjin 2015, 441), but as schools and voluntary associations became increasingly identified with a "leftist" or (less often) "rightist" political position,[7] the political purpose of shows seems to have grown more central, and this was evident in the choice of texts. For instance, as elsewhere in the Chinese-speaking world, *Fangxia ni de bianzi* 放下你的鞭子 (Put down your whip), in which a cruel father whipping his daughter is exhorted by patriots planted in the audience to put down his whip and join the anti-Japanese struggle, became a popular play (Zhang Tao 2008, 99).[8] A picture of a Siantar troupe performing, probably in the early 1950s, a similarly anti-Japanese play, *Guohun* 國魂 (National soul), is also recorded (Huang Shuhai 2008, 146).[9]

As was the case with *xiqu,* the influence of PRC cinema can be felt in the form of plays such as *Bugu niao you jao le* 布谷鳥又叫了 (The cuckoo cries again; 1958) and *Qianwan bu yao wangji* 千萬不要忘記 (Never ever forget; 1964), where films provided the blueprint for the 1959 and 1965 Medan productions (Cao 2007, 59; Liao Zhangran 2007, 209–211).[10] The production of *Liu Sanjie* 劉三姐 (Third sister Liu) in Palembang by a local group, the Hangyou she 航友社 (Aeronatic Amateurs' Association) as well as in Jakarta (in a large-scale collaboration between the Nan'an gonghui 南安公會 [Nan'an Association] and the Xinyi she 新藝社 [New Arts Society]) in the early 1960s shows the same avenue of influence in musical theatre (Zhang Jian 2013, 23; Tang Aili, pers. comm., November 15, 2016).[11]

Pro-PRC schools may have dominated, but pro-ROC schools and organizations had similarly propagandistic activities. Until ROC schools were suppressed in 1958, Sino-Indonesian schools re-created in miniature the war of propaganda plays that was taking place simultaneously on either side of the Taiwan Strait.

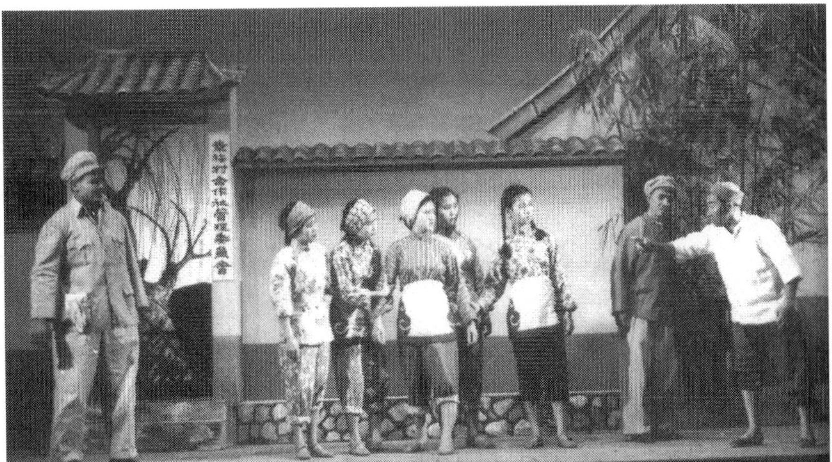

The Cuckoo Calls Again, produced in Medan in 1958. Photo courtesy of Lin Xuehua.

Records from a 1956 Palembang school publication give an example of how pro-ROC schools deployed theatre to advance their political purposes. Using three short comical and musical forms, plays such as *Dangbing shi yingxiong* 當兵是英雄 (It is heroic to be a soldier) or *Wufa wutian* 無法無天 (Without law or morality) satirized Red China while glorifying the ROC and encouraged students to subscribe to the return of the Mainland to KMT control (Nanhua Zhongxue 1956, 35). In the relatively pro-ROC environment of Bagansiapiapi, activity seems to have been more directed towards children's theatre (Chen, pers. comm., November 11, 2016). Even a 1946 ROC film seems to have been made into a Medan theatre adaptation, *Tianzi di yi hao* 天字第一號 (Code name heaven no. 1; Cao 2007, 59). This in turn was an adaptation of the anti-Japanese propaganda play *Ye meigui* 野玫瑰 (Wild rose) by KMT author Chen Quan 陳銓, a script that had been performed by Malang Peranakan Chinese in Indonesian translation as *Mawar hutan* in the mid-1950s. The fact that the play was "amended and shortened to erase much of the explicit propaganda" (Budianta 2012, 267) suggests that one might be wise to remember the possibility that political theatre (in this case pro-ROC) was often altered once it reached Indonesia.

The activities of Bandung dramatist and director Huang Shengda's 黃盛達 (1916–2011) give an idea of the Chinese-language theatre scene in this period in West Java's capital. There too, spoken theatre must have had considerable prominence, for his works *Xiansheng Dama* 先生大馬 (Mister Dama) and *Chulu* 出路 (Escape) were performed in Bandung's premier venue, the Concordia Theatre.[12] A 2011 Chinese-language press summary of Huang's career shows a CCP-oriented repertoire of plays, emerging from a cross section of pro-PRC local community associations:

> [Huang] directed and performed in Guo Moruo' s *Qu Yuan* 屈原 [Qu Yuan], he directed Shengguan tu 升官途 [Road to promotion] for *Nanqiao wenhua xuehui* 南僑文化學會[Southern Chinese Culture Society], the multi-act musical play for the *Huaqiao gonghui* 華僑工會 [Chinese Union] *Youle tudi duoshengchan* 有了土地多生產 [Now that we have land, we can produce more], Funü hui's 婦女會 [the Women's Association] *Shaonian you* 少年遊 [Travels in youth], and Huaqiao zhongxue's 華僑中學 [Overseas Chinese middle school] *Lili cao* 離離草 [The grasses of leaving], as well as the *Jianhua xuexi she* 建華學習社 [Build China Study Association]'s production of Cao Yu's *Thunderstorm* and the *Yurong gonghui* 玉融公會 [the Hokchia Association]'s musical drama, etc. (*Guoji Ribao,* January 6, 2011)

Though not all these plays can be easily traced, the two that can—*Thunderstorm* and Chen Baichen 陳白塵's 1945 *Road to Promotion*—were both works popular in the PRC and aggressively critical of Republican society. The titles of others, such as *Now That We Have Land*, strongly suggest praise for PRC projects and policies, even if no further information is available.

Another theatre figure of this period is Qiu Liuying 邱柳英, who was active in Jakarta and Bandung, in the latter as part of the Southern Chinese Culture Society. His 1949 one-act play *Pinshu* 聘書 (The Employment Contract) is a social tragedy, complete with exploitative boss and dying son (Zhang Tao 2008, 102–103).[13] The story, with its rage against the cruelty of exploitation, would be entirely characteristic of a leftist Chinese play in the same period, and the script at no point shows that it is written by an Indonesian Chinese. The play's legitimacy was derived from and ensured by the creation and production of works that were similar and orthodox in Mainland Chinese terms.

At present only one script has come to light from this pre-PRC period of Chinese-language literature on Java; its paratextual materials permit us to reconstruct something of Batavia's Chinese spoken theatre scene. *Niliu* 逆流 (The Counter-Current), by the otherwise unknown Fei Na 非那, was published in 1947 by the Bacheng Zhonghua xiju xiehui 巴城中華戲劇協會 (Batavia Chinese Theatre Association). Set in postwar Shanghai, the story tells a conventional naturalistic tale of class struggle. The author, who is described by the association's chairman Hu Xuntao 胡訓陶 as having "rich theatre experience," drew his material from events he read in newspapers about China (Hu Xuntao 1947, ii). In a letter, also by Hu, to the Zhonghua quanguo wenyijie xiehui 中華全國文藝界協會 (Chinese National Association of Writers and Artists), the same Batavian organization announced that 30 percent of returns at local events would be dedicated to the support of "cultural people" in China; the other 70 percent would go to local Batavian charities.[14] Describing their own efforts as "childish," the letter requests guidance and scripts including leftist writers' Mao Dun's *Qingming qianhou* 清明前後 (Around the bright and clear festival) and Yang Hansheng's 陽翰笙 *Caomang yingxiong* 草莽英雄 (Rebel hero) from association members (Deng 2002, 186). It is not clear whether *The Counter-Current* was ever performed, although a rather quaint note before the prefaces makes it clear that anyone is welcome to do so, on the condition that newspaper clippings be sent to the association.

Hu was likely a Mainlander and a CCP member, for he also appears in a few memoirs as a member of PRC consular staff (Zhu 1985).[15] More is known about the other man to furnish a preface to *The Counter-Current*, Wang Jiyuan 王紀元, a CCP member and newspaperman who was based in Jakarta between 1945 and 1951. Serving in the PRC bureaucracy for Overseas Chinese upon his return to China, his involvement, like Hu's, suggests the direct influence of the PRC on the creation of local political drama; his preface repeats the party line in declaring that "theatre is mass education, mass entertainment" and that it is "even more important to advocate a theatre movement in Overseas Chinese culture's overgrown Javanese garden." The same text makes it clear that Chinese-language spoken theatre was common in Java, mentioning Surabaya, Bandung, Solo, Semarang, and Cirebon, in all of which places "masses of youngsters were promoting the theatre movement" (Wang Jiyuan 1947, i).[16] Secondary sources show even more hubs of theatre activity—Palembang, Jambi, and Makassar, for instance—often offering a mix of spoken, musical, and *xiqu* productions, and usually connected to schools, dialect associations, and community politics (Huang Kunzhang 1991; Zhang Tao 2007; 2008).

It was North Sumatra that seems to have been the most fervent crucible for Chinese leftist theatre projects. The center of such activity was Medan, though even small towns without troupes were regularly visited by tours of Chinese-language spoken theatre troupes.[17] In Medan, four separate performance groups were founded between 1945 and 1950, running separately for a decade and joining together for some productions from 1961 to 1965 under the name of *Silian* 四聯 (League of Four).[18]

Among the four original groups was the Kunlun juyishe 崑崙劇藝團 (Kunlun Dramatic Arts Troupe), active for fifteen years and reaching a membership of up to six hundred people in its various musical and dramatic associations. Kunlun mostly took their cue from Mainland repertoire (especially after the removal of pro-ROC elements within the society in 1950) with productions such as Cao Yu's *Thunderstorm* in 1959 (for which they claimed a total audience of ten thousand),[19] *Sunrise* in 1962, and, in 1964, *Yedian* 夜店 (Night inn),[20] all held in the General Chinese Association.[21] Kunlun also had some theatrical creations of their own, now presumably lost; some were musical productions (Zhang Minhua 2003, 307–308, 310; Liao Zhangran 2007, 150; Zhang Tao 2007, 201). A 1953 tour took Kunlun through much of North Sumatra, including Tebing Tinggi, Langkat, Kisaran, and Rantauprapat, while in 1956 they visited Java, performing altogether nineteen times in Jakarta, Bandung, Surabaya, and Semarang, as well as on the boat for the sailors. Usually, venues and accommodation were provided by Chinese voluntary associations and schools. In the early sixties, some key theatre workers chose to go to China as part of the general stream of "returnees,"[22] and the activities of various theatre groups, including Kunlun, ebbed. There seems then to have been a modest revival before cultural activities ended in 1965 (Zhang Minhua 2003, 309–311).

Kunlun's final production, *Suwardi* 蘇哇第, was written by Gao Quanjin 高泉錦 and performed in Indonesian right up to August 1965, a month before the fateful regime change. A play with music, *Suwardi* addressed the issue of *pribumi*-Chinese ethnic relations on Sumatra. The plot, now known largely through newspaper reviews of the day and the recollections of participants, revolves around the titular character, a young Indonesian, who throws himself in the river in an attempt to save a Chinese child in Tebing Tinggi. Both drown, and the mother of the child and Suwardi's wife mingle their tears. The local Chinese general association vows to take the widow and children of the departed hero under its wing. Local Chinese-language papers praised the performance for "writing an inspiring and tragic chapter in Sino-Indonesian friendship" (Zhang Tao 2007, 203),[23] and one respondent from the period describes it as being designed to combat Chinese stereotypes about *pribumi* and "show them that Indonesians were also good people" (Chen Dexian, pers. comm., November 11, 2016). Although the audience in Medan was largely Chinese, on countryside tours the audience was about half-Chinese and half-*pribumi;* one can only wonder how they may have felt about Chinese performing, half of them in *pribumi* costume, a story of *pribumi* sacrifice and Chinese beneficence. It was a period of optimism for pro-Beijing Sino-Indonesian associations, and the narrative of local heroism can also be read as a hopeful parable about developing relations with the PRC in the last months of the Sukarno period. It was not to be.

Chinese-language theatre practice in Indonesia, along with the schools and community organizations that generated it, disappeared with the beginning of New Order,[24] and has in Reformasi only been revived in highly limited community settings. Having examined what is presently known about this brief and almost totally erased theatre history in a general way, in the next section I consider two interrelated scripts.

Baren's *Temple of the Five Ancestors*

On February 4, 1942, eleven days before the fall of Singapore to the Japanese, a boat carrying nineteen Chinese writers and intellectuals arrived in the Riau Archipelago. From there, they would disperse through various Sumatran locations, trying to escape the notice of the Japanese, who would soon occupy the Indies as well (Wong Yoon-wah 1988, 11–27). Of these Sumatran exiles, Yu Dafu 郁達夫 is by far the best known, but the exiled Chinese author of the period who most profoundly engages with the history of the region, while also playing a substantial role in its cultural and political history, is Wang Renshu 王任叔, frequently also known by the pen name he had used since 1938, Baren 巴人.[25]

This section focuses on Baren and his 1946 historical drama *Temple of the Five Ancestors* 五祖廟, especially comparing it with the 1959 script of the same name by the leftist Medan Chinese journalist and author Shalihong 沙里洪. To the extent that sources allow, the performance context of both these scripts' productions will also be considered. The scripts are treatments of a late nineteenth-century Chinese labor uprising in the tobacco plantations of Deli, the agricultural region of North Sumatra that surrounds contemporary Medan. The plot of both versions is similar: five young men arrive from Chaozhou under unfair contracts and are exploited by the cruel tobacco-farming system to earn profits for Dutch imperialists. The young men, animated by fervid revolutionary sentiments, kill the Dutch foreman after he has cruelly and unjustly punished an elderly fellow worker. Each of the young men claims to be the ringleader and thus the Dutch court grants clemency to none. They all die as heroic martyrs.[26]

Despite the similarities, the treatments of this same episode reveal distinct political projects, linked both with the historical context of their creation and the backgrounds of its respective authors and performers. Each shall be considered in turn. The story was and is locally well known, though by his own account Shalihong had not read the earlier text.

At the time of his arrival in Sumatra at the age of forty, Baren's literary reputation in Mainland Chinese Communist arts circles was established, and his views on the purpose and aesthetic of literature and theatre were clear. An author in a realistic mode, often using an elevated revolutionary register, he explicitly subscribed to the use of literature as a political tool. In Baren's work, the advancement of the proletariat is the purpose, agent, and theme of literary creation, and its necessary subject is thus misery, noble struggle, and triumph.

Baren was a CCP member from Zhejiang, remembered otherwise for his contributions to 1920s "nativist" literature, for being an active member of various literary associations, including the League of Left-Wing Writers in the 1920s and 1930s, and for his 1924 piece of short short fiction "Blowfish" 河豚子 (Haddon 1994). He knew little of Indonesia before his arrival there during the war. Today, this phase of his work is of substantial historical interest in that it offers a rare view of wartime and revolutionary Indonesia as seen through Mainland Chinese eyes. Later the author of Marxist histories of both ancient and modern Indonesia, Baren distinguished himself by a respectful and informed, if not always nuanced, perspective.

Unusually for his era, Baren took a more than cursory interest in the culture and literature of a Southeast Asian nation, treating, for instance, the folk poetry of Sumatra with respect and admiration and adapting it for use in his works. Unlike local Chinese, he was not embedded in Sumatran race relations or economic concerns, a detachment that allowed him to condemn what he saw as racist exploitation in the business practices of colonial-era Sumatran Chinese.[27] His exoticization of Indonesian peoples, typical for the period, can be problematic and at its worst is reminiscent of European conceptions of the noble savage or the native female; but on the whole his characterization of Indonesians as positive, noble, also often heroic and beautiful, assembled all the necessary traits of the proletariat ideal. Even after his permanent return to China, Indonesia remained a major focal point of Baren's thinking and writing, fictional and nonfictional.

Baren's life in Sumatra was peripatetic. By August 1942, he had moved on to Payakumbuh in West Sumatra, where Hu Yuzhi 胡愈之 and Yu Dafu had settled and were preparing to open a rice-wine distillery (Wong Yoon-wah 1988, 18–19). By October, he was in Siantar, where for three months he "taught revolutionary theory, promoted resistance to the Japanese," and led various anti-Japanese organizations (Huang Shuhai 2008, 124). Due substantially to his influence, the area became known as "Little Yan'an." In the pro-Communist schools, children were taught to sing the songs of Yan'an as well as of the anti-Japanese war (Zhang Minhua 2015, 108). Baren then moved to Medan, where he continued his political teaching and writing, working (unsuccessfully) to unite the Chinese community, which during the war seemed "never to have achieved even the temporary unity that Chinese in Java found in their general associations" (Heidhues 1988, 125). From September 1943, wanted by the Japanese, he hid in the jungle and lived off the land with the support of rural sympathizers. Throughout this time, Baren continued his political writing and activities while also attempting to learn Indonesian.[28]

During the period between the Japanese surrender in August 1945 and the establishment of Republican power in the Indies there was a general vacuum of control. In the area surrounding Medan, this brought about the attacks of a "myriad of irregular troops and criminal gangs that operated under the flag of the revolution, but were by no means under the control of the official Republican army" (van der Veer 2013, 2; see also Reid 2014, 174–175). In 1946, areas in Sumatra effectively controlled by Allied forces were small and limited to parts of Medan, Padang, and Palembang. The remaining area was chaotic, and many Chinese in Sumatra, as on Java, were attacked without provocation. Politically, in the spring of 1946, the nascent Republican state and army were trying to harness and control the violent forces that were overthrowing the traditional aristocracy in a "social revolution," while keeping alternate, often radical, claims to power, at bay (Reid 2014, 228–263).

Chinese press and schools had been closed after the Japanese invasion. With the end of Japanese occupation, widespread Chinese cultural activity again became possible. The Chinese Civil War was at a crucial stage, and securing the support of Overseas Chinese groups was a major concern for both belligerents. The deep gulf between KMT and CCP supporters also roughly indexed the loyalties of Sumatra Chinese onto the struggle going on in the Indies between colonial versus new Republican powers. While leftist local Chinese embraced the Communist movement warmly and regarded themselves as allied to the Indonesian National Revolution, some conservative commercial interests were sympathetic to the KMT in China as well as to the resumption of something like colonial order in the Indies.

During this time, Baren, Hu Yuzhi, and others worked to unite the various covert anti-Japanese wartime societies among the North Sumatra Chinese into a single organization dedicated to preventing the reestablishment of Dutch power.

In August 1945, the Sumatra Chinese Patriotic Democracy Association 蘇門答臘島華僑愛國民主團體 (SCPDA) was founded by the fusion of two anti-Japanese groups, the Sumatra People's Anti-Fascist Alliance 蘇門答臘人民法西斯同盟 and the Sumatra Chinese Anti-Japanese Society 答臘華僑抗日協會. The explicit aims of the new association were to advocate patriotic and democratic principles in order to foster relations between China and Indonesia. Urging the creation of unions, agricultural associations, youth and women's associations, and cultural groups among the Sumatra Chinese, they were ultimately suppressed after a British Indian division took key areas of Sumatra, including Medan, on behalf of the Dutch (Xu Anru 2001, 488; McMillan 2005, 115–117). In opposition to such Communist sympathies was a Chinese association called the Pao An Tui 保安隊 (Peace Protection Corps), formed in Medan in 1946 and also associated with the KMT. It gave itself the mission, in principle, of protecting Chinese property, but was in some cases supported materially by the British and Dutch. Its activities led some Indonesian revolutionaries to conclude that the Chinese sympathized with a Dutch restoration; and indeed, there were other areas of Indonesia where the Chinese were largely friendly to British occupying forces. The region would not fully join the Republic until August 1950 (Willmott 1961, 21–22; van Langenberg 1985, 133–134; McMillan 2005, 55, 60, 71; Tong 2010, 120–121; van der Veer 2013). Most Chinese, in Sumatra as elsewhere, were probably most concerned with avoiding being caught up in the chaos as the Indonesian Revolution progressed.

This was the fraught situation in which Baren wrote *The Temple of the Five Ancestors*. At the time, Medan was under Allied control, while the surrounding areas where the troupe was to tour were occupied by various loosely pro-Republic forces as well as the embryonic Indonesian army.[29] Chinese community associations, long dominated by KMT supporters, were gradually coming under the sway of progressive elements (van der Veer 2013, 58ff.). From Baren's perspective, the political and social revolution in North Sumatra was coming just as final CCP victory was nearing on the Mainland; the time was ripe for Sumatra Chinese to assert their solidarity with the Indonesian Revolution. His script is thus best interpreted as a CCP propaganda piece intended to sway Sumatran views, both Chinese and *pribumi*, towards international proletarian solidarity with the long-term goal of aligning Indonesian interests with the People's Republic of China.

The Historical Foundation and Performance of *Temple of the Five Ancestors* (1946)

Theatre was a natural medium for the period, given widespread illiteracy.[30] Already well known locally for his publishing and political activities, Baren was asked to produce a script by a Medan theatre group called the Xin Zhongguo

Juyishe 新中國劇藝社 (New China Dramatic Society), formed in March 1946 in the circles supporting the Sumatra Chinese Patriotic Democracy Association. New China consisted of young Chinese locals who were dedicated to "using culture and arts groups to promote the deeds of the Chinese people over eight years of resistance to the Japanese, while simultaneously promoting to Indonesia a stance of support for their nationalist independence movement, thus facilitating the harmonious friendship between the two ethnic groups" (Huang Changping 2003, 304). They were, unsurprisingly, also anti-KMT (Heidhues 1988, 125).

The Temple of the Five Ancestors was the group's third play in as many months. The first two also had an evident political purpose and show a tendency to consider Dutch and Japanese actions as colonialist, fascist, or imperialist aspects of an oppressive whole. The first, *Biehou* 別後 (After parting), by New China member Xu Anru 徐安如, had been a political play deriding the *kapitein* system used by Dutch colonial authorities to control the Chinese population,[31] and the second, *Baofengyu zhi ye* 暴風雨之夜 (Stormy night), by Lin Renhuan 林人歡, was an account of Japanese depredations in the Southeast Asian theatre of World War II (Xu Anru 2001, 488). Baren's script, written in April and May 1946, fits comfortably into this ideological program (Xu Anru 2001, 489; Zhou Nanjing 2001, 117; Huang Changping 2003, 304). In China, historical drama was immensely popular among Baren's generation of authors, and so the work shares a certain affinity with the dramas of Guo Moruo (*Qu Yuan;* 1942), which also "used history as a screen on which to project the pattern of the present" (Wagner 1990, 7) or with other early 1940s anti-Japanese historical dramas in Shanghai in the early 1940s (McDougall and Louie 1997, 286ff.). Baren, writing in Sumatra, likewise transparently employed an earlier historical period in order to comment on contemporary class struggles, showing (like Guo) considerable unconcern for historical plausibility.

In his introduction to the published version of the play, Baren reports that he had first read of the relevant events in *Rili jinxi* 日里今昔 (Deli then and now), a probably lost Malay-language work by an otherwise unidentified *pribumi* historian. It seems significant that Baren read about this uprising in a non-Chinese, presumably Malay-language, text. Perhaps it was the fact that the uprising had stirred sympathy in a *pribumi* historian that prompted Baren to conceive of the material as likely to enhance Chinese-Indonesian solidarity.[32] In Baren's words, the author of *Deli Then and Now* had "described the circumstances surrounding the development of Deli by European capital, involving also how *pribumi* attacked the farms and how the Chinese coolies suffered and fled. The author didn't stress these aspects, and only mentioned them in passing. But in the related narrative, I could see that this constituted the united struggle of *pribumi* against the derogation of land and of Chinese coolies against the exploitation of labor. Having gotten a grip on this material, I made critical use of it" (Baren 1996, 457).

Baren, having decided on the plot, set to work. Since the script was for immediate performance, he was not at liberty to conduct extensive historical research, and his script is therefore a work of imagination based on the bare outlines of the case. Indeed, in his later writings Baren acknowledges a good deal of discrepancy between the historical events and his dramatization of them (Baren 1996, 239–247). The play does, however, fit the pattern of labor confrontation in the Deli plantations, with Chinese involvement disproportionately common (Stoler 1995, 67). Baren gives 1871 as the date for the revolt, with the unidentified text of *Deli Then and Now* the presumed source.[33] Although seventy years had passed since the events depicted, attacks on overseers had been fairly common within living memory (Reid 2014, 46); most likely audiences for these plays could have related the story both to the nineteenth-century events and to the immediate conflict (once more, against the Dutch) in which they found themselves.

New China premiered the show with three performances in Medan's Guoda xiyuan 國大戲院 (National Grand Theatre)[34] in May or June as part of a performance that also included the patriotic *Yellow River Cantata* 黄河大合唱.[35] Making some changes, adding revolutionary songs and sketches (including *Put Down Your Whip*) as well as some of their own creations, New China took advantage of the school holidays (many of the actors were teachers) to tour the show in six stops under Republican control—Tinggi, Siantar, Perdagangan, Kisaran, Asahan (presumably in Tanjungbalai), and Brastagi, all in what is now North Sumatra. They performed in each locale one to three times, usually with the help and billeting of local Chinese associations for their forty-member group (Xu Anru 2001, 490; Huang Changping 2003, 305; Su 2007, 17–19).[36] In each new place, they put up posters in both Chinese and Indonesian.

The tour was difficult and daring; at one point the troupe even came under fire, though no one was hurt (Huang Changping 2003, 305). New China would continue performing despite the civil war conditions that reigned in the area requiring them to cross the line between Dutch and revolutionary control (Huang Changping 2003, 306; Su 2007, 17–19). In Siantar, the performance was attended by all the local progressive Chinese associations, and the Chinese General Society "especially invited all the high officials of Siantar government and the officials of the various factions to attend." Along with various fund-raising activities on the part of Chinese associations in favor of "anti-imperialist forces," these are credited with preventing anti-Chinese violence in that city (Xiao Bangjie 2015).

If this is true to any degree, the performance was achieving its stated goal. Both explicitly in the text and directly through the introduction, Baren makes his purposes clear:

> I wanted to borrow the story in order to criticize the thinking of some of my fellow ethnic Chinese (*tongbao* 同胞) who hold an allegiance to impe-

rialism, for this is really one of the reasons for the victory in the colonial war instigated by imperialism and carried out by the Dutch. That was also one of my motives for writing this script. I wanted to borrow their righteous spirit to make an urgent call to fellow Chinese overseas and in China. (Baren 1996, 458)

The audiences were not restricted to the Chinese community and the performance was explicitly intended to "facilitate harmony and amity within the two peoples" while resisting colonialism (Huang Changping 2003, 304–305). Performance practice changed according to the context, with Baren initially writing the characters as Teochew, and actors accordingly speaking Teochew dialect (intelligible to Hokkien audiences), but switching to Malay-Chinese creole for Indonesian or mixed audiences.[37] Indonesian revolutionary songs preceded the play so that when "the Indonesian people heard us, they would know that we sympathized and supported their struggle for independence" (Xu Anru 2001, 490).[38] The troupe members were even recorded singing these songs for the radio (Huang Changping 2003, 306).

Although the original script called for several Indonesian characters to join in the anti-Dutch action, New China figure Xu Anru felt that it was prudent to "temporarily" cut most of the immediate Indonesian involvement, and the script as performed only ever featured Indonesians as peripheral characters: although *The Temple of the Five Ancestors* was a CCP message about the solidarity of Asian proletarian people, in performance it was modified by the judgment of Medan leftist Chinese. Baren's command of Indonesian was never confident, and so when the actors translated his script for performance to non-Chinese audiences, there must have been many adjustments and localizations at the discretion of the actors. In performance, only one *pribumi* character was retained, a young woman, who sings *pantun* and dances *ronggeng* (Xu Anru 2001, 491), to lyrics alternately expressing sympathy for the plight of the workers and urging them to action: "People from China, you cannot go home / No south wind blows yet / Fiery spirits burn your body / Who will be bold enough to kill?" (Baren 1996, 416). Within the context of the Chinese presence in Indonesia, it is significant to have a *pribumi* figure reminding the audience, as the whole play does, that many of the Chinese did not come to Sumatra through whimsy or rapacity, but as victims of Western imperialism.

According to actor memoirs, the play was greatly appreciated by the Indonesian revolutionaries, and the troupe was sometimes even transported in army vehicles (Su 2007, 19). Sumatra governor Teuku Muhammad Hasan[39] even made a request for the performers to continue touring, with costs borne by the government; the troupe declined because most actors were teachers or students and had to go back to work (Huang Changping 2003, 305; Su 2007, 19).[40] Chinese-language accounts make great claims for the effect that performances had on Indonesian audiences by showing them the strength of Chinese solidarity with the Indonesian cause (e.g., Xu Anru 2001, 484) and "making a vigorous contribution to the cause of Indonesian independence" (Su 2007, 19). Given that the play's creators and supporters, not the audiences, are on record, there can be no objective assessment of these claims.

A year after the performances, Baren was captured by Dutch forces and deported, publishing his impressions of the Indonesian Revolution the following year. He had spent the years between 1942 and 1946 on Sumatra, returning as the first PRC ambassador to Indonesia between 1949 and 1951, where—due to diplomatic inexperience and attempts to influence Indonesian politics—his actions caused the "Sino-Indonesian relationship [to reach] its nadir" (Hong Liu 2010, 176; see also Sukma 1994, 41–42). In 1961, he was transferred to the Southeast Asia research center's translation bureau of the Chinese Academy of Sciences. Brutally attacked during the Cultural Revolution, he died in 1972. Throughout the rest of his life, Baren never abandoned the narrative, and the script continued to evolve.[41] According to Baren's friend Zhou Erfu 周而復, his purpose in revising was to "cause the anti-imperialist, anti-colonialist torch of the people of each ethnicity to burn a little brighter" (Zhou Erfu 1986, 5) by increasing the length of the play and including a stronger emphasis on the friendship between the Chinese laborers and the Indonesian characters.

Shalihong's *Temple of the Five Ancestors*

The 1959 *Temple of the Five Ancestors* by Shalihong[42] was written for another of the Medan theatre troupes and performed, thirteen years after Baren's version, in Medan's Chinese General Society.[43] Shalihong's script was not printed until 2007, almost a half-century after its performance, when it was serialized in Jakarta's *Guoji ribao* 國際日報 (International Daily) in six installments of that paper's supplement *Lüdao* 綠島 (Green Islands), accompanied by an introductory note. This brought it for the first time to wider attention outside of the Chinese communities in North Sumatra.

In the thirteen years between the Baren and Shalihong versions of the same story, the political situation and ethnic relations had undergone a fundamental change, with the content and context of the new script reflecting those changes. While the earlier version was intended to articulate Chinese solidarity with the Republic in the midst of its war to prevent the restoration of a Dutch colonial administration, Shalihong was writing just as the ban on alien (i.e., noncitizen Chinese) rural economic activity signaled a shift in the Sukarno government's policy towards Chinese residents of Indonesia.[44] After 1958, those who had chosen to retain Chinese citizenhip could enroll in the remaining (pro-PRC) schools. In Medan, Chinese street names (Shantou Street, Canton Street) would be replaced with Indonesian ones in 1960 (Suryadinata 2004, 76–78; Tsai Yen-ling 2008, 198, 203). To many leftist Sumatra Chinese, this shift seemed like a betrayal. "For the inaugural GANEFO,[45] and at the Bandung Asia-Africa Conference, wasn't it obvious how China helped materially and with manpower, and did it all mean nothing? Even then, during the independence movement, China always stood at Indonesia's side, fully supportive, in line with the shared hopes of the destinies of both countries' peoples" (Yao 2007, 244).

Since leftist organizations strongly identified with the PRC, many North Sumatra Chinese assumed that the support China and local Chinese organizations had shown for the Republic ought to ensure friendly treatment. Instead, in the Medan region it seems that the effect of the ban was particularly harrowing, partly because "pressure from local politicians and businessmen in search of issues to exploit may have been more intense than elsewhere" (Mackie 1976, 97). In Siantar, rural Chinese flooded the city, straining the resources of the local Chinese associations, some of whom brought "the refugees to the local government, demanding humanitarian first aid, relief of the burden borne by the local Chinese general associations, the alteration of Indonesians' discriminatory concepts about Chinese and the contradiction of their claim that Chinese are all big bosses" (Yao 2007, 244). At the same time, years of pro-Beijing education and cultural activities had borne ideological fruit in the Chinese community. The result of this pull of Chinese education and push of Indonesian racial economic policy drove thousands of North Sumatra Chinese to leave for Mainland China. This was the situation—in its own way, no less dramatic than the historical moment in which the narrative was set—in which Shalihong wrote and actors staged this new *Five Ancestors Temple.*

The troupe did not consist of bookish intellectuals. The group's name, Haifeng 海風 (Sea Breeze), derived (according to Shalihong) from the fact that most of the members were by profession fishmongers at the local market,[46] and most shared an ancestral home of Yongchun 永春, a Fujian county in the Quanzhou region.[47] Their particular strengths were in *die luohan* acrobatics and stilt-walking. Although broadly speaking all "progressive" in the terms of the day, respondents agree that while the other three active Chinese troupes in Medan were "intellectual" or school-based, the membership in the troupe was more characterized by "lower-class people" with "low education." They might thus have been particularly drawn to, and felt particularly legitimated in, performing a play about laborers[48] (Qian 2015, 435–436). Shalihong, born in 1930 to recent Meixian Hakka arrivals, was a model leftist Chinese patriot. After leaving high school early, he worked as a vendor in the market and became a schoolteacher in Medan and Bagiansiapiapi, before being invited, at the age of twenty-one, to join the staff of the leftist *Democracy Daily* 民主日報, where he worked for fifteen years until it was closed in the wake of the 1965 regime change.[49]

In such circumstances, the story of the late nineteenth-century historic Chinese uprising provided an opportunity to foster Chinese patriotism and show class struggle. It was not, unlike Baren's version, concerned with bringing either the idea or the non-Chinese people of Indonesia into the story. The local knowledge and context of this script also meant that it was adapted to local Chinese ideology, which was, ironically, more Chinese nationalist than universal Communist. In this version, the North Sumatra Chinese are written not only as the victims and pawns of colonial exploitation but as the proletarian heroes and forerunners of a contemporary struggle.

Shalihong could also draw on different sources, as he spoke fluent Hokkien[50] and could conduct research in a time of relative peace. In contrast with Baren, whose concern was to use a historical event to illustrate what he took to be universal truths about class struggle, Shalihong was writing on the basis of research and background knowledge. The system of indenture had only ended in his own childhood, and in his youth he had met Sumatran Chinese tobacco pickers of the era of the uprising. A local superstition—that the Dutch carriages used always to overturn if they passed the five ancestors' temple—struck him as suitably dramatic material, and motivated him to consider using the incident for a theatre piece. Further research took him to a Labuhan home for destitute and aged Chinese laborers, where he found plantation workers born in the 1880s who were able to provide the detailed account on which Shalihong would base his script.[51]

Shalihong wrote the script, by his own account, out of a sense of commitment to history, realism, and memory as well as a hope of contributing to the "creation of our own scripts" (pers. comm., March 17, 2013). A spectator from the period, remembering the experience almost sixty years later, recalled that the play was "a great success" because it made them "feel like our ancestors had felt the same as us" (*gantong shenshou*) and that "we had suffered the same torment." According to this respondent, the effect produced among the spectators was that "we too had to build the new China and serve the people" (Cheng Gaoling, pers. comm., November 9, 2016).

Unsurprisingly, Shalihong's script is in several ways more local and more historicized than Baren's work. This is apparent, for instance, in lexical elements, which more closely reflect the idiosyncrasies of Mandarin as spoken in Indonesia.[52] Religious observations are more plausibly rendered in the script, and the economic system, as it would have been understood by its victims, is reconstructed in more detail: for example, the terms of the contract, the origins of the men, the possibilities of marriage to local women, and the manner by which workers had been divided into those destined for Bangka tin mines and those headed for Deli tobacco plantations. Shalihong had greater access to the lives of the original laborers, and consequently his script is more realistic and richer in context than that of Baren, who had been in Sumatra for only three years and whose knowledge of Indonesian and Hokkien were imperfect.

Political messaging was directed at the Chinese community rather than at Indonesian society. For one thing, the use of Mandarin effectively excluded non-Chinese from attending. The production was not intended to enlist *pribumi* solidarity; at the same time, the ahistorical linguistic choice was very much in line with sympathy for New China. As another troupe member noted, "our duty was to praise New China, to develop New China's culture" (Zheng Yuanxin 2007, 142). Such praise was to be conducted in the national language as taught in Medan's pro-Beijing Chinese schools.

The play had five performances in 1959. Shalihong was the stage director and also played the role of the Chinese foreman. According to Shalihong, there was an entirely Chinese, though socioeconomically diverse, audience of about three hundred people a night. Knowing that people would not buy the tickets of their own accord, troupe members canvassed businesses and tried to convince the merchants to buy blocks of tickets as a form of support. The proceeds went to the Workers and Farmers School 工農學校, a progressive local school for poor students. Looking back in 2013, Shalihong felt that by that time there was a sense that there were preliminary limits on forms of Chinese expression, and troupe members knew that the authorities would send people to observe the political content. Consequently, there was a certain amount of self-censorship at work, although because the play avoided direct and topical comment, no political interference occurred, as sometimes happened with the more sloganistic varieties of pro-CCP theatre. Within a decade, any room for spoken theatre in Chinese would have disappeared, and this localized, pro-Beijing, "progressive" *Temple of the Five Ancestors* was among its final expressions.

Shalihong's script, subtitled "A History of Blood and Tears of the Overseas Chinese" 華僑先輩血淚史, is clearly an attempt at memorializing the suffering and sacrifices of the first arrivals from "Tangshan." The 2007 reprinting shows that, for the Chinese-language press at least, the bitter history of Chinese labor in Indonesia—now associated with both the nineteenth-century upheaval and the mid-century struggles, and overshadowed by the specter of 1965—is still worth underlining. The temple is now a slightly derelict site in the town of Tanjung Morawa;[53] it remains to be seen whether anyone in Reformasi-era Chinese Indonesia will choose to make new use of an old story.

Just as with *Yindunixiya zhi ge* 印度尼西亞之歌 (Song of Indonesia) Baren created the first epic poem in Chinese set abroad, he also created the first historical drama set among the Overseas Chinese. In the revised versions of the script published after Baren's death in Mainland China (as an independent publication in 1986 and reprinted in his collected works a decade later), the coordination and interaction between Chinese and indigenous revolutionaries is emphasized. By the same token, the "running dog" roles of Chinese middlemen and labor canvassers, as well as the local Indies elites (as expressed in the offstage role of the sultan of Deli) are also more obviously highlighted in the later version. Baren presumably could expect a greater knowledge of Marxist thought from a Mainland reader or audience, but also needed to provide more substantial explication of local circumstances. However, by and large, the three printed versions of Baren's script share a basic ethic of using the rebellion to reinforce proletarian solidarity in the face of Western exploitation, represented by Dutch colonialism. One of the coolies remarks, before his execution, "Malay friends, never mind, in another twenty years there will be another pack of bold young heroes! They can't kill us all" (Baren 1996, 442).

In the Baren scripts, the coolies have a developed (and anachronistic) class consciousness, but they are also impulsive and limited in their goals. There is also a character who personifies a more sophisticated form of resistance and who suggests using the kidnapped foreman for negotiations, proposing solidarity with *pribumi* and routes of escape. But the five coolies are bound by blood oaths made to the tutelary god and can brook no compromise. As such, they represent for Baren a primitive stage of violent resistance against imperialism, to be replaced in Baren's own time by the rational if utopian project of Communism. The proto-communist character, speaking to his *pribumi* friends, foresees the twentieth century much as Baren and the CCP understood it: "Maybe the children and grandchildren of the Chinese coolies will escape the bloody hands of the enemy, and grow up; they will forget how their grandfathers, their fathers were abused, maybe they will instead take the thief as their father, and go serve the enemy! Well, let them remember the cruel deaths of these their five ancestors!" (Baren 1996, 455). Baren's scripts are an attempt at reminding the Sumatra Chinese—even the wealthy—of the proletarian origins of their community, and therefore their duty to the Indonesian revolutionaries, their allies.

This is not the context of Shalihong's script. His tobacco pickers have a racialistic and a nationalistic expression, calling the Dutch "white-skinned dogs" and intent on proving the strength of Chinese people and the "descendants of Chinese people." But their actions are less premeditated and political, and they are driven to violence by a series of offenses against older Chinese workers. While this is surely intended also to highlight Chinese virtues such as *ren* 仁 (humaneness) and *yi* 義 (righteousness), it also establishes a connection with the present day less stridently, nor does it attempt to situate the issues in the context of a global class struggle. The tight plotting and the causal chain in Shalihong's piece give the play some of the mechanism of a well-constructed tragedy. Sold into indentured service, the coolies are forced to sacrifice themselves as a means of maintaining their self-respect. There is also a substantial difference between the texts in that, for Shalihong, the *pribumi* Sumatrans, though appearing briefly as fellow victims, and though helpful to the conspirators as bearers of messages, are not directly implicated, and there is no suggestion that they should band with the Chinese to throw off the yoke of imperialism. Instead, the emphasis is squarely on the historical sacrifices and national pride of the Chinese populations. Shalihong, writing for a working-class troupe, refuses to conflate Chineseness with class, not coincidentally just as the first wave of anti-Chinese legislation in the young Republic was being promulgated. The work is thus a quintessentially Sino-Indonesian work firmly rooted in the historical realities of the place and confronting the ethnic and political tensions of the young Republic. The irony of the narrative is that Shalihong used Sino-Indonesian history to promulgate Chinese nationalism (rather than ethnic harmony in Indonesia); while in Baren's piece a CCP reinterpretation of the same event is deployed to attempt to smoothen local ethnic relations and influence opinion in favor of global communism.

As the two major Chinese-language scripts and productions of their respective periods for which materials are extant, there is little option but to treat these two *Temple of the Five Ancestors* as representatives for the whole period. In a freer Indonesia these works might have become the forerunners of a Sino-Indonesian spoken theatre tradition; instead, as Chinese-language scripts about Indonesia, they remain something of an anomaly, largely ignored in Indonesia as in China. The respective purposes of the two authors—Baren, to unite Chinese and Indonesians as fellow victims and foes of imperialism—the other, to foster a sense of patriotic Chineseness, local but PRC-bound—were both superseded by historical events that would make all local claims of Chinese ethnic nationalism or of proletarian solidarity anathema. This leaves the two texts and performance events as the prelude to a Sino-Indonesian theatre that ultimately did not come about.

CHAPTER 4

The Disguised Beloved

A CHINESE NARRATIVE THREAD IN COMMERCIAL THEATRE

FOR all the importance of traditional and political forms of theatre, no serious attempt can be made to deal with the subject of Chinese performance in the Indies or Indonesia without addressing the nation's rich and varied commercial stage, just as any reasonable account of its genesis will show how Chinese performers and entrepreneurs "played a crucial role in the development of urban modern theatres" (Winet 2010, 60). The new commercial theatre, with its eclectic sources, would become foundational for "modern" Indonesian theatre.

How was the new commercial theatre distinct? One way that the difference can be briefly stated is in terms of venue and function. As in China, the traditional theatre of Indonesia before contact with the West included music, dance, and ritual performance but no theatre that was exclusively spoken. Nor, except for theatricals directed at or performed by colonial Dutch, was there anything resembling a Western theatre building or a proscenium stage: *wayang* most often featured performances on platforms; the Chinese raised stage, for its part, was used only for *xiqu*. In the late nineteenth-century Indies, a touring commercial theatre developed in the cities, influenced by Western, Chinese, and Indian models. Such troupes sold tickets and used the Malay vernacular, performing in tents and theatre buildings for multiethnic audiences. These genres are considered the forerunners of "modern" and "contemporary" Indonesian theatre[1] (Cohen 2006, 1–27); and formally (given, to name only a few features, its "proscenium stage, wing-and-drop set, focused stage lighting"), the influence of European theatre predominated (42), but the influence of Chinese genres and individuals was also powerful and sustained.

The first two chapters of this book have examined how traditional forms of local Chinese theatrical expression (*xiqu* and Sino-Indonesian forms of *wayang*) negotiated and adapted to the changing sociopolitical circumstances of the twentieth and twenty-first centuries, while the third has explored cases of a genre—Chinese-language spoken theatre—that had no opportunity to adapt and thus vanished. The present chapter traces a process simultaneous to all three, although in this case occurring in the mainstream of the Indonesian theatre world rather than in ethnically defined spaces or associations. The process will be examined through a case study: how one Chinese narrative (standing in as a case study for a wide and complex process) was integrated into the commercial theatre as it has developed and thrived from the late colonial period until the present day. This account serves thus both to underline the Sino-Indonesian theatrical heritage that has not received its full due and to illustrate how parallels can be found between Malay/Indonesian-language commercial and Chinese-language ritual theatre developments in terms of ethnic formation, cultural elision, and renegotiation.

Chinese in the Emergence of Indies Cultural Industries

The presence of *xiqu* in the Dutch East Indies was widespread and enduring, and interest in *xiqu* from ethnically mixed audiences in Sumatra, Borneo, and Java is a consistent part of the historical record. As forms of theatre existing simultaneously and in the same places and for overlapping audiences, it was inevitable that influence flowed between the existing practices of *xiqu* and the emergence of a new Malay-language commercial theatre. This cross-pollination is one of many ways in which Sino-Indonesian culture made a signal contribution to nascent Indonesian nationhood.

This influence can be identified, for instance, through the role played by certain persons or groups of people in both genres. According to a leading specialist on Indonesian theatre writing about one of the first major commercial troupes in the last decade of the nineteenth century, "[o]ne might regard the Komedie Stamboel, at least in its first months of operation, as a sort of social club for its Chinese patrons" (Cohen 2006, 58). A number of comparable companies, performing the commercial musical theatre also known as *stamboel,* were also labelled as particularly Chinese and patronized largely by Chinese audiences (277).[2] Chinese patronage, which had been and remained prominent in *wayang* genres and Javanese dances (Pigeaud 1938, 141; Sumarsam 1995, 83–89; Pausacker 2005, 186–193), emerged as a major source of funding for the new commercial theatre, as "it was often Chinese businessmen who had the resources and connections to produce and house urban theatre" (Winet 2010, 60; see also Cohen 2006, 8). Many of the performers, too, were of Chinese origin (Pigeaud 1938, 36). This pattern was by no means restricted to theatre: in several other cultural genres Sino-Indonesian patrons, audiences, and artists were also instrumental. As the related developing industries of commercial music recording and cinema emerged, for instance, the Sino-Indonesian influence was equally crucial (Kartomi 2000, 239–240; Yampolsky 2003b, 25; Sen 2006).

A key figure in commercial theatre's early development was Yap Gwan Thay 葉元泰, the sometime owner of the troupe named Komedie Stamboel (Cohen 2006, 39–41). Moreover, in 1891, that company's first performances, in Surabaya's Chinatown area of Kampung Doro, were held in a theatre that often featured *xiqu* as well as Javanese *topeng* (45). Yap's *stamboel* performers, and other groups that sprang up shortly thereafter, toured alongside Yap's *xiqu* troupes and often shared sets and costumes. Komedi Stamboel was omnivorous in its influences, and alongside Western-derived (and Orientalist) plots such as *Aida* and *The Arabian Nights* troupes also drew on Chinese narratives such as *Ong Ciao Kun* (Wang Zhaojun 王昭君; Cohen 2001, 330; 2006, 104, 279).[3] One might speculate that the Wang narrative, in which a beautiful woman is sent abroad against her will and laments her departure from China, appealed to Sino-Indonesian nostalgia for an imagined homeland.[4]

Literary production in Malay was another area where Chinese influence was strongly felt. As a prominent Dutch Sinologist remarked about Java in 1891, "very few Chinamen are to be found able to read Chinese books," but translated "Chinese tales and novels are greedily read by natives" (Schlegel 1891, 148), creating a market for translations and adaptations in local languages. In the words of one Sino-Indonesian intellectual of the period, "all substantial Chinese novels could be read in Malay before the outbreak of the Pacific War," adaptations and translation that "sold like hotcakes, despite the high price one had to pay for them" (Nio 1947, 14), and even if some of the earlier translations showed "less attention to the value of style, sentence structure and word choice" (Nio 1943, 171). Chinese Indies writers were influential figures in the translation not only of Chinese works into Malay, Javanese, and other languages but also of European literatures, including drama. Familiar to various degrees with the popular commercial stage, the development of realist drama in Europe, and the debates surrounding theatre modernization in China, in the 1910s and 1920s Sino-Indonesian intellectuals became pioneers in attempts to bring literary drama to the Indies modern stage. These fixed scripts (without the improvisation typical of the commercial stage), appearing in Sino-Indonesian magazines or in book form, were intended for Malay-speaking Chinese amateurs who were literate but not used to improvisation. Indeed, the "model of an amateur nationalist stage featuring literary drama appeared first in Indonesia within these Chinese opera derma troupes" (Winet 2010, 61). "Opera derma" could be translated as "charity opera," as their revenues were usually raised for Chinese community or patriotic causes. Plots were predominantly set in the Sino-Indonesian community and were concerned with the moral and social obligations of the community and the individual, though a few plays touched on the political situation in China. Formally, they owe an obvious debt to European theatre, notably Ibsen's social dramas, but it is probable that some of its authors were also inspired by developments in contemporary theatre in China, texts of which were widely available in the Indies. Along with the melodrama and comedies of the commercial theatre, this more earnest theatre represents another strand that would contribute to the development of modern Indonesian theatre.[5]

The full acknowledgment of Chinese involvement in the theatre and in the other projects integral to the development of national culture (such as modern literature), however, was largely suppressed during the New Order years, becoming what one scholar has called a "spectral genealogy" from an "unimagined community" (Winet 2010). The Chinese presence, which had been central to the development of all the arts as the movement for nationhood coalesced, was in retrospect elided as Suharto-era intellectuals and academics wrote the cultural history of modern Indonesia into existence. In the area of theatre research, the principal exception are the works of Jakob Sumardjo, who, in books such as *Perkembangan Teater Modern dan Sastra Drama Indonesia* (The Development of Indonesian Modern Theatre and Dramatic Literature) gave due credit to the theatrical contribution of Chinese Indies artists, patrons, and intellectuals (Sumardjo 1992, 110–127).[6] By and large, however, accounts of the Chinese contribution to Indies and Indonesian commercial theatre were ignored or noted incidentally in peripheral or piecemeal fashion; this deficiency has only partially been remedied by contemporary scholars.

How is one to approach the question of Chinese narrative influence on Indies and Indonesian theatres, when Chinese stories are numberless? Some of the Chinese stories that circulated in the Indies are particularly associated with southern Fujian, where most Sino-Indonesians can trace their roots,[7] and comparison with puppet repertoire in southern Fujian and Taiwan suggests that emigrants largely replicated the narrative universes of that world. Certainly, the puppet theatre partook of the same narrative corpus as the translations and adaptations of Chinese fiction, most of it consisting of mid- to late-Qing historical martial stories, which appeared in Malay, Javanese, and other archipelagic languages from the last quarter of the nineteenth century.

One way to focus a conversation on the role of Chinese stories in the archipelago, and thereby to trace how Chinese threads are initially woven into local performance fabrics on Java and Bali, and from there into a national performative imaginary, is to trace one particularly successful narrative through its Indies and Indonesian career. The most obvious candidate for this role is *Liang Shanbo and Zhu Yingtai* 梁山伯與祝英台, often abbreviated in the Chinese-language world as *Liang-Zhu* 梁祝. It is known in Indonesia and Malaysia by various spellings based on its Hokkien pronunciation, most commonly *Sampek Engtay* 山伯英台.[8]

In Western languages the story is also known by variants of the title *The Butterfly Lovers*.

This is among the best-known stories of the Chinese stage (and screen), most frequently appearing in various genres of *xiqu*. The narrative has earned its fair share of scholarly attention, including several overviews and collections of essays in Chinese, as well as Wilt Idema's 2010 selection of annotated English translations with an introduction. As will become apparent, it has also substantially filtered into a wide variety of Indonesian genres that do not trace their performance tradition to a Chinese origin. As such, it is both example and symbol of the Chinese contribution to Indonesian theatre.

Sampek Engtay

A brief synopsis of the story, which is usually set in what is now Zhejiang Province during the Eastern Jin dynasty (AD 265–420), will help orient unfamiliar readers.

The talented Zhu Yingtai, youngest daughter of a distinguished and affluent family, convinces her parents that she ought to be educated in the classics like a boy. Disguising herself as a man, she meets Liang Shanbo on the way to a famous school, where they both prepare for the imperial exams. They pledge themselves to friendship and remain inseparable during their years of study. Zhu's gender goes undiscovered during their schooling, but—increasingly attracted to him—she ultimately attempts to arrange a match with Liang. Frustrated by Liang's failure to understand her insinuations that she herself is a nubile young woman, she ultimately arranges a marriage between Liang and a fictional sister. By the time Liang eventually does come to understand that Zhu is a woman and delightedly agrees to the marriage, she has already left the school. He seeks out her family home in order to ask for her hand in marriage. However, in the interval Zhu's parents have betrothed her to a wealthy local ruffian. Liang perishes of lovesickness, and Zhu visits his tomb on her way to her wedding ceremony. Supernaturally, his tomb opens, and Zhu throws herself in. After it has closed over her, a pair of butterflies emerge, flying heavenwards. Thus, though denied happiness on earth, the lovers are joined in the afterlife. Despite the substantial plot variations over the various iterations, theatrical, textual, and cinematic, this general structure has remained fairly consistent.[9]

In China, the story was already being put to use for performance purposes during the Song and Yuan dynasties (Idema 2010, xiii–xxi; Quinn 2013, 337). It existed in a wide variety of Chinese performance genres and is particularly associated with the Zhejiang genre *yueju* 越劇, for which it was one of the principal narratives in that genre's foundational 1920s (Jiang 2009, 48–51). In modern times, the story has proven amenable to ideological interpretation by various streams of Chinese social reformists as an illustration of the evil done by arranged marriages, understood to be a failure of "feudal society." The story has been adapted over twenty times for the large and small screen, never more successfully than in the Shaw Brothers' 1963 *huangmeixi* film, known in English as *The Love Eterne*, starring Ivy Po Ling 凌波 and Betty Loh Ti 樂蒂. It has also been an inspiration for fiction by the contemporary prominent Jiangsu author Su Tong 蘇童 ("The eighteen leavetakings" 十八相送) and furnished the material for one of the most-performed pieces of Western-style classical music in the PRC.[10]

Recent stage versions include a *kunqu* production (with a script by Academia Sinica academician Tseng Yong-Yih 曾永義, produced in Nanjing by the Jiangsu Kunju Theatre 江蘇省崑劇院); an excerpt performed for PRC leader Xi Jinping and his guests at the 2016 Hangzhou G20 Summit; and the Zhejiang *yueju* opera version that opened Bangkok's 2015 International Festival of Song and Dance. The story has also been selected, in one of the Chinese official cultural establishment's crazes for enshrining a canonical number of masterpieces, as one of the Four Great Folktales; and, due to the equally powerful mania for generating equivalences with the West, also as "China's Romeo and Juliet."[11] The push to have the narrative enshrined as a UNESCO Oral and Intangible Masterpiece of Humanity seems, however, to have failed (see also Idema 2010, xxxvi).

It is impossible to establish when the narrative might have arrived in the Indies.[12] Certainly, it was familiar in the southern Chinese areas from which migrants largely departed, and is recorded in the southern Fujian region in the mid- and later nineteenth century, as well as in Taiwan in the early twentieth century; several singing manuscripts of this narrative from this period are extant (van der Loon 1992, 77–83). Since it appears today in the repertoire of several of the *xiqu* varieties that were popular in the Indies, including *gaojiaxi*, *gezaixi*, and *chaoju*, theatre may have been one of the avenues of its transmission. The narrative probably moved, in textual as well as theatrical and storytelling forms, into the archipelago from the mid-nineteenth century onward.

Towards the end of the century, it featured prominently in that period's press boom: in Javanese alone, versions of the story are known to have been printed in 1873, 1875, 1878, 1880, 1902, 1928, and even after independence (Quinn 2013, 339–349; Salmon 2013b, 240). A Malay version by Boen Sing Hoo 文信和 (pen name of Tan Tjien Hwa 陳振華) was published in 1885,[13] with reprints in 1892, 1902, and 1922 (Salmon 1981, 155–156), and between 1890 and 1895 another version by The Tin Lam 鄭丁蘭 went through three editions. Print versions in other archipelagic languages appeared slightly later: a Balinese *gaguritan* verse version is known from 1915 (Quinn 2013, 339), to some degree interlarded with Javanese poetry from another narrative, some of it untranslated (Marrison 1987, 482). The official Dutch East Indies organ Balai Pustaka published a Javanese version in 1928 and a Madurese version in 1930 (Oetomo 2013) while a version in

Makassarese, by Liem Kheng Yong 林慶容, appeared somewhere between 1928 and 1936 (Hamonic and Salmon 2013, 364, 371).

Evidently, the story was familiar throughout the Indies. Later publications are largely recensions or revisions of earlier Indies versions rather than translations from a Chinese version, in which language it is in any event not defined by a single classical text. Many Indies versions are likely something between adaptation and translation, and unsurprisingly, Indonesian adaptations, both textual and theatrical, have taken considerable liberties with the original material. Early in its Indonesian career, the story began to be substantially domesticized (Quinn 2013).

Through contact in the Indies, the narrative also entered Dutch. In 1902, the "Chinese-Malay fairy tale" (Tonnet 1902, 165) "De Gele Kapelletjes of Sam Pek en Eng Tay" (The little yellow butterflies or Sam Pek and Eng Tay) was published first, with illustrations, in the Haarlem monthly *Woord en beeld* (Word and image). Then, in May of the same year, it was republished, in ten installments and without illustrations, in the Dutch-language Indies daily *Bataviaasch nieuwsblad.*[14] The author, Martine Tonnet, was a Haarlem woman who resided for some time in the Indies and would go on to write on *wayang orang* and Indies archaeology. She provides a frame story in which her student, Soen, "my little Scheherezade," the sixteen-year-old daughter of Chinese merchants in the Indies, has in the past recounted various Chinese stories to the author. Soen is prompted to tell the story of Sampek and Engtay by the appearance of yellow butterflies. Tonnet claims to have combined Soen's account with a translated version in Malay to produce her own text[15] (Tonnet 1902; *Bataviaasch nieuwsblad,* May 5–20, 1902). Thus, by the turn of the century, it seems the story had become familiar to residents of Java regardless of ethnicity.

To the Stage and Back Again

Sampek Engtay as a narrative appears in predecessor forms of commercial theatre in the second half of the nineteenth century, when Chinese communities around Bogor performed it as part of a practice called *wayang cerita,* which was financed, written, and performed for local Chinese and used Chinese instruments (Cohen 2001, 322; Jedamski 2008, 477–478). *Wayang cerita* can be considered a hybrid genre and was performed not on stages but (unlike *xiqu*) on the ground; the fact that some such troupes were all-male, however, could suggest a *xiqu* influence.

Then, in the first years of the twentieth century, the Singapore-based *bangsawan* company Indra Zanibar, "the premier popular theatre of the entire Malay world" (Cohen 2002, 111), presented the narrative in Surabaya (1902), Medan (1906), and Penang (1909) (*De Sumatra Post,* September 3, 1906; Sooi-Beng Tan 1989, 235). The best-known domestic commercial theatre of the Indies at the turn of the century, August Mahieu's Komedie Stamboel, also made use of this narrative, and the whole spectrum of commercial theatre relied to some degree on the familiarity with Chinese stories such as this one for its development.

Sampek Engtay, no doubt in various forms, remained in repertoire in commercial theatre throughout the first half of the twentieth century. A troupe called Soei Ban Lian, founded in 1911, granted top billing to the actress Teng Poi Noi, who played male roles and was particularly well known for her rendition of Sampek (Sumardjo 2001, 218).[16] The Malay Opera Siti Hawa in 1928 was another troupe that performed a musical version of the narrative for a performance at the City Gardens Theatre in Surabaya (*De indische courant,* June 4, 1928), while the company of the prominent Sino-Indonesian entertainer Fifi Young staged a *Sampek Engtay* in Batavia in 1947 (*Nieuwe courant,* September 22, 1947).[17] A newspaper report from 1951 shows an Indonesian-language performance of *Sampek Engtay* organized by Chinese amateurs through the Chinese organization *Hua Chiao Lien Ho Hui* 華僑聯合會 (Overseas Chinese Association) to sold-out audiences (*Soerabaijasch Handelsblad*, November 1, 1902; *De Sumatra Post,* September 3, 1906; *Bataviaasch Nieuwsblad,* October 26, 1918; *De Indische Courant,* June 4, 1928; *Het Dagblad: Uitgave van de Nederlandsche Dagbladpers te Batavia,* November 11, 1947; *Algemeen Indisch Dagblad: de Preangerbode,* April 23, 1951; Cohen 2002, 111).

In parallel to these musical versions was the presence of the narrative on the Indies silver screen. The early Sino-Indonesian commercial theatre world was deeply interlocked with the burgeoning Indies film industry, and many producers, writers, and actors were Chinese. It is thus not surprising to find a version of *Sampek Engtay* among the early films of the period. Released in 1931, it was directed by The Teng Chun 鄭丁春 and seems to have met with substantial success. The film was one of several Chinese-themed talkies that allowed The to expand his business (Said 1992, 101). A 1951 drama, *Antara Tertawa dan Airmata* (Between Laughter and Tears) by prolific Semarang Chinese director Fred Young, was also advertised as being inspired by the narrative, with actors drawn in modern dress and in opera-style costumes sharing the advertising space (*Java Bode,* January 22, 1952).[18] Furthermore, films from the Chinese world were also accessible to Indonesian audiences. For instance, in 1955 a film of the narrative was shown over several months in various Indonesian cities (*De Preangerbode,* March 31, 1955; *De Locomotief,* May 31, 1955), which, judging from photographs, was most likely the 1953 Mainland Chinese *yueju* movie starring Yuan Xuefen 袁雪芬. Jakarta's left-wing *Shenghuo bao* even ran an article instructing progressive youths to interpret the film as a denunciation of feudal gender roles and arranged marriages (February 2, 1955).

The itinerant commercial theatre influenced regional theatre practices, and it was probably in this way that *Sampek Engtay* crossed genres, apparently particularly in Bali, though the 1915 Balinese text may well have contributed to the genre's early popularity. The story had moved into the Balinese sung drama *arja* in the first two decades of the twentieth century and was instrumental in creating the *arja* repertory system (Bandem and Deboer 1983, 29–30). By the late 1920s, it was "perhaps the most popular arja tale" (Clendinning 2017, 173), and *arja* performances of the story were depicted by at least one renowned Balinese painter (Cooper 2007, 34). In the version described by Beryl de Zoete and Walter Spies in 1938, the heroine (now called Sentai) travels by motorcar (198), and the lovers appear after death before the Hindu deity Indra in heaven, asking for rebirth, which is granted them. They foil the villainous bridegroom Ma Tjoen and are happily married (de Zoete and Spies 1938, 322–323; Covarrubias 1937, 251).[19] By this time, in contact with *stamboel,* the action was also being presented "against a background of real painted streets" (214). I Wayan Dibia, writing of his childhood (ca. 1950s), remembers that costuming concessions were made in view of the subject material, with some characters being in "white trousers and shirts, rather than traditional Balinese dance costume" (2012, 487). The narrative had also become a common narrative for *legong,* a Balinese dance usually performed by two or three young girls, by the 1940s (Ong 1943, 218).[20]

As *drama gong,* a Balinese vernacular spoken genre, it was popular by the 1970s, having been transmitted (since the 1950s at the latest) at least partly through *gaguritan* poetry (Hooykaas 1963, 384; Putra 2008, 102, 107). In the first decade of the twenty-first century, the story was frequently heard on Singaraja radio in metrical form, and sometimes also in Denpasar (Putra 2009, 262). According to Balinese scholar I Nyoman Darma Putra, "the melodramatic theme and the long process of Balinization have made the story feel as authentic [as] other local stories" (ibid.), and there are now fourteen different versions in circulation. Although it was "popularised through theatre performances, nowadays this role has been partly taken over by printed texts and kidung interaktif" (ibid.), a radio program to which callers phone in to sing or recite verses.

If Bali has adopted the narrative in many genres, the story has not been ignored in Javanese regional theatre either. It has left its traces in *gendhing tayub,* a Malang-area style of dance music, in East Java's regional theatre *ludruk* (East Java), and Central Java's *ketoprak* and *dagelan mataram,* where it sometimes becomes a comic free-for-all with particular mileage derived from the transvestism. In *ketoprak,* the story probably appeared by the 1930s and is attested at various points during New Order, including for a televised 1990 production (Sumardjo 1992, 62; Labrousse 2002, 46–47). It has also made its way into Javanese-Western hybrid musical forms such as *campursari* and has been used as material for pop music in Balinese and Javanese.

Chinese versions of the story are largely pitched as tragicomedy built around the inherent suspense and dramatic irony of mistaken gender. Several of the Indonesian regional drama versions, however, have a risqué streak, to the point that in Indonesia the narrative is considered characteristic of "the very rude, bawdy farce" (Kwee 1978, 227), perhaps partially by association with the "rude transvestite theme" otherwise familiar in local Javanese theatre (ibid.). This streak of humor may have developed quite early; for instance, a 1922 version has Sampek discovering that Engtay is a woman when he sees her breasts while she is bathing in a river (37). There are also rather absurd interventions. For instance, a 1970s version in *ketoprak*, a humorous Javanese form of theatre, has the rich, undesirable bridegroom appearing with five neckties on and accidentally wearing his mother's shoes, going on to confuse the bride with her mother. Presumably, this sort of slapstick comedy aims to exaggerate the difference between the oafish bridegroom and gentlemanly Liang (Quinn 2013, 347). The relationship between the Indonesian iterations and the story as performed in the Chinese world has become remote.

Teater Koma and other Contemporary Versions

One local observer, writing in 1947, remarked of the narrative that "many theatre groups have it in their repertoire" (Nio 1947, 14). Similarly, in 1948, a newspaper overview of the Indonesian stage would use *Sampek Engtay,* "which appears in the repertoire of various stage companies," as an example of how the Chinese influence on the Indonesian stage (and literature) had gone deeper than the European (*Nieuwe courant,* October 18, 1948).[21] Indeed, it is hard to point to any European story that, even now, is more familiar. Although the narrative seems to have lost prominence by the third quarter of the twentieth century, textual and theatrical reimaginations of *Sampek Engtay* in Indonesia have reemerged since then.

One notable adaptation was a 1990 book by OKT (Oey Kim Tiang 黃欽長)[22] who, having been principally active as an author and adaptor of *kung fu* novels in the 1920s, was eighty-five when he published *Sampek Engtay,* working from the Chinese text of Zhang Henshui 張恨水.[23] Its Indonesian subtitle, *Romantika Emansipasi Seorang Perempuan* (The romance of a woman's emancipation), likely shows the influence of Communist Chinese interpretations of the legend, the "politically correct reading of this narrative" in which the heroine "stands for female emancipation, equal rights for both sexes, as well as faithfulness in marriage" (Altenburger 2005, 167). OKT had, after all, worked at the pro-Beijing newspaper *Sin Po* before the Suharto period (Setyautama 2008, 272).

OKT seems, moreover, to have been motivated to create a "correct" version by a dislike for the way the narrative had developed in Indonesia, particularly due to the fact that in various Indonesian adaptations Engtay reveals that she is a woman by allowing a glimpse under her clothes (ASA 1990, xiv). The introduction also links the work to the status of women in Indonesia and states that the principal icon of early women's rights in Indonesia, R. A. Kartini, "reputedly also read the story *San Pek Eng Tay*" (xxv). This positioning—deeply embedded in Indonesian history yet receptive to new influences from China as well as at pains to make an association with non-Chinese identity and history—suggests both the concern with authenticity existing among the Sino-Indonesians (where all cultural products are measured against an imagined Mainland Chinese norm) and the obligation to perform a distinct but loyal and integrated identity for an Indonesian state.

The idea that the narrative was principally a call for female emancipation had reached Indonesia fairly early. The journalist Kwee Kek Beng had already deplored in 1948 the changes he had noted in the stagings of the *Sampek Engtay* narrative, believing that romance had obscured the "story's mission," namely "the importance of education for women" (Saidi 1991, 18). In New Order, a different message was discovered in the narrative: in the terms of Betawi cultural critic and sometime politician Ridwan Saidi, in a chapter for a basically assimilationist tome entitled *Nonpri di mata pribumi* (Non-indigenous people [i.e., Sino-Indonesians] in the eyes of the indigenous), one 1988 adaptation was a great success for its ability to turn the principal characters into WNI (Warga Negara Indonesia; Citizens of Indonesia), a New Order euphemism for Sino-Indonesians. In his view, through its pungent humor, the production had succeeded in dissolving the distinction between Chinese (*nonpri*) and indigenous (*pribumi*) (18–19).

The adaptation in question was that of Teater Koma. Founded by Nano Riantiarno[24] in 1977 in Jakarta, Teater Koma is renowned for producing theatre critical of the status quo in a format that has "combined slangy Jakartan jargon, transvestite actors and roles, earthy humor . . . and Broadway style songs" (Bodden 2010, 279).[25] Raucous and eclectic, the company is an heir to *stamboel* and the other forms of early commercial theatre, a period and a genre in which Riantiarno has also shown an interest as a director and dramatist.[26] The company has also generally been considered to represent "the rise of a more commercially oriented middle-class" while also "expressing some of the key general social and political concerns of large segments of that class" (Bodden 2010, 334n5). Consequently, it more than once became the target of Suharto-era monitoring and interference (Ian Jarvis Brown 2001, 190). Run by Nano and his wife Ratna out of their family home, the company's work has attracted scholarly attention at home and abroad, and his *Opera Kecoa* (Cockroach Opera), *1983,* and *Bom Waktu* (Time bomb) have been translated into English. Characters in Teater Koma are often members of society's underbelly—prostitutes and small-time crooks—who nevertheless are more honorable than the government officials who shamelessly exploit them.

During New Order, Teater Koma produced two Chinese-themed plays, *Sampek Engtay* and the later *Opera Ular Putih* (The white snake opera, 1994).[27] *Sampek*

Engtay premiered in Jakarta on August 27, 1988, and was written and directed, like many of Teater Koma's works, by Riantiarno himself. This version transplants the setting to Batavia, with the heroes hailing from the Banten localities of Pandeglang and Serang, apparently to keep the distances within plausibility for colonial Java. In preparation for the production, Riantiarno and his circle of actors travelled to observe life in the Chinese areas of these Banten towns, as well as in a Jakarta Chinese temple in the Teluk Gong area, a process that Riantiarno humorously likened to obtaining Indonesian ID cards (KTP) for the two protagonists.[28] At Teluk Gong, the cast witnessed a *xiqu* troupe performing and drew inspiration from the costumes and the actors' dedication (Janarto 1997, 221, 227).[29]

Beginning with *Sampek Engtay*'s initial run, Sino-Indonesians have been a substantial proportion of the audience, some of them even "dress[ing] for the occasion in traditional Chinese clothes," a phenomenon that evidently surprised Riantiarno himself (Blussé 1991, 5). During fieldwork in 2012 and 2013, I frequently met people from various parts of Java who had travelled to Jakarta particularly to watch the show; some respondents told me that the original production mattered to them especially because it featured *barongsay* (lion dancing) in the theatre at a time when such practice was prohibited on the streets.[30] In general, however, it is largely the narrative that shows a Chinese influence, while the style of performance, dance, and music all owe greater debts to local theatre such as *masres* (from Riantiarno's native city of Cirebon) and the Jakarta genre *lenong* (Janarto 1997, 226). Costumes and sets are in a vein of "Chineseness" that draws on other Sino-Indonesian depictions. In a 2005 semi-theatrical interview, Riantiarno connected the Batavian setting with the Chinese history in that city in the colonial period, since that is "when the Chinese influence was greatest" (Teater Koma 2005, 4), suggesting in a later television interview that it was specifically set in the 1860s (*Da Ai* 2013).

In 1988 and 1989, Teater Koma's *Sampek Engtay* was performed over three dozen times on Java: premiering in Jakarta, at the prestigious Gedung Kesenian Jakarta (Jakarta Art Building), it went on also to Surabaya. Riantiarno, though interrogated by BAKIN (the Suharto-era State Intelligence Coordination Body) on the day of the premiere, was able to secure permission for the show by promising not to display Chinese characters, include *barongsay* in the wedding scene, or otherwise visually indicate the Chinese dimension of the play. Riantiarno also had to offer assurances that no members of Teater Koma hailed from China (Ian Jarvis Brown 2001, 196–197; Paramita 2015). The show went on to sell out its initial run and was forced to add more performances.

Teater Koma's luck did not hold. In May 1989, after a dress rehearsal, the education and culture department of the North Sumatra provincial government prevented the company from performing the piece at the Tiara Convention Center in Medan, even though the same office had already given permission for the

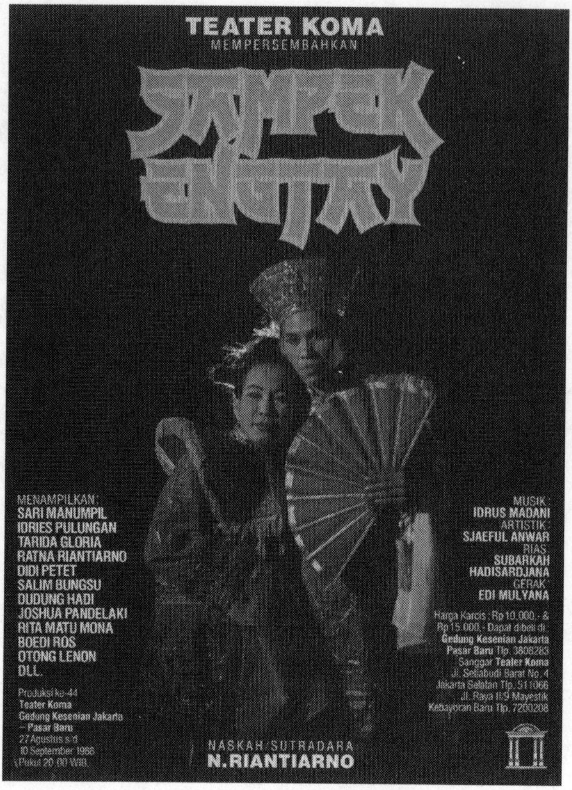

The poster of Teater Koma's original production of *Sampek Engtay* 1988. Photo courtesy of Teater Koma.

performances (Asia Watch 56). Although the exact reasons are not known (Ian Jarvis Brown 2001, 197), the event can be conceived as part of a "highly publicized series of confrontations between the Indonesian state and a number of theater groups over performances banned by the government" (Bodden 2010, 1). Despite the wider context of theatrical dissent,[31] and even though the official objection was that the show was in contravention of the values of Pancasila, this intervention should also be contextualized in terms of the ongoing ban on Chinese performance in Indonesian culture, which was allegedly "incompatible with the national character" (Heryanto 1999, 173). Some observers also connected it with the ban of the visiting Taiwanese *jingju* troupe mentioned in the first chapter (Mély G. Tan 1991, 118; Asmara 1995, 172). As Riantiarno himself interpreted the events, "*Sampek Engtay* was banned because of the sensitivity of the New Order government over the Chinese community. The Chinese were often suspected of being Communist agents, and most of their cultural expression was banned. But actually this work is just a classic love story, there's no political criticism" (Riantiarno 2003, 119). In other words, the political aspect the local government found offensive was not the specific content but the acting of a Chinese story per se. The prominence and size of Medan's Chinese community, the relative strictness of provincial authorities compared to their Jakarta counterparts, the correspondence with a national holiday, and Riantiarno's own Chinese background have all been mooted as factors in this ban.[32]

The text of *Sampek Engtay*'s prologue gives some idea of how the play incorporates its Chinese material. In the New Order context, it can be read as an attempt to minimize the Chinese nature of the story. The first line, read by the *dalang* (himself an inherently Indonesian role, as he is the traditional leader of a *wayang* performance) runs: "This is one love story among the millions of love stories that have existed since the creation of the earth. We all know the story of Qais and Laila, a pair of amorous beetles buried in the desert sands of Arabia. Roro Mendut and Pronocitro is a popular love story from Java. Romeo and Juliet, a love tragedy à la Europe, told through flowers and poisons, and able to jerk your tears dry" (Riantiarno 1999, 8). This enumeration of *Sampek Engtay* as one of the world's great romances, alongside those of Romeo and Juliet as well as Roro Mendut and Pronocitro, is a commonplace in China as in Indonesia and is mentioned also in the preface to OKT's work (OKT 1990, xiii; see also Idema 2010, xi).[33] It also could operate as a defense against the production of a specifically Chinese play by situating it as part of a global heritage, or as a Chinese variant of a love story that is familiar also in Europe and Indonesia. The *dalang* goes on to note that it is

> an old work which has already become a legend, the product of the daydreams of a poet whom I do not wish to name. This is: *Sampek-Engtay* from Batavia.
>
> SERVANT: (*Shouting*). Silly, you're being silly, Mr. Dalang. Don't be such an embarrassment. Everyone knows the Sampek-Engtay story came here from China. (8–9)

The text mischievously points out the obvious: that *Sampek-Engtay* has roots from outside Indonesia; and also that one might be tempted to dissemble a little in this regard. It continues in the same vein:

> SERVANT: Aren't we going to perform *Sampek Engtay* tonight? We've already got our costumes. If we are, tell us in which way we're going to perform it: Chinese, Batavian, Sundanese, European, or American?
>
> DALANG: Wait a moment, wait a moment. Didn't I already say just now, *Sampek-Engtay* is from Batavia? Because that's what the playwright of this version wants, who moreover is also the director. (10)

Since the abolition of restrictions on Chinese culture, interest in the play has increased, with the script being published in 1999 (Pustaka Jaya) and 2004 (Galang Press). Moreover, "Chinese" readings of the play have become more available as the play has been revived, in 1999–2000 and 2013 for longer runs, as well as for one-off shows in Medan and Yogyakarta in 2002 and 2004, respectively. On its Yogyakarta restaging in 2004, literary critic Faruk HT expressed appreciation for the Teater Koma version because it challenged conventional narratives about money-hungry Chinese, although he also took the opportunity to lament the absence of Sino-Indonesian writing about the contemporary community. One might counter that it is *Sampek Engtay*'s remoteness of period as well as its indiginizing adaptation, however, that made the play feasible during the New Order period. On the other hand, Ariel Heryanto sees in Faruk's objection the influence of "several western countries" with its writers, who are "expected to be preoccupied with their own ethnicity, and write primarily about, and for, their own ethnic communities" (Heryanto 2004, 78). Heryanto sees little attraction in an ethnic-focused interpretation; Riantiarno would likely agree.

Audience response, however, does not always follow suit. An ethnically conscious reception was also accorded to the play, for instance, when Riantiarno worked with Singaporean actors to stage a production there in 2000. The performance was in an English translation by Rangga Bhuana (son of the Riantiarnos) and much of the Betawi humor was rewritten for local audiences (*The Straits Times,* November 28, 2000). Emphasizing the fact that Riantiarno is "ethnic Chinese," the *Straits Times*' Arthur Sim felt the need to explain the "liberties" taken with the familiar Chinese story, casting it in terms of "Javanese music and comedy" (*The Straits Times,* November 28, 2000). Another reviewer, generally positive, found the setting confusing, wondering whether viewers were to consider themselves in "Mainland China? Indonesia? What?" (*The Flying Inkpot,* December 1, 2000) The actress playing Engtay, Elaine Cheah, reported that Riantiarno had put the wild humor in context by suggesting that actors "think of Sampek Engtay as a Steven Chow movie," thus linking the play's comedy with the Hong Kong actor's distinctive wackiness, familiar throughout the Chinese-speaking world.

Chinese-language responses are even more likely to highlight an ethnic essentialism. In a 2013 news profile by Da Ai, an Indonesian television company owned by the Taiwan-based religious charity Tzu Chi, the Mandarin-language voice-over, which identifies the play as *huaju* (i.e., "spoken theatre" in the Chinese modernist tradition), also claims that Teater Koma's repertoire has been defined by its "bringing several Chinese classic stories onto the Indonesian stage" and the fact that it "interprets ancient Chinese culture in Indonesian language," thus eliding the performance style and textual adaptation, both of which move the production very far from the narrative as presented on the Mainland Chinese stage (*Da Ai* 2013).

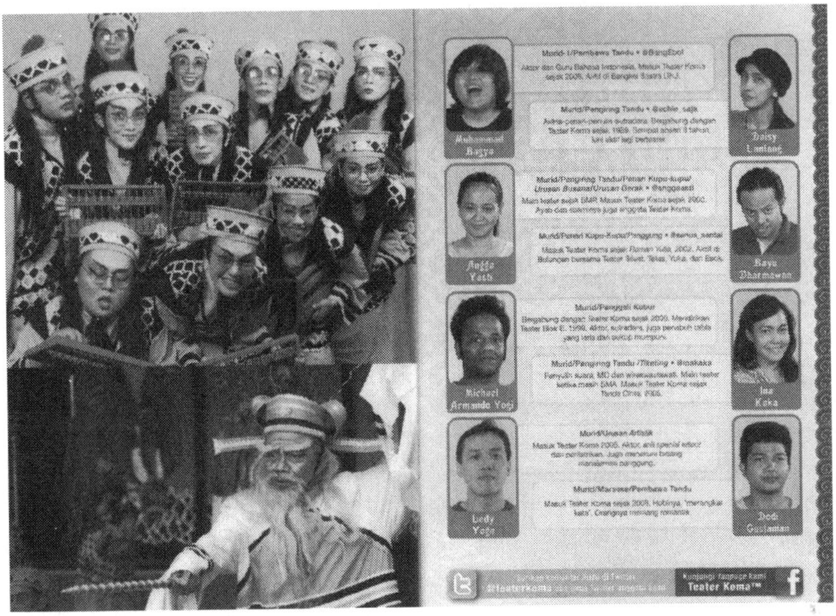

Students and teacher from the program of the 2013 *Sampek Engtay* revival. Photo courtesy of Teater Koma.

Riantiarno has further gone on to highlight, in a way similar to strategies employed by *potehi* troupes and patrons, the story's integrationist potential, suggesting that the play shows that "the Chinese are one of our tribes," stressing his point both in content (the Chinese as an Indonesian *suku*) and in form (by use of the pronomial "our").[34] Teater Koma's version of *Sampek Engtay* is part of the same tendency to identify and celebrate Chinese performance as a constituent of a larger Indonesian practice.[35] With its confusion of identity and star-crossed love story, some have also taken it to be a metaphor of "interracial relationships" between Chinese and non-Chinese in Indonesia (Noor and Tranggano 2003, 102). Ethnic interpretations have persisted, and some have pointed to the play as remedying a situation wherein Sino-Indonesians have "been left without cultural and nationalist expression in the context of their existence in Indonesia" (Malna 2010, 181).[36]

In a 2010 text, later repurposed as an introduction to a book of his translations, Goenawan Mohamad, one of Indonesia's best-known essayists and most respected cultural figures, writes in defense of books. Between reference to Karl May's *The Death of Winnetou* and *The Brothers Karamazow,* Goenawan writes that in his childhood during the early Republic his "tears fell for Sampek and Engtai who died in the story that I heard some of the workers at the cigarette factory beside our house reading aloud in turn from a book written in Javanese" (Goenawan 2015, "Books: A Preface"). One could hope for no better illustration of the story's indigenization than this evidence of widespread oral and communal transmission without reference to its Chinese origin.

The range taken on by the *Sampek Engtay* narrative can be used to symbolize the Chinese strand in modern commercial Indonesian theatre. It is expressed in a wide variety of genres, was subject to (but survived) the New Order restrictions, and is now enjoying a renaissance. Insofar as *Sampek Engtay* is a story of misapprehended romance and failures of communication, its themes, too, can lead us back to the ethnic dynamic. At the same time, as Ian Jarvis Brown aptly remarks, in the Indies and Indonesia "classic Chinese stories were not the sole property of any one group" (2001, 53). Recognition of the narratives as part of Indonesian heritage rehearses the integration of Sino-Indonesians in the national narrative.

Has the reception and development of this narrative been exceptional in the archipelago and in the Malay-Indonesian world more generally? Does it make sense to ask why it "enjoyed such enduring popularity in the Malay-Indonesian archipelago and not elsewhere"? (Chin 1991, 138). Quinn suggests that it may have benefited from similarities with Indonesian narratives (such as *Roro Mendut*), which also involve love suicides, but this does not explain why, unlike other Chinese narratives, it seems to have made little impression on the Japanese stage, where love suicides are a dominant trope.

It is at least worth entertaining the hypothesis that an explanation is to be found in the long history and integration of Chinese people in the Malay-Indonesian world, so that theatre, storytelling, and eventually cinema existed alongside printed texts as media of culture. It is worth considering whether Japan, Korea, and Vietnam, and (later) the West might be relatively more influenced by Chinese texts (as opposed to principally oral traditions and narratives), leading to the closer reproduction by academics, literati, and translators of the literary canon as established in China. In Southeast Asia, by contrast, Chinese communities were both more numerous and frequently bicultural, and, certainly in the nineteenth century, the printed word was less dominant than oral media.[37] Transmission of Chinese culture was not overwhelmingly the domain of literate elites.

Any such distinction must, of course, be nuanced, both by the large amount of print material based on Chinese narratives in the Malay world, and by the paths through which oral sources also influenced East Asian and Western theatre; nevertheless, the length and breadth of heavy migration as a bearer of culture does seem to provide a certain contrast with the relative "thinness" of textual transmission. Even a familiar story, like that of the Monkey King, remains more marginal and ethnic in English than *Sampek Engtay* in the Malay-Indonesian world. Such considerations may even lead us to consider whether reception of Chinese culture in general has been more "literary" in the Western countries where much translation (overwhelmingly so until the last few decades) has occurred through sinology, and more "oral" in the Southeast Asian world, where the text was only one part of the many ways, including theatre, storytelling, and puppetry, in which major narratives were received.

As demonstrated in other chapters, the identification of Chinese elements within an Indonesian work is a recognition of a vein of inspiration that enriches rather than detracts from Indonesian theatre historiography. The deep assimilation of many Sino-Indonesians, whether historical or contemporary, need not be in tension with an abiding interest in Chineseness, and Overseas Chinese works can be fruitfully examined from a sinological perspective without appealing to ethnic essentialism. It is, one hopes, possible to investigate the contribution of Chineseness to Indonesian modern theatre without suggesting that Chineseness is in any way a detraction or a distraction from these works' importance in Indonesian theatre history. Indeed, close attention to Chinese strands running through Indonesian spoken theatre history highlights the richness of Indonesian commercial theatre's sources and inspiration.

CHAPTER 5

Alumni Networks and Hybrid Dances

SINO-INDONESIAN VOLUNTARY ASSOCIATIONS AND PERFORMANCE

PERFORMANCE is far more than theatre in its most packaged and self-conscious forms. For that reason, performance theorists and practitioners have long questioned the barriers between stage and society at large. Because "minority comes into existence in the very act of representation" (Tripathy and Padmanabhan 2014a, xi), minority groups in multiethnic societies are deeply concerned with managing perceptions of their group and how their actions will be interpreted by majority populations, the state, the notional homeland, and other diasporic communities. Preceding chapters have traced the evolution of Sino-Indonesian formation and negotiation of identity in the overtly theatrical spheres of *xiqu* and *wayang,* and considered cases in political and commercial theatres. Less theatrically framed venues for performativity will now be examined: in this chapter, community performance is considered; in the next chapter, religious and ritual performance.

It is useful to incorporate community and religious organizations' public events into a book on Sino-Indonesian performance of identity, not least because framed theatre has never been entirely extricable from these community organizations. Most, if not all, of the performances discussed in the preceding chapters have depended on Chinese association networks for their funding, organization, audiences, and publicity. Chinese diasporic theatres anywhere in the world emerge from geographical, social, cultural, religious, educational, and political associations. Attention to the performative aspect in Sino-Indonesian voluntary associations allows a better understanding of the sociopolitical and economic structures that produce the public image of the minority group.

Community performance in Sino-Indonesian communities is amateur and usually occurs incidentally as part of a larger festive program, usually including a meal. For these events, tickets may be sold, usually to benefit the organizing charity or an associated cause. Other events are outward-facing, presenting the Chinese community to a larger Indonesian society. Since community performance "facilitates creative expression of a diverse group of people" and is "communally created" rather than being the product of an individual (Kuppers 2006, 4), such forms of performance can make an enhanced claim to representing a broad variety of interests and subgroups. Karen Ahlquist, approaching the amateur chorus as a community, points out that such organizations can "assert artistic and educational achievement, aesthetic merit, and social, national, religious, or ethnic identity" (Ahlquist 2006, 2).[1] Civic events are among the situations where Indonesians are most likely to encounter performances of Chinese identity. As Tan Chee-Beng notes of large Overseas Chinese communities (such as Indonesia), "social organizations are able to exert considerable influence over inter-community affairs and inter-community relations," while also helping to "promote the social, cultural and political interests of the Chinese" (Chee-Beng Tan 2004, 50).

After restrictions were placed on Chinese communal expression during the early Suharto years, Chinese organizations, including schools and publications, were banned and communal life was severely curtailed.[2] Any organizations that persisted had to assimilate, or be seen to do so, by modifying their names, structures, and purposes in order to be or appear more Indonesian (Liao [Suryadinata] 2002, 18–19). By the 1980s there were "extremely few permitted family associations, religious associations, medical and hygienic associations, entertainment associations, etc" (Ding 2009b).[3] Chinese societies had been known, along with the Chinese press and Chinese schools, as the "three pillars" of the Chinese community. The banning of Chinese voluntary societies during New Order constituted a deliberate crippling of the community's means of self-expression.

In the last few years of New Order, the ban on Sino-Indonesian associations weakened, allowing the emergence of several new organizations. One of the most visible and positive outcomes for Sino-Indonesians in the past two decades has been the opening of the public sphere to Chinese organizations. Since the beginning of the Reformasi period, over five hundred Sino-Indonesian organizations have emerged or reemerged,[4] causing one Sino-Indonesian activist to write that "Chinese associations and trilingual schools have sprung up all over the country like bamboo shoots after the rain" (Liu Jiesheng 2010, 117). Some churches, colleges, charitable organizations, or sporting groups are not officially designated as being Chinese but are dominated by members of Chinese origin; sometimes their activities are marked as Chinese in linguistic or cultural terms.[5] Operating through these associations, Chinese groups in this new period have benefited from the "activation of extensive transnational networks" (Nagata 2003, 369) that had been dormant or covert during the Suharto years.

While usually regarded positively by Sino-Indonesians, Chinese voluntary associations can be perceived critically by the general Indonesian population, for whom "the formation of exclusive informal groups and social associations of which the membership are predominantly Chinese" (Susanto 2010, 71) is often taken as evidence of Sino-Indonesian arrogance or aloofness. Not least for this reason, many Sino-Indonesian organizations explicitly encourage "ethnic Chinese to actively assimilate to mainstream [Indonesian] society" (Ding 2009b), although the actual terms of such integration are rarely spelled out.

The activities of Sino-Indonesian voluntary associations can be read as the most explicit and organized expression of a general contemporary Sino-Indonesian trend to perform loyalty and cultural hybridity. It is no coincidence that Chinese-language publications and public discourse prominently refer to Indonesia as *zuguo* 祖國 (native country) or *woguo* 我國 (our country) and to other Indonesians as *xiongdi minzu* 兄弟民族 (brother ethnicities) or *youhao minzu* 友好民族 (friendly ethnicities). At the same time, members of these groups are committed to retaining a distinct Sino-Indonesian identity, and concerns about community aging are often voiced as fears of the extinction of this identity. The aims of these organizations may be framed in sociocultural terms, but they typically are also concerned with the status of Sino-Indonesians within the Indonesian polity, and as such possess political goals and attitudes (Hoon 2011a, 77–79).

Points of interaction between Chinese and non-Chinese Indonesian groups and individuals often occur under the auspices of Chinese community organization events. Chinese Indonesian associations support charities and relief efforts; political candidates visit them and solicit their support in invited addresses. Such organizations also represent the Chinese community at state celebrations and at civic events such as music festivals and book fairs. At the same time, they often invite local representatives of the PRC, including embassy, army, and Confucius Institute staff to their events. In these ways, voluntary associations operate as the mediators of Indonesia for Mainland China, and vice versa.

The activities of these organizations are also the elements of daily life that are most overtly marked as "Chinese" for members. Sino-Indonesians overwhelmingly use Indonesian or other local languages in daily life and are surrounded largely by *pribumi* in their professional lives, in their ordinary activities, and to a variable degree also in their social lives. These organizations thus strengthen ties within the Chinese community, reinforce ethnic identity, provide space for language and culture instruction, and create avenues for the Chinese population to interact with (or perform for) Indonesian society as a unit. The general reluctance of younger Sino-Indonesians to participate in voluntary associations is often interpreted as a sign that Sino-Indonesian identity is weakening, although it is also possible that the younger generation is simply less interested in civic associations of any kind, or that their interest may grow as senior positions become available to them.

Sino-Indonesian community organizations pursue a variety of different goals and determine membership according to varying principles. The following ten categories for Sino-Indonesian associations in the Reformasi period may be useful:

1. Educational (teachers' or alumni associations)
2. Ancestral (based on ancestral origin)
3. Clan- or surname-based
4. Cultural
5. Economic
6. Women's organizations
7. Charitable
8. Political
9. Recreational
10. Religious

Organizations representing these types are present in one way or another in Bandung, from which the following case studies are drawn. In practice, many of these organizations cannot be easily defined by a single such category. The typology presented above must therefore be understood as identifying tendencies within a deep integration of organizational purposes. Association membership, drawn from a finite pool of identifying, community-oriented Sino-Indonesians, overlaps as thoroughly as the scope of activities.

Performance Activities of Bandung Voluntary Associations

Bandung is the capital of West Java and the metropolis of the Sundanese cultural area. West Java has featured an extensive Chinese presence since before the Dutch arrived in the early seventeenth century, especially on the northern coast. Chinese communities in the early colonial period were concentrated around ports, especially Cirebon, while the Sundanese economy remained largely centered on small-scale dry-field agriculture.[6]

Over the period of Dutch colonialism, the tea, coffee, and quinine plantations of the Pasundan highlands increased the interaction between Chinese and Sundanese peoples. Under the British, in 1812, a marketplace was established in Bandung, and a small number of Chinese were active there. In 1820, however, the Chinese were prohibited from settling in Priangan, and a series of other restrictions all but eliminated the Chinese presence in Bandung. The area was also under an opium ban, the commodity then most associated with a Chinese merchant presence (Tunas 2007, 28–32). While in "Batavia the Chinese were considered an inseparable part of the town," in Priangan they were considered "a potential threat that might conflict with the VOC trade monopoly by secretly buying the crops from the native peasants" (Tunas 2007, 22).

In the later nineteenth century, however, the rise of Bandung as a center of commerce was substantially connected to the growth of the Chinese trading population, especially after the railway arrived in Bandung in 1884. Throughout the first half of the twentieth century, colonial censuses show the Chinese population at around 10 percent of the rapidly growing city, reaching 40,000 of a total 437,000 in 1945 (Smail 1964, 7). A 1954 Taipei publication put the number close to 100,000 with over 70 community organizations (about 30 percent of which were Taipei-oriented, and the rest Beijing-oriented; Chen Yiling 1954, 7). The 2010 census, which reports over 80,000 Chinese in Bandung, is probably an underestimation. Even so, that would make it the seventh-largest concentration of Chinese in Indonesia (Arifin et al. 2016, 11); another 45,000 or so live elsewhere in West Java (Arifin et al. 2015, 97). Despite the openness of Reformasi, however, acknowledgment of Chinese interaction with, and contributions to, local culture remains uneven and uneasy.

There is also, as in most areas of Indonesia, a history of anti-Chinese sentiment. In 1945–1946, as the Indonesian revolutionaries fought Dutch and British forces, ending in the horrific, era-defining "Bandung Lautan Api" (The Bandung sea of flames),[7] Chinese were treated with suspicion and, later, kidnappings and killings at the hands of revolutionaries were widespread (Smail 1964, 95, 107). Though many Chinese were also killed in British bombings, most eventually sought refuge in the British-occupied zone of the city (116, 128), leaving the impression on many revolutionaries that they were allied with colonial forces.

Anti-Chinese sentiment did not end with independence. A major riot hit Bandung in 1973, in which hundreds of Chinese homes were damaged or destroyed. The violence evolved from a traffic incident and was possibly further fanned by the military.[8] As in other parts of Indonesia, the West Java Chinese are likely to be looked upon by *pribumi* as aloof from society: a Western musicologist opined in 1990 that the two communities "normally make a point of keeping themselves separate" (Williams 1989, 181), and such barriers have not fallen entirely. Purdey found eight instances of violence in West Java between 1996 and 1999, of which half involved Bandung (2006, 219–220). My Sino-Indonesian respondents in Bandung continue to report mild but pervasive discrimination, especially in interactions with bureaucracy and police that result in the payment of small bribes.

The majority of local Sino-Indonesians explicitly identify themselves as patriotic Indonesians and are native speakers of Sundanese. The exhibits of Museum Sri Baduga in Bandung, the largest museum dedicated to Sundanese culture, indicate Chinese influence present in everything from gigs to the wedding costumes of Karawang. According to Chang-yau Hoon, young Sino-Sundanese may use slang terms like "Cina Sunda" or "Cinsun" to describe themselves (2011, 167).[9] Cultural mingling is not new, although the development of a self-conscious Sino-Sundanese identity may well be.

Today, Chinese identity in Bandung as it can be formally apprehended or encountered is built around a variety of interpenetrating civic organizations. These are sometimes branches of national organizations, sometimes loosely affiliated with groups in other cities, and sometimes wholly autonomous. A very few have a particular sociopolitical platform for Chinese minority identity, such as the West Java branch of Perhimpunan Indonesia Tionghoa (INTI) 印尼華裔總會 (Association of Chinese Indonesians), which was founded in 1999 and is committed to an integrationist view of the Chinese presence in Indonesia. As always, the "restored liberties" of the Reformasi period "are being negotiated in accord with local political and cultural dynamics," (Hui 2011, 247), and consequently organizations have a high local specificity as well as more national Sino-Indonesian concerns.

In one way or another, all types of voluntary associations are engaged in performance: a badminton club, as well as a political society or a literary association, has a performative aspect. When a voluntary association hosts Chinese or transnational diasporic organizations, it usually presents local Indonesian arts, often performed by Sino-Indonesians.[10] Activities of Chinese associations are consistently reported in Chinese-language newspapers such as *Guoji ribao* 國際日報 (International Times) and the Chinese-oriented Indonesian-language publications such as *Jiaxiang* 家鄉 (Hometown), as well as receiving more sporadic attention from the local Indonesian-language press. The exercise of charity, both for the alleviation of poverty and for disaster relief, is prominently noted in association publications and given as evidence for good interethnic relations. This section provides an overview of some of these associations and performances in greater detail in order to examine how Bandung associations combine attachment to local identity with expressions of loyalty to the Indonesian state.

Tongxianghui 同鄉會 Performances

Chinese society, especially the later *totok* immigrants, was substantially organized by dialect groups in the late colonial period; however, intra-Chinese distinctions faded drastically under New Order. Nonetheless, place of origin in China remains the nominal organizing principle for some of the most influential organizations, a feature inherited from a late imperial Chinese "ideological connection between native-place identity and Chinese identity" (Goodman 1995, 13). Today, although membership has become more flexible and porous, organization leadership is still drawn from among those who can trace the pertinent ancestry.[11] Since several local place organizations own buildings, one of their important functions is to provide the rental space for other organizations, such as the annual fund-raising festivities of various alumni associations, several choirs, weekly karaoke meetings, *wushu* and table-tennis groups, and so on.

The two most prominent ancestral-origin organizations in Bandung belong to the Hakka and the Guangzhao (Cantonese) associations.[12] The Bandung branch of the Hakka Friendship Association, founded in 2000, is a large and influential group, with annual meetings drawing over four hundred members. The same association held the 11th World Congress of Lee Families 世界李氏宗親總會 in 2003.[13] Relations with Mainland China are an important element of this group's activities, and delegations attend the World Hakka Conference on a regular basis. In 2012–2013, the Hakka Association invited the performers from Mainland China and Taiwan whose visit is noted in chapter 1. Connections to Hakka regions of Guangdong, especially Meizhou, are an important part of the association's activities, with visits from Meizhou officials balanced by Hakka Association trips to China. A 2012 trip, for instance, saw over two hundred Bandung Hakka travelling to important places of origin such as Meizhou and other places of Sino-Indonesian interest such as Quanzhou. Within Java, the local Hakka Association arranges tours to visit regional temple festivals or to visit Sino-Indonesian tourist draws such as Sam Po Kong 三寶宫 in Semarang, where the (purported) visit of Zheng He is commemorated. A weekly club for Hakka Association elderly provides karaoke singing and entertainment under the rubric of activities for "Joyful [Old] Age" 樂齡, and trilingual (Indonesian-Mandarin-English) middle and elementary schools are also associated with the institution.[14]

The full name of the Bandung Cantonese association is Yayasan Mutiara Kemakmuran Sejahtera[15] 萬隆廣肇福利銀會 (Bandung Guangzhou-Zhaoqing Welfare Association). This group is known for hosting the best *wushu* organization in the city, as well as table tennis, fitness dancing, and tai chi groups. As with other Chinese associations, the group is committed to assertions of loyalty to Indonesia, producing, for instance, Chinese-language books such as *Chengzhang zhong de Yinni* 成長中的印尼 (Indonesia in the Process of Maturation). They also have their own choral group, besides sometimes organizing Cantonese *yueju* karaoke.[16]

The program of one of their events provides an example of the content of a typical Chinese community association performance: in March 2013, the Cantonese association celebrated the opening of its new building and the seventy-fifth anniversary of its 1937 establishment. A Chinese-language newspaper reported: "Yu Wenji and Xie Fengzhu sang a Cantonese opera song together, and then the association's women's chorus sang three songs, 'Dust on the Great Dragon' 蒙塵的巨龍, 'Dreaming of Camel Chimes' 夢駝鈴, and 'Ondel-Ondel'."[17] The program was rounded off by children's performances (*Qiandao ribao,* March 20, 2013). The first of these songs is by the 1980s Hong Kong singer Cheung Ming Men 張明敏,[18] known for his ethnic nationalist songs. The second is a 1984 song by ROC-

Taiwan icon Fei Yu-ching 費玉清, which can be fitted into the category of "Western" exoticism (i.e., Xinjiang), while the third is a folksy song about a certain kind of large puppet in Betawi (i.e., Jakarta local) festivities. This mix of programming combines pan-Chinese patriotic music of the 1980s with Indonesian elements. The popularity of this mix, drawing on repertoire thirty or more years old, across all Sino-Indonesian organizations also reflects the advanced average age of its members.

Local place associations are more complex than their geographical origin may suggest, and the phenomenon does not operate only in a unidirectional fashion. Sino-Indonesians in Hong Kong, Taiwan, and Mainland China also create associations akin to local place organizations, though based on Indonesian rather than on Chinese places of origin (Wang and Wong 2007, 195).[19] Furthermore, these associations then publicly perform Indonesian-style or -inspired songs or dances, or wear Indonesian clothing on formal occasions, as part of their "returned sojourner" (*guiqiao*) identity (e.g., Yinni guiqiao xiehui 2009, 237). Such associations even exist within Indonesia for internal Sino-Indonesian migrants from a particular region: for instance, Chinese from localities such as Bagansiapiapi or Singkawang who reside in Jakarta have their own organizations there, showing the regional power of Indonesian identity even among nominal "co-ethnics."[20] Although local place organizations are built around the principle of a homeland in China that might seem to exalt that essentialist identity over a local one, they also provide an opportunity for noting the flexibility, contextuality, and tenacity of Sino-Indonesian identities.

Alumni Association Performances

The system of Chinese-language schools was an important feature of Sino-Indonesian life in the early Indonesian Republic, structuring society according to economic class and political tendency in a time of nation building. In the post-Suharto era, alumni associations have regained an important place in the rhythms of Chinese community life, allowing cohorts of pre–New Order schoolmates to reestablish their links (Sai 2006, 58–63). Several choirs, dance groups, and *angklung*[21] groups are also organized according to original school membership, even if in practice most accept non-alumni members. Major reunions are held for graduation anniversaries, with commemorative books often printed for the occasion. These collect anecdotes about favorite teachers, reproduce school songs, and document in text and image important visits and service and cultural activities in the school (see Sai 2006, 239–252). Because the Sino-Indonesians are themselves something of a diaspora, there are a number of alumni associations in Jakarta, Hong Kong, Taipei, Guangzhou, Hangzhou, and Beijing that are represented or send congratulatory messages on such occasions.[22]

One of the defining activities of such groups is known as *arisan* 銀會, which deserves notice as a distinct Sino-Indonesian version of an Indonesian practice. The *arisan* is an Indonesian system of rotating savings and credit; usually engaged in by a small circle of friends, it is a "widespread, traditional form of informal finance" (Martowijoyo 2004, 237). In the Bandung Sino-Indonesian alumni organizations, however, it is instead done on a large scale, with the proceeds derived from the *arisan* used for community celebrations and performances. For instance, in one alumni association, every member must pay 240,000 rupiah a month, creating a large interest-bearing fund.[23] At the end of the year 200,000 of it is returned to each member. The remainder of the capital is added to the interest and used to generate a quarterly rhythm of banquets and shows, also called *arisan*. Performance contents themselves resemble the local place association shows—sentimental Taiwanese Mandarin songs of the 1970s and 1980s, Sundanese- and Indonesian-language favorites, CCP songs.

One of the major alumni associations in Bandung is that of Sekolah Menengah Hua Chiao 華僑中學 (Hua Chiao Middle School/Yayasan Citra Cemara). Like other Chinese associations, the organization was able to establish itself in the late New Order. It was, however, careful to disguise its purpose of Chinese-language education. As one executive explained: "Under the regime of the so-called 'New Order,' it was impossible to use the name 'Hua Chiao Alumni Association.' After years of deliberation, we dared to take the lead, and so on October 3, 1993, we announced the formation of the 'Evergreen Foundation' [勁松基金會]. From then on we have resolutely set a cornerstone for the revival [of Chinese-language] education" (*Guoji ribao*, July 4, 2013). Later, this foundation established a bilingual Chinese-Indonesian primary school and junior high school and began to offer a high school program in 2017/2018. Their activities include "choir, *Mulan* martial arts,[24] *tai chi*, dancing, social dance, painting and calligraphy, and *angklung*," along with "recreational activities to develop and transmit Sino-Indonesian culture and social welfare" (ibid.).

By maintaining alumni networks, even for schools that have not been reestablished, the alumni associations foster a community identity through amateur performance while also generating funding for contemporary educational activities and retaining links to Sino-Indonesians abroad and elsewhere in Indonesia, all the while negotiating the demands of Chinese cultural identity and Indonesian political loyalty.

Cultural Society Performances

A variety of Sino-Indonesian cultural societies exist in Bandung, including choirs, Chinese-language literary associations, and orchestral and dance groups. Since they deal with culture, these organizations are especially strongly marked by the negotiation between various available identities. The repertoire and activities of one organization, a Chinese choir, provide an illustration.

Paduan Suara Kota Kembang[25] 花城歌詠團 (Flower City Choir), a mixed-voice choir, was founded in 1995, taking its name from a well-known nickname for Bandung. At the time of its foundation, Suharto was still in power, and the choir was conceived of as a low-key way to revive Mandarin-language vocal music in a period when restrictions were relaxing.[26] Since Reformasi began, the choir has increased in public prominence, although the advanced age of its members makes long-term viability a concern. Performing songs in Mandarin, Sundanese, and Indonesian, Kota Kembang is not the only Chinese choir in Bandung, but according to the choir leader Soeria Disastra 卜汝亮,[27] the group has deliberately defined itself through its frequent cooperation with Indonesian cultural organizations. Disastra stated in an interview that "we were born and raised here, work here, and may die here," adding that the healthiest Chinese organizations are those willing to blend with *pribumi* society" (Disastra, pers. comm., January 10, 2013). According to him, the purpose of Kota Kembang is to emphasize the identity of Chinese-Indonesians as a constituent ethnicity of Indonesia.

This concern with being clearly and patriotically Indonesian is reflected in the choice of songs such as "Lemah Cai" (Land and water—i.e., the Sundanese homeland) and "Hariring Bandung" (The spirit of Bandung), repertoire in Sundanese that can be classified as "lagu *tembang Sunda*," drawing both on Sunda's *tembang* tradition[28] and on the popular music influenced by Sundanese tradition, known as *pop Sunda*.[29] These songs are balanced by Chinese-identity (and often enthusiastically pro-PRC) songs such as "Yangguang lu shang" 陽光路上 (On the sunlit road), which includes lines such as "scientific development shows the direction for harmonious China," and is principally associated with singer Peng Liyuan 彭麗媛, the wife of Xi Jinping.

Kota Kembang's experiences are roughly mirrored in those of Red Sunset 夕陽紅,[30] a Medan organization that reemerged from members of one of the pre-Suharto musical associations, Shio Yih. By the late 1980s, members had begun to gather informally in homes to sing old Chinese songs and new ones they had transcribed from shortwave broadcasts from Beijing. As soon as Reformasi started, they began to perform publicly, almost exclusively at the meetings of Chinese voluntary associations. Their director Cheng Gaoling 程高齡, a veteran of Medan's lively pre-Suharto cultural establishments, estimates that their number was between sixty and seventy at that time, with upwards of twenty annual performances.

By 2016, due to old age, they were reduced to a few dozen members and gave only a few performances a year. They performed at an international festival in Guangzhou in 2010, representing Indonesia, and wherein Cheng astonished a Russian choir with his knowledge of the Soviet choral repertoire dating from the

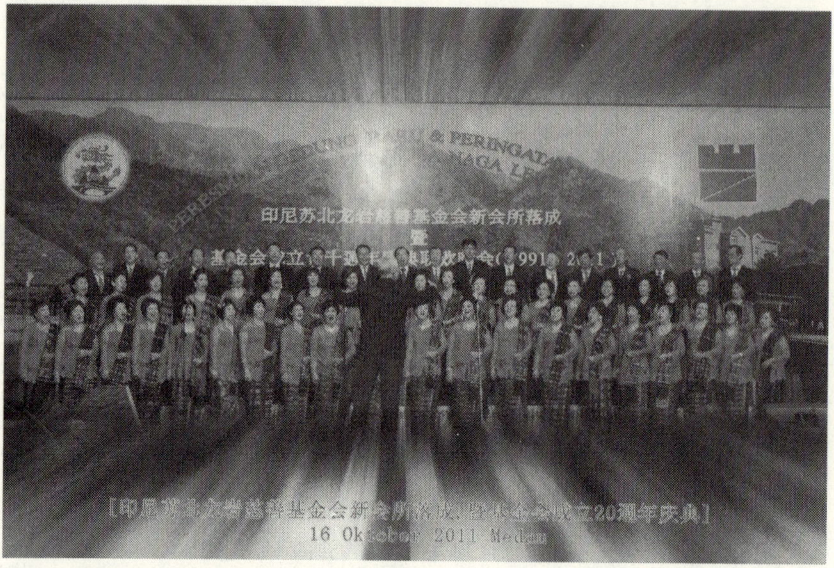

Medan choir Red Sunset performing at a community event in *kebaya* and suits, Medan, 2011. Photo courtesy of Cheng Gaoling.

period before the Sino-Soviet split. The prestige of this visit led to an invitation from the *bupati* (regent) of the nearby Karo Regency, an occasion for which they arranged and performed a Karo song (Cheng Gaoling, pers. comm., November 9, 2016).

This duality of repertoire is representative of cultural association attitudes and is reflected more systematically in the rules for larger Chinese choir festivals in Jakarta, where every group has to present one song in Indonesian and one in another language, for the most part Mandarin (although some prefer English songs; see also Stenberg 2018). Sometimes Indonesian and Chinese nationalisms can appear side by side, as when, at the 2012 Pameran Buku Bandung (Bandung Book Fair), a Chinese Bandung *angklung* troupe played, first, the Indonesian national anthem, followed immediately by the Chinese Communist patriotic song "Wo de zuguo" 我的祖國 (My native land).[31]

From Chinese Subethnic Identities to Indonesian Local Expression

The sketches above give an account of the different strategies Sino-Indonesian groups make use of to negotiate a position for Chinese culture and identity within the Indonesian state. The following section shows how some Chinese groups have come to adopt and express a locally unitary Sino-Indonesian identity. The availability for local identities—in this case, Chinese and Sundanese—can be delineated by tracing the history and activities of one Bandung organization, Yayasan Dana Sosial Priangan 萬隆勃良安福利基金會 (Bandung Priangan Welfare Foundation).

The primacy of Priangan among Bandung Chinese associations, even today, must partly be accounted for by its seniority, as it was founded in 1976 and consequently has operated over four decades, including the last twenty-two years of New Order.[32] Its ability to organize and provide space for assembly during the Suharto years made it something of a covert rallying point for Sino-Indonesians. Its operations were possible because anti-Chinese restrictions exempted (or tended to be interpreted as exempting) life-cycle or (in Indonesian terms, necessarily) religious events such as marriages and burials (Setianto 2010, 84).[33] Traditional Hakka and Hokkien burial ceremonies being quite elaborate, it was and is important for the community to ensure the availability of an affordable space in which mourning and wake can be conducted, thus relieving the stress on families to take care of funeral arrangements. However, while Priangan did and does indeed operate as a burial society, it was also viewed by members as an opportunity for the Chinese community to gather with official approval. At present, Priangan funeral facilities and the crematorium it owns continue to be widely used by the Chinese community, including adherents of several religions; however, Priangan has long since expanded beyond these activities. In Indonesian, however, the whole complex is still generally known as a *rumah duka* (funeral home).

The credit for the foundation of Priangan goes largely to Surya Widjaja 李湘生 (1917–1984). Born in the Hakka-majority Guangdong region of Meixian, Widjaja arrived in Bandung in 1930. According to his children, still closely involved with the organization,[34] Widjaja's project was bedeviled not only by New Order restrictions, but also by the conflicts between regional groups, especially Hakka and Hokkien, within the Bandung Chinese community.[35] However, by 1976 the space for Chinese communal life was very small, and the willingness of Widjaja and other initial leaders to welcome all Chinese into the organization allowed it to become established as central to a semiofficial communal life. Widjaja spearheaded an effort to buy two thousand square meters not far from Bandung's center.[36] An altar known as the Hundred Families' Hall 百氏祠 was opened in 1984, used especially for equinoctial ceremonies. Today the complex features, among other things, a small incense altar; a library and a museum for the Chinese contributions to Indonesian culture, society, and politics; chess tables; a karaoke room; staffed tea service on Sundays; a banquet room; a lecture series; and rental space for massage, pharmaceutical, and medical services. Despite the variety of activities and services on offer at Priangan, its official raison d'être remains unchanged.

As one member remarked on the occasion of Priangan's thirty-fifth anniversary, "all Chinese had to unite in order to overcome difficulties and establish the foundation" (Hou 2011, 83). Chinese-language media praised Widjaja for uniting diverse Chinese factions and subethnic groups under a single roof for the common good, despite New Order pressures. The same event acquired a different emphasis in an Indonesian-language publication such as *Jia Xiang:* "To realise his dream, Surya [Widjaja] assembled philanthropists to found a charitable foundation based on Pancasila, regardless of race or religion, and with a mission to strengthen regional ties and friendship between all layers and clans of Chinese ethnicity, to serve the state and nation of Indonesia" (*Jia Xiang,* April 22, 2014).[37] Ambivalence is still necessary for addressing Chinese cultural enterprises, couched as it is in language on the charitable rather than the ethnic basis for the foundation and justified by claiming Pancasila as inspiration.

Organizing publicly as a Chinese association in Indonesia means that philanthropy must be foregrounded. One of the major purposes of such Sino-Indonesian organizations, as Susy Ong has noted, is to demonstrate a "charitable nature," which allows "its ethnic Chinese members to gain moral legitimacy" (Ong 2008, 106). As one of the Priangan founders, Wu Yuanchang, commented: "everyone was really active to do things for the public, for my father always said: if we want to exist long-term, we have to take care of our relationships with the local people. When there's a disaster, we have to stretch out a helping hand" (Xu Mingfang 2011, 79). In my interviews, several Priangan members were eager to point out that the charitable association had done much to improve the development of the surrounding neighborhood, and indeed Priangan records—held in its library, which is open to the public—are full of annual reports describing how donations of money and food began to be given to local *pribumi* families and organizations. On festive occasions such as Eid, National Holiday, Christmas, and Chinese New Year, Priangan donates clothing and food to orphanages, old folks' homes, institutions for the blind and the handicapped, as well as to organizations for the poor. Disaster relief, especially in their home province of West Java, is another concern. Since 1981, the federation has sponsored education initiatives and provided funding for Gerakan Nasional Untuk Orang Tua Asuh (National Foster Parents Association). These attentions do not go unnoticed by the authorities. Priangan has garnered the praise of West Java politicians for its good works, with then governor Ahmad Heryawan lauding the association as one of the province's most humanitarian charities. Such successes, however, are noticed mostly in the Chinese-language press (*Guoji ribao,* August 29, 2013).

Priangan's museum, like the larger (recently opened) Hakka-focused museum in Jakarta's iconic Taman Mini Indonesia Indah,[38] is an effort to shape the public image of Sino-Indonesians. Called the Sino-Indonesian Historical Memorial Museum 印尼華人歷史紀念館, it presents historical pictures and documentary materials as well as pictures and posters featuring Chinese Indonesian accomplishments in various fields of endeavor. The museum is focused on representing the community in two parallel ways: through the achievements and richness of Chinese culture generally; and the contributions of Sino-Indonesians to the Indonesian nation.[39] Thus, visitors are greeted on entry by four large posters dedicated to Chinese-Indonesian badminton stars.[40] The military is represented by John Lie 李約翰, an important naval commander (and gun smuggler) in the Indonesian National Revolution and, since 2009, a National Hero of Indonesia.[41] Recent Sino-Indonesian cabinet ministers such as Kwik Kian Gie 郭建義 and Mari Elka Pangestu are also represented. Meanwhile, discriminatory New Order legislation, like anti-Chinese violence and sentiment, are almost entirely elided. Thus, rather than dealing directly with the complexities and contradictions of Sino-Indonesian history, the museum opts for a feel-good account of Chinese contributions to Indonesia, supplemented by information about Chinese arts and festivals, and pictures of Sino-Indonesian batik patterns and *wayang potehi*.

While the museum is clearly intended to instruct Chinese Indonesians about their heritage and imbue them with a sense of pride, it is also directed at non-Chinese Indonesians. For instance, Priangan invites Bandung schoolteachers for free tours, in the hope that they will bring school groups. It also creates an opportunity for local politicians to show amity to the Chinese community. During the 2013 West Java gubernatorial campaign, for example, the candidate for vice-governor, Teten Masduki, visited the museum, followed by gubernatorial candidate Rieke Diah Pitaloka herself the following month. Both candidates assured Priangan executives that they would "look after ethnic Chinese" (*Shangbao Indonesia*, January 20, 2013). In such cases, Priangan seeks to convey a positive narrative to the general Indonesian population via the intermediaries of schools and politicians.

Dancing Sino-Sundanese Identity

While Priangan shows the process of cohesion that produced a Sino-Indonesian identity to supersede dialect and regional differences, other groups have focused instead on Bandung Chinese as contributors to the local Sundanese culture and arts. As in the Javanese cultural region, Sino-Indonesians played a role in the patronage of Sundanese traditional music, for instance *tembang*, even if it seems there have been few Chinese performers (Williams 1990, 249). Sino-Indonesians were indispensable for the retailing and wholesaling of Sundanese music from at least the 1930s (Ridwan 2010, 10). One specialist in Indonesian media studies found that, in 1997, "most production houses and recording studios in Bandung [were] owned by an Indonesian of Chinese descent" (Jurriëns 2004, 69). Although this constitutes on the one hand a contribution to Sundanese culture, it has also been met with resentment, for instance from competing studios run by ethnic Sundanese (Jurriëns 2004, 71). Though less well documented than Sino-Javanese or Sino-Betawi cultural products, Sino-Sundanese cultural activity has produced and continues to produce examples of hybrid performance, forming one constituent of Sino-Indonesian performance.

One organization that confronts and confounds expectations regarding the Chinese community and expresses a Sino-Sundanese identity in a performative fashion is Padepokan Pasundan Asih 巴巽華 (Loving Sunda Studio), founded in 2002. The central figures behind the organization are Tan Deseng 陳勵成 (b. 1942) and Ibu Ade (1936–2012). Tan Deseng, also known as Tan Déséng, Mohamad Deseng, or (according to the Hokkien pronunciation of his name) Tan Li Seng, was born into a large Bandung merchant family interested, but not professionally engaged, in the arts. As a child he watched *wayang golek* and *gamelan,* then learned the harmonica and was taught to play the flute and read music by a brother; another brother played Chinese instruments. His father intended that he go into business, but instead he dropped out of a local Chinese high school and dedicated himself to a career in Sundanese music.[42]

Tan is acknowledged as a "leader in the field of Sundanese music" (Ridwan 2010, 73). As a Sundanese musician, he has impeccable credentials, having learned from some of the region's most accomplished masters, including Ki Oyok and Mang Suarta, and especially *kacapi* with the master Adjat Sudrajat.[43] Before long he was performing in groups on the guitar, *kacapi,* and *suling,* in styles both traditional (*tembang Sunda Cianjuran*) and hybrid contemporary (including *ketuktilu* and *kliningan*). As an arranger, he adopted Sundanese music to Western instruments and arranged Sundanese songs in rumba, samba, or rock styles (Ridwan 2010, 78); as a performer, he devised a guitar tuning for Sundanese music (95).

With friends, Tan founded the *kacapi* group Bhakti Siliwangi,[44] and with it and other associated groups, he toured the West Java countryside for several years. He achieved local renown and was invited to collaborate with famous musicians including Titim Fatimah, Euis Komariah, and the *jaipongan* singer Tati Saleh, also working on the arrangement of music for the last's films. In 1970, he cofounded a recording studio, producing thousands of master tapes of Sundanese traditional music. He is known in cultural circles as a versatile performer as well as a composer of his own *kawih.*[45] He is thus distinguished by a long career at the heart of traditional Sundanese music, exhibiting a considerable range and virtuosity. In one musicological text, Tan takes a hard line on tradition in Sundanese music, considering that tuning scales, language, and structural elements "made Sundanese songs irreconcilable with international pop music" (Jurriëns 2004, 124).[46]

The cofounder of Pasundan, Ibu Ade, was not a professional musician, though she was a well-known performer in Chinese community circles, specializing on the *guzheng* 古筝 (a kind of zither).[47] Until her sudden death in 2012, she frequently performed at Chinese community events, attired in formal Sundanese dress (*kebaya Sunda,* a blouse worn with a dress, and distinguished from Javanese varieties by the collar). She first assumed a leadership role with Pasundan, forming a bridge between the Chinese associations and Tan, who had lost contact with formal Sino-Indonesian society during the New Order years. Reformasi having cleared the way, the opportunity appeared to create an organization that would represent an ethnic Chinese contribution to Sundanese arts.

In over a decade of activity, Pasundan has engaged in dance, instrumental, and vocal music, as well as theatre. Performing in Sundanese, Chinese, and mixed styles, its goal is explicitly stated as the promotion of a Sino-Sundanese identity and cultural exchange. Through the exertions of Ibu Ade, Pasundan managed to enlist a number of community organizations to support its efforts, with a 2004 newspaper advertisement listing Priangan, the Hakka and Cantonese associations, the Evergreen Foundation, Chinese-language radio, and several other individuals and organizations as its sponsors. More recently, the group also received support from ethnic Chinese parliamentarians. The principal audience has been Bandung locals, both Sundanese and Chinese, but Pasundan has also been engaged in refining Mainland Chinese understanding of Sino-Indonesians through performances in Guangdong, Shanghai, Nanjing, Beijing, and Kunming, stirring interest because members were "mostly Chinese, but they were promoting Sundanese culture" (*Shijie ribao,* May 4, 2004).

The performances are hybrid both in terms of context and content. For instance, a Malaysian Chinese blog, interviewing Pasundan chairman Liang Tze Hai 梁志海, describes Tan's artistic achievement as follows: "besides promoting traditional Sundanese music, Tan Deseng is adept at mixing Sundanese and Chinese music together, creating a new genre of artistic culture." Liang cites particularly the song "Pearl of the East" 東方之珠, which Tan orchestrated for Sundanese instruments and which "in Indonesian ears, feels so familiar, so easy to accept" (Zheng Zhaoxian 2008).[48] In one Pasundan performance, I saw the Chinese performers in Sundanese dance costumes transition from a Sundanese *jaipongan* recording to a Mandarin pop song without altering the manner of their dance, and Bandung academics report performances of *tembang sunda Cianjuran* (classical Sundanese accompanied songs) using the *guzheng* (Hermawan 2014, 83).

Fortunately, thanks to the efforts of Liang and Tan as well as the ongoing support of Bandung Chinese associations, Pasundan has survived the death of Ibu Ade. When the group was invited to perform in 2013 at the STSI Bandung (now ISBI Bandung), the premier post-secondary institution of the Sundanese arts, Tan explained the mission and artistic philosophy of the Pasundan group in between numbers. At the end of the three-hour show, the head of the arts institution, Endang Caturwati, praised the group's fused style as unique and invited

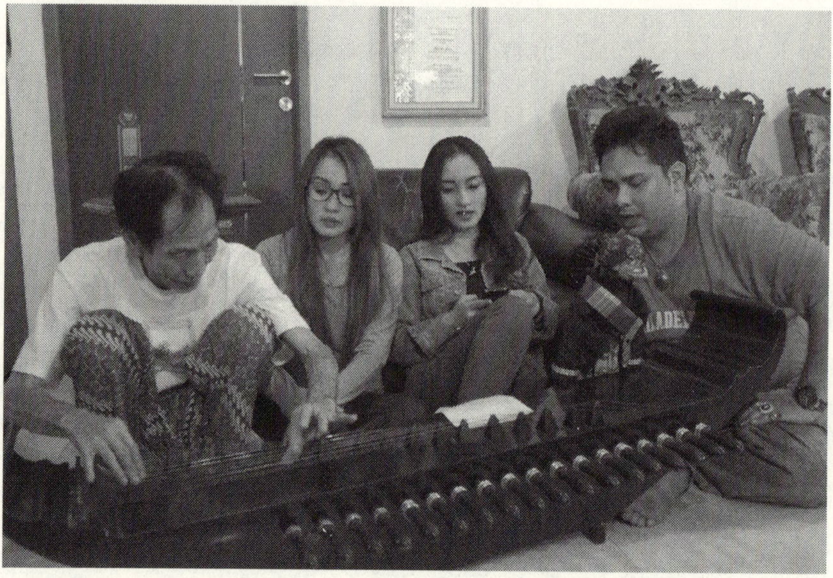

Tan Deseng (*left*) accompanies family members on the *kacapi* in a song of his composition; on the right is his grandson, a *dalang* in the *wayang golek* tradition. Photo courtesy of the editors of kebudayaanindonesia.net, a site of Indonesia's Ministry of Education and Culture. Copyright Ministry of Education and Culture and the General Directorate of Culture.

Tan to return soon. The local Chinese-language media reported her remarking that the students ought to be grateful to their ancestors for the richness of their musical heritage and stressed the importance of their carrying on the tradition. Inevitably, she also commented on the notability of a non-Sundanese person being so skillful and passionate about Sundanese tradition (*Guoji ribao*, May 2, 2013).

Articles about Tan show that the element of Chinese identity is inescapable in the reception of his practices and performances. Tan himself has always been resistant to the Chinese label, remarking, "If I am born in Indonesia, eat rice and drink water which comes from the mother earth, even father children in this country, and then I like Indonesian arts, especially Sundanese arts, may I not deepen my knowledge and even develop the values of Sundanese culture?" (Hermawan 2014, 83); and, in another interview, stated that, while "my physical traits show that I am of Chinese descent, my soul is truly Sundanese. I was born and get my daily bread in Sundanese lands" (*Kompas*, February 27, 2001, in Ridwan 2010, 81).

In his ambivalence towards the special status conveyed upon him as an ethnic exception, some of Tan's thinking and comments resemble New World discourses on minority, including a strong resistance to stereotypes or narratives that exclude the descendants of migrants from authenticity or indigeneity. On the other hand,

Tan cannot reject a communal Chinese identity, as the powerful organizational apparatus and financial support of West Java Chinese communities also provide many of his performance opportunities. This means that his career has been beset by a certain irony, in that his Chineseness has probably both helped and hindered him. Even positive Indonesian attention tends to engage him on the point of his Chineseness—Tan's first quote above is from an article about *pendatang* (immigrants), though his family has been in the region for over one hundred years. On the other hand, the article takes a step beyond the usual essentialism by referring to him as "a Sundanese artist of Chinese descent" (Hermawan 2014, 83), perhaps showing the influence of Western discourses of ethnicity and identity.

In my own 2013 conversation with him, Tan himself referred to the issue when he pointed out that, after a life spent in the Sundanese arts, he had not rated an entry in the *Ensiklopedi Sunda* (The Sunda Encyclopedia), though he had, on the other hand, been included in the *Tokoh-tokoh etnis Tionghoa di Indonesia* (Ethnic Chinese personalities of Indonesia). His ethnicity's double-edged sword—granting special attention while withdrawing authenticity—is felt in the last sentence of that profile: "People say that Deseng is more Sundanese than the Sundanese themselves" (Setyautama 2008, 348).

A Different Kind of Model Minority?

On the occasion of the Hakka Association's tenth anniversary, its honorary chairman Chen Fusheng 陳富聲, noted that the organization had "made an outstanding contribution for our fellow Hakka, for Chinese associations, for Indonesian society, winning glory for Bandung's Hakka" (Chen Fusheng 2010, 10). The current chairman, Wu Yuanchang 吳元昌, stated the goals of the organization as follows: "to be loyal to the Indonesian motherland, advance Hakka benevolence, strengthen economic contacts, boost culture and education, unity and mutual assistance, and collaborate for a general welfare" (Wu 2010, 8). Meanwhile, the group's choir sings the praises of its native city: "Bandung, city in our hearts / Your every liter of air / Is steeped in the fragrance of flowers" (Huang Yinggu 2010, 70).

The Association, like Pasundan and similar projects, like those of Hesheng Zhongyue tuan 和聲中樂團 (Harmony Chinese Music Troupe) or recent collaborations between *guzheng* player Fransisca Agustin and Daya Mahasiswa Sunda (Sundanese Student Power), demonstrate how Sino-Indonesians not only perform loyalty to Indonesia and to Indonesian culture but also pursue and adopt local identities. Performing local identities fosters closer ties with the local majority population with whom Sino-Indonesians interact and breaks down stereotypes about the alleged exclusivity of Chinese communities. Focusing on the Sundanese aspects of Sino-Indonesian cultural production encourages the Sundanese majority to accept the population as "local Chinese"; potentially, this makes the Bandung community seem less foreign than a more abstract national idea of the Chinese in Indonesia.

The regional, the immigrant, the ethnic, the discourses of origin, constitution, authenticity, nativeness, all are perpetually intertwined and performed, with loyalty shown equally to the Indonesian state and to Chinese language and culture. When Kota Kembang sings in Sundanese in Jakarta, or when Priangan hosts equinoctial rituals, or when a Hakka organization makes a donation to poor neighbors for Eid al-Fitr, the community is enacting the performance of a particular kind of minority—charitable, pious, cultured, friendly, both loyal to the Indonesian state and integrated into local culture. Though very different from the North American context, there is a way in which Sino-Indonesians, like a certain generation of Chinese in North America, have been concerned to represent themselves as a model minority—with the frustrations and constraints inherent in that role.

And yet, perhaps because the Sino-Indonesians protest their loyalty so consistently, it is evident that the image of the patriotic constituent ethnicity that Chinese associations attempt to project is still often translated in Indonesian writing, press, and society as one of intimate outsiders. This is the flip side of Pramoedya Ananta Toer's formulation regarding Chinese Indonesians: "Orang asing yang tidak asing" (Foreigners who are not foreign). There is no doubt that Pramoedya had the best of intentions in coining this phrase, which he used in his defense of Chinese Indonesians, *Hoakiau di Indonesia* (1960; Overseas Chinese in Indonesia). And yet, a "foreigner who is not foreign" does not by that token become a native. On the contrary, such a person risks remaining, to the unsympathetic eye or the overly categorical mind, merely a particular, a curious, even an inauthentic, kind of foreigner. This persistence of narrative strangerhood both dogs and motivates the public expressions of Sino-Indonesian identity.

CHAPTER 6

Deities on Parade

SINO-INDONESIAN RITUAL PERFORMANCE

It is the Lantern Festival, known in Indonesia as Cap Go Meh 十五暝,[1] Bandung, 2013; on a stage outside the host temple, playing to an audience occupying a few rows of temporary seating, students from the Sundanese dance program of STSI are performing *jaipongan*.[2] Next, Pop Sunda favorites are rendered by another student group before they transition into the Republican-era Chinese New Year standard "Congratulations" 恭喜恭喜, performed in Mandarin but infused with Sundanese rhythms.[3] Farther up Cibadak Road, the historical focal point of the Chinese neighborhood, vendors sell the contemporary icons of cultural China: plastic dragons with glowing eyes, marionette lions, mandarin clothes and caps for children, as well as the usual street foods (with a special emphasis on pork satay),[4] toys, and clothes, while karaoke stalls blare Chinese pop songs subtitled in Indonesian-Mandarin romanization.[5] Up the street, a group of little girls in *qipao* are being judged for a beauty contest.[6] Meanwhile, inside the temple, accessible only to lanyard-wearing temple members and participating delegations, the statues of the visiting gods are being presented on cushions to the temple leaders and to the host gods, accompanied by ceremonial gong strikes and obeisances made, incense in hand.

When the parade begins, it does not look like Lantern Festival in any other Indonesian region, or for that matter any other part of the world: the procession is led by a variety of Sundanese performance groups. These included stilt-walkers (*egrang*) from Karawang, *kuda renggong*,[7] and *sisingaan*,[8] as well as a marching brass band, broadly in the Western style.[9] Two dozen or so members of the Batalyon Kaveleri 4, a Bandung-based cavalry battalion of the Indonesian Army, follow close behind.[10] Dressed in clothing meant to evoke classical China, they wear the tasseled hats of Qing officials, with "soldier" 兵 *bing* inscribed on the backs of their shirts.[11] A sea of Indonesian flags in their hands, the soldiers precede

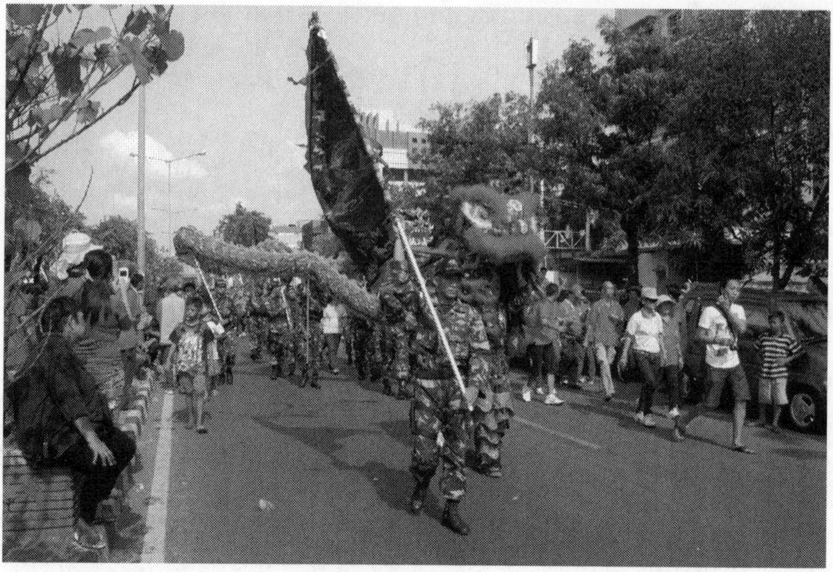

Fat Cu Kung procession in Jakarta, 2012. Photo courtesy of Kristyna Cilkova.

the Sino-Indonesian temple delegations with their palanquins (*joli*), *barongsay*, drums, and gongs. Altogether, the temple delegations number over five thousand people representing fifty-seven temples, all but a few from Java (*Pikiran Rakyat*, March 3, 2013).

The presence of Sundanese performance highlights the local character of the celebration and the attention the temple pays to the way it is perceived by the state as well as by the broader society in Bandung, yet transnational Chinese networks are also visible. One prominent example of this is the "Electric Techno Neon God" 電音三太子 troupe from the southern Taiwanese city of Tainan,[12] which, though strangely at odds with the largely "traditional" character of the procession, proves popular with fellow participants and audience. Their presence seems important to many temple members, too, for several express gladness at this group's participation on the grounds that it symbolizes the connection to a homeland most of them have never seen. Linguistically, things are a struggle: the Taiwanese performers, speakers of Hokkien and Mandarin, have to communicate with most temple officials in simple English, given that the overwhelming majority of Bandung temple members speak no Chinese language, though they are fluent in both Indonesian and Sundanese.[13]

While the Electric Techno Neon God could only be a product of our times, the celebration of Cap Go Meh itself boasts a venerable pedigree in Indonesia. Well over a century and a half ago, in the colonial Indies, the same Chinese festival was already a major part of the colony's calendar. Aquasi Boachi, the remarkable Ashanti prince who became an engineer in the Dutch colonial service, wrote the following in 1855:

> 12th of February. Tjap-Go-meh (Joy Festival) called Tepekkonn[14] by the Javanese. This festival is celebrated in different ways. In some large cities, the children of the distinguished and affluent are drawn in pretty, endearing, richly decorated little carts by people through the alleys, accompanied by a numberless wealth of candles and bright, beautifully colored lanterns and some music, to singing and clangor and terrible drumming on the *gemmbreng* [gong]. Thousands of rockets and fireworks are set off. In other places all manner of sea monsters (sea snakes, horrible fish, etc.), ships and groups of people and animals etc. of different sizes are made out of colored paper and borne on scaffolds to display throughout the city. These scaffolds are illuminated by thousands of candles and multicolored lanterns, and the bands and the cymbals pass by them, making a deafening music. Thousands and thousands of rockets and fireworks are set off, and, combined with the shouting and rejoicings of the people, they make a cannon-like din. Distinguished and base people move through the streets or gather on the balconies of Chinese houses to watch this strange procession. The Chinese houses are open, and Europeans as well as inlanders [i.e., Javanese] are allowed freely in and served with tea, arak, beer, and baked goods at no cost. (Boachi 1856, 295–296)

Other mid-nineteenth-century colonial sources, including almanacs and newspaper articles, confirm that Cap Go Meh was a central festival for the Chinese of the Indies at that time (e.g., Chen Menghong 2009, 70), and, according to Boachi, Chinese communities on Java defrayed the expenses communally (Boachi 1856, 296).[15] The (presumably Chinese) author of a 1871 *syair*[16] in honor of Siam's King Chulalangkorn wrote that "in this year there are two Cap Go Meh," flattering the royal youth by comparing his visit to the year's biggest festival (Salmon and Lombard 1981, 134).[17] Cap Go Meh was popular among colonial Chinese and non-Chinese inhabitants alike, with festivities involving *wayang potehi, wayang kulit,* and *wayang klitik,* not to mention dancing (Kartomi 2000, 284–285; Pausacker 2005, 187–188; Matthew Isaac Cohen 2006, 37–38; 160). Reports from the late nineteenth-century Malay-language press show that Eurasian-, Malay-, and Arab-inflected performances were included alongside those by Chinese groups (Abeyasekere 1983, 25).

Dutch-language newspapers reported on the festival on a regular basis throughout the colonial period, even if accounts until the late nineteenth century could, on religious grounds, be censorious (e.g., *Bataviaasch Handelsblad*, January

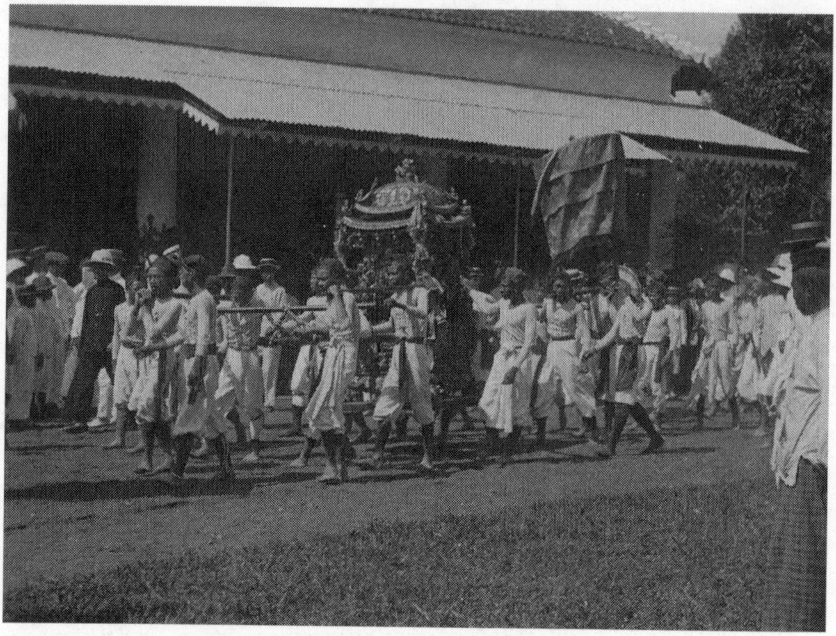

Late colonial Cap Go Meh procession, probably in Malang. Photo by Neville Keasberry (1866–1940). Courtesy of the Rijksmuseum, Amsterdam.

29, 1862). In the twentieth century, the festival served as the inspiration for at least two of Indonesia's highest-regarded modern painters, Basuki Resobowo and Sudjojono, and the festivities provided the premise for Kwee Tek Hoay's 1930 comic play *Nonton Tjapgome* (Watching Cap Go Meh).[18] It is clear that there are certain elements of continuity between the colonial period and the early twenty-first century: the festival's importance, its communal spirit, and its cross-ethnic audience, for instance.

But there are limits to the similarities. Like all other forms of visible Sino-Indonesian culture, public Cap Go Meh festivities were officially banned under New Order, a proscription followed especially strictly on Java. Its reemergence in the current Reformasi period is credited to the openness of the Gus Dur presidency and is usually cited as part of the revival of public Chinese culture in Indonesia alongside other festivals such as Imlek and Qing Ming (Ceng Beng) as well as iconic practices such as *barongsay* (Heidhues 2006, 90; Aizawa 2010, 48). In many ways, now Cap Go Meh is a peculiarly Sino-Indonesian event, with its own foods, practices, and beliefs.[19] Today, important events to mark the holiday occur across the archipelago from Palembang and Bangka to Manado (e.g., Taal 2002, 189–190; Jacobsen 2006, 82). By contrast, for many Mainland Chinese today, Lantern Festival is minimally important; nor does it feature prominently in the communal lives of Chinese communities in North America, Europe, or Australasia.[20]

The rise, fall, and reemergence of Chinese temple festivals linked to the lunisolar calendar as an element of recognized Indonesian life mirror the metamorphosis undergone by the Sino-Indonesian community more generally. The celebrations in the colonial period were the organic expression of a community that perceived itself and was categorized by the colonial authorities as alien, while one way of reading contemporary celebrations is as performances to celebrate Chinese identity as a component of the local culture and of the Indonesian state. Moreover, despite the triumphant narrative of a post-Suharto cultural revival that surrounds reports on Sino-Indonesian temple festivities, these celebrations are also sites of tension between Chinese communities, non-Chinese Indonesians, and the state. This chapter will examine Chinese temple celebrations in two locations (Bandung and Singkawang) in order to show these ritual expressions in public spaces as a crucial part of the ongoing Sino-Indonesian negotiation of identity.

International Connections and Rituals Revived

Though neither the oldest nor the largest Chinese temple in Bandung, Vihara Dharma Ramsi (VDR) 靈光寺 is at present the most public, open, and active of local Chinese Tridharma organizations.[21] Its role as host for the most visible Chinese festival in West Java, the Cap Go Meh festival and procession, has increased its prominence and prestige. Established in 1952, VDR's founders were Daoists arriving from the Guangdong area of Meizhou 梅州, a core Hakka region. Though temple officers themselves are uncertain of the details, the founders likely arrived from Lingguang Temple on Meizhou's Yinna Mountain 陰那山; in any event, the Meizhou temple, which shares the same Chinese name, is considered its mother temple. Guan Gong 關公 is the temple's principal deity, but the temple is distinguished by its prominent observance of the cult of the ninth-century Fujian monk Pan Liaoquan 潘了拳, also known as the Ashamed Patriarch 慚愧祖師.[22] This cult, which is not common in Indonesia, highlights the origins of the temple's founders, as Pan established the mother temple in a core Hakka area.[23] By lineage, the temple is thus clearly Hakka, much like some of the prominent Bandung community organizations described in the previous chapter.

However, as in the nonreligious voluntary associations, Chinese regional and dialect identities have coalesced over the last half-century and been replaced with a pan-Chinese (or Sino-Indonesian) identity.[24] Although Meizhou Hakka members still are an important factor in VDR leadership and membership, respondents agreed that the congregation is no longer split along the various Chinese subethnicity lines present in Bandung: Hakka, Hokkien, Hokchia, and

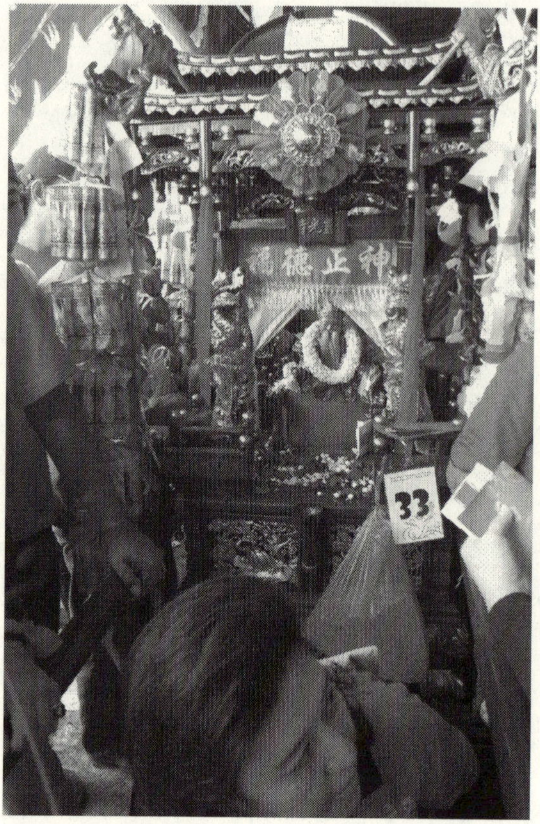

Fude Zhengshen, representing the Bandung temple Vihara Dharma Ramsi, prepared for the Fat Cu Kung procession in Jakarta, 2012. Photo courtesy of Kristyna Cilkova.

Cantonese groups. Members of all these origins are represented in the VDR congregation, and the thoroughgoing erasure of Hokkien and Hakka language among people under the age of sixty means that dialect is used only rarely at VDR events.[25] The once vivid intra-Chinese divisions, whether Hakka/Hokkien or *totok*/Peranakan, are not live distinctions for most congregants.

The revival of VDR since Reformasi is closely connected to both national and transnational networks, in part because many practices were not directly transmitted within the congregation following the New Order's prohibitions. Consequently, practices have been recently transferred from elsewhere, sometimes further evolving to suit the needs of the community. For instance, one of the temple's *locu* 爐主 (ritual leaders and incense masters) received training in Singapore. Another temple officiant is a local who speaks little Chinese but reads the prayers (from phonetic transcriptions) in Hakka; he is assisted by a monk, originally from Jakarta, who studied scripture and practice in Guangdong. Sino-Indonesians from Central Java who have migrated from smaller centers to

Bandung for economic reasons have been crucial in establishing and developing ritual practice, with the result that VDR's public activities have become substantially revitalized through the influence and assistance of Tek Hay Kiong 澤海宮, a very active Tegal temple.[26] Networks allow for a great deal of mutual assistance between temple members, who travel to attend each others' events, share resources, offer billets to one another, and donate funds to construct new temples or expand existing ones (see also Hauser-Schäublin 2014, 103–104).

Sino-Indonesian temple members have also been sending members abroad for conferences for over a decade (Hoon 2011a, 55); VDR members made use of new connections to Taiwan to take a delegation of over ninety people to Taiwan in August 2013 for a Buddhist meeting (*Yinni shangbao*, September 14, 2013).[27] The anthropologist Brigitta Hauser-Schäublin reports that some Sino-Balinese groups have commissioned and imported furniture and *kimsin* 金身, the ensouled statues of divinities, from Mainland China (2014, 105).[28] In recent years, officials from Meizhou have visited VDR twice, and a temple group from Bandung has arranged tours to visit Lingguang Temple in Meizhou, with tourist information for potential pilgrims readily available within the VDR. There can thus be no doubt that one of the effects of Reformasi has been to reestablish temple networks with southern China and Taiwan.

The current practice of religious rituals and festivals must therefore be understood as a revival enabled not only by the relative liberality of this period of Indonesian ethnic politics but also by the ensuing revitalization of national and transnational Chinese connections. In every detail, temples are establishing their rituals and their festivals through a combination of local memory, input from other Sino-Indonesian temples, and influence from both other locations in the international diaspora and from a diversity of possible Chinese homelands.

Institutionalized Religion as a Producer of Chineseness

To understand how and why religious organizations express ethnic identity, it is necessary to return to the issue of how Chinese religions are organized in Indonesia. There, temple ritual is one area in which "Chineseness" is the distinguishing element of both a religious and an ethnic minority.[29] It is, moreover, a community whose public presence has in recent history been monitored and curbed, and whose public activities continue to attract scrutiny. For this reason, rites and religious festivals are today among the most powerful ways in which Chinese communities perform identity for the larger society, not least because Chinese festivals are more easily accessible to the public than community-hall events or ticketed theatre performances. Like all other aspects of Sino-Indonesian lives, religion and ritual have a complex relationship to "Chineseness" as conceived elsewhere in the Chinese world, and the public events of Chinese religious organizations are therefore a way for the congregation members to perform Sino-Indonesian identity for each other, the general Indonesian population, officialdom, and the global Chinese diaspora.

Chinese religion and belief systems present a formidable academic corpus in Chinese, other Asian, and Western languages. The religious makeup of Chinese in Indonesia diverges considerably from that of other Chinese communities, both in its formal grouping of various Chinese practices under "Buddhism" and in its relatively large proportion of Catholics, Protestants, and Muslims. Its religious profile is also highly distinct from those of other ethnic groups in Indonesia.[30] Since the minority is in a position of performance vis-à-vis the dominant majority, Sino-Indonesian temple events must negotiate an ethnic Chinese identity within the Indonesian polity.

At the same time, and as the description of the Bandung Cap Go Meh procession should make clear, the content of religious events is locally Sundanese as well as "Chinese." Political, social, cultural, and economic processes have caused substantial divergence between religious practices in southern China, Taiwan, and Southeast Asia, and the religious practices of Overseas Chinese communities such as the Sino-Indonesians must not be modelled as deviating from a norm established and maintained in a motherland. Rather, the various evolutions of such practices should be respected in their own subjectivity—that is, on their own terms—and not as deficient vis-à-vis the politically endorsed "authenticity" of Chinese ritual elsewhere. The increasing convenience of both real-life and mediated interaction with Chinese communities elsewhere influences the further development of Sino-Indonesian religious life and contributes to a process that one might consider another re-sinicization[31]—that is, a renewal of ties to a perceived Chinese "center."[32] This development can be seen as a religious counterpart to the linguistic and social re-sinicization projects under way that originate from the PRC itself, all of which can be linked to China's increasing economic and political importance.[33] The possibility of reading re-sinicization as a move away from loyalty to the Indonesian state or identity also generates tension in the community and controversy surrounding use of this terminology in academic discourse.

For many Indonesians, the temples are "the bastion of Chinese culture" (Suryadinata 2004, 129), and for many Sino-Indonesians temple life can also, as one Tridharma official declared, "awaken their identification and feelings with their own people and motherland" (Tsai Tsung-te 2015, 88). This purported association with "China-centrism" can be a liability (Coppel 1983, 107). Chinese temples have been recognized as playing a role of maintaining Chinese identity throughout the Suharto years, when religious activity provided one of the few legitimate arenas for its expression (Hoon 2009a, 91).[34] As noted in chapter 1, it is probable that the Sino-Javanese puppet theatre *wayang potehi*, for instance, would have disappeared had it not been legitimized as a temple-bound religious practice.[35]

Who and what is performed during such events has been substantially dictated by government policy towards religion. For one thing, ritual performance is usually sponsored by Chinese institutions with the express permission and, increasingly, the approval or support of local authorities. Since New Order, the Indonesian state has presumed to register the religion of all its citizens, partly "to prevent the re-emergence of Communism" (Hoon 2011a, 43). This was deemed "especially necessary" for Chinese Indonesians, given the historic suspicion that Sino-Indonesians are sympathetic to communism and therefore atheism (Ong 2008, 97). In the words of anthropologist Lyn Parker, the constitution "guarantees religious freedom but not the freedom not to be religious" (Parker 2010). The parameters of Indonesian religious policy, especially the official requirement of identifying a religion on identity cards, has created a great many paper Catholics and Protestants on the one hand[36] and generated a strain of monotheistic Daoism and Buddhism on the other.[37] In recent years, it has also made Indonesia one of the only places in the world where one meets people who self-identify as Confucians.[38] Adherents of Sino-Indonesian temples, however, are usually registered as "Buddhist," even if the actual deities they are dedicated to are predominantly Daoist.[39] In contrast, traditional Chinese religions in Mainland China and Taiwan have no formally defined congregation or membership, no dogmatic doctrine, typically no sharp delineations of cults or practices, or any prohibition against mixing religions. Han Chinese faithful in Mainland China need not as a rule be concerned with how their practices might define ethnicity or perform identity for a general public.[40]

The more formal organization of Sino-Indonesian religion has its roots in the colonial period a century earlier. Confucianism in the colony was formally founded as a religion in 1918 (Suryadinata 2005b, 79), and during the 1930s certain Indies Chinese intellectuals began to push for ideological reform of Chinese religions, combining Confucianism, Daoism, and Buddhism to form a religion called San Kauw 三教 (the Three Teachings), later known by its Indonesian name of Tridharma. The movement, which also incorporated aspects of Peranakan Chinese culture and had some monotheistic traits, was, at least in part, an attempt to secure the Chinese identity of Indies Chinese and ran parallel to the foundation of Chinese schools and other organs of Chinese nationalism.

New Order provided a new impetus for temples to organize in a way that showed "that their religion was compatible with *Panca Sila*," one aspect of which was monotheism, in order to "demonstrate their commitment to the Indonesian state" (Iem Brown 1987, 108). During the Suharto years all aspects of an explicit Chinese identity were under threat, but, likely because the Suharto regime felt that "Buddhism was more Indonesian than Confucianism" (Suryadinata 2005b,

83),[41] various practices were subsumed under the Buddhist category, including Tridharma. Certain temples felt that only joining Tridharma organizations would prevent their closure (Tsuda 2012, 392). Tridharma's explicit embrace of Pancasila can be taken as an example of how some Chinese organizations have "presented them as committed to a nationalist vision" (Ramage 1995, 114).

Furthermore, from 1965 to 1978, Confucianism was deregistered as a religion (Suryadinata 2005b, 79–83), meaning that most adherents were registered as Buddhists (Iem Brown 1987, 117n27). "Buddhism" has in this way become an umbrella term for Sino-Indonesian religious practices, although the use of "Tridharma" in the names of its principal associations underlines the syncretic history and practice of "Buddhism" in Indonesia. In the 1980s, perhaps dissatisfied with the overt Chinese identity of temples, the Suharto regime attempted to further convert Chinese temples, usually known as *klenteng*, into *vihara*, which were supposed to stress the practices, iconography, and Indian origins of Buddhism (Suryadinata 2005b, 83–85). The transition was, however, often nominal (Suryadinata 2014, 32–33), and many *klenteng* are only formally known as *vihara* (at least in Indonesian).[42]

The process of registering citizens by religion and collecting the diverse beliefs of Sino-Indonesian temples under one single category cemented the connection between temple activity and Chinese identity and made temples the principal sites for expressions of Chinese culture under New Order. Indeed, one of the attractions of belonging to Tridharma is that it provides structure for the Sino-Indonesian community, as the "organisation unites Chinese, regardless of their social standing, throughout Indonesia and especially their temples, or *klenteng* or *bio*"[43] (Hauser-Schäublin 2014, 103). It is thus the authority of the Indonesian state that, by providing a single legitimate category for beliefs originating from China, associates temple activity with Chinese identity and permits the celebration of Chinese rituals and festivals such as Cap Go Meh. Though this categorization essentially assembles all Chinese practices under "Buddhism," the (now somewhat relaxed) imposition of Indic terminology such as *vihara* simultaneously delegitimizes (and effaces) Chineseness (see Suryadinata 2005b).

Although Reformasi and especially the initiatives of Gus Dur to abolish anti-Chinese legislation can be credited in a general way for the reemergence of Chinese festivals in Indonesia, the specific local revival of any particular festival is to be sought in the interaction between local officialdom and the Chinese religious communities. At the very least, permission must be sought and granted for parades, and the police must assure security. The Cap Go Meh festival is organized by VDR, but it is represented as an organic expression of Chinese belief or tradition; its contemporary revival was not originally the result of a temple initiative. According to temple officials, the impetus for the festival arose around 2010 when Dada Rosada (mayor of Bandung 2003–2013), meeting with members of the Chinese organizations, asked why none of them had ever applied to hold the Cap Go Meh parade. Rosada mentioned that even small places in West Java such as Cianjur and Sukabumi had revived the festival and wondered why the provincial capital, Bandung, was lagging behind? The VDR chairman thereupon took it upon himself to organize the temple congregation, muster support from the other Chinese organizations, and prepare the application for the festivity, which was duly accepted.[44]

Official support remained visible through the 2013 festival, which I attended, with posters of Dada Rosada and his wife featured on advertisements for the "Cibadak Street cultural festival." This naming omitted direct mention of Cap Go Meh, although it continued to be called so by VDR members, non-Chinese spectators, and the media.[45] After the morning events, including prayers and the arrival of several sedan chairs from other temples, Mayor Rosada and his wife visited the temple. Inside, Rosada donned the red VDR polo shirt worn by members and volunteers. Then, remarking that "the Cap Go Meh festival indicates that culture can forge unity and cohesion between the *pribumi* people and the Tionghoa [i.e., Sino-Indonesian] people" (*Pikiran Rakyat,* March 3, 2013), he went on to praise the event as emblematic of Bandung's cultural diversity, stressed the Sundanese elements of the parade, and defined Bandung as a home for both Muslims and non-Muslims. Meanwhile, the local press celebrated the event, remarking that "Hopefully this celebration will be continued. Because in that way, culture in the city of Bandung will become more and more diverse" (*Galamedia,* March 3, 2013).

Despite the success of the celebrations and the official support for Cap Go Meh in 2013, in the days following there was some anxiety for the future. Parliamentary elections were to be held in April 2014, presidential elections in July 2014, and the late calendrical date for Cap Go Meh that year, March 5, meant that the celebrations would not be held the following year in order not to raise tensions during an election period. Furthermore, Dada Rosada was nearing the end of his term,[46] and neither the identity nor the attitude of the new mayor was known.

In retrospect, these fears seem to have been unfounded, for the new mayor, Ridwan Kamil, opened the event in 2015, again putting on the same red polo temple shirt. According to media reports, the size of the event was comparable to that of 2013, and new Bandung temples have joined in the organizational efforts. All in all, the one-year hiatus seems to have done no harm, and if anything the public space permitted to Chinese celebrations has expanded. That the hiatus was deemed necessary, however, and the sense that the festival is dependent on the goodwill of local leadership, points to the dependence of Chinese public expression on the friendliness of the local authority and the lingering uncertainty of Sino-Indonesian public expression.

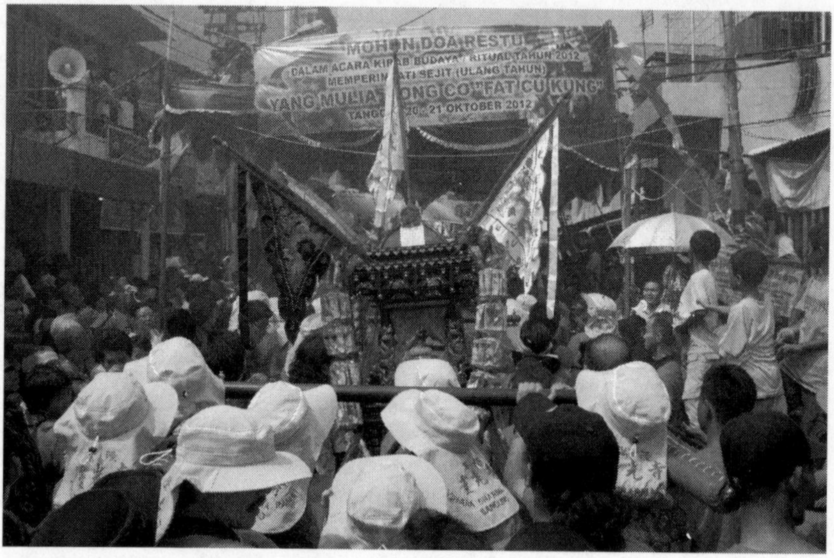

Fat Cu Kung procession in Jakarta, 2012. Photo courtesy of Kristyna Cilkova.

Returning the Visit: VDR in Jakarta

It is the birthday of Fat Cu Kung,[47] October 21, 2012, in Glodok, Jakarta's Chinatown. Just as VDR welcomes temple delegations from throughout Java to Bandung, it too sends delegations to allied temples throughout Java. Now, members of VDR are passing through the narrow roads of this neighborhood before issuing onto the wider major streets, taking turns carrying the palanquin that holds a VDR *kimsin*. As far as I can see ahead or behind, other palanquins, drummers, dancers, and *ondel-ondel* are parading. Over the ten kilometer route, vehicle traffic has been stopped and crowds line the streets. Throughout these four hours, members of the public approach us to slip red envelopes into the wads of golden sacrificial money that fixed the god's position, to bow to the palanquin, dance, take photos with temple members, or, in symbolic participation, to shoulder the palanquin for a short time.

The average age of temple members must be somewhere around sixty. As they tire, their places carrying the palanquins are taken by the Sundanese young men and adolescents who live near VDR. Many of these are also members of the temple's dragon and lion dance teams and are frequently hired for temple events in Bandung and for trips. As the day wears on, even these younger men sometimes have to balance the palanquin on a small wooden bench carried along for this purpose. On the other hand, sometimes the palanquin purposely lags behind in order to create a gap with the palanquin ahead so the carriers can execute a short, exhilarating sprint. Behind the palanquin is a small set of gongs on a wagon with a drum on the side, played alternately by temple members and the Sundanese adolescents, providing the varying rhythm of the march. At one point, the delegation sings "Halo, Halo Bandung," a song commemorating the heroic spirit of Bandung during the Indonesian National Revolution and a moment of civic pride in the midst of a Chinese religious procession.[48] The networks to which the temple belongs are always apparent: as the route passes by or near other Glodok temples with which VDR maintains good relations, among them Jakarta's historic Kim Tek Ie 金德院 (Indonesian name: Vihara Dharma Bhakti) temple,[49] the palanquin is raised while members of the friendly temple, waiting to greet the VDR delegation, cheer.

The host of this October 2012 festival was Bio Fat Cu Kung 法主公廟, a temple located in Glodok and described by one anthropologist as "really just the cramped front room of a private residence at the end of a cul-de-sac" (Chan 2010). The Fat Cu Kung festival is a recent revival, and 2012 was the first time VDR had participated. The festival schedule called for visiting temples to arrive in the morning, eat lunch, and set up in a covered space near the temple to prepare the palanquins.[50] Leaving early in the morning, the VDR had travelled from Bandung to Jakarta by bus and returned to Bandung in the evening after the procession (*kirab*) concluded.[51] The VDR deity, who had been driven in from Bandung in a special car the day before, spent the night in the host temple. In this case, VDR's representative[52] was the Earth God, Fude Zhengshen 福德正神.[53]

While the palanquins were being readied, small *kimsin* arrived, accompanied by the ceremonious striking of gongs. Their progress narrated by loudspeaker, temple leaders brought in the sculpture of the deity through noisily enthusiastic crowds (largely, though far from entirely, Sino-Indonesian). Security guards were busy keeping back those who tried to force themselves forward, intent on touching the *kimsin*'s clothing as the deity passed by. After the Earth God had been presented to the host deity, Fat Cu Kung, he was brought to the palanquin and secured in place with wads of sacrificial money so that, when the palanquin swayed violently back and forth in the procession, he would not come loose.[54] As all the other teams went about the same work, the small crowded space, normally a parking lot, filled with incense smoke and busy temple faithful.

During the presentation of the visiting deities to Fat Cu Gong, the Sino-Indonesian politician Ahok,[55] then vice-governor of Jakarta, appeared. Amid a barrage of cheers and photographs, the crowd swelled forward with the same desire to touch his clothing as had been apparent with regard to the *kimsin*. The festival occurred less than one month after Ahok's successful candidacy as running mate to then governor-elect Joko Widodo, and posters of both men's faces were ubiquitous in Glodok.[56] Newer posters also contained messages expressing the politicians' good wishes for success for the festival. Television reports of the festival that evening would focus largely on Ahok's visit to the parade, stressing his position as the most prominent Sino-Indonesian politician.[57] It was clearly an emotional moment for many of the parade participants, not least because some political opponents had attempted to use Ahok's ethnicity against the ticket (Suaedy 2014, 115–116).[58] Ahok's appearance at an overtly Chinese public event seemed to indicate that such celebrations would henceforth be not only tolerated but endorsed by local government. No one foresaw that within five years Ahok would become governor, then be imprisoned for blasphemy.

Temple Events and the Public Face of Chinese Identity

Regular ritual events are a baseline of community interaction and identity performance. A key activity for VDR is participation in a growing network of religious processions (*kirab*). Parades are typically held on the occasion of a festival celebrating the birthday or ascension of the temple's principal deity. Various temples allied to the host temple send teams by bus, car, or airplane, bearing sculptures of their deities on a palanquin. *Kirab,* referred to as *xunyou* 巡遊 or *youshen* 遊神 in Chinese, has its origins in the practices of Hokkien and Hakka temples. Such practices have experienced a revival in Fujian since the 1980s (Dean 1993, 1998), and have never stopped being a feature of Chinese festivals in Taiwan, Malaysia, and Singapore (Boretz 2003).

In Indonesia, the network of parades has reemerged and undergone sustained expansion since the end of the New Order era. In 2012, VDR, by no means the most active of such temples, sent palanquins to *kirab* in Jakarta, in the Central Javanese localities of Kudus, Welahan (although there they only observed ritual, as the area was flooded), Semarang, Cilacap, and Tegal. In 2013, the nearby West Java town of Ciamis was added to their itinerary, which in 2012 had been cancelled, due reportedly to opposition from the local branch of the Front Pembela Islam (Islamic Defenders' Front).[59] Another local *kirab,* in Indramayu, cannot usually be attended, as their festival also honors Zehai Zhenren 澤海真人 and the schedule thus conflicts with the large *kirab* in Tegal, to which they are committed. Similarly, attendance is not possible at Sukabumi or Purwokerto, given that their *kirab* falls very close to VDR's own major annual event, the Cap Go Meh festival.

Relations with the majority population is a constant consideration for Sino-Indonesian temples. As the preceding chapter on community performance demonstrated, the Chinese community in Bandung is substantially affiliated to Sundanese language and identity. Since the temple is a considerable physical presence in the predominantly Sundanese Cibadak neighborhood,[60] it plays a role in how Sino-Indonesians are perceived by non-Chinese locals.[61] In the densely populated urban landscape of Bandung, the twice-monthly communal prayers are visible to passersby and audible to neighbors. After the completion of regular rituals, vendors often gather outside the temple grounds to derive business from the crowd as they exit. Less regular rituals, such as "life release" *fangsheng* 放生 (a Buddhist practice that consists of the freeing of captive doves in the temple courtyard), are also certain to be observed by neighbors. The temple is a hub of economic activities in the vicinity, with its ongoing production of its own devotional materials such as sacrificial money and its patronage of the maker of devotional paper materials next door. Planned expansion of the temple means that liaison with neighborhood groups is imperative.[62] Temple activity is thus a major way in which neighbors, local officials, visitors from elsewhere in the Chinese world, and potential congregants will construct their ideas of the local Chinese community.

The ritual year at VDR is marked by regular public events. Following the lunisolar Chinese calendar, evening observations and joint prayers are held on the first and fifteenth of every month, as well as volunteer-prepared food and general socializing on the following morning.[63] During joint prayers, the congregation, convoked by a gong, performs three obeisances: first, it kneels and kowtows towards the outside, then to the Ashamed Patriarch, and finally to Guan Gong as the temple's principal deity. Wine and meat are offered by leaders of the congregation to the deities, and all members of the congregation burn three sticks of incense at each prayer. Gongs, prayers, and socializing are audible from the street and from neighboring houses; passersby and vendors are certain to see elements of both the ritual and the social events.

Besides events, temple-produced objects, visible both in the temple and in congregants' homes and businesses, also act as mediations of the Sino-Indonesian identity promoted by the temple. A major example is the annual calendar issued by the temple, hanging in many Bandung Chinese homes and businesses, which provides another concrete example of how the temple shapes its public image. Other Chinese holidays, observed with special gatherings at the temple, are indicated, as are national holidays, whether Muslim, Christian, Hindu, or patriotic. The calendar's pages feature the Western months most prominently, but, like most others calendars in Indonesia, it includes, besides the Chinese reckoning, also the Javanese days of the week, as well as the date according to Javanese and Arab systems.[64] Chinese-owned or -affiliated organizations and companies project their support of the temple in the pages of the calendar through advertisements: these include a local, largely Chinese, Hash House Harrier[65] club as well as footwear, electronics, and furniture companies, not to mention bookstores, travel agencies, and bakeries. With their profoundly heterogeneous system, incorporating pre-Muslim Indonesian, Muslim Arab, Western Christian, and Chinese reckonings, these objects, hanging in the congregants' businesses, homes, and various community associations, signal the integration of the Chinese community, faith networks, and sponsors into the society, as well as the claim of the Chinese to be indigenous and constituent to Indonesia.

Another highly visible point of interaction with, and representation towards, the non-Chinese community is VDR's *barongsay* team. *Barongsay*, the Indonesian term for the Chinese lion dance, is one of the iconic performances of Chineseness in diaspora. Its popularity today makes it a product "of mass consumption in post-Suharto Indonesia" (Hoon 2009a, 90). The heavy migration of southern coastal Chinese populations has meant that specific regional practices such as *barongsay* have come to stand in for the entirety of China abroad, even though they have been (until recently) unfamiliar in many parts of China.[66] *Barong*, the emblematic Balinese lion dance, is reckoned by some as part of the same family (Bandem and deBoer 1981, 119–120), although that there is a historical relationship is doubtful.

Despite its ubiquitous practice throughout the late colonial period and its ritual purposes, the *barongsay* lion dance, along with other Chinese performance styles, was officially suppressed during the New Order period.[67] At the beginning of the Reformasi period, the reappearance of *barongsay* performances for Imlek in 1999 was reported in the newspapers and on television, signalling the shift in the political climate. Since then, *barongsay* has reemerged as a common feature of the Indonesian urban environment, and larger cities such as Bandung now have several *barongsay* troupes, in loose competition with one another. It has also featured prominently in revivals of Chinese culture in Bali and Sumatra (Sooi-Beng Tan 2007, 70–72; Hauser-Schäublin 2014, 99). As with Cap Go Meh celebrations, *barongsay* is today being deployed to represent Chineseness as well as the Sino-Indonesian contribution to Indonesian culture.[68] Economically, it is perhaps justifiable to regard its new ubiquity as part of "the pervasive commodification of Chineseness" (Sai and Hoon 2013, 15) and the reduction of the complexities of Chinese regional practice to a few standardized icons.

The VDR *barongsay* troupe is under the leadership of Eric Mintardja (Liem Ming Tjiang), whom I interviewed on several occasions in 2012 and 2013 in order to understand the role of *barongsay* in the temple's interactions with its neighbors. At the time a youthful seventy-year-old, he was born in Bandung of Hokchia descent and has been participating in the temple since the beginning of Reformasi. Mintardja, whose responsibilities at the temple involve working with the local neighborhood association and the administrative community group (*rukun warga*), explains his volunteering for the temple as a result of his concern for neighborhood youth. The most fulfilling feature of this work for him is as a *barongsay* and dragon-dance teacher for local Sundanese children.[69] Mintardja believes that his work integrates the temple more into the life of the neighborhood than do other temples in Bandung and is thus less likely to cause resentment among non-Chinese populations.

Consequently, unlike *barongsay* such as those run by some Bandung Chinese restaurants, the temple does not run its *barongsay* for profit. Another result of consideration for local feeling is that Mintardja's team does not perform riskier tricks that other groups execute for higher fees.[70] As the local Sundanese children are paid for the performance, there is also a financial incentive for Sundanese families, while *barongsay* activities also grant the temple substantial positive coverage in the press. A 2015 example praises Mintardja and VDR for fostering Sundanese youth practically and spiritually while keeping them out of trouble (*Suaka-Online*, February 9, 2015). However, inevitably, the relationship also involves managing moderate friction with neighbors and parents. On one disappointing occasion, a talented child in whom the temple group had invested considerable time and energy was prevented from continuing with the VDR *barongsay* because, late in the day, his father objected on religious grounds to his son's participation with a temple organization.

At present, while *barongsay* performance is an active way of representing the temple to the local population in positive ways, such as being hired for weddings, business openings, and private events, its ritual meaning has probably been occluded for most audience members. Only for the elders does the dancing still have the principal purpose of dispelling bad fortune as it did in their youth, when they might have been called to perform at intersections where there had been collisions or at factories where accidents had taken place. For them, *barongsay* is a means of correcting cosmic imbalances and preventing disasters, whereas younger members are more likely to consider it the embodiment of local identity or a Chinese entertainment intended to project a particular way of being Chinese—integrated, colorful, festive—for a broader audience.[71] This shift from ritual performance to political, economic, and social relationships is part of the broader shift towards conscious enactment of Chineseness. The folding of ritual into a wider range of sociopolitical goals will also be evident in the second case study.

Singkawang Cap Go Meh: A Gate of Safety and Prosperity?

Singkawang, West Kalimantan, Cap Go Meh, 2013,[72] the fair on the field of Stadion Kridasana, otherwise the football stadium for third-league team Persiwang. Since Chinese New Year, about half of the football pitch has been occupied by stalls selling jewellery, tattoos, and T-shirts proclaiming variations on "I ♥ 山口洋,"[73] soda, sausages, toys, ice cream, and so on. At night, the stage is occupied by the emcees' merry repartee in Hakka, sometimes interspersed with Indonesian, as they introduce the various performances: a Mandopop singer who travelled from Malaysia; local dancers invoking the harmony of Dayaks, Malays, and Chinese; *wushu* demonstrations from Singkawang's martial arts schools. A large audience stands watching, makes space for a picnic, mills about on the pitch or gazes from the stands, sometimes crying out responses to questions of the emcees, such as *Are you having fun?*

Fairgoers who tire of the performance can pay 10,000 rupiah (at the time, roughly US$1) to enter an enclosure, passing through an enormous gate in red and gold on a thin wood façade. Above the gate hangs a reproduction of *Congregation of Immortals at the Jade Pool* 瑤池會仙圖, a mythological theme painted in 1995 by Liu Yuyi 劉宇一,[74] while the back features an image of the three star deities.[75] On the side panels are reproductions of more landscape and waterscape paintings—impressions of "traditional China." The enclosure's outside-facing walls are inscribed with quotes from Confucius, the *Daodejing*, and (more than any other) the Taiwanese Buddhist nun Cheng Yen 證嚴, founder of the international Buddhist organization Tzu Chi 慈濟.[76] In the grassy yard behind the gate, a statue of the Guanyin Buddha towers on a lotus surrounded by a fountain. At the side, plastic pink-and-white plum blossoms[77] are strung with lights that will produce strobe effects at sudden, equatorial nightfall. And—doesn't the structure look familiar?—*Is* the gate a meagre miniature of Tiananmen, the Gate of Heavenly Peace? But, approaching, one finds that instead it is inscribed with the characters Ping'an men 平安門, translated with reasonable accuracy on the gate as Pintu keselamatan dan kesejahteraan kota Singkawang (Gate of safety and prosperity of the city of Singkawang).

This variation on a famous name catches the attention. I was informed by someone familiar with the organizing committee deliberations that the inclinations had been split between an older and a younger group. While the older generation was eager to show links with political as well as cultural China, the younger members were more oriented towards an Indonesian identity and reluctant to host anything suggesting the People's Republic. The old guard retaining control, the previous year's festival had featured a reproduction of the Great Wall of China. Younger members, who desired a closer working relationship with the Malay-controlled municipal government, felt that Cap Go Meh ought to move toward defining itself more as a local West Kalimantan and Indonesian festival. The initial choice of Tiananmen produced local unease, an unsurprising result in a city where monumental representations of Chinese culture have provoked unrest before.[78] *The Pontianak Post,* in an article unsympathetic to the project, quoted a leader of the patriotic organization Pembela Tanah Air (Defenders of the Homeland) as saying: "We really support CGM. CGM is an asset for tourism in Singkawang. But we don't like foreign concepts being brought to Singkawang" (January 31, 2013). Another warned that the structure could make it seem as though Singkawang Hakka was "establishing a state within a state" (*Kal Bar Times,* February 1,2013).

Ultimately, the municipal government balked at the structure, which had been commissioned by the committee without consultation. In the end, an uneasy compromise was made to keep the structure but change the name. The head of the committee, Bong Ci Nen, told the media that "this miniature old building, resembling a temple, is something we have made in order to bring a stronger feeling of Chinese New Year to the celebrating people" (*InfoPublik*, May 2, 2013), sidestepping the issue. Nevertheless, Malay respondents I spoke with during the visit considered it to be a replica of Tiananmen, and it was also reported that way in some media (*Rakyat Kalbar*, February 13, 2013). This gate of safety and prosperity was certainly an uneasy compromise.

Siting the Singkawang Hakka

The Jakarta journalist Kwee Kek Beng claimed in 1951 that West Kalimantan "is the most Chinese part of Indonesia," where "even many Indonesians understand Chinese" (*Java-bode*, July 18, 1951).[79] His words were echoed over fifty years later by a local, who wrote that "it might be difficult to find this Chinese rhythm of life in any other region of the country" (Wen 2007, 52). The density of the Chinese population had earned the area nicknames such as "Little China," while the local Hakka have been called "Chinese among the Chinese" (Heidhues 1997, 201). One recent dissertation on Singkawang Chinese "circuits of mobility" went so far as to call it "a Chinese town in Indonesia" (Hertzman 2017).

What New Order failed to do, however, is perhaps being achieved by economic development and improved transportation: the incorporation of Singkawang Hakka into an Indonesian imaginary as well as a transnational network of ethnic Chinese. The preceding sketch, as well as the account of Hakka marionettes in the first chapter, show how festivities in Singkawang are pulled in two different directions: between a powerful recognition of Chinese identity and transnational loyalties in one of Indonesia's linguistically and culturally most conservative Sino-Indonesian communities, and the need to represent its culture as a component of Indonesia's multicultural tapestry.

The scale of the Singkawang celebrations and the use of municipal buildings are indications that these are larger and more generously supported events than those described in Bandung. As has been noted throughout, Sino-Indonesians have "never been a homogeneous group" and "[r]egional and class diversity partly accounts for their heterogeneous self-identification" (Hoon 2011a, 4). It should be evident in this case, as in the previous chapter on community organizations, that Sino-Indonesian performance is heavily influenced by the particular regional atmosphere and culture. The way of being Chinese in Kalimantan is a different proposition from the Sundanese inflection of

Chinese identity in Bandung, as a brief overview of the West Kalimantan Chinese context can show.

West Borneo was profoundly marked by the arrival of Hakka gold miners in the eighteenth century. Malay rulers encouraged Chinese to come for mining purposes but proved unable to control them (Heidhues 2003, 12). Early Hakka mining federations, known as *kongsi* 公司, were substantially independent of Dutch control and exerted a measure of control over Malay and Dayak populations in their territories.[80] The bulk of the Singkawang Hakka[81] population descends from these miners, many of whom, especially in the early stages of settlement, had married local women. Nevertheless, because of the territory's high proportion of Chinese population, as well as the distance from urban centers and state power, intermarriage did not result in the same degree of acculturation as that which occurred in Java. Two campaigns by the Dutch East Indies Army (1822–1824, 1850–1854) against the *kongsi* and the suppression of a last uprising (1884–1885) put an end to Chinese political power in West Kalimantan. However, the *kongsi* remain powerful historiographical touchstones for Sino-Indonesian communities,[82] and local Hakka are fiercely proud of having preserved "their language and culture in a way unknown in other parts of the archipelago" (Heidhues 2006, 266–267).

The province of West Kalimantan, covering the Western part of the Indonesian portion of Borneo, has one of the highest proportions of Chinese population in Indonesia. According to the 2000 census, it was a close second in Chinese proportion of total population (9.62 percent, after Bangka Belitung). In absolute numbers West Kalimantan represented almost 15 percent of the Chinese Indonesian population), second only to Jakarta[83] (Ananta, Arifin, and Bakhtiar 2008, 27). What little success Sino-Indonesian political parties have had in recent years has also largely been in West Kalimantan (Hoon 2011a, 85). Unlike other Sino-Indonesians, most West Kalimantan Chinese are of Hakka or Teochew origin, while the Hokkien population—the majority origin of Javanese and Sumatran Chinese—accounts here for a much smaller proportion. The use of Hakka as the predominant Chinese language, and a codominant language overall, in Singkawang, is a legacy of the mining populations and is unusual even in a broader Southeast Asian context.

Within West Kalimantan the urban areas of Singkawang and Pontianak are the most heavily Chinese. Smaller populations in rural areas still exist despite military-sponsored ethnic violence in autumn 1967 that targeted the Chinese of interior West Kalimantan, killing hundreds and driving tens of thousands to the cities (Purdey 2006, 19–20; Tanasaldy 2012, 140–153).[84] At 186,462 inhabitants in the 2010 national census, Singkawang was the fifty-eighth-largest city in the nation and the second largest in West Kalimantan. Population numbers differ by source, and the population is subject to fluctuation, given that many Singkawang people, especially the Singkawang Hakka, migrate to work in Jakarta, Taiwan, Malaysia, and elsewhere across Asia in and to the West.[85] With a Chinese plurality in the urban area, and with conservative figures showing the proportion to be around 40 percent, Singkawang likely has the highest proportion of Chinese population among Indonesian cities, judged by historian Mary Somers Heidhues to constitute "a majority or near-majority" (Heidhues 2006, 266–267).[86] The most recent census data found Singkawang Regency the only area in the country where Chinese formed the plurality (Arifin et al. 2016, 12).

In such a distinct social environment, the performance of Hakka groups in Singkawang is necessarily also distinguished by a characteristic subethnic Chinese culture and a regional Indonesian identity. Though it is not wrong to say that the Hakka of Singkawang "wear their Chineseness like a badge" (Chan 2009, 115) and true also that they are theoretically and emotionally invested in China (which they frequently refer to by the elsewhere antiquated name of Tangshan),[87] their identity is in large part organized around and determined by local and transnational Hakka formations and allegiances rather than along either pan-Chinese or pan-Indonesian lines.[88]

Not surprisingly, they consider themselves as substantially separate from other Sino-Indonesian groups. For instance, Jakarta-resident Singkawang Hakkas reported mixing little with local Jakarta Chinese, as they are likely to be "often teased by Jakartans because they either have a 'Chinese' accent when speaking Bahasa Indonesia or lack knowledge of Jakarta slang" (Hoon 2011a, 59).[89] They are also most often of a different economic class:[90] as one respondent explained in a Jakarta focus group: "People around you [in Singkawang] have nothing ... unlike those Chinese in Jakarta ... who throw money around ... dining and staying at luxurious hotels" (Dawis 2009a, 89).[91] One of my Singkawang respondents, having studied in Semarang and Jakarta, commented that he felt no closer to his Java-Chinese fellow students than to Javanese *pribumi*. Though respondents estimate that there are perhaps over a hundred thousand Singkawang people in Jakarta, they form their own formal or informal associations rather than integrating into Chinese Jakarta circles. West Kalimantan Chinese associations in the capital number over forty-five.

New Order policy also had a distinctive effect in West Kalimantan. Farther from the centers of power and representing a higher proportion of the population, Chinese populations in this region were less readily reorganized according to national directives. According to local respondents, Hakka temples in Singkawang, though formally integrated into the structure of official "Buddhism," in practice often did little more than add a small Buddha figure and/or a sign in Indonesian to their existing temple. These places of worship also remained "well-kept ... centres of activity" (Heidhues 1997, 204).

Nor have the institutional structures of contemporary Tridharma been as

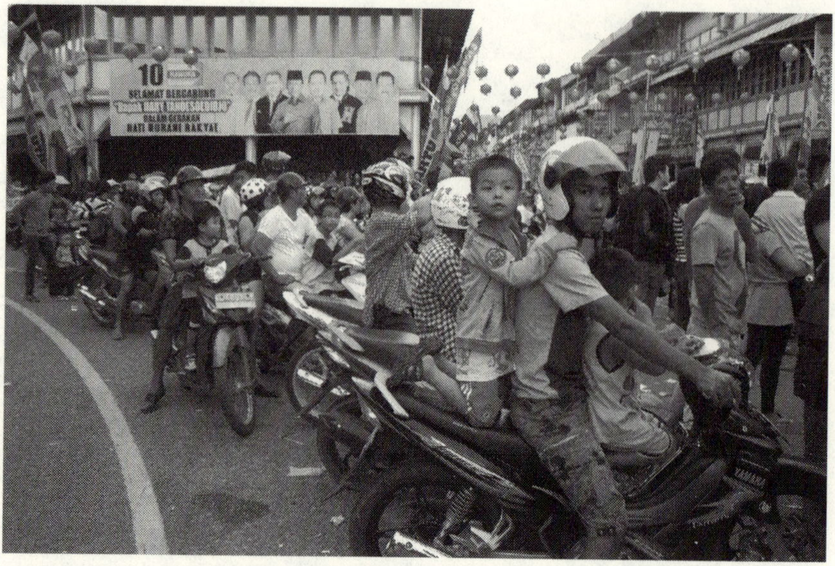

Spectators line the roads in anticipation of Cap Go Meh in Singkawang, 2013. Photo courtesy of Elisabeth Kramer.

powerful as on Java, and the practice of Chinese religion seems both more pervasive and less formally organized. Syncretism is expressed not through any strong Buddhist influence but through the localization of deities and noticeable interaction with local Dayak and Malay systems of belief.[92] The Chinese temple itineraries on Java, like those described at the beginning of the chapter, do not extend to Kalimantan: rarely do such festivals include, invite, or integrate Kalimantan Chinese communities.[93]

The official municipal line, as well as habitual press coverage, present an image of harmonious interethnic coexistence in Singkawang.[94] This representation is as much an aspiration and a discourse as a reality. In daily interaction racialist thinking is common on all sides.[95] When I visited a Singkawang Hakka home on the day after arrival, a new acquaintance told me that the Malays are "very stupid"; another Chinese respondent, living in Java, prepared me for the visit by telling me that development of Singkawang was impeded by the presence of "savage peoples." I was warned several times by local Chinese respondents against making friends or sometimes even speaking to "native people," while on the other hand I was told I could confer my trust on Chinese because they "wouldn't do anything bad."[96] The recent history of regional ethnic clashes—both the massacres of Chinese by Dayaks in the 1960s and the anti-Madurese violence of the Sambas riots in the late 1990s—informs ethnic dynamics, even if these are muted or circumvented in daily conversation.[97]

Singkawang Hakka identity is to a considerable degree socially and institutionally distinct from other groups of Indonesian Chinese, combining particularity drawn from an atypical migration history with the hybridity of their long history in Kalimantan.[98] As one anthropologist notes, Singkawang Hakka can even deploy "stereotypical characterizations of [other] groups of Chinese Indonesians, and Chinese in other nations" (Hertzman 2017, 145n61). The local celebration of Cap Go Meh can be read, among other things, as an expression, a performance, a celebration, and also a negotiation of that ethnic-local identity. The audiences are not only the local Dayak and Muslim populations, but also the municipal, provincial, and national authorities charged with incorporating Chinese ethnicity into a harmonious narrative. They are also the ethnic Chinese—mostly from Java, but also from Singapore, Malaysia, Hong Kong, and Mainland China—who have come to experience an exotic Chinese spectacle, and whose interest can be derived from identifying it as strange, authentic, or antiquated.

Cap Go Meh as a "Unique" and "Authentic" State-Sponsored Festival

Outside Kridasana stadium on the morning of the Cap Go Meh procession, groups of drummers are holding banners honoring their home temple or sponsoring company. Spirit-mediums, known as *tatung*, dance on swords, pierce their cheeks with skewers, chant, brandish stage weapons, gesticulate.[99] Some in the parade shoulder spirit altars; others, dressed in military attire, carry *choi lam sin* 菜籃神, vegetable baskets that are capable of divination and carrying messages from other spirits.[100] This year, 747 *tatung* are registered, including participants as young as fifteen (*Pontianak Post,* February 24, 2013).

Although spirit divination is common throughout Hakka culture, Singkawang's Cap Go Meh procession is highly distinctive, with media reports and tourism pitches usually focusing on the spirit-mediums, the *tatung*.[101] The most detailed account of the practice asserts that "the influence of spirit mediums over the lives of people is all-encompassing" (Chai 2017, xiii). There are both Chinese and Dayak *tatung*, and the spirits who possess them may also be Chinese or Dayak. During the parade, each medium is preceded by flags or altars bearing the Chinese names of the possessing spirits, some of which are those of specific Daoist or Dayak spirits, but more of which bear generic names. The *tatung* themselves stand on chairs, dressed in military costumes, and—in a state of trance—gesticulate, balance, scream. Many have pierced their cheeks, ears, or lips with skewers; on the ends of some skewers, oranges are impaled. The practice demonstrates the ability of the divinity to enter battle and represents the strength of the divinity, not a sacrifice on the part of the worshipper (see also Chan 2006, 111–112). Some *tatung* give detailed accounts of their "master" spirit, whereas others are less specific, or reported that they were possessed by successions of different spirits.[102]

The Cap Go Meh procession has the purpose of purifying the town at the beginning of the new year, with the parade of spirits serving to frighten away the evil spirits through demonstrations of bravery and prowess. Many of the costumes worn by mediums resemble military attire,[103] and some of the mediums possessed by Dayak spirits wear feather headdresses and carry dead chickens in their mouths.[104]

By and large, Singkawang Hakka regard the rituals of Cap Go Meh as a necessity. One retired schoolteacher remarked, "You can't fake being a *tatung*. Our fortunes depend on their efficacy." The commodification of ritual has in this case thus not displaced belief in its efficacy, although it was the view of some respondents that the principal procession, due to its prominence as a tourism event, was losing potency.[105]

As the ritual is commodified, *tatung* and the procession have been assigned a new role as well—as markers of authenticity. In 2013, the Dayak governor, Cornelis M.H. of West Kalimantan, drew special attention at the opening of the Cap Go Meh parade to the *tatung*. According to Cornelis, "*tatung* were forbidden by Mao [Zedong] during the Cultural Revolution in the country of China. Perhaps Singkawang is the one and only area where *tatung* perform in the festival of Cap Go Meh" (*Detik*, February 25, 2013).[106] After the event, he suggested that "in order

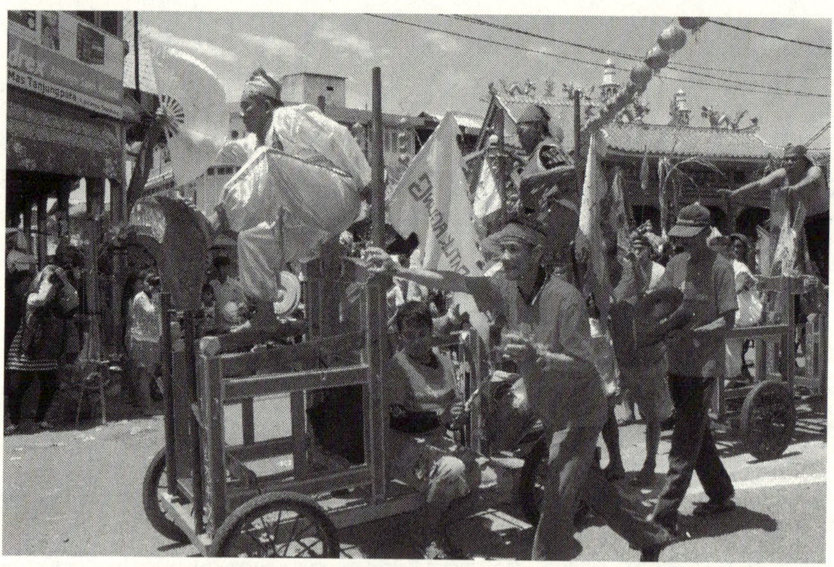

Tatung on a spirit chair with musicians. Cap Go Meh, Singkawang, 2013. Photo courtesy of Elisabeth Kramer.

for it not to be imitated or copied by other nations, Cap Go Meh will soon be listed by UN bodies such as UNESCO" (*Kal Bar Times*, February 26, 2013), raising the intriguing if improbable prospect of Indonesia applying for intangible cultural heritage status on behalf of an ethnic Chinese holiday. These quotes from the province's highest elected official are revealing about how contemporary West Kalimantan authorities wish to present their Chinese festivities: namely, as a practice eradicated from China but retained in Kalimantan, and therefore both locally specific and marked by superior authenticity.[107] Nevertheless, it is clear that the Singkawang practice of Cap Go Meh is a very complicated and hybridized descendant of a practice the Hakka brought with them to Borneo.[108]

Materials from the principal temple, the destination of the parade, show twin (and contradictory) claims being made for both "genuine" Chinese tradition and special hybridity: *tatung* feats are "replicating Chinese tradition and mixed with... Dayak culture. This assimilation is only found in Singkawang" (Vihara Tri Dharma Bhumi Raya 2013). Both Chinese and non-Chinese respondents frequently emphasized the singularity of Cap Go Meh in particular and of Singkawang in general by calling it "unique," usually setting Singkawang Chinese culture up in contrast to the People's Republic of China, where, according to this discourse, such displays "no longer" occur.[109] Both claims can be validated to a certain extent: trance behaviors in Hakka rituals are well known both in Mainland China and in diaspora (Chai 2013), and trance is an important part of Dayak spirit-medium practices (Jay 1989); and, as with many other aspects of popular religion, much of Hakka ritual was indeed suppressed under Mao (Myron L. Cohen 1991).

Examining how Cap Go Meh presents as both a defining display of Chineseness and as an officially approved local performance practice shows how Chinese performance can be integrated into a core local identity. If, as related earlier, the Singkawang puppetry form of *wayang gantung* is endangered by its reluctance to integrate into the structure of Indonesian arts as defined by officialdom, one might suppose that the celebration of Cap Go Meh faces a similar challenge as it is a cultural expression of the same community. However, quite the opposite is the case. Like *wayang potehi*, Cap Go Meh practice has undergone substantial formal change, although, in this case, in addition to acting as a sociopolitical performative tool for the local Chinese community, it also becomes an instrument of the region's touristic development. So while the modernization of Singkawang has all but eliminated one branch of local Chinese culture (*wayang gantung*), it has revitalized, promoted, and adapted another (Cap Go Meh celebrations).

The practice's absorption into wider networks of pan-Chinese influence, especially tourism, and its accommodation with local Indonesian authority, have allowed Cap Go Meh to become a defining feature of the city. Its transformation merits attention as an example of the integration of a Chinese ritual performance into an Indonesian city's self-perception. Thus, while Bandung has provided us with an example of how a small minority can represent its rituals in a majority Sundanese city, Singkawang can indicate how the rituals of a regional Chinese plurality can be integrated into a narrative of local culture for, among other things, economic purposes.

Once a purely communal and ritual affair,[110] the procession is now under municipal control, a process that was completed not without acrimony (Chan 2009, 116; Ong et al. 2017, 49). Local respondents gave the following oral chronology, which allows us some idea of the decades-long negotiations between municipal authorities and Chinese community organizations. Informants confirmed having gone to temple grounds for Cap Go Meh in the late 1980s and early 1990s.[111] Before 1996, Cap Go Meh had been held at the city's central temple, which "occupies the heart of the city from a geographical perspective and also the heart of the people from the social, historical and cultural perspectives" (Chai 2017, 12).[112] From 1996 to 2000, the celebration moved to a temple in Roban on the outskirts of the city; it was held at the bus station for one year in 2001. After 2001, the parade proceeded along the main street in Singkawang. In 2006, the procession started from city hall, but in recent years it has begun at Kridasana stadium and led to the *tuapekong* temple. Despite its reestablishment in the civic landscape and recognition of its value as a tourism event, local Chinese still often voice the opinion that the local government regards Cap Go Meh as an expression of foreign culture.

Organizers and municipal officials are continually looking for ways to attract more attention and tourism. Hui writes that "celebrations have grown to comprise a whole series of events in recent years" (2011, 281), with seven events planned for the year he reports on, 2006. Much publicity was garnered in 2010, when Singkawang Cap Go Meh celebrations had three records certified by the Semarang-based Indonesian World Record Museum (MURI).[113] In 2012, the parade reportedly contained the "longest dragon in Asia." It has only expanded since then: the 2013 official program, besides private initiatives, featured a lantern-decorating competition, the stadium performances, opening and closing ceremonies, and the Miss Shanghai Beauty Pageant. Visible throughout the city were entries to the decoration competition, not unlike North American Christmas-light exhibits, showing mechanical snakes, hanging couplet scrolls (*duilian*), and in one case the Indonesian text *Kita Semua Bersaudara*—"We are all brothers"— hung above the diorama like a title.

As the celebration has grown, its original ritual character has also altered. An American missionary reported that, while posted in the area in the 1970s, he and his wife were forbidden to take photographs of *tatung* for fear of robbing them of their "life power," so he was astonished to learn that nowadays *tatung* are freely pictured in the media. Older Singkawang residents also lament that authenticity (and therefore efficacy) were degrading. Indeed, some complained that some participants were using illicit magic and that, rather than undergoing genuine possession by spirits, they were inducing trances by burning spells and drinking the ashes in liquid.[114] Syncretic practices were also vanishing: an older Catholic Chinese woman, for instance, told me of her regret that the *tatung* would no longer dismount from their spirit chairs and bow respectfully before the church, as they had in her youth. Some locals explained to me that the rituals held the day before the actual parade, in which the various *tatung* visit the central temple of the town in order to "clean the roads" (*xilu*) had now become more important—because more authentic—than the parade itself (see also Chai 2017, 91).

Cap Go Meh as a Civic and Multiethnic Project

Hui notes that the state in Singkawang has appropriated culture as an artifact of tourism and is encouraging the performance of multiculturalism (2001, 279–280). Cap Go Meh is now one way in which the city and the province market themselves. Local and national officialdom is firmly committed to Cap Go Meh, and its public pronouncements are a visible feature of the city in the lead-up to the festival. Then president Susilo Bambang Yudhoyono, in his capacity as chairman of the advisory board to the Democratic Party and pictured with West Kalimantan members of his party, wished Singkawang citizens a Happy New Year and Cap Go Meh in Indonesian and Chinese; on the other side of the same billboard, the wishes for Christmas and the New Year could still be read. Other billboards from politicians and businesses, as well as a few outside churches, were scattered about the city. The local papers trumpeted the many tourists as well as the presence of Jakarta-based foreign diplomats (e.g., *Rakyat Kalbar*, February 13, 2013).

Official approval of the festival is intimately connected with Cap Go Meh's potential as an economic asset. The 2013 celebrations were featured on the Garuda Indonesia website and magazine as highlights of the Indonesian tourist scene, despite the fact that Singkawang has no airport. Several respondents expressed the wish that Cap Go Meh would revitalize the local economy or help Singkawang "Go Global." Local newspapers emphasized the tourists of many different nations who would be converging on the city. Spectators thronged the street and ice cream vendors did a roaring trade. Hotels were fully booked and prices rose above 100 percent; many locals converted their homes to accommodate tourists. One ice cream vendor told me that he did five times as much trade during the week leading up to Cap Go Meh than in an ordinary week.

The year I attended, 2013, marked the first celebrations under a new local government's administration. From 2008 to 2012 the city government had been headed by a Singkawang Chinese lawyer returned from Jakarta, Hasan Karman 黄少凡, supported by Megawati's PDI-P party. His election was seen as "rais[ing] Chinese political aspirations and enthusiasm to a new level" since it "was the result of direct votes of the Singkawang Chinese, which further emphasized the role Chinese could play in the direct *pilkada* [direct local executive elections] in other regions with a significant Chinese population" (Tanasaldy 2015, 459–460). In autumn 2012, Karman, however, was defeated by the former mayor, the Malay Awang Ishak, representing PAN (National Mandate Party), a Muhammadiyah-based Islamic party and supported by Golkar, the former governing party of Suharto. In that election, three Chinese candidates ran, but Ishak was the only Malay. This resulted, according to locals, in a Chinese vote split, while the Malay-Muslim vote was unified. Some Chinese respondents were bitter about this perceived lack of political solidarity among the Chinese.[115]

As a result, some respondents, both Chinese and non-Chinese, expressed the opinion that in 2013 Cap Go Meh would not be as "lively" with a Malay mayor, pointing to, for instance, the engagement of less-well-known performers for the Kridasana stage or the cancellation of some events (such as a bodybuilding competition). Several respondents opined that the rainstorm that had literally dampened the parade in 2013 was due to supernatural displeasure at the election of a Malay mayor. On the other hand, it cannot be denied that Ishak's first tenure as mayor had been the first major period of growth for Cap Go Meh as a tourist event, and that all of his official pronouncements on the festival have been celebratory.

Along with the government, newspaper reports emphasized that Cap Go Meh was no longer just for Chinese but for citizens of every national background; the sentiment among respondents, however, seemed to be more ambivalent. While plenty of non-Chinese locals were happy to visit the stadium or watch Cap Go Meh, it was still not uncommon to hear more guarded sentiments being expressed. In 2013, for instance, the comments of a prominent local *da'i*[116] on Cap Go Meh were: "We have our own way, and they have their own way. We have our own culture, and they have their own culture. Each culture should go its own way alone in order to maintain itself and not attain conflict" (*Equator News*, January 27, 2013). Indeed, the FPI also erected banners in 2012 and 2013 telling Muslims that it was forbidden for religious reasons (*haram*) to watch Cap Go Meh.[117]

Such religious separation has its effects on municipal policy. Muslims—in the Singkawang context, mostly Malays—are not permitted to sign on as *tatung*, and one Malay respondent reported being harassed as result of his participation.[118] In Pontianak, Malay-Chinese relations have been a frequent stumbling block for Cap Go Meh festivities, with the mayor banning *tatung* from 2011 (Tanasaldy 2013, 102) and the local FPI director stating in 2013, "We request there to be no *tatung* in the city of Pontianak, and if there are *tatung* in Pontianak we will break up the event." His objection, as reported in the media, was grounded not only in the idea that the spectacle was unsafe for children, but also that "lion dances and *tatung* are cultures that have been brought in from outside Indonesia" (*BeritAnda*, February 15, 2012). However, in Singkawang, the importance of Imlek and Cap

Go Meh both to the spiritual life of the city and to the livelihoods of its citizens means that it cannot be easily dismissed,[119] and religious prohibitions appear to have limited effect, even when they are a source of anxiety.

Notwithstanding the genuine belief system in which Cap Go Meh in Singkawang remains centrally implicated, the present performance is also designed to create a Sino-Indonesian flair for returnees and (mostly ethnic Chinese) tourists. Sino-Indonesian actors and their non-Chinese fellow citizens exploit genuine cultural difference—produced by a community that for generations has been outside the mainstreams of Chinese culture, Indonesian politics, and development economics. The windfall that tourism can bring means that in this case modernization and globalization both reinforce and incorporate public religious practice rather than weakening it. As one local remarked to me, "the rise of Cap Go Meh is the result of the [Malay] Ishak government trying to develop the economy while making Chinese people happy." One of the best opportunities for revitalizing the West Kalimantan economy revolves around tourism focused on the performance of Chinese identity.[120]

That this is possible is a statement of how Indonesian identities are broadening to include a view of the Sino-Indonesian minority as integral, distinct but belonging. It speaks also to the way in which cultural and religious practice are more and more beholden to economic and touristic interests. As in China, official approval must be paid for through overt political expressions of loyalty. At the same time Cap Go Meh clearly also partakes in the loyalty-signalling of other festivals, such as when the governor of West Kalimantan remarked at the 2006 festival that "Chinese citizens are citizens that possess the same status, rights, duties and responsibilities as any other citizen of Indonesia" (Hui 2011, 87). The ambivalence of participants can perhaps be symbolized by the fact that, although the parade regulations stated that all *tatung* had to include Indonesian flags in their train, this regulation was only patchily followed.

As Singkawang residents begin "imagining [themselves] as part of a globally significant, transnational Chinese diasporic community" (Ang 2001, 78), it becomes more feasible for them to integrate into Sino-Indonesian and global Chinese networks. Paradoxically, this integration into Chinese networks is substantially effected by the marketing to international Chinese tourists of a display noteworthy both for its deviation from contemporary Chinese or Sino-Indonesian norms and for the participation in it of non-Chinese peoples.[121]

Location, Location, Location

Singkawang Hakka and Bandung's Vihara Dharma Ramsi (VDR) congregants are nominally part of a single group that is often totalized as Chinese Indonesians. Yet their practices, while sharing a position in Indonesian discourses of multiculturalism, are determined as much by local conditions as by their cultural inheritance. As anthropologist Marianne Holm Pedersen has observed, "Ritual performance does not necessarily symbolise relations to one's place of origin: it may also be a means of creating social relations and belonging in the place where one is currently living" (2014, 4). Holm Pedersen's observation is true for her respondents, Iraqi Shi'a women in Denmark, but it is equally apt for Sino-Indonesians, whose practice of Chinese religion is mediated by this community's long history and deep indigeneity.

Sino-Indonesian religious performances have socioeconomic and cultural as well as ritual meanings. As in other multicultural countries today, Sino-Indonesian practices and identities are being incorporated "into the rituals of the city, and the Indonesian nation state itself" (Prasetyo 2016). As with Sino-Indonesian cultural products such as *wayang potehi* or Sampek Engtay, there is a growing willingness to consider Chinese religious festivals an element of Indonesian life, even if this phenomenon also reveals tensions and provokes an illiberal resistance.

The activities of temples and community organizations in West Java and West Kalimantan described here indicate the diversity of Sino-Indonesian ritual performance. While different specific practices would have been found had the selected sites been Hokkien-speaking Bagansiapiapi with its boat-burning festival or the Hinduism-inflected Chinese temples of Bali, it is generally apparent that Sino-Indonesian religious practices can be considered both "resuscitated" and "historically anchored" performances of an ethnic minority (Prasetyo 2016). The processes of incorporating Chinese performance into Indonesian culture operate at different speeds according to the contexts of local culture and interethnic history and are part of the larger incorporation of Sino-Indonesians into a conception of the Indonesian people. Practices that were formerly considered the preserve of a specific religious-ethnic community can now be not only permitted but endorsed by Indonesian authorities. At the same time, such performances benefit from and strengthen transnational pan-Chinese networks. Tourism from elsewhere in the Chinese world and participation of foreign Chinese organizations in Sino-Indonesian events show that it is not just Indonesians but also ethnic Chinese from throughout Asia who are the intended audiences of these performances.

Religious parades, such as the Tamil Hindu processions in London studied by Ann David, can show how "signs of greater confidence in outward display are part of specific aspects of religious pluralism and of identity-marking of minority groups, signalling cohesiveness and strength," not only to members of the local or transnational in-group, "but also to other religious groups and the local community" (David 2012, 462). Sino-Indonesian ritual performance practices throughout Indonesia are being revived, interpreted, and readapted for ideological integration into concepts of both local and national culture. They are conscious of the image they project of both a general "authentic" Chineseness and an integrated, specifically regional, community identity. Authorities of Reformasi-era Indonesia incorporate these performances into narratives of ethnic harmony and diversity, even if the reality is never quite as tension-free as the parade would have you believe.

Conclusion

HINDSIGHT AND PROSPECTS

THE era of unreflective fieldwork is, thankfully, over. The researcher must attend not only to the ethics of methodology but also to his/her own positionality and the biases that inevitably come along with it. Some of the biases contained in this book are regional, a function of the serendipities or mishaps of fieldwork, of the personal introductions allowing me to be present for a certain performance or to gather a particular kind of material. Research conducted among Chinese communities in other parts of Indonesia would necessarily have produced different images and narratives, and despite the now voluminous work published on the national community (usually focused on Java), many areas remain academically underrepresented or even ignored. Hui Yew-Foong, considering the same phenomenon at the regional-local level, writes that, if he "had gone to places like Sanggau, Sintang or Ketapang, or taken up what may be considered peripheral vantage points, the story told would probably be quite different" (2011, 304). The same is true of this work, or of any book attempting to deal with the complexities of Sino-Indonesian experience. Writing on Indonesia may correct or complicate prevalent assumptions about "Chineseness" on a regional or global scale; at the same time, overgeneralizations about Sino-Indonesians inevitably do a disservice to overlooked communities: a view cannot be both focused and comprehensive.

Other biases are a result of my personal or educational background, my preexisting sympathies, and those of the circles in which I move. My academic training and research before embarking on this project in 2011 had been divided into work on the fields of Chinese performance—especially *xiqu*—and on Overseas Chinese communities. My ideas on the two topics were isolated from one another, and I thought of them, when I did manage any kind of academic introspection, as options between which I would eventually have to choose. I wrote academically about related fields of Chinese performance, from puppetry through pop culture, working mostly on Jiangsu and later Fujian forms; and when I had the opportunity, I conducted fieldwork in the border cities of the Russian Far East, then in Chinese communities in Brazil.

I did not yet see any opportunity of combining or reconciling my interests in the study of migration and of performance. Even when I first became interested in the Chinese Indonesian minority's specific performance forms—beginning with the scanty materials then available on *wayang potehi*—I realized only gradually that such topics not only permitted but demanded simultaneous investigation into Chinese theatrical practices and Chinese identity. As my work developed, I began to move from attempting to document instances of Sino-Indonesian performance to considering how these performances might be interpretable as the most performative articulation of a century-long Sino-Indonesian negotiation of identity. I had to critically reexamine the ideas I might entertain about being Chinese, picked up as much from years spent living in Beijing, Nanjing, Hong Kong, and Taipei as from any readings. Chineseness evidently found radically different expression in Indonesia; and my ideas of what the content of performance was in Chinese theatre had to adjust to the idea that, in Indonesia, the audience was never entirely Chinese, and even when it was "Chinese," seldom Chinese in the senses I was familiar with from my time in other Chinese environments.

Like all other social identities, minority is performatively defined. There are, of course, the literal performances—the way in which a minority presents itself in festivals, parades, theatre, concerts, and films—that belong to the collection of organized and acknowledged "shows." For a minority, these are interpreted (and are performed with the knowledge that they will be construed) as a conscious, often "traditional," expression of ethnic identity. But they are also expressions of that group's position vis-à-vis the population at large. The phenomenon of performance is a thread that runs through minority experiences, not only in officially designated performance arenas. The individual or small group is often assumed—even compelled—to stand in for the whole population; a representative or ambassadorial role is attributed to it. I myself have felt this as a *laowai* in the Chinese world, a *bule* in Indonesia, an *angmao* in Singapore, a *gwailo* in Hong Kong, a returnee (ex-expat? a *gui laowai?*) in Canada, a Canuck in the United States, a diasporan in Israel, a Jew in Europe.[1] In each of these roles (and it is worth noting how the terminology of performance inevitably elbows its way into any talk about ethnicity) I was expected and usually found to have tastes or behaviors characteristic of (hugely diverse) sets. These identities, which I have alternately rejected, borne grudgingly, or tried (in vain) to ornament with asterisks, were not natural to me until I was placed in a society that had prepared a category for me; these experiences, in turn, influenced self-perception. The process is uncomfortable even when it is not accompanied by prejudice.[2] Whether it is voluntary associations, religious groups, theatre troupes, or schools, the gaze of the majority must always be negotiated. The unrest surrounding the Ahok trial was only the most recent reminder that there is also and always a political aspect to the Chinese minority performance in Indonesia. This political aspect has become one, though of course not the only, lens through which any Chinese public display can be interpreted.

I do not think it was always so. By and large, the Chinese presence in the Dutch East Indies was not self-conscious before the sinicization movements of the early twentieth century. The first two chapters have demonstrated that traditional Chinese theatre, both human and puppet, was in frequent performance throughout the late colonial archipelago and was attended by many different audiences well into the Sukarno years. Though they featured in accounts of local color, there is little to suggest a community managing its image; for one thing, the Chinese were not expected to display loyalty to anyone except a usually abstract China. Taking *wayang kulit Cina Jawa,* which adapted the most symbolic form of Javanese *wayang* in order to represent recognizably Chinese stories, as an example, nothing about the project suggests that this was a conscious negotiation of Chinese identity rather than the organic expression of a highly talented Yogyakarta bicultural artist.

The move that occurs gradually over the twentieth century is one that distributes the concept of an audience. Rather than a concern for the immediate physical audience attending a particular show alone, Sino-Indonesians have increasingly had to consider how their performance will be diffused among state and majority audiences via a series of shows and displays that, in sum total, amount to the performance of being minority Chinese in modern Indonesia. Unsurprisingly, a highly self-conscious iteration of a particular kind of Chinese performance was created by Mainlander Baren, who sought to use the history of the Chinese to unite Sino-Indonesians and *pribumi* as victims of colonialism and imperialism, turning them into heroic rebels. Shalihong's treatment of the same subject, while also leftist, lays Chinese claim to the land without integrating it into or relating it to *pribumi* nationalism, indeed without much concern for *pribumi* views. Shalihong's writing seems to propose a strategy of nonconfrontational difference—which might have been a tenable minority position if Indonesia had developed as a federal state without the nationalist pressures that were felt at the beginning of New Order. As it is, the spoken theatre these two authors represent must largely be regarded as the beginnings of a political, Chinese-language spoken theatre that might have been.

After the beginning of New Order, all forms of Chinese performance were under constraint and the threat of extinction. Only those that developed successful strategies of ethnic self-representation could continue. *Xiqu* was all but eliminated, and only one Chinese puppet form, *wayang potehi,* was performed widely and continuously. The restrictions of New Order, indeed, caused it to become increasingly temple-based, and ultimately—as the community lost almost all capability to use Chinese—it adopted the Indonesian language and began to be performed by non-Chinese. The irony—that suppression resulted in the deeper integration of Chinese arts and stories into Javanese society—is not lost on its patrons and practitioners. In the current freer Reformasi period, *wayang potehi* has now evolved into a powerful tool for expressing Chinese identity within a united Indonesia. *Wayang gantung,* on the other hand, was preserved less by adaptation than by remoteness from effective control of Chinese activity. Having failed to adapt to Indonesian identity or state expectations, it has limited use as a tool of Sino-Indonesian identity; and since it cannot compete with newer forms of entertainment, it is on the brink of extinction. It may yet survive, and if it does, it will be specifically on the basis of its increasing incorporation into the system of *wayang;* this will likely be accompanied by some degree of hybridity.

While the avenues for *xiqu* or Chinese-language spoken theatre expression were largely closed to Sino-Indonesians, there remained room for Chinese narratives on the Indonesian-language stage. This is strikingly the case of the Sampek Engtay narrative, which had become integrated into various Indonesian genres and has been taken up, time and again, in the late colonial period, under New Order and in the present day. When it presented itself too overtly as Chinese, however, it could be suppressed. Chinese community organizations, once again under the exemption granted to religion, could subsist in a semipublic fashion—until, as New Order drew to an end, they once again appeared as choirs, literary societies, local place societies, and so on. In remoter areas, such as Jombang and Singkawang, uneasy and shifting arrangements allowed parades and festivals to subsist.

The space for all Chinese-culture-oriented performance having opened up in the Reformasi era, there has been a flowering of Sino-Indonesian performance, from temple festivities and Cap Go Meh parades to Teater Koma's newer China-themed productions and the Sino-Sundanese performances of Tan Deseng or of Kota Kembang. While all these performance types are enabled by the current permissibility of performing "Chineseness" openly, they must also all continue to navigate a vulnerable minority identity in a precariously liberal and precariously multiethnic state. Patriotism, charity, and hybridity are highlighted; appeals are made to officially approved concepts of cultural diversity or *wayang.* Chinese performance is being presented as an integral part of Indonesia; and an attempt is being made to dispel the stigma of foreignness while retaining ethnic distinctiveness. Whether the Sino-Indonesian profile towards which such performance works becomes the prevailing view in Indonesian society, or if, on the contrary, this account becomes simply a moment of unwarranted optimism from one historical moment, the second decade of the twenty-first century, is an almost wholly open question. Less optimistic analyses are, it must be said, increasingly available.

Now that the era of New Order has passed, it can be confidently asserted that

Chinese Indonesians have contributed to all aspects of Indonesian theatre, from the most traditional *wayang* to the most contemporary drama. In some instances, these contributions are not marked as "Chinese," and nothing is to be gained by dwelling on the ethnicity of the authors, artists, and practitioners. Frequently enough, however, elements of Chinese performance and narrative have been drawn into their performance, and Indonesian multiculturalism is, one hopes, now robust enough to acknowledge this contribution as an important part of the Indonesian national fabric.

Having viewed and charted the development of Sino-Indonesian performance through a sociopolitical lens, I hope that the extent and breadth of the Chinese component of Indonesian performance speak for themselves. There is one regret that must be acknowledged and set aside to be dealt with on another day or by another writer: paradoxically, the effect of studying the hybridity of Chinese communities is to showcase their Chineseness; and the risk of examining performativity in a social context is to subordinate culture to politics. The risk in defining the community by its divergence from another, more "authentic" Chineseness, is that thereby the categories of ethnicity and nation-state are reimposed. At the same time, it is these categories and limits that make such studies possible at all. In order to reveal the contributions of Sino-Indonesians, it seems necessary to consider the kinds of definitions of Chineseness that many Sino-Indonesians would rather see disappear. Like many a paradox, this one can be partially defused through its acknowledgment. It is my hope that this unfortunate failing is partly redeemed through the deployability of this work for other purposes and the other directions it tends to support: hybridity, integration, and transnational cultural exchange, as well as the relevance and ubiquity of performance, of theatre, of culture.

There is another shadowy presence: while the field of performance studies is always political, it is always also economic. Behind the public performances of Chinese communities is contained an old and dangerous current surrounding Sino-Indonesian public performance in Indonesia: largesse in the service of a public festivity (with Chinese culture, as here, imbedded) can also be read as ostentatious display.[3] That is to say, presenting a village festival with Javanese arts, door prizes, and *potehi*—visibly sponsored by a local Chinese businessman and performed by the troupe he pays—may be intended to stimulate liking for local Chinese culture; yet it may also play a role in reinforcing existing cultural stereotypes. This paradox, too, may be insoluble, and remains a dissonant element within the celebration of much public Chinese performance. Sino-Indonesians cannot afford to lose sight of the still powerful stigma assessed to them; much of their performance of charity is designed to correct the long-standing racist stereotypes of the Chinese exploiter. As with the reception of international aid in developing countries, however, the dispensation of charity can also incur resentment and charges of arrogance.

As the Chinese as an ethnic group are being politically and ethnically accommodated into a national narrative of Indonesia, the performance history of the country should also be revised to include a greater awareness of the Chinese integral contribution to Indonesia's performing arts. It has been too long "an uncomfortable area of inquiry which is rife with popular misconceptions based on centuries of perpetrated racist thinking" (Kartomi 2000, 275). To Indonesian friends and colleagues I must have seemed somewhat narrow-minded in the process of this research, as my focus (and my field of competence) compelled me to look largely at Chinese forms and to take an interest in a musician like Tan Deseng primarily in terms of his complex Chineseness. This narrative of Chinese performance in Indonesia is by no means intended to grant Chinese culture a privileged place in the historiography of Indonesian performance—to replace one chauvinism with another. It is a function of my own background as a student of Chinese theatre that my contribution to Indonesian studies must focus specifically on Chinese aspects of performance. I argue for the persistent influence of Chinese performance in Indonesia in support of views—held by Indonesians of all ethnic backgrounds who support a pluralistic national identity—that regard the Chinese presence as a contribution to Indonesia's cultural fabric, not as a challenge to it.

Another limit to this work comes as a pleasant surprise. Sino-Indonesian performance has usually been absent in works on the Chinese of Indonesia, with a few performance genres or iterations directly addressed in only a small number of articles and books. It seemed possible that I would arrive in Indonesia and find little or nothing to write about. Instead, I am now in the position of realizing that this study is only a preliminary to any number of productive avenues of research. In fact, I have had to pass over many forms of Chinese performance in Indonesia, including Batavian orchestral and dance forms,[4] the historic visits of Chinese-American magicians[5] and Shanghai cabarets,[6] the recent presentation of Sino-Malaysian Buddhist musicals,[7] as well as local Sino-Indonesian performative phenomena, such as Sino-Indonesian Muslim preachers[8] or the practices of open-air public Chinese karaoke or beauty pageants.

Finally, if I have managed to indicate some of the richness and diversity of Sino-Indonesian performative culture, it is only because the culture proved to be an exceptionally open and welcoming one, and because at every turn I was assisted in my work by the generous spirit of the artists, patrons, scholars, audiences, and organizations presented in these pages.

NOTES

Introduction

1. Contemporary migrants from China to Indonesia do not constitute a large group, although the presence of Chinese laborers particularly has recently been an Indonesian media flashpoint. However, temples quite frequently engage migrant or visiting religious staff from China, often recruited in ancestral places and charged with performing the "authentic" rituals. On other kinds of recent migration from China, see Hew 2017.

2. The scene belongs to the *Pipa ji* 琵琶記 narrative. The convoluted publication and performance history of this work, attributed to fourteenth-century author Gao Ming 高明, have generated a substantial subfield of Chinese theatre and drama studies. It remains a major narrative in *kunqu* repertoire and has been translated and/or adapted into numerous foreign languages, including a Surabaya-published Malay version held in Leiden (Louw 1934).

3. These include a plot to launch a rocket attack on Singapore from Indonesian territory (uncovered in August 2016), a November 2016 petrol bomb attack on a monastery in Singkawang, and the burning and plundering of temples in Tanjungbalai (North Sumatra) in August 2016, reportedly because Meiliana, a Sino-Indonesian woman, protested against loud calls to worship from a mosque. In August 2018, she was sentenced to a jail term for blasphemy.

4. The most prominent recent conflict has been over the waters around the Natuna Islands, with skirmishes between the Indonesian navy and PRC vessels in June 2017.

5. For instance, this important difference has largely established a barrier between Asian studies and Asian-American (or other hyphenated) studies, which the latter especially is reluctant to break down. There is an inherent anxiety in studying diaspora that, by emphasizing connections with an ancestral land, is likely to delegitimize that community in the eyes of the "receiving" society. It is partly on account of such an anxiety that I am eager to stress that in applying a Chinese emphasis here (not least as a result of the limits of my own capacities) I reject any suggestion that there is tension with any given work's or tradition's full "Indonesian-ness."

6. This spurious association between an entire class and an entire ethnicity remains a common, and rather dangerous, feature of anti-Chinese feeling.

7. As Leo Suryadinata has pointed out, the tendency to label Sino-Indonesians as a trading minority has meant that they are treated "as if they have neither culture nor literature" (2004, 149). Indeed, the association of Sino-Indonesians with economics is in part a *result* of

restrictions on Chinese culture (Budianti 2007, 172). In my own experience, I am reminded of a Bandung Chinese couple, both of whom had been young teachers at Chinese schools in the early 1960s, who told me they had entered into the gravel business only because their chosen profession was closed to them.

8. For instance, Suryadinata's excellent *The Culture of the Chinese Minority in Indonesia* makes no substantial reference to theatrical or musical performance.

9. The temple in honor of Zheng He in Semarang, Sam Po Kong 三寶洞, has become a major cross-religious place of veneration and an important symbol of the antiquity of Chinese presence in Indonesia. Also worth noting is the fact that central Javanese Chinese apparently associated Zheng with a figure from Javanese mythology (Pigeaud 1938, 92). There is, however, no evidence in contemporary Chinese records that Zheng He visited Semarang.

10. It is worth mentioning that the Javanese annals made no mention of their ethnicity, and that it was the Dutch records that note a distinction (Kumar 1987, 609).

11. In Blussé's view, the massacre was a result of diverging economic interests between the VOC and the Batavia Chinese, writing that an "interplay of several factors such as economic depression and gross ineptitude... temporarily spoiled the institutionalized modus vivendi" (1986, 96).

12. The interest stemmed at least partly from the fact that Balinese women, being Hindu, could prepare and eat pork (Vickers 2012, 44).

13. It is possible, though controversial, to extend this analysis earlier into Indies history. Ann Kumar suggests "that the seeds of nineteenth- and twentieth-century anti-Chinese feeling were already present in the economic dominance and consequent legal privilege that the Chinese had acquired as early as the second half of the seventeenth century" (1987, 613). The prevailing approach among historians seems to be, however, to deal with anti-Chinese sentiment as emerging principally from late colonial ethnic categories and interactions.

14. It seems to me that South Africa and Indonesia share a legacy of race strife based partly on a Dutch colonial heritage of hard race distinctions that divided up the population into three groups (white, intermediate, native) and apportioned rights accordingly. In the words of Ariel Heryanto, such labels are "a colonial legacy that post-colonial dominant groups decided to impose upon silent Others in order to assert an identity of self" (Heryanto 1998, 100).

15. One might cite religion, population size, economics, and international relations as starting points for considering these differences. See also Heryanto 1998; for the Indian community of Indonesia, Myutel 2017; and, for a comparative view between Chinese and Indian communities in Indonesia, Myutel and Sandkühler 2015.

16. In the late colonial period, the Japanese (as was also the case in the Shanghai foreign concessions or, later, in apartheid South Africa) achieved "symbolic social and political parity," while Chinese communities did not have "the leverage to pry it from the colonial administration," causing considerable resentment (Lev 1985, 62; Willmott 1961, 17).

17. Anthropologist Emily Hertzman, working on Singkawang Hakka communities, "decided not to use these terms because they are inaccurate in the case of Singkawang where individuals display characteristics of both processes of long-term, multi-generational assimilation and acculturation into Indonesian society, as well as persistence and preservation of Chinese language and traditions" (2014, 194n2).

18. Anti-Chinese violence was not the subject I was researching, but it inevitably emerged as I engaged in fieldwork. For instance, in the course of a temple visit in 2013 I met an old Sino-Indonesian man in Kuningan, West Java, who explained some wall paintings on the temple walls. These depicted how the two neighboring Chinese in the communities of Ancaran and Kedungarum had both been burnt to death in temples and buried in a ditch. Evidently, many

atrocities have basically disappeared from the historical record. More recently, I encountered a poem by the Chinese-language Bandung writer Ming Fang 明芳 recounting how she encountered a similar oral history of a massacre in West Java in much the same incidental way. For a translation, see Stenberg 2017.

19. Sukarno also recognized the Peranakan, though not the *totok*, Chinese, as part of the Indonesian nation (*bangsa*) in 1963. This was reversed by Suharto on the basis that, unlike other ethnicities, the Chinese had no place of origin in the archipelago (Liao [Suryadinata] 2002, 11).

20. It remains a matter of some dispute whether Chinese were or were not disproportionately victimized nationwide in the initial stages of the crisis. In certain local cases, especially in West Kalimantan and Aceh, the evidence is irrefutable that the violence had an ethnic dimension (Bertrand 2004, 63–64; Purdey 2006, 14).

21. Many Sino-Indonesians believe that this is still the case with ID cards, and there seems to be some evidence that a particular sequence of numbers on these cards still differentiates Indonesians of Chinese descent from *pribumi* (Weeratne 2009, 118).

22. This resulted in the considerable migration of Sino-Indonesians out of the PRC and to Hong Kong, Taiwan, and back to Indonesia. If Overseas Chinese who move to China are (probably unwisely) termed "re-migrants," there is thus a considerable population of those who are re-re-migrants.

23. *Cina* was once an unloaded term in the Malay-speaking world. In Indonesia, it acquired offensive connotations in the Suharto years. Tionghoa 中華, based on Hokkien pronunciation of "Chinese" in its cultural sense *Zhonghua*, is now used for the ethnicity, and Tiongkok 中國 for its geographic equivalent. These terms were first introduced by THHK at the beginning of the twentieth century (Budianta 2007, 172). In recent years, the term "China," in its English pronunciation, has gained popularity; this is also the usual Malay-language way of referring to the PRC, while Malaysia and Singapore Malay retain *Cina* for language, culture, and people. Lately, even the untranslated English term "Chinese opera" has gained some currency in Indonesian (e.g., *Harian Analisa*, January 15, 2006).

24. The lateness of this last date is also a reminder that the Dutch East Indies were in many regions a recent administration with small numbers of officials and variable social penetration.

25. The national language of Indonesian is much closer to Malay as spoken on Brunei and Malaysia than it is to the native languages of Timor and Flores, let alone to the unrelated Papuan languages.

26. For instance, Malays, Timorese, and Papuans cross international borders.

27. Ariel Heryanto pointed out that the Sino-Indonesians could be seen as one of four "major 'Others' of the New Order Self," the others being the Western world, Communism, and fundamentalist Islam (Heryanto 1998, 97). The other three, it is worth noting, are situated, as concepts, largely outside Indonesia.

28. In the original, the subject of this quotation is minority rights, but the observation can be aptly extended to attempts to define a minority.

29. Winet's focus in his book *Indonesian Postcolonial Theatre: Spectral Genealogies and Absent Faces* is not on Sino-Indonesian theatre, although he acknowledges the influence of *xiqu* and the importance of Sino-Indonesian businessmen and dramatists. The omission or understatement of Sino-Indonesian performance is only slowly being redressed and, even though the genres appear in his work only in passing, Winet's term of "spectral genealogy" (itself derived from other scholars such as Pheng Cheah) is aptly applied to the relationship of several Sino-Indonesian genres and narratives.

Chapter 1: Delighting Verie Much in Playes and Singing

1. One might note, for instance, the practice of *chaoju* in the Thai language, or the predominance of non-ethnic Chinese performers in Manila *gaojiaxi* 高甲戲.

2. Unless one includes puppetry, treated in chapter 2 as a separate family of arts.

3. Even Nano Riantiarno, whose dramatic work has dealt with both the heritage of Chinese theatre and the early Indonesian commercial theatre, elides the presence of Chinese *xiqu* theatres in the colonial Indies, acknowledging only classical China (i.e., Confucius and Laozi), along with the theatres of Korea and Japan, as an undefined influence on "Classical Indonesia before 1885" in his chart of "The Spread of Theatre" (Riantiarno 2011, 25).

4. Chinese-language scholarship sometimes dates the presence of *xiqu* in the Indies to the early Qing dynasty, namely the mid-seventeenth century, without giving sources (Zhou 2007, 52); Scott may be the ultimate origin for this dating, although his account would actually be, in Chinese chronology, late Ming rather than early Qing.

5. However, *xiqu* history can be traced even earlier in the Philippines. The sixteenth-century Manila Dominicans attempted to excommunicate those (Chinese and Spanish) who attended Chinese theatricals on the grounds of superstition and idolatry, though the success of their efforts of preventing attendance is not known (Irving 2010, 210; Chia 2011, 269).

6. The page reference here is to the English translation, which is from the French rather than the original Dutch. The passages can be found in the original Dutch on pages 365–66 in the 1714 copy digitized by the University of Utrecht, as well as on Google Books, and include the guess that "the play itself stages one or the other of the stories from their idolatrous worship" (365).

7. As Abeyesekere notes, it is likely that certain practices (such as gambling) permitted by the authorities for Chinese festive purposes, were also enjoyed by Europeans and *pribumi*. Festivals would also have provided an opportunity to bribe colonial officials in the guise of gifts (1983, 25).

8. A French translation, with context, is also available (Salmon and Lombard 1980, 293–295). Several of these visits were previously noted there and in van der Loon 1992, 26–27.

9. It is not clear why Thorn uses "mountebank exhibition," as mountebank shows were in Europe largely associated with medical quackery; it may carry a whiff of disrepute for the female performers, or Thorn may simply be using the word to suggest exoticism (see Wiles 2003, 117–118; Katritzky 2007, 81–82).

10. This was a punitive venture against a village on the western coast of what is now Aceh, Kuala Batee (Quallah Battoo in the Western-language records of the day), which had killed the crew of an American merchant ship.

11. Social dances like *ronggeng*, along with *topeng* and various forms of *wayang* (human and puppet), were certainly among the many performance genres on Java that benefited from Chinese patronage in the nineteenth century (Pigeaud 1938; Kunst 1973, 142, 166, 244; Seltmann 1976, 51–76; Sumarsam 1995, 83–89; Kartomi 2000, 280–289; Cohen 2006, 38; Ross 2013, 25–26). In fact, the expression of the same opprobrium from VOC officials suggests that "these kinds of entertainment were available and were enjoyed by the same public" (Salmon and Lombard 1980, 273), and indeed there were also VOC efforts specifically to try to restrict Chinese Peranakan (acculturated and mixed Chinese Indonesians) access to *tandhak* dance performances by inflicting high entrance fees (Kartomi 2000, 281). There was thus likely an influence of Chinese genres on *ronggeng* both artistically and economically. On the other hand, there is no reason to exclude the possibility that Warriner is describing *xiqu:* stage farce and ribaldry and disrepute were common in *xiqu,* especially before the Communist Revolution; and female-to-male stage cross-dressing has a long heritage in China (Chou 1997, 133–135) and remains common today.

12. Another writer's account of the visit of the *Potomac* also mentions "mountebank exhibitions" among the Chinese of Batavia, but that author was not present for the Indies leg of the voyage, and the similarity of the language suggests he is paraphrasing Thorn (Reynolds 1835, 304).

13. Major (*majoor*) Tan, a leading merchant and tax farmer, was the leading officer of the Chinese Council of Batavia, the Kong Koan 公館. This was a "semi-autonomous organization, in which from the eighteenth to the twentieth century the local elite of Batavia's Chinese community joined hands to supervise and coordinate social and religious matters" (Blussé and Chen 2003, 1).

14. She was impressed neither with the vocal performance ("they screamed the text monotonously and without feeling, with appallingly squawky voices") or the "graceless" movements. In her description of their gait there is an unmistakable description of *xiqu* steps (*taibu*): "they raised their feet as they marched as high as they could, and placed them again on the ground with all their force" (Pfeiffer 1856, 190). Pfeiffer probably was in agreement with the general views of colonial society when she remarked that "when one reflects that these warriors are played by young girls" the gait appears "disgusting and immoral" (190).

15. This name is now often written, according to modern orthography, Kwasi Boakye. He was an Ashanti prince and mining engineer who lived for half a century in the Dutch East Indies.

16. For a record of *gezaixi* visits to the Indies even during the wartime years, see ZGXQZ 1993, 54.

17. Jeremy Taylor, writing of Amoy-dialect films, notes that the "imagined space of the Nanyang was overlaid . . . with a complex network of colonial and postcolonial boundaries" that determined how the film industry operated. The same was true of theatre troupes, many of them also from the Hokkien-speaking regions. At the same time, Chinese-language sources often conflate the entire region into "Nanyang," which often diminishes the amount of information that can be derived from sources on troupe travel.

18. The Indonesian career of this particular story, sometimes referred to in English as *The Butterfly Lovers* but better known in Malaysia and Indonesia as *Sampek Engtay*, will be examined in chapter 4.

19. There is some dispute surrounding this genre. Teochew communities as well as Hakka communities claim it, and wealthy members of both groups often invited troupes to perform it in Southeast Asia. In recent history, however, the Hakka claim has predominated.

20. It might be that this is the same troupe of which Yeo How Jiang 楊浩然 remembers the following story, which took place in the late 1920s: on the way back from touring in the Indies, the troupe ran out of money and sold their costumes to the Singapore Hakka Association (Yeo, pers. comm, October 28, 2016).

21. According to exhibition materials of the Teochew Puppet and Opera House 潮藝館, Penang. The "mid-century" conjecture derives from the fact that the actress Yeoh Cheng Imm 楊清音 is reported to have visited Indonesia; she had begun performing at the age of eleven, in 1936.

22. As Cantonese people and language were often referred to as *kongfoe* (presumably from an older name for Guangzhou, Guangfu 廣府), it is likely that references to "*wajang kongfoe*" in Makassar and Batavia in the 1920s and 1930s also refer to *yueju*. There is evidence that *yueju* performers sometimes visited from Hong Kong (*NDNI*, October 13, 1936; Wirawan 2013, 197–198).

23. Rees speaks of a "court language," and it seems likeliest that this refers to the elevated *guanhua* 官話 speech of *xiqu* characters in *waijiangxi*, then a popular genre among Hakka. Yuan Bingling (2000, 86) thinks this circumstance, and the fact that the Hakka genre *Hanju*

had not yet developed, may be a reason to believe troupes were coming from Singapore or elsewhere. However, various Hakka genres (which predate the later term *Hanju*) were being performed in Guangdong in this period (Li and Zhang 2012), even if the genres and terminology were fluid. *Waijiangxi* was widespread among both Hakka and Teochew communities.

24. Chinese orchestras remain active there today. Besides Mandarin and local Kalimantan songs they perform music that is "close to songs for ancient Chinese opera" (Yulianto 2013; DVD).

25. The building was confiscated by the military and the "crawl-space beneath the . . . performance stage" was converted "into a torture-chamber" where prisoners could not stand, sit, or lie down. Among other things, this earned the building the name of the "Bastille of Medan" (Tsai 2008, 247–250, quotation on 249).

26. As with other genres, the influence of cinema is probable: all of the plays mentioned by Linbai—*Chen San Wuniang* 陳三五娘 (Chen San and Wuniang; 1961), *Gao qinfu* 告親夫 (To sue a husband; 1961), *Su Liuniang* 蘇六娘 (1959), and *Huoshao Linjianglou* 火燒臨江樓 (The burning of Linjiang Temple; 1960)—were opera movies in the same period, and local respondents confirm having seen at least some of them.

27. Why, the reader may wonder, was there more *chaoju* than Hokkien theatre in whatever form, given the local predominance of the Hokkien language? One theory advanced by respondents was that *xiqu* was in general more popular in the countryside, and that the countryside around Medan had a high proportion of Chaozhou people. This, perhaps, would also explain why there is a modest history of Chaozhou puppetry in the Medan area but only visiting troupes for Hokkien puppetry.

28. Nio Joe Lan noted about this performer that she was "popular especially among Batavian Chinese ladies" and that "Malay poetry about her was published" (1943, 266).

29. Although efforts to connect *xiqu* to charity seem to have intensified at this time, there were precedents a generation earlier for using *xiqu* performance to generate funds for relief of the Chinese "fatherland" (e.g., *Bataviaasch Nieuwsblad*, June 26, 1915).

30. Also known as Ko Tsu-kuang, Kah narrowly escaped Java when it fell to Japanese forces the following year. The ship he was fleeing on having been bombed by the Japanese, he survived thirty-six hours on a raft before being picked up and taken to Australia, where eventually he was attached to the ROC legation in Canberra (*Goulburn Evening Post*, June 16, 1944).

31. The China Instituut was founded in 1936 by "mainly Dutch-educated Indonesian-Chinese and other Sinophiles from the European and Javanese communities" and published a journal that also included at least one article on *xiqu* (Kartomi 2000, 294).

32. Given that Jambi and Palembang Chinese populations are overwhelmingly Hokkien, presumably the performance style was in that dialect, although by this time *gaojiaxi* may have been supplanted by *gezaixi*. The prominence of the Wang Baochuan narrative in the *gezaixi* repertoire might support this supposition. Writing at very much the same time, Ong (himself Dutch-educated) notes that Western-educated Indies Chinese might be getting their Chinese literature through translations into Western languages, noting especially H.-I. Hsiung's 熊式一 translation of the Wang Baochuan narrative into English, and its Dutch translation *De geborduurde bal* (The embroidered ball; Ong 1943, 219). Dutch newspapers show that Hsiung's script, translated by Charlotte Köhler, premiered in the Netherlands in September 1935. The English "original," premiered a year earlier, was probably the earliest Chinese attempt to stage a *xiqu* story in the Anglophone world (Mao 2014, 47–62). Although it seems to have attracted no attention, except for a passing mention by Nio Joe Lan (1943, 265), the story had been translated into Malay and published in 1904. A copy of this book, which renders Xue Pinggui as Siek Peng Koei, is held in Leiden.

33. Mei Lanfang, prominently deployed in cultural diplomacy by the early PRC, would cross paths with Indonesian notables visiting the PRC in the years following independence, most

notably Hatta shortly after his retirement as vice president (*Java Bode*, October 8, 1957). The reporter refers to Mei as an "actrice." Did he fail to notice that Mei was a man?

34. One such translation, into Dutch, was performed in 1940 in Batavia and Buitenzorg (now Bogor) by members of the Hsing Chung Hui 興中會 (Revive China Society) youth association. That story, presumably performed in a spoken theatre style, consists of a simplification of the Diaochan 貂蟬 episode of the Three Kingdoms. In this version, however, Diaochan commits suicide as soon as she has sent Dong Zhuo 董卓 off to his bloody end. The story, entitled *Tiauw Sian* (a Hokkien romanization of Diaochan) was authored by Tjoa Tjien Mo and published in a publication of the China Instituut (Tjoa 1941). His other Dutch-language plays and novels, as well as some Malay journalism, are recorded by Claudine Salmon (1981, 359). Kwee's reference to the work of Vincenz Hundhausen, the German poet who settled in Beijing and translated, sometimes with the help of the Germanophile poet Feng Zhi 馮至, certain key texts of Chinese drama and poetry, not least *The Peony Pavilion* 牡丹亭 and *The Lute* 琵琶記, suggests that the projects of certain Chinese Indonesians were to some degree influenced by contemporary international projects intending to raise the status of Chinese classical theatre or culture more generally (see also Walravens 2000).

35. "Hokkien opera" in Singapore usually means *gezaixi;* but other suggestions of *gezaixi* performance in Java in this period are missing. In the absence of any clear mechanism for transmission, this type of performance may also have been musical theatre in Hokkien, with a degree of Chinese musical knowledge and instrumentation.

36. Stories concerning Xue Rengui, a Tang general, were popular throughout the Qing dynasty and became prominent in nineteenth-century Indies print and stage. For further details about this narrative's career in the Indies, refer to chapter 2.

37. These are the sisters Su Wen 蘇文 and Guo Bingling 郭冰玲 (Liao 2007, 20–28).

38. Actors were native speakers of Hokkien and had some experience in theatre (Han 2007b, 67). Even in Mainland China, *xiqu* genre terminology was in a bit of a state of flux in the 1950s, and "Hokkien opera" 閩南戲 is not a conclusive term, as it referred to *liyuanxi* at one point in Mainland China, and to *gezaixi* 歌仔戲 in Singapore. Another piece that Xu directed, *Taohua Crosses the River* 桃花搭渡, strongly suggests *gaojiaxi,* while another, *The Married Couple Watches the Lanterns* 夫妻觀燈 is a piece best known as *huangmeixi,* a genre little known in Indonesia except through film (ibid.). Further pieces, described only as "regional theatre" 地方戲, might usually suggest *jingju* repertoire (Qin Xianglian 秦香蓮 and Little Shepherdess 小放牛; 291). It may be that Xu simply instructed students in a kind of general *xiqu* technique, to which they sang in Mandarin. The general sense of respondents that the genres were musicals 歌劇 in dialect suggests that the genre qualities of *xiqu* types (musical system, prosody, dialect, orchestral accompaniment) were not highly defined.

39. The choice of repertoire and genre often suggests the popularity of *xiqu* movies in this period, even when the movies may not have been shown. A production of *Chen San and Wu Niang* in Jakarta in 1957 was explicitly inspired by the reform of the opera in China, which would have been most widely known by the film of the same year (Taylor 2018, 180n97). For instance, a Hong Kong *yueju* movie of *The Western Chambers* 西廂記 was produced in 1959; Xu directed it in Medan in 1961 or thereabouts, since the unified theatre group Silian 四聯 that performed it was only formally established that year (67, 85). The connection with cinema is even more strikingly shown by the production of *Third Sister Liu* 劉三姐 by Silian as well (66), as this musical would not have been familiar except through the influence of film.

40. The generic vagueness is notable here too, in that *Chen San and Wuniang* was performed, billed as *liyuanxi,* in both Hokkien and Mandarin versions ("Fujian liyuanxi Chen San Wuniang," unpaginated). One would usually think of the genre as being too bound to Hokkien

to admit of a Mandarin without becoming a different genre. My thanks go to Jeremy E. Taylor for sharing scans of relevant pages from *Nanyang Post* with me.

41. All three of the titles mentioned by Fu (2012) as being performed by groups in Sumatra in the 1960s had been made into popular movies between 1958 and 1963. Xiaoxing 晓星, an author from Binjai, in the Medan region, also recalls seeing *chaoju* performances in Binjai temples in the 1960s (Xiaoxing, pers. comm., November 1, 2016).

42. This is somewhat surprising, given the genre's popularity in Malaya and Singapore.

43. Apparently, a high proportion of *nanyin* practitioners in Jakarta or Surabaya, even today, are people of Bagansiapiapi origin (Chen Dexian, pers. comm., November 11, 2016).

44. It is not entirely clear why; one theory is that the initial performers were touring Singaporean *gezaixi* actors who elected to stay; or perhaps an unrelated group decided to capitalize on the renown of the name.

45. Titles include *Nasibnja satoe zangeres* (The fate of a female singer; *Bataviaasch Nieuwsblaad,* February 25, 1939) and *Boenga Roos* (The rose; *Bataviaasch Nieuwsblaad,* December 9, 1938).

46. At least one Hong Kong–based Indonesian Chinese also produced Amoy-dialect films (Taylor 2011, 79–80), but this history may be irrecoverable (135).

47. There are few accounts of the gradual disappearance of troupes. Chinese academic publications as recent as the 1990s suggest that *xiqu* was still being widely performed in Indonesia, but field research does not bear this out. It seems probable that these accounts of *xiqu* as an ongoing practice rest on pre–New Order sources, whether textual or interview. Another misunderstanding occurs when Indonesian genres such as *ketoprak* (Central Javanese popular theatre) or *arja* (Balinese sung theatre), which have a history of drawing on Chinese sources but are not generically derived from Chinese theatre, are labelled in Chinese-language texts as a form of *xiqu* or even *jingju,* despite having none of their characteristics. Some care is thus necessary when assessing the occasional claims in Chinese scholarship that *xiqu* is a flourishing practice in Indonesia.

48. Indonesia was the last stop on a seven-country Southeast Asian swing for forty-four members of the China National Drama Troupe 中華國劇團 (*The Straits Times,* October 4, 1989), a name given to *jingju* troupes (in this period always members of the Fu-hsing National Drama Troupe), who were sent on tours abroad via the Education Ministry of the ROC's Bureau of International Cultural and Educational Relations 國際文化教育事業處. The troupe was meant to perform an abridged version of *Lady White Snake* 白蛇傳 and *Meeting at Gucheng* 古城會. As a result of the cancellation, of which the actors were informed as they waited in the lobby for transport to the theatre for the first rehearsal, the troupe spent a week of tourism in Yogyakarta and Bali before moving on to Australia. The president of the National Fu-hsing Dramatic Arts Academy 國立復興劇藝實驗學校, Wang Jing-hsien 王敬先, made a special trip to Bali to comfort and encourage the snubbed actors. The actors, however, report that the unexpected holiday was much enjoyed, and they personally experienced no anti-Chinese sentiment (Chang Yu-chiao, pers. comm., January 19, 2015; Tsao Fu-yong, pers. comm., October 15, 2016). The resumption of diplomatic ties with the PRC in 1990 may have eliminated problems with diplomatically arranged shows from the Mainland. In any event, the Beijing Central Song and Dance Troupe 北京中央歌舞團 was performing in Jakarta by September 1992 (*Harian Indonesia,* September 8, 1992).

49. Wang (2011, 322–323) reprints an article from the state-owned and -controlled Chinese-language paper, *Harian Indonesia,* by Lin Qinghai 林清海. Lin notes that he often listened to *minju* tapes, and that the visit was a "rare opportunity." After returning home from the performance, Lin writes, "my heart was beating wildly, and it was impossible to calm it."

50. *Bianlian,* initially a *chuanju* (Sichuan opera) technique for use in specific repertoire,

has made a global career that largely divorces it from its *xiqu* origins. For a few years, one Bandung Chinese couple has been making a specialty of *bianlian*, and Sino-Indonesian newspapers report efforts to integrate the technique into Cirebon mask dancing (*tari topeng Cirebon*; *Guoji ribao*, December 12, 2013; and June 9, 2016).

51. In this case, Hunan Normal University and Taiwan's best-known *gezaixi* troupe, Ming Hwa Yuan, were the visitors.

52. While the Chinese name (Hakka Friendship Association) indicates its Hakka affiliation, the Indonesian name (Foundation of Love and Hope) refers to its charitable role. This divergence in names for different linguistic audiences is extremely common among Sino-Indonesian associations.

53. The troupe is among the most prominent in Fujian Province, and has been decorated nationally on several occasions. As it happens, Zeng's mother is a Sino-Indonesian from Ambon who "returned" to Quanzhou as a young woman.

54. Similarly, I was asked by a Bandung luxury restaurant to approach Mainland Chinese *xiqu* performers to travel to Indonesia to provide fifteen minutes of *xiqu* for Imlek 2014.

55. These were apparently the Capitol and the Guoda 國大 theatres.

56. Cunyi was a broader Cantonese arts group founded in the early 1950s and initially specializing in lion dance (Liao 2007, 285; Li Meirong, pers. comm., November 5, 2016).

57. *Guan Hanqing* was derived from Tian Han's 田漢 drama of the same name; the last was a film version of Tong Dik Sang's 唐滌生 Cantonese *yueju* script. The same holds true of their 1962 production of *Snow in Midsummer* 六月雪, which had been filmed in 1959. For the influence of Chinese cinema on spoken theatre, see chapter 3.

58. The Medan consulate undertook a high level of propaganda activity, both among Indonesians and the local Chinese community (Hong Liu 2010, 158, 160). Other respondents suggest that the consulate, through the Chinese General Society, exercised a considerable amount of control over the content of spoken theatre groups (see chapter 4). Many local Chinese respondents remember with excitement the visits of PRC cultural delegations, for instance, the visit of the Nanjing-based Qianxian Gewutuan 前綫歌舞團 (Frontline Song and Dance Troupe) in 1965, only months before the fall of Sukarno (*Guoji ribao*, September 21, 2012).

59. I have, however, not seen any reference to performance in the last five years. It seems probable that Tan has retired.

60. His late brother Chen Xinrong 陳新榮 was also a *yueju* performer; other members of the troupe today include his wife and other Medan Cantonese transplants to Jakarta. Its performances consist mostly of mall and restaurant events, generally centered on Chinese festivals. In terms of repertoire, there is some indication of Indonesian influence, in that the troupe is reported as performing a Sie Jin Kwie (i.e., Xue Rengui 薛仁貴) show, which is especially popular in Indonesia.

61. Reports from Penang also suggest that Thailand *chaoju* troupes are a source of competition in Malaysia.

62. The *chaoju* version was concerned with the episode in which the fabulous bird Jataya attempts, unsuccessfully, to prevent the abduction of Sita by Ravana (Javier Li, pers. comm., October 28, 2016).

63. Singapore's Chinese Opera Institute was also invited by then Solo mayor Joko Widodo to perform a *yueju* 越劇 version of *Handan meng* 邯鄲夢 (Dream of Handan) at Mangkunegaran Palace in 2008 (Cai 2011b).

64. In response to local Chinese criticism that a Malay culture festival had ignored the pluralism of Tanjungpinang, *xiqu*, likely from Singapore, was one of the events arranged (Faucher 2007, 451).

65. Locally, the troupe uses "Opera Hok Kien," and the Indonesian-language media tends to use variations on "Wayang Orang Tionghoa." Although the troupe recognizes that it is part of *gezaixi* in Chinese terms, the local Chinese-language terms are simply either *xi* 戲 or *renxi* 人戲, perhaps both in analogy to "wayang orang" and in distinction against the *potehi* genre, now locally extinct. In the occasional printed materials, such as in Palembang's Chinese monthly *Palembang Hengpo* 巨港興報 (e.g., *Jugang xingbao* 58 [2016]), the term *minju* 閩劇 is also used, as *min* is short for Fujian; this usage exists also in the Singaporean Chinese-language press. This, however, is not the same form as *minju* as known in the Mainland, where it refers to the Fuzhou-dialect genre.

66. The oldest local *gezaixi* veteran, Tang Nantong 唐南通, estimated that Huaqiao had been active from 1948 to 1964, and remembered that there had been a teacher from China involved. There was also a Cantonese opera troupe, Qunsheng Troupe 群聲劇社, active in ca. 1955–1965, which performed at the General Chinese Association 華僑總會 rather than at temples. There seems to be no documentation for the Palembang troupes except for the scripts brought from China. Some older respondents remarked that they had burnt photos at the beginning of the New Order period when houses had been searched for Chinese-language materials.

67. Much like Cunyi in Medan at roughly the same time, Xiongfeng's theatre activities were an expansion of their existing lion dance troupe.

68. The police remain a presence at Tridharma Arts festivals, ostensibly to provide security, and temple officials had no alternative but to come to terms with them in the usual way. Suharto-era performances were especially dependent on the establishment and maintenance of relations with local police, and changes in personnel might cause performances to be cancelled.

69. This remains the case also with *gezaixi* performances for temple festivals in Taiwan. According to several of the younger Tridharma Arts actors, they find the Hokkien used in Fujian and Taiwan quite difficult to understand as Palembang Hokkien is distinct; this is part of what makes improvisation necessary, because the lines used in Taiwanese *gezaixi* are not natural parlance for them. The scene summaries, improvisation, and the assistance of offstage actors also closely resemble recent *gezaixi* practice in Singapore (Lee 2009, 62–68).

70. As related above, Ming Hwa Yuan visited Bandung in 2012, attracting an audience that literally had no idea what the troupe or the genre was; in Palembang, however, they are idolized in the Tridharma Arts circles.

71. This temple is also known as Baiyun Ting 白雲亭 and is a daughter temple to a temple of the same name in Anxi. South Sumatra rehearses at another daughter temple in Karya Baru 七公里.

72. Typically, the troupe adds on another performance as a voluntary donation to the gods. The chief rival entertainments for the local temple festivals are karaoke or variety shows, and some temples have gone back and forth between the options.

73. Because all the actors either have other work or are students, the troupe has had to refuse some touring invitations, including to Jakarta. Interestingly, a young actor also reported being hired as an extra for a couple of weeks by a PRC company touring around Medan, which featured actors from "various provinces" and performed in Mandarin, with otherwise "the same music, the same stories" as *gezaixi*. I have not been able otherwise to identify this troupe, but it may suggest that there are more PRC troupes operating seasonally in North Sumatra, and that not all of them are Hokkien.

74. For instance, the series of performances I witnessed between November 15 and 18, 2016, was hosted by Liong Toh Kiong, which is a daughter temple of a Tang/Theng clan temple in the Anxi town of Wenquan 溫泉. Today Anxi is a county under the Quanzhou municipality,

although its own identity remains strong. Anxi networks have also long been active in Singapore, and have contributed to the ancestral region's institutions (Hue and Dean 2016, 188).

75. Locals reported that only four or five of the fourteen local temples have been inviting the troupe; Yang Fuxing estimated the activity of the troupe at seven or eight engagements a year, for two or three nights each. At the time of my visit in November 2016, there were rumors of a possible merger between the two troupes.

76. The rule was explained to me by both Acit and actors as a way to avoid offending the gods, who might take umbrage at women actors' menstrual cycles.

77. Long-term, however, the reported decline of Hokkien among the youngest generation of Palembang Chinese may prove a challenge for the groups' viability. On the other hand, there was a large group of attentive children and a high proportion of young actors. Local media reports that the troupe uses Palembang Malay in its performances, but actors and Acit both told me that this was only ever a few utterances, to amuse the audience. Youngsters who are not competent in Hokkien are given walk-on roles; backstage language use does seem to divide generationally between Hokkien and Malay/Indonesian. Increasingly, Indonesian translations of the scene summaries were projected above the screen.

78. The editor of *Palembang Hengpo*, Armin E.S. 潘振勝, himself a Hokkien transplant from Medan, suggested to me that the history of Chinese farming in Palembang might contribute part of the explanation, as theatre was one of the principal amusements during periods of agricultural inactivity. The heavy concentration of clan-based temples and the relatively long history of Palembang Chinese may also provide a greater impetus for theatre vis-à-vis Medan.

Chapter 2: Glove, String, and Shadow

1. The presence of rod and shadow puppetry in China has prompted some scholars to suggest that China is the ultimate origin for many kinds of Southeast Asian puppetry genres, including *wayang*. While guesswork is hard to disprove, there remains no evidence that *wayang* has Chinese origins, and no reason to assume it (Zhou Nanjing 1987, 215–216; Fan Pen Chen 2003, 41–42).

2. The term "white people's *wayang*" was in the nineteenth century also applied to Western drama (Matthew Isaac Cohen 2007, 571).

3. Nio Joe Lan still uses it this way ("wajang Tiongkok") in his 1962 work on Sino-Indonesian literature (3, 11).

4. The term *wayang* is even applied, in Indonesian-language texts, to Chinese puppetry forms that have no connection to Indonesia (e.g., Soelarto and Albiladiyah 1980/1981, 6; Wulandari 2009, 7–11).

5. See, for instance, the stories of Tan Hong Boen 陳豐文 (1905–1983).

6. For instance, the *wayang kulit dalang* Ki Sabdhosutedjo (Tee Boen Liong) or Widayat Djiang (Tjioe Bian Djiang), both from East Java.

7. *Budaixi* and *potehi* are the romanizations of the words for "cloth-bag theatre" in Mandarin *pinyin* and Hokkien, respectively. Western scholarship on China (in recent decades committed to *pinyin*) has tended to use the former term, while non–Chinese-language scholarship focused on Southeast Asian practices adopts the latter, now increasingly expanding to *wayang potehi* in the Indonesian context. Given the persistence of misunderstandings regarding the name, it may be useful to offer some explanation: early scholarship in Dutch variously translated the Chinese term as "linen-bag theatre" (Hazeu 1897) and "play of the linen bag" (Moens 1949), proposing that the term came from a bag hanging beneath the stage (De Groot in Hazeu 1897, 92–93), from a bag puppets were brought out of (Serrurier 1896, 141), or from a bag that

the puppeteer would have worn during performance, with an opening at the top for the puppets (Moens 1949); van Groenendael's summation of these interpretations of the terms of origin has often been followed by Indonesian scholars who, like early Dutch scholars, were not examining the terms from a Chinese-language perspective (van Groenendael 1993, 14–15). However, the three Chinese characters (cloth [*bu/po/* 布]-pocket/bag [*dai/te/* 袋]-theatre/show [*xi/hi/* 戲]) for the genre are transparent, and the usual derivation of the name lies in the fact that the bodies of the puppets are made of cloth, forming a kind of pocket for the puppeteer's hand. Western languages refer to this kind of puppetry as "glove" ' puppets (as opposed to rod puppets or marionettes), but the Chinese word means "cloth pocket," and the name of the genre seems as self-explanatory to Chinese speakers as "glove puppet" does to English speakers. Since van Groenendael (1993, 13–16) also provides the doubtless correct explanation (that the pocket/bag refers to the body of the puppet), furnished by puppetry specialist Robin Ruizendaal, Indonesian sources today tend to provide the whole range of explanations; but there is little reason to assert the earlier guesswork alongside the standard Chinese explanation. In Chinese, *potehi* is also known as *zhangzhongxi* 掌中戲 (theatre of the palm of the hand); older Sino-Indonesian puppeteers in Indonesia also used this term. *Mu'ouxi* 木偶戲 is also sometimes used, though since this means "wooden puppet theatre," it does not provide a distinction from marionette forms. Consequently, the three state-sponsored puppet troupes in the ancestral region of southern Fujian today feature confusing terminology: the *potehi* troupe in Zhangzhou 漳州 is called the Mu'ou Jutuan 木偶劇團 (Wooden Puppet Troupe); but the Quanzhou Mu'ou Jutuan 泉州木偶劇團 is a marionette troupe, while the *potehi* troupe in Jinjiang 晋江 is called Zhangzhong Mu'ou Jutuan 掌中木偶劇團 (Palm-of-the-Hand Wooden Puppet Troupe).

8. This makes Javanese evidence for the genre, as will become apparent further on, very early by comparison. For that evidence too, however, the existing account is from a twentieth-century source, citing a source that is now lost.

9. Indeed, with the decline of Singaporean *potehi*, various forms of Indonesian puppetry tradition may operate as sources of influence and inspiration to them (Lin Jia 2009, 142).

10. Chinese and hybrid puppetry certainly exists in Thailand, including the *hun lek* marionettes (made by Bangkok Chinese starting in 1878), and the Hainan-inspired *hun krabog* rod puppets (made by Thais starting from the late nineteenth century), which performs *Three Kingdoms* repertoire (Chandavij and Pramualratana 1998, 58–83, 94–105; Reynolds 2001, 131).

11. Specifically, the *Nawaruci* text cited in chapter 1, and that does not make clear whether the entertainment provided was performed by humans or puppets.

12. Zhou Nanjing (1987, 216) makes a claim that *potehi* was being performed in "Banten and Jakarta" in the seventeenth century, but does not provide a source.

13. Dutch descriptions of the art as "chineesche poppenkast" (Chinese puppet-box) clearly suggests *potehi*'s box-like stages, several of which have been preserved in Java from the nineteenth century.

14. This remains a highly speculative association, along with all others suggesting that genres of *wayang* were influenced by Chinese puppetry at a formative stage. A Dutch source notes that the Javanese referred to a Chinese puppetry form as "wajang-golèq" (Poensen 1873, 163). This was almost certainly *potehi*, given that it was performed in a high register of Chinese by "full-blooded Chinese" (ibid.) and its stage resembled European puppet stages; however, this lexical point is no reason to presume a relation between *potehi* and *golek*. Even presuming that Poensen has committed no error, this is most likely a case of linguistic approximation by analogy.

15. Use of the word itself is a sign of acculturation, borrowing the term as it does from the Javanese master-artists who lead other forms of *wayang*. For *potehi*, the Hokkien-derived term *sehu* 師傅 is also used.

16. The venture failed in 1899, and the man behind it returned to his previous employ at the Komedie Stamboel.

17. The earliest reference here derives from van Hasselt's information that *wajang* meant to Padang people "Javanese or Chinese box puppetry."

18. Usually, the ensemble consisted of ten people and performed the same repertoire, according to the same summaries, as those used by the *gezaixi* troupe. Performance petered out in the late 1950s because it was less popular than *gezaixi*; Ong was associated with the Xiongfeng troupe (Ong Kok Kie, pers. comm., November 15 and 19, 2016; Tang Nantong, pers. comm., November 16, 2016).

19. It is worth noting that the narratives listed in 1954 (*Three Kingdoms*, *Xue Rengui*, and *Investiture of the Gods* and *Qu Yuan*)—are, except for the last, very much the same type of repertoire one sees today (*Java-Bode*, June 4, 1954).

20. According to Matthew Cohen, Malay and Hokkien were already being combined in *potehi* in late nineteenth-century Surabaya (Cohen 2006, 39), but the more widespread move seems to be mid-twentieth century.

21. For names and areas of activity of mid-century *potehi dalang*, see Purwoseputro 2014, 44.

22. The information on Thio is based largely on my interview with him in January 2013, while corroborating via Kuardhani (2012, 95–97), Tsai Tsung-te (2015, 75–76), and *The Jakarta Post* (April 9, 2000; March 20, 2009; and October 11, 2010).

23. The Tridharma Arts troupe in Palembang has also incorporated this melody into their *gezaixi* performances, which is one of only a handful of melodies they use.

24. These are generally referred to by the Javanese *wayang* term *suluk*, designating, in *wayang kulit*, a kind of "mood-song" sung periodically by the *dalang* to generate a particular atmosphere. Generally, characters who first appear in Chinese theatre (including puppetry) explain who they are and what they intend. These fixed Hokkien phrases have been retained in *potehi*; the term *suluk* has been applied to them by analogy in *potehi*.

25. I am indebted for this observation to Robin Ruizendaal, who thinks the relative conservatism of marionettes may have its roots in the greater ritual importance.

26. The lotus flower apparently recalled the banned organization BAPERKI, often associated with Chinese Indonesian leftists.

27. While Santoso is still active in Tulungagung, and the Gudo practice will be discussed later, it would seem that there is no longer a Kediri group.

28. Similarly, John B. Kwee, writing in 1996, reports that the *dalang* had to obtain permission to perform and were advised to refrain from insulting or political humor and "about ten minutes during the performance [had to be] allegorical in regard to the development program" (1996, 47). Difficulties are reported regarding New Order performances in Malang and Semarang as well (Purwoseputro 2014, 50).

29. Guangze Zunwang is a local deity particularly associated with Nan'an 南安, today a county-level district of Quanzhou. In life, he was a tenth-century miracle-worker in Anxi and Nan'an, and during the twelfth century the figure received a title from the emperor (Dean 1993; Jack Meng-Tat Chia 2013; Tan 2015, 360). Temples, many of them also with Fengshan 鳳山 (Phoenix Mountain) in their names, are common in Taiwan and Southeast Asia, especially Malaysia. Among the other temples devoted to this god is the Surabaya temple where *potehi* is performed (Tsai Tsung-te 2015, 78). The central temple in Nan'an was rebuilt with money from Singaporean adepts in 1978 and has been controlled by local government since 1980 (Tan 2015, 362). That temple hosts lucrative visits from Southeast Asian adepts, and in 2013 a delegation from the Gudo temple made the trip to Nan'an for such a pilgrimage.

30. It remains, however, common for *dalang* to mimic a Chinese accent for certain charac-

ters or at certain points (see Purwoseputro 2014, 113), so that one may see a Javanese performer, the star employee of a Sino-Indonesian patron who labels the show as 100 percent Indonesian, mimicking a comical Chinese accent while performing a Chinese narrative.

31. The result of the 2012 reconciliation between rival claimants of this title was that the author of this text, Sinuhun Tedjowulan, relinquished his claim to the title of Susuhanan, assuming a royal consultative role. However, the process of reconciliation has been marred by ongoing disputes (*Tempo*, September 1, 2013; *The Jakarta Post*, July 11, 2017).

32. Didik Nini Thowok's Chinese name is Kwee Tjoen An 郭春安, and his childhood memories likely refer to the 1960s, given that he was born in 1954. The Chinese-language press in Indonesia has recently called him the "Mei Lanfang of the Indonesian arts world," a reference to the fact that he generally dances women's roles (*Yinhua ribao*, November 1, 2016).

33. Gus Dur, especially, is often featured in Sino-Indonesian community events. In 2017, the Gudo temple advertised its temple festival with the image of, and a quote from, Gus Dur (who was born in nearby Jombang): "The more different we are, the clearer the point of our commonality."

34. Because other *wayang* forms predate the nationalist movements that instituted Indonesian as the archipelago's unifying language, they were once all performed in languages such as Javanese, Balinese, and Sundanese. *Wayang potehi*'s switch to Indonesian may tap into the fact that, as with spoken theatre, "the use of Indonesian is the identifying characteristic of being modern and national" in contrast to "most performances [that] are unscripted and performed in regional languages" (Gillitt, 2010, ix). More broadly, as "a linguistic symbol for the Indonesian nation, the language [Indonesian] also betokens the unification of diverse ethnic groups with varying socio-cultural backgrounds" (McGlynn 1998, 85).

35. Unlike the city of Mojokerto, these villages have no substantial Sino-Indonesian presence.

36. It is worth noting, however, that Pak Yensen is not a *klenteng* member, being a Protestant.

37. This name is in use also among Mainland and Taiwanese Hakka (and does not distinguish between glove puppets and marionettes). The character *qiao* 樵 would seem to refer to the wood used to carve the puppets, although sometimes the character *jiao* 醮 also is found, which would more directly indicate ritual practice. The Mandarin marionette terms *tixian mu'ou* 提線木偶 or *kuileixi* 傀儡戲 are known only to those who have spent time in Chinese-speaking territories

38. The term *wayang gantung* will be used here, since it is what the reader is most likely to encounter outside the Chinese-speaking world (in which the genre has almost entirely escaped mention).

39. This is a county of Longyan; the place-name Shanghang is also used as a genre name.

40. Shanghang and Liancheng are both counties belonging administratively to Longyan, but each has a substantial local culture and identity.

41. Records of marionettes appear in Taiwan by 1835, although these are Hokkien rather than Hakka practices (Lai Dengming 2014, 85). Current Hakka practice is centered around Taoyuan; a second family of Hakka puppet troupes, using gloves rather than marionettes, has developed in Yunlin and is a result of Hokkien *potehi* tradition being adopted and adapted by Hakka troupes. It is also worth mentioning a Singkawang woman, Ye Sushan 葉蘇珊, who is also working in Hokkien *potehi* in Yunlin assisting her husband, though there is no indication that she is connected to Singkawang marionette traditions. A Taiwanese TV reportage on Ye is available at https://www.youtube.com/watch?v=y7nsJuLR5Aw (accessed October 10, 2018).

42. Tjin's children, like other West Kalimantan Hakka, have left to go to Jakarta or Malaysia

for work (see also Hui 2011, 264n51). The youngest son, who was minding the family house in Singkawang when I visited in 2013, said "nobody even asks about *wayang gantung* here anymore. There's nothing for me but to go sell vegetables in Malaysia."

43. Both the orchestra and the marionette troupe are essentially family businesses, including besides his wife and children also his elder brother. For over forty years Tai has provided the female voice for marionette performances, while Tjin himself does the male voices. Other members of the troupe each take on one marionette. Older performers were all taught by Tjin's father.

44. Indeed, the only Western-language mention of *wayang gantung* of any length are the notes provided by Margaret Kartomi about a performance she witnessed in 1992 (Kartomi 2000, 312n22). She saw many of the same performers who are still active today. However, the group—at thirty—seems very large compared to the present usual complement of eight to ten and occasionally twenty.

45. Suharto himself in 1969 called for the help of *dalang* in supporting government policy (Pausacker 2004, 128), and it became common nationwide to include family planning in *wayang* performances during the Suharto era. For examples in other forms of *wayang*, see Terrence (1997, 151–125, 156–157) and Weintraub (2004, 5, 153–154).

46. As with *potehi*, Indonesian authorities are not mistaken about the ritual aspect of Singkawang marionettes, and indeed ritual purposes are typical of southern Chinese string puppetry. Kagan (1978, 74) also notes it among Hakka practitioners in Hong Kong. The belief among marionettists is that marionettes are imbued with supernatural powers, capable of bringing good or bad luck, and useful especially for exorcistic purposes. One way of thinking of the faithful's attitude (in the following quote, in the Singapore Hokkien community) may be that an adept "worships the gods who are dancing as puppets" (Margaret Chan 2006, 136). Singkawang marionettes are also considered to be able to move or speak on their own. For that reason, before a performance or before taking out the puppets to be shown, they must be treated with reverence, given meat or eggs, and offered incense and joss paper. The ritual occurs ten to fifteen minutes before the show. If the ritual is not completed, the performance will not go smoothly, or a dangerous mishap may occur. If the performance is taking place in the countryside, chicken blood must be spread on the puppets, because the countryside spirits are stronger than their urban counterparts. If it occurs in the city, the recitation of a spell is sufficient. One story was repeated to me on several occasions: in 2008, while Shin Thian Chai was visiting Jakarta for performances, Chen's Lirang house caught fire. Neighbors reported hearing the puppets calling for rescue. Although the house was burnt to the ground, twenty puppets were saved from the house due to their calls for help.

47. Karaoke is also a direct competitor with *xiqu* for temple business in Palembang.

48. For a report on marionette participation in 2011, see *Guoji ribao*, April 11, 2011.

49. This phenomenon will be dealt with at greater length in chapter 6.

50. Interaction between marionette and human troupes is documented in historic Mainland Hakka tradition, with marionettes having pride of place (Lai Dengming 2014, 83).

51. This sort of interaction between Sino-Indonesian puppet and human theatre was noted also by Thio Thiong Gie, and in a way this influence still operates, for instance, in the adoption of *wayang potehi* and *wayang kulit Cina-Jawa* by contemporary theatre practitioners such as Teater Koma. Similarly, in Penang *potehi* practice one finds the movement of many retired Penang *gezaixi* performers into *potehi* troupes (Sooi-Beng Tan 2016, 25–26).

52. Tangshan or "Tong san" 唐山 is, and was, familiar in Chinese communities in Malaysia and Indonesia as a metonym for China, and Tangshan songs are associated with Hakka identity (Hui 2011, 222; Leo 2015, 73).

53. For Indonesians not from Java or Bali, the association between Indonesian culture or identity and *wayang* may seem to elide national diversity in favor of a Java-centric perspective.

54. *Wayang kulit* refers to the leather shadow puppets on Java. The "Cina" in the title is something of a terminological throwback, since "Cina" is now often generally regarded as an ethnic slur and is dispreferred in favor of Hokkien-derived Tionghoa (Chinese) and Tiongkok (China) or English-derived "China" (see also Hui 2011, 9–12). As a result, one may now find "Wayang kulit China-Jawa" instead of "Cina-Jawa." Alternatively, the terms "thithi" or "titi," have also been used, apparently as an onomatopoeic word referring to the percussion. However, since this term has also been used for *potehi*, it may also lead to confusion, to avoid which *wayang kulit Cina-Jawa* will be used here. A recent exhibition and its catalogue opted for *Wacinwa* (i.e., ***Wayang Cina Jawa***), which has the advantage of eliding the offensive term through amalgamation into a new one; a further 2015 publication followed suit.

55. Contrary to previous sources, *Wacinwa* gives the dates of Gan's life span as 1895–1967. It is not clear whether this constitutes the introduction of an error or a correction of previous sources. The same holds true of *Wacinwa*'s assertion that Gan Ing Kwat was the grandfather of Gan Thwan Sing rather than his father. In some sources, Gan's name is also spelled Gan Dhwan Sing and Gan Thoan Sing. The Chinese characters for any names in the family remain unknown.

56. Given the genre's similarity to, and obvious inspiration by, other *wayang kulit* practices, it might be considered a particular, Chinese-infused, subvariety of *wayang kulit*; or, on the model of *wayang revolusi* (revolutionary *wayang*) or *wayang wahyu* (revelations *wayang*), it might be considered an independent form of *wayang*.

57. Angst was a Swiss zoologist (and once the director of Germany's largest monkey park, nearby). Beginning in 1973, Angst had collected approximately 20,000 *wayang* puppets by 2011 (Cohen 2018). Selections from the collection, including some *wayang kulit Cina-Jawa*, were published in *Wayang Indonesia: Die phantastische Welt des Indonesischen Figurentheaters*; the 2014 exhibition catalogue *Wacinwa: Silang Budaya Cina-Jawa* provides images of many of the other set, held at Sonobudoyo.

58. Seltmann had been a leading German scholar of South Indian puppet forms and extended this interest to Indonesia in the 1970s and 1980s.

59. Judging by what is known about the original number of puppets (according to Seltmann [1976, 55], Gan initially had approximately 400 leather and 130 cardboard figures, the latter becoming necessary due to the rise of leather prices during World War II), those presently in the Sonobudoyo and Yale collections represent the overwhelming majority of those ever produced. Replicas of the puppets can be seen also at Jakarta's Wayang Museum, another indication of the incorporation of Chinese forms by Indonesian *wayang* institutions. Apparently, Gan's other scripts are lost, burnt by his family after the 1982 death of his son (Mastuti 2004, 6). His son had assisted his father in performance but not deemed himself capable enough to serve as *dalang* (Seltmann 1976, 55).

60. Tsai Tsung-te reports that Gan studied in Habiranda, the well-known *wayang kulit* school (2017, 52).

61. This date is universally used, apparently taken from the *gunungan* (mountain) *wayang* in the Uberlingen collection, in which the date made is indicated as 1925 (Prasetya 2014a, 9). Although Kartomi's insistence (286) that there must have been a tradition preexisting Gan's work is reasonable, there are no records or artifacts to support this (see also Pausacker 2005, 195). Similarly, the use of Chinese puppets as models is possible but not demonstrable; and Kartomi's belief that a Chinese orchestra similar to *potehi* was in use, is not the view of Mastuti

or the Sonobudoyo curators, who believe that musically the genre was similar to *wayang kulit purwa* (Ontoro 2014, 22–23).

62. Similarly, *wayang potehi* and the Palembang *gezaixi* all employ summaries rather than full scripts.

63. According to Seltmann (1976, 54) some of the scripts were also used for *wayang wong*.

64. Contrary to common belief, perhaps especially in Indonesia (where shadow puppets are assumed by many to be a unique national invention), shadow puppets are historically found in many parts of China, including in the Fujian and Guangdong regions from which Sino-Indonesians partially descend (Fan Pen Chen 2007, 232–233; Yeung 2007, 64, 68). Soelarto and Albiladiyah state (1980/1981, 6) that Chinese leather-puppet shows were being performed on Java, but do not identify any sources suggesting their presence in the 1920s or 1930s, though they do reproduce pictures of a Chinese *piyingxi* puppet (1980/1981, 51), presumably found on Java. Earlier references to Chinese performing *wayang kulit* on Java are interpreted by both Seltmann (1976, 53) and Soelarto and Albiladiyah (1980/1981, 6) as potentially referring to Chinese shadow puppetry. The researcher Annie Katsura Rollins, a specialist in Chinese shadow puppets, suggests that these puppets "look heavily influenced by Chinese shadow puppet traditions, but also are clearly tied to *wayang*" (pers. comm., February 23, 2016), citing size and the removability of the head. Similarly, Seltmann judges the puppets to be "by no means images of Javanese figures. Their similarity with these latter is to be found only in the technical sense and in the effect achieved through the workmanship" (1976, 55). Riharyani (2015, 40–41) reproduces Chinese and Cina-Jawa puppets side by side, showing influence was likely considerable—even greater, indeed, than *wayang kulit purwa*. This is an area requiring further research from material culture scholars, and it may also be possible to recover textual evidence of Chinese shadow puppetry in the archipelago.

65. Namely, in Gan's transliteration, *Thig Jing Nga Ha Ping She* 狄青五虎平西 (Di Qing and the five tigers pacify the West), known in Javanese as *Rabenipun radja Tig Tjeng* (The marriage of King Di Qing).

66. For instance, Di Qing, Xue Rengui, and Zhao Kuangyin are all categorized as Qing military romances, "apparently intended for a less well-educated audience" (Idema and Haft 1997, 229) than the more famous Qing novels such as *Rulin waishi* or *Honglou meng*. Xue Rengui does seem to have predominated in the Sino-Javanese narrative universe. Mastuti, tabulating 119 Sino-Javanese texts, finds that almost one half, 53 of 119, are Xue Rengui narratives (Mastuti 2011, 51).

67. One of these, *Song Taizu san xia nantang*, is an anonymous, now forgotten, martial Qing novel from the 1860s and 1870s. It is a sequel to *Feilong zhuan* (Story of the flying dragons), an eighteenth-century novel that, among other things, gives an account of the rise of Zhao Kuangyin (Idema and Haft 1997, 225). *Feilong zhuan* had been translated in the Indies by 1887 (Salmon 1981, 354).

68. Likely based on the Ming novel of that name by Wu Yuantai 吳元泰.

69. Translated into Malay by 1901 (Salmon 1981, 354–355, 477).

70. It is worth noting that nineteenth-century and early twentieth-century shadow puppet scripts in Taiwan show much of the same repertoire, including the focus on Xue Rengui (Schipper 1979, 13–19). There may have been a direct influence from Hokkien shadow-puppet repertoire, or else—like Thio Thiong Gie—Gan may simply have absorbed the same stories through printed translations and oral sources.

71. Between 1954 and 1960, the Solo-born comic-book author Siauw Tik Kwie 蕭德貴, under the pen name of Oto Suastika, produced *Sie Djin Koei* comics for various Java newspapers. Some of these were reprinted in book form, most recently in 2009 (Setyautama 2008, 323).

72. Ketoprak versions include a 1970s play produced by Mujiman Atmo Priyatno and staged by Ketoprak Saptamandala. All the characters acquired Indonesianized names: Sie Jin Kui became Joko Sudiro; his son Xue Dingshan/Sie Teng San became Sutrisno, and so on. Adaptations based on these characters have continued, including a television version (Ketoprak Sayembara, 2001) and a radio miniseries (Radio Republik Indonesia Yogyakarta, 2004).

Chapter 3: Five Ancestors, Twice Over

1. The most active group may be Medan's Xiyanghong Juyishe 夕陽紅劇藝社 (Red Sunset Performing Arts Society), which performs occasional skits along with its usual singing and karaoke events (*Guoji ribao*, February 7, 2012). See also chapter 5.

2. Probably the most important Chinese-language Indonesian author working in Chinese was Hei Ying 黑嬰. Though the best-known part of his oeuvre are 1930s stories written and set in Shanghai, he wrote considerably about his native city of Medan. See Zhang 1995.

3. The particular piece of European theatre listed in the source, a Palembang Chinese school, is Molière's *L'Avare* in (or adapted from) a 1926 translation by Gao Zhenchang 高真常; the comedy was Song Chunfang's 宋春舫 1935 *In the Fog* 五里霧中, usually classified as a comedy of manners.

4. Evidence exists, for instance, in the form of a program of a 1938 patriotic performance, in Siantar, of the Siantar Chinese Arts Troupe 先達華僑國術團 (*Huaqiao lishi wenxian dang'an guan*, n.d.)

5. These scripts seem to have been easily available. A 1948 Jakarta bookstore newspaper ad shows three Cao Yu plays, *Thunderstorm* 雷雨 (1934), *Sunrise* 日出 (1936), and *The Wilderness* 原野 (1937) among the books for sale (*Xinbao*, September 9, 1948). Veterans of Medan troupes reported that they had formerly found scripts without difficulty in bookstores, and smaller North Sumatra localities bought theirs in Medan.

6. The author Shi Huawen 石華文 and director Li Zhiping 李志萍 do not seem to be well known otherwise. The piece, described as a social satire, mocked conservative male social attitudes through the story of a lascivious boss who insists that all his employees be young unmarried women.

7. Somewhat amusingly, the factions were popularly known in North Sumatra as blue-ass 藍屁股 (KMT) and red-ass 紅屁股 (CCP).

8. Troupes were sent out throughout China to perform this piece, mostly outdoors on street corners, in a project of national salvation. It was shown also at Roosevelt's wartime White House and famously painted by Xu Beihong. Its authorship is complex and disputed (Lai Him Mark 2010, 110; Tang 2016).

9. *The Soul of China* was a 1948 Hong Kong–made Mandarin film adapted from a 1937 script. *Zhengqi ge* 正氣歌 (Song of righteousness), by well-known dramatist Wu Zuguang 吳祖光.

10. Several other shows also appear to be adaptations of PRC films, such as, for instance, *Xin juzhang dao lai zhiqian* 新局長到來之前 (Before the arrival of the new secretary; 1956), even if the dates of the Medan productions are not known (Cao 2007, 59). The same holds true of the society in Binjai, which produced *Sanmao xue shengyi* 三毛學生意 (Sanmao studies business; 1958). One Medan show, *Fengyu Niucheshui* 風雨牛車水 (Tumultuous Kreta Ayer, known in its movie version as *Rainstorm in Chinatown*) is about Singapore and might reflect either connections within Nanyang or inspiration from Mainland China. However, even *Tumultuous Kreta Ayer* was written and performed by Mainlanders for a Singapore tour (Cao 2007, 59; Lim 2016, 79). Even if a certain film had not been shown in Medan, the popularity a film generated among Mainland Chinese spoken theatre groups may have meant that these were the

scripts most likely to arrive in Medan. There is also evidence that Singapore-based song-and-dance troupes visited Indonesia at least until the 1950s (Lai Bojiang 1993, 170).

11. Liu Sanjie is a legendary figure who was renowned for being "thoroughly educated in the classics and history and especially good at making up songs," defeating all comers at song competitions (Loh 1984, 167). The 1961 film—which transformed the character into the heroine of an "educational comedy of class struggle" (170)—was one of the greatest successes of early PRC cinema (Loh 1984).

12. Now the Gedung Merdeka (Freedom Building), this building was the conference hall of the Bandung Asia-Africa Conference of 1955.

13. It may be that this text is now lost. Xiamen University's Zhang Tao 張桃 has seen this manuscript when it was kept in the library at the Sino-Indonesian Writers' Association (印華寫作協會 Perhimpunan Penulis Tionghoa Indonesia). But the original, it seems, was destroyed in a recent flood at that library; and Zhang's photocopy has been lost in a move.

14. Deng's text also reproduces a message from the Chinese National Association of Writers and Artists to the editor of Batavia's *Xinbao* 新報, almost certainly Ang Yan Goan 洪淵源, though either Deng or the original letter mistakenly writes Runyuan 潤源. The Association thanks the Chinese on Java, thanking them for their donations and for "caring so much for the motherland's cultural workers" (Deng 2002, 185). The message, having been passed to Republic of China Consul-General Tsiang Chia Tung 蔣家棟, had reached them through diplomatic channels.

15. Most dramatically, Hu was dispatched to the crash site of Air India's *Kashmir Princess*. The plane had crashed, likely as part of an assassination plot against Zhou Enlai (who was not on the aircraft) as he travelled to the Asia-Africa Conference in 1955.

16. As with many features of Chinese performance, no direct connection seems to have been made with activities on the other islands at this point.

17. Among these groups was Siantar's New People Musical Theatre Society 新民歌劇社, which between 1956 and 1962 travelled to Jakarta, Bandung, and various places in Sumatra such as Tarutung, Bukittinggi, and Padang (Lu 2003, 313–315; Huang Shuhai 2008, 158). Frequent trips such as these took advantage of a wide network of pro-PRC schools that spanned Java and Sumatra. Some Medan troupes made trips to remote Chinese fishing villages, while Binjai's Minhua juyishe 民華劇藝社 (People's Chinese Dramatic Arts Society) toured more locally. It is worth noting that this network existed partly because many members of the various troupes were originally from more remote communities.

18. The groups all soon "turned into patriotic societies," that is, became committed pro-CCP organizations (Zhang Minhua 2015, 433). In addition to the three groups discussed in this chapter, the fourth was the Xueyi juyishe 學藝劇藝社 (Shio Yih Dramatic Arts Society), the chorus of which was the most active. Li Huanqing's 李煥清 lyrics of the song "Yinzhong Youhao wansui song" 印中友好萬歲頌 (Ode to ten thousand years of Sino-Indonesian friendship) reflect the political rhetoric of most of the performance groups, as do the opening lines "Indonesia China / China Indonesia / Separated by Oceans, / But hearts joined forever. / We have both experienced aggression / and our good hearts both want peace." For information on this group, see Liao Zhangran 2007, 107–134; for the song, 126–127. Some members had travelled to China to study music (and at least one to Italy), and the scores they used were mostly Communist songs imported from China. It is perhaps also worth noting that one of the artistic genealogies of this troupe leads to European colonial society, from the person of Käthe Botterweg-Schmieden, a soprano who had studied in Leipzig and taught piano and voice in Medan from at least 1933, to a number of the students who would later found Shio Yih. Botterweg-Schmieden seems to have been living in Jakarta in 1952 when she was invited to Bandung for a concert by

the Ta Hsioh Hsioh Sing Hui, so her engagement with Chinese musical associations in Sumatra and Java seems to have spanned at least two decades (*De Sumatra Post*, April 2,1933; *De Preangerbode*, April 19, 1952; Lin Longfei 2007, 156). Shio Yih's theatre section produced at least one play, *Wang Xiuluan* 王秀鸞, a 1945 musical by Fu Duo 傅鐸, initially written for the Communist-controlled Central Hebei Military Region (see deMare 2015, 189, 224).

19. *Thunderstorm* ran in Medan from May 21 to 30, 1959. One Medan respondent told me that many people had gone to see the show three or four times, and the house was always full. Actors were trained by an enthusiast who had read about theatre production from books. Another respondent, who had attended a pro-Taipei school, remarked that those who did not adhere to leftist pro-PRC dogma were not welcome at the performance. The same man described his ROC school shows as "less political" and written by teachers and students. See also Liao Zhangran 2007, 176–185.

20. This 1945 play by Ke Ling 柯靈 and Shi Tuo 師陀 was based on Gorky's *The Lower Depths*. Kunlun cites a 1963 Beijing revival in its program, but the 1947 film may also have made the story familiar (Liao Zhangran 2007, 196).

21. A 1960 production of *Peking Man* 北京人, another Cao Yu play, was cancelled because troupe members instead assisted with refugees, presumably from the effects of PP10/1959. Many of these refugees left for China (Zhang Tao 2007, 201).

22. Medan, where communities largely spoke Chinese languages and leftist patriotism was strong, had an especially high rate of "return" to the PRC (Godley and Coppel 1990, 181, 183).

23. The section on *Suwardi* in Liao collates material from three papers, these being Jakarta's *Zhongcheng bao* 忠誠報 (Loyalty News), and Medan's *Geming ribao* 革命日報 (Revolutionary Daily) and *Huzhu hezuo ribao* 互助合作日報 (Cooperative Daily).

24. Oei Tong Pin's 黃東平 1979 script *Hongxi* 红溪 (Red stream), printed in the eighth volume of Oei's collected works in 2004, takes (like also Remy Sylado's Indonesian-language play *9 Oktober 1740, Drama Sejarah* [October 9, 1740, a historical drama]) the 1740 Batavia massacre as its topic, and in both its historical material and its use of Dutch colonials to stage Chinese and Indonesian solidarity, has some similarities with the work of Shalihong. Since the play seems never to have been performed, it must be considered peripheral to Chinese-language Indonesian dramatic history.

25. Baren (1902–1972) was born in Zhejiang Province, near Fenghua 奉化. After graduating in 1920, he became a schoolteacher and began to publish creative work two years later. In 1923, upon the invitation of Zheng Zhenduo 鄭振鐸, Baren joined the Wenxue yanjiu hui 文學研究會 (Literary Research Society). His first major literary success came when his 1925 short story "Pibeizhe" 疲憊者 (The tired), the narrative of a peasant forced into beggary, was anthologized by Mao Dun. The following year saw the publication of his first collection of fiction, *Jianyu* 監獄 (Prison). A member of the CCP since 1924, Baren travelled to Japan in 1929, where his studies focused on sociology and proletarian literature until he was deported in October of the same year. In 1930, he became active in the Zhongguo zuoyi zuojia lianmeng 中國左翼作家聯盟 (League of Left-wing Writers). Arrests and brief periods of imprisonment occurred for political reasons on three occasions in the 1930s. Upon release (through the intervention of Chiang Kai-shek's intimate Mao Sicheng 毛思誠) Baren became active in the Chinese Association of Writers and Artists 中國文藝家協會, one of the disputed attempts to create a successor group to the disbanded League of Left-wing Writers. He also played a major role in the Case of the Seven Gentlemen that protested the arrest of seven figures of the Jiuguo hui 救國會 (China Salvation Council).

26. Baren wrote four versions of the play, all now in the possession of Baren's son Wang Keping 王克平. The second (*Five Hanged Coolies* 五個被吊死的苦力) and the third (which reverts to the original name) are contained in the 1996 drama volume of Baren's collected works; the

second was also republished in Zhou Nanjing 2001. *Five Hanged Coolies* was written over a month's time in 1947 and seems to have been intended also for performance again in Sumatra and perhaps publication, a project made impossible by Baren's imprisonment in a camp (August) and deportation (October) by the Dutch.

27. In fact, had Baren himself not been Chinese, his language on the subject might nowadays expose him to the charge of racist caricature. As it is, it reads as a harsh Communist sketch of the merchant bourgeoisie and as such prefigures the attacks that would later be launched in the PRC against returned Southeast Asian Chinese students.

28. Wang Qianyu 王謙宇, a Chinese Indonesian now resident in Shenzhen, printed a short memoir of Baren in Siantar in 1946 in the online journal *Xianda tongxun* 仙達通訊 (Siantar Messenger): "Baren spoke Indonesian badly, with a ridiculous Ningbo accent, but his accomplishments in terms of written Indonesian really made a person prostrate with admiration. He might not be the first person to discover Indonesian folk songs, but he was certainly the first to bring them into Chinese literature" (Wang Qianyu 2012).

29. Allied control in Medan was, from October 1945, substantially exerted by Japanese forces under British command. Dutch forces did not arrive until October 1946 (Roadnight 2002).

30. Indeed, it is interesting to note that the Japanese propaganda authorities during the occupation had also sponsored Acehnese plays highlighting their history (both recent and remote) of anti-Dutch resistance (Reid 2014, 116).

31. According to this system, a prominent member of the community "was granted the rights to manage community affairs regarding religions and customs" (Suryadinata 1993, 80–81), a system that persisted into the twentieth century. Towards the end of the colonial period, "Chinese nationalists considered these officers as symbols of Dutch interests and tended to pay them no regard" (81).

32. Presumably coincidentally, Indonesia's most famous author, Pramoedya Ananta Toer, also used Sumatran Chinese coolie labor, particularly in Sumatra, as grounds for claiming Chinese contributions to Indonesia and interethnic solidarity in his 1960 work on the Chinese of Indonesia (Pramoedya 2007, 181).

33. Shalihong considers 1871 and 1889 as possible dates but concludes that the date cannot be conclusively demonstrated (Li 2015, 47–48). Moreover, sources suggest that, historically, seven Chinese laborers were executed.

34. Along with the Capitol Theatre, this was one of the Chinese community's principal entertainment sites. Besides spoken theatre, they also hosted Cantonese opera and literary events.

35. Composed by Sinn Sing Hoi 冼星海, the *Cantata*, which premiered in 1939, is the best-known piece of Western-style classical music from the Yan'an period and has been called "by far the most convincing synthesis of Western and Chinese musical idioms" (Wong 1984, 125). It has also been claimed that "no other work . . . demonstrates so close a tie between music and political power" (Yang 2005, 87). *The Yellow River Concerto*, on which it was based, became a bravura piano piece during the Cultural Revolution and is regarded as one of the PRC's central pieces for orchestra.

36. Su Wen, who participated in the show, includes both a list of the sequence of segments (one of which is *The Temple of the Five Ancestors*) for the performance when on tour and also the names of the cast (Su 2007, 17–18).

37. One actress' recollection differs in this somewhat, in that she recollects the performance as being in Hokkien in Medan, although both agree that Medan audiences understood the play when performed in Chinese, while a "special language" had to be developed for the tour (Su 2007, 19).

38. A list of songs from the tour included "Tanggal Tujuh Belas" (The seventeenth [of August], in reference to the Proclamation of Independence the year before) and "Sang Merah Putih" (The Red-and-White, in reference to the national flag), as well as an Ambonese folk song, "Hela Rotan." Liao Zhangran (2007, 16) provides a score in numbered musical notation for the former song. "Bengawan Solo" was a popular song on New China's Java tours (Zhang Minhua 2015, 421–422).

39. Hasan was officially governor of Sumatra (at that time the whole island was considered a single province by the Republic of Indonesia) but of course did not exercise all that much control over the island, being "effectively limited to a liaison function between the Japanese, the British, and the *kerajaan* [Malay royalty] on one side, and the fighting *pemuda* on the other" (Reid 2014, 183). He had moved his government to Siantar because Medan was in Allied hands; even there he was almost ousted by a coup from the left in April 1946 (261–262).

40. Apparently there was considerable difficulty crossing back into the Allied territory of Medan, solved only after two weeks by the intercession of the General Chinese Association (Su 2007, 19).

41. Zhou Erfu, before his departure to visit Indonesia with Zheng Zhenduo in 1955, paid a call on Baren, then resident in Beijing. Baren asked him to visit the Temple of the Five Ancestors, which to his regret Baren himself had never seen. Zhou did so, recording the names of the historical figures and gathering supplementary information from local Chinese informants. Baren used Zhou's account, revising his script to include the accurate historical names (Baren 1996, 1–10).

42. In his professional life, Shalihong goes by his original Chinese name Li Jing 李靖, and in Indonesian he is known as Sinshe Rusli. As a writer and journalist, he has used many pseudonyms, the most common of which is Shalihong. This is the name used for the 2007 printing of *Five Ancestors Temple* as well as several works published by Shalihong in Hong Kong in the 1950s and early 1960s, such as *Zheyang yanjing* 遮陽眼鏡 (Sunglasses), *Bali fengguang* 峇厘風光 (Scenes of Bali), *Yinni fengguang* 印尼風光 (Scenes of Indonesia), and *Yu Dafu taowang ji* 郁達夫逃亡記 (Chronicle of Yu Dafu as a fugitive). He has published on a weekly basis in the Chinese-language press of Medan or Jakarta from 1951 to 1966 and from 1975 to 1990 (during the New Order years in the only officially permitted Chinese-language paper, the *Harian Indonesia*), and again from the foundation of the *International Daily* in 2001 and was still writing in 2018.

43. After his departure, though a few copies remained in the area, Baren's script was almost wholly unknown to Chinese Indonesians. Though he was aware that Baren had dramatized the same event, Shalihong's purpose in writing the play was not to mimic or re-create Baren's version but to dramatize the historical events for his own purposes. Not surprisingly, the two scripts feature substantial differences. In Shalihong's estimation, much of his audience would have not seen the Baren play, though all were aware of the temple.

44. Sukarno's presidential Regulation No. 10 (PP10/1959) had "an appalling effect on the entire minority community," leading to an exodus of Chinese Indonesians to China (Lev and Lev 2011, 177; see also Tsai Yen-ling 2008, 197–198; Lin Xuehua 2009, 145–148; and Tong 2010, 123).

45. While the 1955 Asia-Africa Conference remains widely known, GANEFO (The games of the emerging new forces) have now been mostly forgotten. The inaugural games were held in 1963 in Jakarta, and the support of the PRC was indeed substantial. The author's logic seems to confuse the time line, given that PP10 was promulgated before China's involvement in GANEFO; nevertheless, it is striking that PP10 was put into effect at the same time as such warm support was being offered by the PRC to Sukarno's Indonesia.

46. A complementary explanation is provided by another member, who notes that a sea breeze produces "great waves" (Zheng Yuanxin 2007, 142).

47. Much of the activity was therefore focused on the local Yongchun Society 永春公所.

48. Shalihong had met the group at a pickup game of badminton, and the group had begun with stilt-walking exhibitions. Those activities had eventually developed to include solo and choir concerts, skits, and dances both Chinese and local Indonesian. Besides their one production of Shalihong's *Temple of the Five Ancestors*, they performed no other spoken theatre.

49. He moved to Jakarta in 1973, where he still lives today and practices as a doctor of traditional Chinese medicine in Glodok. As a journalist and amateur historian, Shalihong conducted archival research, fieldwork, and interviews in Medan from the beginning of his career in the 1950s to his departure in 1973.

50. Though Shalihong is himself Hakka, the dominance of Hokkien in much of North Sumatra has long made that language a Chinese lingua franca.

51. A principal informant, A'er, is pictured in the 2007 *International Daily* printing of the *Temple of the Five Ancestors*.

52. For instance, his script introduces Indonesian Chinese vocabulary from the period: "dun" (gulden), "xian" (cent), "kontrakt" (contract), "babi hutan" ("wild boar" in Malay, used as a term of abuse), as well as Indonesian Chinese vocabulary such as "huanqian" 還錢 for paying (rather than returning) money. By contrast, Baren's script contains a number of lexical items (perhaps most prominently the pronouns *an* 俺 and *zanmen* 咱們), which are not much, if at all, used among Medan Chinese or in the various southern dialects the coolies would have spoken.

53. According to local sources, the graves were moved in 1972 on account of the expansion of the city. A local businessman is reported to have had bad dreams in which he saw a certain place; when the dreams were interpreted for him, he collected donations for the building of a new temple to house the graves at that location. When the temple was completed, the dreams ceased (Huaiying 2015, 94–96).

Chapter 4: The Disguised Beloved

1. Although use of these terms is hard to avoid, it is important to call attention to the fact that *xiqu* and *wayang* are both innovative, productive, and adaptive systems and in that sense are no less contemporary or modern. As such, the use of "modern" to designate "Western-origin" theatre risks being both disrespectful and inaccurate. However, this usage is difficult to avoid, and rather than resort to contortions that might communicate less well the object of inquiry, it seems best to continue using the term for the nonce, though bracketed by this caveat: inevitably, contemporary "traditional" theatre has also defined itself in relation or opposition to the "modern" theatre that has emerged over the last century (Cohen 2016).

2. Consider, for instance, the report from a 1900 Semarang newspaper about "wajang tjina Stambool," which was "very well attended, mostly by Chinese and their ladies," and was standing-room only (*De Locomotief*, June 11, 1900).

3. Translations of Wang Zhaojun had been available in Malay since 1884, and Salmon notes that this Chinese princess has also expressed her plight in Malay *pantun* form (Salmon 2013a, 21). The Peranakan Chinese group PERTIP in Makassar also produced a Wang Zhaojun story (under the name *Ong Tjiao Koen*) in 1952. Described as *sandiwara*, it is likely that this was an Indonesian-language musical drama (PERTIP 1953, 72–73). The author thanks Dr. Yerry Wirawan for scans of the relevant pages.

4. Certainly, the narrative has always attracted political interpretations and (setting aside classical versions) was adapted in one form or another by major twentieth-century figures such as Guo Moruo, Cao Yu, and Hu Shih 胡適. In 1925, Cantonese opera troupes in Los Angeles

performed the same narrative to benefit those who had gone on strike in Shanghai's anti-imperialist May Thirtieth Movement (Rao 2016, 216). Perhaps the story was being employed on Java also to remind Sino-Indonesians of their ties and duties.

5. For studies of Kwee Tek Hoay, a representative author of this period of Sino-Malay drama as well as an author of fiction and a prominent figure in the development of Chinese institutional religion, see Kwee 1980 and Lin 2011. Kwee's work has been reprinted and revived on the stage a number of times since the beginning of Reformasi (Bodden 2007, 121).

6. Doubtless this is largely what attracted the attention of Bandung Chinese-language author Lin Wanli 林萬里, who translated excerpts of another work, *Kesusastraan kaum Peranakan-Tionghoa* (The literature of the Chinese-Peranakan community), for publication in Hong Kong in Chinese in 1998.

7. One such example is *Chen San Wuniang*, known in Indonesia as *Tan Sha Go Nio*, a story closely associated with Quanzhou and Teochew narrative traditions, and from which two cities the two protagonists hail. A translation was published in Malay in Semarang in 1886, adapted or translated by Boen Sing Hoo (Lombard-Salmon 1974, 168). A version from 1906 by Batavian translator Tjiong Hok Long 鍾福龍 is also known, although no copy is apparently extant (Salmon 1981, 474–474; 2013c, 256, 268). There was also a *syair* (traditional Malay poetry in quatrains) on the subject in 1896, 1902, and 1930 (Kwee 1978, 37; Maier 2006, 18). Today, however, the story is largely unknown in Indonesia outside of the older generation in North Sumatra, which is both Hokkien-speaking and grew up with Chinese theatre; and among the Hokkien speakers of Palembang, where it is still in *gezaixi* repertoire. The same risqué features that appear in Liang Shanbo also are noticeable in this narrative, and also without parallels, to my knowledge, in Chinese sources. Kwee notes, presumably of the 1922 printing, "a rather indecent bedroom scene, where Tan Sha not only made love with Go Nio but also with her maid" (1978, 39).

8. It has also received considerable interest in minority areas and in Korea. According to one scholar, "[t]exts of the Liang-Zhu tale are found in Zhejiang, Jiangsu, Shandong, Shanxi, Hunan, Guizhou, Henan, Guangxi, Fujian, Sichuan, and Liaoning provinces as well as among ethnic minority groups such as the Miao, Zhuang, Yao, She, Tujia, and Gelao" (Cho 2014, 249). It entered Korea six hundred years ago, featuring in "Korean shaman ritual narratives and local lore" (211).

9. For instance, some adaptations have made the two lovers reincarnations of other famous lovers, such as the Wang Xiliang and Meng Jiangnü, or the Weaving Maiden and Buffalo Boy (Idema 2010, xxii).

10. This is *Liang Shanbo yu Zhu Yingtai xiaotiqin xiezouqu* (1959) 梁山伯與祝英台小提琴協奏曲 (The butterfly lovers' violin concerto) by Chen Gang 陳鋼 and He Zhanhao 何占豪. Chen and He drew on *yueju* for inspiration, hoping to naturalize the violin for a wide (and ideologically appropriate) Chinese audience (Melvin and Cai 2004, 210–211).

11. This tiresome and inaccurate equivalence is at least sixty years old; apparently Zhou Enlai, having screened the *yueju* film in Geneva for British Prime Minister Anthony Eden, called the story "the Chinese *Romeo and Juliet*" in 1954 (Gao 2004, 236).

12. Unsurprisingly, alongside the Indonesian forms considered in this chapter, the narrative has had a parallel career on the Malay Peninsula. In 1963, a late example of Sino-Malay *sya'ir* in Singapore took the story as its subject matter (Salmon 2013d, 294), and a 1964 printed version by Yim Weng Kwok is also known in Penang. The Malay singer Saloma, popular in the 1960s, had a version of the song in her repertoire, and *bangsawan* productions have been mounted from the colonial period to the present day (Sooi-Beng Tan 1993, 35). A 2006 version by the Dama Malaysia Orchestra mixed modern Western art music and *huangmeidiao* influ-

ences, with narration in English, dialogues and lyrics in Mandarin, and subtitles in both (Loo and Loo 2012).

13. The existence of the Boen translation is, rather amusingly, also recorded in advertising verse of the following year (Lombard-Salmon 1974, 171–172).

14. Usually, Chinese narratives make no special reference to the butterflies' color. One can speculate that Tonnet intended it as a reference to the "yellow race."

15. The translation Tonnet cites in *Woord en beeld* is an 1897 adaptation from a "Chinese poem" made by Yap Goan Ho 葉源和 and published in Batavia. Yap was a translator and publisher (Salmon 1981, 370–371), although this translation of *Sam Pek Eng Tay* has not, it seems, made its way into catalogue listings.

16. It is common for the character of Liang Shanbo to be performed by a woman in several *xiqu* genres as well; the success of female Sampeks in the Indies may reflect to some degree the influence of *xiqu*.

17. It seems probable that Fifi Young's version is that to which Nio Joe Lan referred when he wrote, in 1947, "only a few months ago, we have seen [*Sampek Engtay*] performed by a Malay theatre group in modern dress and four acts" (Nio 1947, 14).

18. Since the film is likely lost, it is not clear exactly of what the connection consists.

19. De Zoete and Spies differ slightly from Covarrubias as regards dating. While the former claim that the story entered *arja* just before World War I, the latter gives 1924 as the date and writes that such performances started as "bastard performances with actors in European clothes playing on mandolins," which may suggest something *stamboel*-like. "Eventually," wrote Covarrubias, "these stories became thoroughly Balinese" (1937, 251).

20. Some of the accounts of the origin of this genre, which has both a palace pedigree and a village practice, credit Chinese individuals with key roles in its development (Davies 2008, 196–198). One famous elder teacher, Davies reports, "did not hesitate in declaring that legong had come from China" (197). There do not seem, however, to be texts that support this account, and at present the academic consensus supports an origin in the Balinese eighteenth or nineteenth century (see Vickers 2009).

21. The author, who is not named, makes it clear that he regards the relative strength of Chinese influence on the Indonesian stage as "regrettable."

22. His work was usually published under this abbreviation, or as "OKT."

23. An edited English translation of this work was also produced in 1991 by American Stanley R. Munro, entitled *The Eternal Love: The Story of Liang Shanbo and Zhu Yingtai*. Evidently, Munro and OKT were trying to highlight very different aspects, or uses, of the Liang-Zhu story.

24. Typically, Riantiarno speaks of Indonesia as "us" and the Chinese community as "them." He has been identified in academic and journalistic writing as being Chinese Indonesian, both locally and abroad, and it is not a background he has ever refuted. However, it is clear that, while he has considerable interest in Sino-Indonesian materials, Chinese ethnicity is for him personally by no means an identity marker.

25. Unsurprisingly, it was also one of the adaptations too risqué for OKT's taste.

26. Most notably in *Opera Prima Donna* (1993). Many observers saw the plot, about an older *bangsawan* prima donna's refusal to cede to a younger star, as a parable about the late Suharto years.

27. There was a television show and a popular novel on the same topic about the same time. In the story of White Snake, no amount of goodwill, cultivation, or devotion to her human husband can free the protagonist from her identity as a snake. Some have seen parallels between this story and the travails of Sino-Indonesians, given that "the core theme that runs through

it is a defense of individuals victimized by official norms and hostile treatment due to their descent!" (Heryanto 1998, 107). An Indonesian prose version of the story also appeared in 1994, with one scholar also suggesting that it can be read as reflecting "a community cautiously optimistic of their place in an Indonesia recovering from ethnic conflagration" (Khor 2014, 301).

28. Whether or not this is Riantiarno's intent, there is a certain irony to this reference to identity cards, since the fact that Sino-Indonesian ID cards were once (and perhaps still are) identified by distinct numbers on their cards was a source of bureaucratic racism causing "[e]xtra paper-work and fees... in any legal dealings with the public service" (Heryanto 1998, 101). Many Sino-Indonesians still report such experiences.

29. As noted in chapter 1, a *xiqu* performance in Jakarta in the late 1980s would have been rare, but not inconceivable. The Chinese of this neighborhood are largely from Bagansiapiapi, and so Riantiarno and his actors may well have seen a Sumatran group rather than a Betawi Chinese practice.

30. Thus, in the 1999 post-Reformasi revival, the return of the *barongsay* became a highlight and a feature mentioned by Sino-Indonesian respondents as a special attraction (Ian Jarvis Brown 2001, 200).

31. For instance, in 1990, Riantiarno's own *Opera Kecoa* (The Cockroach Opera) and *Suksesi* (Succession) were also banned in 1990; a large-scale tour of Japan, planned for 1991, was kiboshed after all preparations and payments had been made (Ian Jarvis Brown 2001, 193–195; Bodden 2010, 322).

32. The subsequent bans of two subsequent Riantiarno shows—the play *Suksesi* (Succession), about a royal family's squabbles to succeed the king and a new production of *Opera Kecoa*—probably had as much to do with the satirical content of the plays, although the stated reason was because the company supposedly had not applied for permission to perform.

33. Tonnet, with her vastly different field of reference, had instead compared the story to the wildly popular Rousseauist late eighteenth-century French novel *Paul et Virginie*.

34. Naturally enough, performance of the narrative as *potehi* is also known (Tsai Tsung-te 2015, 83), though it is not a core part of repertoire.

35. As such, it is analogous with the profile that *wayang potehi* has been acquiring, as detailed in chapter 2. It comes as little surprise, then, that Teater Koma has made use of *wayang potehi* in its recent *Sie Jin Kwie* trilogy (Bachmid 2011, 36).

36. The recent revivals of *Sampek Engtay* are only a part of the way Teater Koma is recovering Chinese narratives. Alongside the creation of the *Sie Jin Kwie* trilogy, which has made use of *wayang potehi* elements in service of a quintessentially Sino-Indonesian narrative, the revivals of *Opera Ular Putih* (The white snake opera) should also be considered, which can be read as a New Order parable of Sino-Indonesian identity. The flourishing of Chinese-themed work reflects not only a new freedom to deal with these themes, but also the direct support of the Sino-Indonesian business community.

37. Wilt Idema, a specialist in late imperial Chinese drama and fiction, has also remarked that Southeast Asian translators and adaptors "largely shunned the 'literary novels' and overwhelmingly opted for works written in a very simple and straight-forward idiom" (Idema 1989, 584).

Chapter 5: Alumni Networks and Hybrid Dances

1. This listing can serve as a reminder that the treatment of various organizations' performance here is not meant to elide the variety of their composition, aims, or genres. For the purposes of this section, however, they will all be regarded in the light of the ways they negotiate their performance of Chineseness.

2. The claim, indeed, is sometimes made that communal life disappeared entirely. Given the interpenetration of religious and communal life, the informal side of communal life, and the fact that several currently existing organizations have roots that predate the Reformasi era, having survived in various accepted or tolerated forms (charity, religion, sporting) through the New Order era, this claim should always be qualified. Even a Chinese press persisted, in the form of the government-controlled daily *Harian Indonesia* (Indonesia Daily), simultaneously a tool of oppression and a means of maintaining community (Hoon 2006b).

3. Despite the blanket ban, some organizations, as the history of some of the organizations presented below shows, were able to continue operating. As always in Indonesia, there was considerable regional disparity (Heidhues 2006, 87).

4. For comparison, Huang estimates that there were perhaps two thousand in 1958, with three-quarters identified with Beijing and a quarter with Taipei (Huang Kunzhang 2005, 312). Today, no definitive survey is possible, as many groups are informal, overlapping, or inactive (Ding 2009a).

5. According to a 2003 study, only one organization was then mandating Chinese ethnicity as a condition of membership (Giblin 2003, 357).

6. Since some readers will be approaching this work from a China studies background, a few words about Sundanese culture may be appropriate. According to the 2010 census, there are over 36 million Sundanese people, overwhelmingly in West Java (34 million), where they form the majority. This makes the Sundanese the second largest ethnicity of Indonesia, at 15.5 percent of the national population (smaller only than the Javanese). There are also substantial Sundanese migrant populations in Jakarta (1.5 million) as well as smaller groups in Central and East Java, Lampung, and elsewhere throughout the archipelago. At the margins, especially in its relationship to the coastal cultures of Cirebon and Banten (usually considered closely related but distinct ethnic groups), definitions of Sundanese culture and language may be debatable, but at its core it is generally considered a more Islamic, less stratified, and historically more agricultural and less centralized culture than that of the Javanese. There are, for instance, no close Sundanese equivalents to the courts of Yogyakarta and Solo or the empire of Majapahit. The cultural region did not have a real urban center until the Dutch establishment of Bandung and its rise as a transport hub and light-industry hub in the nineteenth century. Jakarta, located in the historic Sundanese cultural area, has been so diversely populated, and developed so independently, that its Betawi culture and ethnicity are not considered to be Sundanese, although the contribution of Sundanese to its genesis is crucial. For Chinese influence and acculturation in Cirebon with reference to the arts, see Pigeaud 1938, 114.

7. In this incident, revolutionaries torched the city rather than let it fall to the British. By one estimate, six hundred Chinese homes and stores were burnt in this fire, many targeted by revolutionaries (Smail 1964, 153).

8. Barker (2009, 65), quoting Bandung papers of the period, reports "some 1,520 houses . . . damaged or destroyed," while a dictionary of Overseas Chinese lists 914 homes destroyed or burnt, as well as another 80 in nearby Cianjur (Zhou Nanjing 1993, 31). On the role of the local military leaders, see Crouch (2007, 312).

9. It should be noted that "Cina" is considered rude by many Sino-Indonesians, partly because of association with the offensive Japanese *shina* 支那, a term associated with Japanese imperialism (Fogel 1995, 66–76). Nevertheless, it retains wide usage in Indonesia, including in academic, though no longer usually in official or diplomatic, contexts. Typically, Sino-Indonesians prefer "Tionghoa" (for the ethnicity) or "Tiongkok" (for the nation), based on Hokkien pronunciations of *Zhonghua* 中華 and *Zhongguo* 中國. An increasingly popular alternative is "China," using the English pronunciation.

10. For example, at the 2006 World Chinese-language Flash Fiction Conference in Bandung, both "Sundanese dance" and *jaipong* were featured alongside a Lantern dance performed by the Sino-Indonesian Evergreen Dance Troupe (Dongrui 2006, 233).

11. Bandung's Chinese place-of-origin demographics are atypical for Java, having larger Cantonese and Hokchia backgrounds than most parts of Java and a smaller proportion of Hokkien descendants, who otherwise dominate Sino-Javanese migration history. The most organizationally active regional groups are the Hakka.

12. That is, the Guangzhou 廣州 and Zhaoqing 肇慶 prefectures of Guangdong.

13. On this type of convention, Chee-Beng Tan (2001, 229) notes that they formalize "the existing informal economic network that had been important to ethnic Chinese businessmen since the nineteenth century" and that it is "primarily a formal occasion for gathering, dialogue and listening to views of scholars and relevant speakers." Members of the Lie/Widjaja family hold high posts in both the Taiwan-based World Headquarters of the Lee Family 世界李氏宗親總會 and the Indonesian Meizhou *huiguan* 印尼梅州會館. This is the same Lie/Widjaja family that is prominent in the foundation of Yayasan Dana Sosial Priangan, described below.

14. This section relies both on fieldwork interviews and on the YHK publication Yinni Wanlong *Keshu lianyihui chengli shizhounian jinian tekan 2000 nian-2010 nian* (Special commemorative issue for the tenth anniversary of the Bandung, Indonesia Hakka Association, 2000–2010).

15. The reader who reads both Chinese and Indonesian will have noticed that neither YHK nor YMKS have names that are direct translations; YMKS' Indonesian name means "The Pearl Prosperous Welfare Association," while the Chinese name refers to the Guangzhou-Zhaoqing area of Guangdong Province. Similarly, YHK means "Foundation of Hope and Love" in Indonesian, but simply "Bandung Hakka Benevolent Association" in Chinese. This follows an established New Order–period practice by which Chinese organizations in Indonesia gave names unrelated to their Chinese (generally place-name) titles, and thus ostensibly had a non-Chinese purpose.

16. Today, these seem to be the only regular local *xiqu* activities of any kind in the city.

17. *Ondel-ondel* are "larger-than-life, papier-mâché dolls, usually paraded around during Jakartan festivals or as part of lifecycle ritual celebrations, such as a circumcision or marriage. They are meant to represent ancestral spirits that look after the community" (Winarnita 2014, 85) and are often considered emblematic of Betawi (i.e., Jakarta) culture. The genre, like many Betawi forms, has a syncretic aspect that includes Chinese influences—Augusta de Wit's work, for instance, shows them as part of a Chinese funeral march in 1912 Batavia (de Wit 1912, 49). Recent work has noted the complex politics of representation when the genre has been sanctioned by Indonesian authorities for performance abroad by Chinese Indonesians as a representative of national culture for consumption by a foreign (in their case, Australian) audience (Winarnita and Araujo 2016).

18. Like most Chinese Indonesians, Cheung actually traces his ancestry to southern Fujian, specifically the major city of Quanzhou. This fact is likely more of a peculiar parallel than a consciously made association.

19. This line of thought leads Wang and Wong to propose the idea of home as a "circular process" for such (re-)migrants.

20. This migration generally occurs through family connections and produces concentrations within Jakarta in terms of both geography and economic sector (Hertzman 2017, 110–114).

21. Recognized by UNESCO on the Representative List of the Intangible Cultural Heritage of Humanity, *angklung* is a "musical instrument consisting of two to four bamboo tubes sus-

pended in a bamboo frame, bound with rattan cords" (UNESCO 2010). Although practiced also outside of West Java, *angklung* originated in and is most closely associated with Sundanese culture, in the form of a "traditional Sundanese outdoor processional bamboo rattle ensemble strongly associated with rural fertility rituals" (Williams 1990, 153), Such groups are common also in the "diaspora" of Sino-Indonesians in the Chinese-speaking world. See, for instance, the pictures of Hong Kong–based alumni associations performing *angklung* and Sumatran dance in Huang Shuhai 2008 (238–239).

22. As noted in the preceding section, these alumni associations can effectively function as *tongxianghui*.

23. This kind of *arisan* has replaced the older rotating savings and credit system, which is perhaps a sign of weakening community solidarity (Koning 2007, 146–147).

24. *Mulan* martial arts 木蘭拳, named after legendary heroine Hua Mulan 花木蘭, are a variety of martial arts invented in the late 1980s by a Shanghai practitioner especially for the use of girls and women. Its presence in Bandung is only one sign of the influence, often through DVDs, of China-based martial arts and calisthenics on the physical practices of Sino-Indonesians.

25. "Kota Kembang" means "City of Flowers" and is a familiar nickname for Bandung.

26. Karaoke activities began at Priangan in 1994, and in general Chinese-language music seems to have become publicly permissible at about this time (Yinni Wanlong Boliangan Fuli Jijinhui 2011, 153). Suryadinata (2004, 81) noted a relaxation in Mandarin education at about the same time.

27. Disastra is well known in Sino-Indonesian–language teaching, literary, and dramatic circles as well, having published both Indonesian translations of Chinese poetry (collected in 2006 as *Tirai Bambu*) and Chinese-language essays on the Sino-Indonesian condition, such as *Wo mei jianguo Zhongguo de yueliang* 我沒見過中國的月亮 (I have not seen the moon over China; 2010) and *Qiandao zhonghua ernü* 千島中華兒女 (Chinese sons and daughters of the archipelago; 2012), both with the Yinhua Wenxue she 印華文學社 (Sino-Indonesian Literary Press).

28. This is the most classical and aristocratic of Sundanese music genres, in which the voice is accompanied by an "18-string zither (*kacapi*), a smaller 15-string zither (*rincik*), an end-blown bamboo flute (*suling*), and occasionally a 2-string bowed lute (*rebab*)" (Williams 1990, i).

29. The repertoire shows considerable overlap with Muslim Sundanese ensembles when performing in secular contexts (Pätzold 2011, 186). For the musical features of *pop Sunda* that are drawn from tradition, see Williams 1989.

30. According to Cheng, they chose their name because "although already in middle age, they were still full of vigor."

31. The song, written for a 1956 Korean War film, has become a staple of patriotic repertoire. The song, which refers to American soldiers as "wolves" to be met with "hunting guns," also became the subject of a mild media kerfuffle in 2011 when classical pianist Lang Lang 朗朗 teamed up with jazz legend Herbie Hancock to play it at the White House dinner where President Obama hosted Hu Jintao, then the paramount leader of the PRC (*New York Times*, January 21, 2011).

32. Of course, there were still many restrictions. According to respondents, during the early period, all visible writing had to be in Indonesian, and Chinese characters were not permitted to be retained even in religious contexts. As a crematorium society officially without ethnic or religious affiliation, Priangan was in principle available to anyone. Sundanese Muslim respondents, of course, rarely availed themselves of these services because of religious prescription against cremation. The Priangan commemorative video in their museum also shows various foundation officials discussing how the local Chinese community slowly shifted from

traditional burial to cremation, under the same sorts of space pressures that have caused this shift in Mainland China, Taiwan, and Hong Kong.

33. Besides religion, health and sports were also exempt (Setianto 2010, 84). Heidhues (2003, 253) also notes the presence of Chinese burial societies in Kalimantan under New Order.

34. Since 2002, Widjaja's youngest son Li Zhenjian/Herman Widjaja has been the head of the organization. At the same time, he is also the head of the Li Clan organization (Marga Lie) and the Bandung branch of the international Taiwan-based Buddhist organization Tzu Chi 慈濟. This group has been prominently active throughout Chinese Indonesia since 1993 and is another way in which Chinese Indonesians demonstrate charity for Indonesian society at large, distributing rice to the poor and helping with medical services under the cooperation of the armed forces (see also Ong 2008, 106).

35. These separations between Hakka, Hokkien, and Cantonese were felt throughout Chinese communities in Indonesia, but have been slowly weakening since the mid-century. For an example of convergence in Jakarta Chinese education in the early Republic, see Sai 2006, 122.

36. The financial investment was of course substantial; Widjaja himself donated 10 million rupiah, other individuals contributed 46.3 million rupiah, and thirty-seven ancestral organizations combined gave a total of 66.16 million rupiah. The initial building covers 860 square meters. Besides being cofounder along with Chen Fusheng 陳富聲 and Liang Baxiu 梁拔秀, Widjaja was also the first president and served second and third terms before his death in 1984. In 1983, the foundation bought another 8,000 square meters.

37. Itself an interesting expression of Sino-Indonesian positionality, *Jia Xiang*'s predominantly Indonesian-language contributions are often written by non-Chinese freelance journalists, with the effect that information about the activities of various Chinese communities is transmitted among Sino-Indonesian individuals through the words of *pribumi* authors.

38. For the importance of this institution in the codification of Indonesian national identity, see Hitchcock 1998. For the significance of the building of the Hakka museum in Taman Mini, see Heidhues 1996 and 2017 and Setijadi 2016.

39. It is one of several Sino-Indonesian museums that have appeared in recent years, including in Cirebon and Tangerang. Jakarta's Indonesia Hakka Museum was opened by then President Susilo Bambang Yudhoyono in 2014, who declared that it would be an object of pride not only for the ethnic Chinese but for the Indonesian nation (*Tempo*, August 30, 2014).

40. One researcher found that the ethnic background of Indonesian Chinese badminton stars did not substantially figure in their public perception, although they were able to "use[] their influence to call attention to issues which particularly affected the Chinese community" (Colin Brown 2006, 92).

41. It seems probable that Lie's posthumous elevation to National Hero was intended as a friendly gesture to Sino-Indonesians. As presented in the museum, one would not surmise that Manado-born Lie was, in his time, known for his devout Christianity as well as Indonesian patriotism. For *LIFE* magazine in 1949, he was "the strange Christian captain with guns, bazookas and Bibles" (*LIFE*, September 26, 1949).

42. Despite his long immersion in Sundanese culture, Tan still speaks reasonably good Mandarin due to his early Chinese schooling. This would later prove useful on tours of Mainland China.

43. Naturally enough, these artists are mainly familiar in Indonesia, and especially in West Java. They do, however, provide Tan with an important local pedigree. The people in this section can be found in the following reference books (with page numbers). In *Apa Siapa Orang Sunda* (Rosidi 2003): Adjat Sudrajat (28); Euis Komariah (158); Tati Saleh (387); and Tan Deseng himself (383). For information on music genres and styles, see *Ensiklopedia Sunda* (Rosidi

2000): *degung* (187), *jaipongan* (296–297), *kawih* (334), *ketuk tilu* (346–347), *kliningan* (349), and *tembang Sunda* (656–657). For instruments, see *kacapi* (316–317) and *suling* (613) in the same work. Tan also features in *Tokoh-tokoh etnis Tionghoa di Indonesia* (348).

44. The name is itself a proclamation of identity, meaning "Loyalty to Siliwangi," a central Sundanese culture hero.

45. An adaptation of the more classical *gamelan degung, kawih degung* developed in the 1970s and 1980s with the addition of *kawih*, that is, light vocal music (Williams 1989, 112). Williams' article describes the profitability of composing and performing *kawih degung* in the 1980s, but that heyday is now long gone.

46. Jurriëns is here summarizing Tan's 1989 essay on regional pop songs in an essay compilation called *Apa itu lagu pop daerah* (What are regional pop songs?; Tan Deseng 1989).

47. Tan's several names reflect Hokkien, Mandarin, Sundanese, and Muslim influences and perspectives. Bearing a similar multiplicity of Sino-Sundanese identities, Ibu Ade was also known by several names. "Ibu Ade" (Mother Ade) referred to her marriage to Ade Tjahyadi 林財興 (or Tjahjadi; or Cahyadi), a prominent Bandung businessman and a standing vice-chairman of the International Association of Hokchia Clansmen 世界福清社團聯誼會. In Chinese print, she was most often known as Mrs. Lin Caixing 林財興夫人 or, in Indo-Hokkien, as Ny. Lim Chay Hin. Her maiden name, Tatty Muljati or, in Hokkien, The Sioe Ing 鄭秀英, also appeared. In this community, names too are contextual, being inscribed with different aspects of identity depending on context and language.

48. Once again, the choice of repertoire is not quite dissociable from the cultural products of Chinese nationalism: "Pearl of the Orient" is primarily associated with an upbeat view of Hong Kong's future after its retrocession and was sung during the handover ceremony (Brand and Ho 1999, 233).

Chapter 6: Deities on Parade

1. The term is also current in Malaysia and Singapore where, however, spelling conventions render it Chap Goh Meh or Mei. The name means "fifteenth night" and is rendered according to Hokkien pronunciation. Today, the festival is most often known in China and Taiwan as *Yuanxiaojie* 元宵節. *Yuan* refers to the first month of the Chinese calendar, and *xiao* means night; the holiday marks the first full moon of the year.

2. At the time Sekolah Seni Tinggi Indonesia Bandung (Indonesian Higher School of the Arts, Bandung): it changed its name in 2014 to Institut Seni Budaya Indonesia Bandung (Institute of Indonesian Cultural Arts, Bandung).

3. The song, by Shanghai tunesmith Chen Gexin 陳歌辛, was composed for the first Chinese New Year after the Second World War, in 1946. Like the Sino-Indonesians listening to the song in Bandung in 2013, Chen was celebrating the return of Chinese festivities after a disastrous and bloody hiatus.

4. In a Muslim-majority city such as Bandung, pork is substantially associated with Chinese cuisine.

5. Standard *Hanyu pinyin* was not widely used in Indonesia in the generation of Mandarin speakers now in their sixties and seventies, and of course many of that generation know no characters. As a result, the popular Mandarin-language songs, dominated by Teresa Teng (Deng Lijun) and other largely Taiwanese stars of the 1970s and 1980s, are generally subtitled for karaoke in a transliteration that is modelled on *Hanyu pinyin* to a degree but replaces unfamiliar phonemes like *x* and *q* with letters *s* and *c*, respectively, approximating Indonesian orthography.

6. Perhaps this display was inspired by the annual, very popular Koko Cici event in Jakarta, where the Sino-Indonesian community chooses a youth ambassador for the year. The terms *koko* and *cici* are derived from the Hokkien pronunciation of "elder brother" and "elder sister," respectively. The *qipao*, being a northern dress adapted to Shanghai Republican style, was probably worn by very few in the Dutch East Indies; it is only one of many examples of the symbols that have acquired an ahistorical and uncritical association with "authentic" Chineseness.

7. A performance form, originating in Sumedang, in which *pencak silat* martial arts are mixed with the horse-dance *renggong*. Considered a relatively recent practice, it has been incorporated into circumcision ceremonies (Hellman 2003, 16–17).

8. In *sisingaan*, a dance where four porters carry a lion on which a boy or boys are seated. Apparently originating in anticolonial sentiment (with the Dutch represented by the tamed lion), it has latterly been incorporated into the circumcision ceremony and has been used also for independence day parades (see Hellman 2003, 16–17, 84–86).

9. Marching bands have been a prominent feature of musical life on Java since the colonial period (Sumarsam 2013, 88–92).

10. The battalion belongs to the military district of Siliwangi, the leadership of which was implicated in anti-Chinese riots in Bandung, such as those of 1963 and 1973, as noted in chapter 5 (Mackie 1976, 102; Crouch 2007, 312). Their presence in a Chinese procession in Bandung thus has symbolic importance.

11. At intersections, boy scouts are deployed to manage crowds and help the procession navigate traffic. Their participation also shows temple outreach to, and alliance with, civic power structures to ensure the success of the procession. The Indonesian scouting movement dates to 1912, and groups function "as seedbeds for raising loyal national cadres and winning popular support" through "their attachment to larger institutions, be they royal courts, nationalistic movement organizations, religious organizations, political parties, armed forces or government" (Semedi 2011, 20–21).

12. This is the dominant name in English news reports, though a more accurate translation might be "electronica prince troupe." The "prince" refers to Nezha 哪吒, the third son of general Li Jing 李靖 (and therefore "third prince" *san taizi*). Nezha is a familiar figure in Hokkien temples, but also as a figure from children's animation such as the PRC's *Nezha naohai* 哪吒鬧海 (Nezha conquers the dragon king; 1979). Neon God troupes first became popular on account of their appearance in the opening ceremony of the World Games, hosted in Kaohsiung in 2009 (Sheng 2013, 392). Their cartoon-inspired design and electronic music have proven popular in Taiwan and for representations of Taiwan abroad, including the 2010 Shanghai Expo and festivals in Toronto and Los Angeles. Hailing from Tainan's Sinying Taizih Temple 新營太子宮, the troupe continued their Indonesia tour with events at Plaza Indonesia, one of Jakarta's most prominent malls, and at a temple event in Cianjur (*Guoji ribao*, February 27, 2013).

13. In contexts such as these, where Chineseness is foregrounded, the inability to speak Chinese is experienced by many Sino-Indonesians as humiliating. As Hertzman notes about Singkawang Hakka, this humiliation can be expressed "as anger at the Indonesian government, embarrassment, and a sense of personal failure, as well as frustration with not having one's Chineseness recognized and affirmed by other groups of ethnic Chinese" (2014, 159).

14. This is likely derived from *dabo gong* 大伯公 (now more often written *toapekong* in Indonesia), that is, an honorific of the Earth God *Tudi gong* 土地公 (see also Chai 2017, 15–16). In Indonesia, however, the word *toapekong* is sometimes applied generally to images of deities, and in some areas to temples. Perhaps in Boachi's time it also applied to the festival.

15. Boachi's account is not wholly reliable: Cap Go Meh occurs according to the lunisolar

calendar, not, as he claims, on a fixed date of the Western calendar; nor does its name mean "Joy Festival."

16. Along with *pantun*, one of the principal poetic forms of the Malay world. Based on a four-line stanza, the *syair* was a popular genre among Indies Chinese, and various Chinese narratives appeared in this genre in the late nineteenth century and early twentieth century.

17. The importance of the festival is unsurprising, given that the event, occurring on the fifteenth day of the Chinese New Year, is also among the principal festivals of the southeastern coastal regions of China, to which most Sino-Indonesians trace their ancestry.There is no classical source for the Lantern Festival, but it was already hugely popular in Fujian during the Ming dynasty and traces its origins to the Tang dynasty or earlier (Szonyi 2002, 141–142).

18. In this play, a man is forbidden by his parents-in-law to take his wife with him to go see the Cap Go Meh festivities because it is deemed improper for them to hold hands in public. Instead, he takes a friend disguised as a woman. His wife, in turn, asks a friend to disguise herself as a man. All of them meet at Cap Go Meh in their disguises, quarrel jealously, and then realize the ridiculousness of the situation. They go home and remonstrate with the parents about the old-fashioned mores they are expected to observe. It may be that Kwee had some exposure to *xiqu*, for the cross-dressing and mistaken identity are quite similar to some plots of traditional southern Fujian theatre, and the Lantern Festival setting is familiar from plays such as *Chen San and Wuniang*.

19. One such case is the Sino-Javanese rice-cake dish called *lontong capgomeh* associated with the festival. Indeed, it is differentiated only slightly (being wrapped in coconut leaves rather than banana leaves) from the *lontong* eaten at the end of Ramadan (Sidharta 2011, 114). Then President Susilo Bambang Yudhoyono invoked the same food as an example of Sino-Indonesian fusion at a 2007 Chinese New Year celebration in Jakarta (Dawis 2009b, 167–168).

20. It remains, however, a substantial celebration in the Hokkien area from which many Sino-Indonesians trace their origins.

21. Descriptions of temple activities in Bandung derive largely from the roughly nine months I spent as an observer-participant at VDR. In this capacity, I attended festivals "at home" in Bandung as well as away in Jakarta, Tegal, Kudus, and Ciamis. Because the congregation is aging, and palanquin processions, especially, require substantial physical exertion, I was welcomed not only as a Mandarin-speaking student representing a Mainland Chinese university (at that time I was a doctoral student, with a scholarship from the Chinese state, at Nanjing University) but also as a youngish man willing to travel and physically assist with the somewhat demanding business of processions. My association with the group thus afforded me the opportunity for semi-structured open-ended conversations with members of this temple, its employers, and attendees of its events, as well as, through its various excursions, opportunities to speak to the members of temples elsewhere in Java and, to a certain extent, with spectators. In Bandung, I also conducted a number of interviews of Chinese and non-Chinese respondents in the days following Cap Go Meh. For specific questions regarding the membership, activities, and history of VDR and other Bandung temples, I interviewed and later corresponded with officers of VDR. They also made some of their documentation available to me, and I supplemented these perspectives from information in the local newspapers reporting on Cap Go Meh and other festivals. The account presented here is further informed by observations at a considerable number of community events, meetings, gatherings, concerts, and festivities to which I was either invited or that were open to the public.

22. The legend attached to this name relates that Pan's great humility prompted him to instruct a disciple to write this name on his gravestone.

23. Accounts of local appeals in Meizhou to Pan to relieve droughts and suppress bandits continued into the twentieth century, and today visitors continue to ask for his help in business, health, and love. Dozens of temples have also been built in his honor in Taiwan, principally in Nantou (Xie Chongguang 2012). As a deified Buddhist monk venerated according to Daoist practices, Pan is also the kind of syncretic figure who raises questions about the proper drawing and even the usefulness of such boundaries. For an example of how a Fujian-based Daoist cult spread within China and to Southeast Asia, including Indonesia, see Dean 1998.

24. Setijadi (2015, 148) notes that this is also a factor in the new increase of Mandarin-learning among young Sino-Indonesians.

25. Mandarin has made only a limited return to usage in the temple, the result of various language programs. Younger learners of Mandarin tend either to nonreligiosity or Christianity, and in the aging congregation there are few Chinese speakers of any kind.

26. The close links between Tek Hay Kion and Vihara Dharma Ramsi during a temple visit to Tegal in May 2013 led the Bandung temple to acquire a new *kimsin* of Tek Hay Kiong's principal deity Zehai Zhenren. His cult has little or no history in Bandung, and—as a maritime deity in a mountain city—its presence is counterintuitive, but the relations between temples has primacy. Tek Hay Kiong is in turn deeply connected to PRC temples, the *locu* having learned his practices in Hubei's Wudang Mountains 武當山. Though certainly Wudangshan is deeply associated with Daoist history and practice, the communities that founded these temples on Java were overwhelmingly of Hokkien and Hakka origin. Consequently, the particular Daoist practice that is learned in twenty-first-century Wudangshan is unlikely to closely resemble anything their ancestors brought from coastal China during the period of large-scale Chinese migration to Java. Tsuda (2012, 395–396) notes influences from Mainland Chinese Daoist publications as well as training in Singapore at Tek Hay Kiong.

27. They attended even though the organization—Chunghwa's International Great Merciful Water Association 中華國際大悲咒水功德會 in Taoyuan County—is committed to a canonical Buddhism remote from VDR's Daoist practices.

28. In 2015, I accompanied and translated for Sino-Indonesian temple officials visiting temples in Taipei's Wanhua district. Besides tourism, the visitors told me that one purpose of their trip was to collect materials to inspire their own upcoming temple renovations in East Java.

29. No conflation between the Sino-Indonesians as a whole and the smaller set of Sino-Indonesians who practice some form of Chinese religion is intended. However, for that considerable portion of the Sino-Indonesian community that follows some form of Chinese religious practice, ethnic and religious minority status are being performed simultaneously. The same may be true to a degree of Protestant and Catholic Sino-Indonesians, but generally their practices are less public, and to some degree less likely to be read as representing the ethnicity as well as the religion. Nevertheless, as recent scholarship has shown, this intersection is also productive, for instance, with regard to business and to education (Koning 2011; Hoon 2011b).

30. Indonesia is largely Muslim. However, many ethnicities, including the Batak, the Nias, the Dayak, the Papuans, the Toraja, the Manadonese, the Timorese, and the inhabitants of Flores are predominantly Christian. Protestantism and Catholicism are thus both less associated specifically with a Chinese identity than "Buddhism," adherents of which are almost exclusively Sino-Indonesian. Also, from an Overseas Chinese studies perspective, there is also something of a division in terms of positionality of the Chinese between Muslim and non-Muslim Southeast Asia: while the majority of Chinese populations in the Philippines, Thailand, Vietnam, Cambodia, or Laos adhere to the majority religion, the majority of Chinese in Indonesia (whether Protestant, Catholic, or adherents of Chinese religions) belong to religious as well as ethnic minorities.

31. As discussed in the introduction, re-sinicization is primarily associated with the goals of the Tiong Hoa Hwe Koan and other associations of the early twentieth century in the colonial Dutch East Indies. At that time, developments in technology and in Chinese as well as Indies politics fostered a new nationalism among the Indies Chinese. The rise of the People's Republic, the freedom of Reformasi politics, and the convenience of both travel and the Internet are today re-sinicizing some younger Sino-Indonesians.

32. One example is the influence of Taiwan-based Buddhist organizations, most notably Tzu Chi. Adepts or temple officials who visit China and Taiwan are clearly interested in applying what they learn to Sino-Indonesian temple life. That said, there are minor strains of Indonesian Buddhism that recognize alternate centers, deriving their inspiration, not from Chinese Buddhism, but from Tibet and Japan (Hui 2011, 189) or from Thailand.

33. I am thinking here of the formal interventions such as Confucius Institutes as well as the resumption and expansion of travel, education, cultural, and clan contacts, enabling exchanges with Chinese-majority polities.

34. Hoon points out that Christian churches also played an important role in maintaining Chinese identity, although it is less often examined, probably because Christianity is considered to maintain a certain distance from Chinese tradition (Hoon 2011a, 55–56).

35. The Christian *wayang wahyu* has also been practiced to a substantial extent by Chinese artists, but it is not obvious whether or not it has played a role in maintaining Chinese identities or even cultural practices.

36. Several of my Bandung respondents reported never having set foot in a church, despite their official registration as Christians. Pausacker (2007) notes the case of a Sino-Indonesian Tegal couple where the woman is Protestant and the man Catholic according to their identity cards, but who awaited the re-registration of Confucianism in 2006 as an official religion before being wed as such.

37. This is no doubt in part because the official ideological foundation, Pancasila, mandates monotheism. For this process, see Suryadinata 2005b, 85. There is no way of measuring how many Sino-Indonesians adherents of Chinese religions subscribe to a form of monotheism, but it does not seem to be an unusual interpretation.

38. In China and Taiwan, individuals often acknowledge the importance of such Confucian concepts as filial piety in their value system and behavior, but because Confucianism is not usually regarded as a faith there, few if any people would identify religiously as "Confucianists." See also Pausacker 2007.

39. Temples generally honor a principal deity in the great hall, with secondary figures in the side altars and in the side or back halls. The pantheon is large and the laying of emphasis variable; a secondary deity in one temple may be a principal one elsewhere, and some deities are to be found in one manifestation or another in almost any Sino-Indonesian temple. One deity may be considered particularly good for improving fertility; another for business success; a third for studies. In China and Taiwan, these diverse and overlapping systems of religious practice are fluid, polytheistic, and nonexclusive.

40. On the other hand, contemporary Taiwanese religious observations, occurring in the context of a heated and protracted debate about the island's political and cultural identity, can sometimes very much contain elements of performative "Taiwaneseness."

41. This is due to the precolonial presence of Buddhism in the archipelago.

42. It is common for temples, like Chinese voluntary organizations, to have Indonesian names for public use. A Chinese-derived name, most often Hokkien and not necessarily semantically related to the official Indonesian name, is often more commonly in use among the congregants.

43. "Bio" is the Indonesian rendering of the Hokkien pronunciation of Mandarin *miao*, a standard word for temple.

44. This procedure must be repeated every year; obtaining permission remains enough of a concern that the bureaucratic reference number is sometimes shown on public posters near the events and is also affixed in the temple's communal dining area.

45. Other recent observances of Cap Go Meh have also downplayed the Chineseness of the festivals in the material. Take, for instance, the strategy in Bogor, where the 2017 festival was advertised as "Pesta Rakyat Bogor CGM" (CGM Bogor Folk Festival), while the 2018 materials opted for a similar English version: "Bogor Street Fest CGM."

46. Not long after his term ended, he was given a ten-year sentence for corruption.

47. The deity Fa Cu Kung or Fat Cu Kung (法主公) is Zhang Shengzhe 張聖者, the commander of the Eastern camp in the netherworld (Pregadio 2008, 2:1071–1072). This dark-faced figure is associated with migration from Yongchun, a county now administratively a part of Quanzhou (Chee-Beng Tan 2015, 373), and he is thought to offer protection from disease. In spirit processions, he may manifest as three bodies, each with a black beard, but made up with red, green, and black faces (Chan 2006, 48).

48. There is, however, also a bitterly ironic aspect to this song whenever it is sung at Bandung Chinese events, as some revolutionaries directed their aggression at the Chinese. As Mary Somers Heidhues remarks, the song "proudly recalls the *lautan api* [sea of fire], but in reality, the fires targeted the Chinese minority, one they blamed for profiting from Indonesian suffering under Dutch or Japanese rule" (2012, 386).

49. This temple, among the oldest extant Sino-Indonesian places of worship, was gutted in a March 2015 fire during preparations for Cap Go Meh. Despite the substantial damage, the temple was open during Cap Go Meh because, as the security coordinator told the *Jakarta Post*, "this is the home of Chinese-Indonesians" (*The Jakarta Post*, March 3, 2015).

50. The preparation of the palanquins occurred in a space immediately adjacent to the Catholic church Santa Maria de Fatima. This church, converted from an older Chinese residency, is notable for its Chinese stone lions and Mandarin-language mass.

51. Temple delegations travelling from farther afield, mostly temples of Central or East Java, generally stayed the night in Jakarta.

52. The Guan Gong sculpture had to remain at VDR, where birthday celebrations for Star Lord of the Northern Dipper 北斗星君 and Star Lord of the Southern Dipper 南斗星君 deities were ongoing. According to VDR members, *jiaobei* 筊杯 block divination had been used to determine who should be sent in Guan Gong's stead.

53. Fude Zhengshen is an honorific of the Earth God (Tudi gong), translated as "Orthodox Deity of Blessing and Virtue." He is "often compared to a local official" since he is "a low ranking member of the celestial bureaucracy" (Pregadio 2008, 2:999). His cult is very common among Nanyang Chinese communities, perhaps because invoking the Earth God was a way for migrants to affiliate themselves with land overseas.

54. Some consider this swaying to be involuntary, a result of the divinity's great power (Chan 2006, 70).

55. Formally, Basuki Tjahaja Purnama 鍾萬勰. Ahok 阿勰 is a nickname derived from the Hakka pronunciation of the last character.

56. Joko Widodo was governor for only two years before becoming president of Indonesia, making Ahok automatically governor of Jakarta. As president, Joko Widodo's attendance at a Cap Go Meh festival in Bogor in 2015 was much celebrated in Sino-Indonesian communities.

57. Ahok was not the first Sino-Indonesian to reach the rank of vice-governor; that honor goes to Christiandy Sanjaya, elected to a 2008–2013 term in West Kalimantan, where Chinese

are one of the largest ethnic groups, and where he ran with the Dayak gubernatorial candidate Cornelis M.H. When Joko Widodo was elected president of Indonesia in 2014, Ahok became the first Sino-Indonesian governor. He had accomplished another first in 2005 when he was elected the first Chinese district head on Sumatra. That post, in East Belitung, was later held by his brother (Tanasaldy 2015, 447).

58. There also remain concerns among Chinese Indonesians that Ahok's actions could, if they became unpopular, provoke a backlash against the community (Setijadi 2016, 5). The narrative that Ahok was benefiting ethnic Chinese at the expensive of poor (largely *pribumi*) Jakartans began to gain traction by April 2016 (Herlijanto 2016, 1).

59. The attitude of Chinese Christians is not always friendly either. One VDR respondent recounted that during the 2012 Cap Go Meh parade a Chinese Christian had virulently remonstrated with viewers not to watch it, as it was a parade of monsters and demons. The respondent, a Chinese temple member, noted with satisfaction that it was Muslim *pribumi* spectators rather than VDR members who made the man conclude his tirade and leave.

60. The area is in central Bandung, a short distance from the city's *alun-alun* (central lawn square) and principal mosque. There were likely Chinese in this area as early as the British interlude (1811–1815), and it became known as part of the "Chinatown" (*Pecinan*), which accounts for the high density of Chinese temples (Tunas 2007, 75–90). However, today the Sino-Indonesian community is scattered throughout the city, and no neighborhood features a majority Chinese population.

61. Compared to Chinese churches, the temples are both more spatially integrated and locally involved, even if temples (as opposed to churches) are likely to be considered more "essentially" or originally Chinese. It is an intriguing paradox that the ethnically identified religious community is apparently more open and embedded than the Christian churches, with their universalist aspirations.

62. Moreover, VDR has been enlarged several times since the 1950s, and, during my fieldwork in 2013–2014, was again in the process of seeking funds from members to enlarge its grounds.

63. After this, more than a few of the congregation members move on to secular Chinese social activities in the afternoon of the kind described in the previous chapter. VDR, for instance, is not far from Priangan, and the membership of the two organizations overlaps substantially.

64. Some calendars also include a "Chinese year," which is apparently an Indonesian invention and is modelled on Christian (since the birth of Jesus Christ) and Muslim (since the Hijra year) timekeeping since the birth of Confucius. The year 2016, for instance, is the year 2567 according to this calendar. This may also be the place to remark that the Islamic terminology, too, is sometimes applied to Confucius in Indonesia. Notably, he is widely identified as a *nabi*, the term usually reserved for the prophets of Islam. Consider how distant from the usual understandings of Confucianism is the sentence "For the adherents of the religion Confucianism, he [Confucius] is recognized as a prophet," which has been in the opening paragraph on the Indonesian Wikipedia entry for "Confucius" since 2005. Similar accounts appear regularly in the press or in popular works on religion. It seems likely that the terminology dates specifically from the foundation of the Tiong Hoa Hwe Koan in 1900. As Lea Williams remarks, "the attempt of the THHK founders to messianize their patron is but one more example of Chinese acculturation to the Javanese environment" (Williams, n. 13, in Tek Hoay Kwee 1969, 6). It may also be, as Williams noted elsewhere, that the messianic quality of Indonesian Confucianism is related to the fact that its revival "was born of experience with Christianity" (Lea E. Williams 1960, 192). Chang-Yau Hoon even remarks that some "Chinese-Indonesians celebrate Imlek

[i.e., Chinese New Year] as a sacred day that commemorates the birth of Confucius, just as Christians celebrate Christmas to remember the birth of Jesus Christ" (Hoon 2009b).

65. Founded in prewar Malaya by British colonial officials, the Hash House Harriers have evolved, predominantly but not exclusively in Asia, to find "new life as centers for postcolonial activities for international workers and their families" (Hindman 2013, 178). Today they are usually Western expatriate-dominated noncompetitive walking and hiking organizations, associated also with drinking during or after activities. In Bandung, however, and it seems in much of Indonesia, HHH clubs are Sino-Indonesian-dominated walking and charity organizations, usually concluding with food and multilingual karaoke, and with no alcohol.

66. Today, dragon and lion dance have been adopted and standardized by the PRC national cultural and sports establishments. This substitution of a national standard for specific regional or subethnic practices is something that is repeated across food history, iconography, religious practices, and many other fields of cultural activity. These politically endorsed standards are then borrowed into diasporic communities, often overriding local practices.

67. Nevertheless, *barongsay* was still, respondents assert, performed in some areas behind closed doors. It also featured in Nano Riantiarno's 1988 *Sampek Engtay*, and the opportunity to see the *barongsay* on stage was a major draw for Sino-Indonesian audience members.

68. Hui relates, for instance, that it was included in a rice ritual of the Salako Dayaks in West Kalimantan, alongside Dayak and Javanese performances (Hui 2011, 289–290). A similar absorption of *barongsay* occurred in a photo exhibit, where it appeared alongside *wayang kulit*, *jatilan*, and *wayang wong* in a photo exhibition. Visual anthropologist Karen Strassler noted that it is "being incorporated into the Indonesian pantheon of *asli* [i.e., autochthonous] cultural arts" (Strassler 2010, 69).

69. The employment of non-Chinese performers for *barongsay* is widespread. Anthropologist Margaret Chan writes about the practice in Jakarta that "[m]ost of them are made up of non-Chinese youths, many of whom must be Muslim. But religion does not come into the picture. If the Chinese will pay for perfunctory performances of lion dance at their place of business, then the youths see no problem in quite literally dancing to that tune" (Chan 2010). Most often, the non-Chinese youths will be earning low wages; in many cases, the owner of the troupe (and its equipment) will be earning substantial profits from the performance.

70. An example cited by Mintardja is post-hopping (*meihua zhuang* 梅花樁), in which the children leading the dragon or the *barongsay* jump from post to post. As the posts can be very high, a fall could lead to serious injuries.

71. Consequently, many *barongsay* troupes no longer have temple affiliations and are instead connected with sports groups, restaurants, or community associations. Even for the temple group, it is clear that *barongsay* as practiced today constitutes as much a re-creation as a continuity. Mintardja and certain other older temple members are old enough to remember *barongsay* practice before the New Order period and describe the performance as vastly different. During their childhoods, in the early independence period, all the performers would have been Chinese, and the dragons were made out of a rattan frame and a cloth skin, as opposed to the plastic now in use. There were four dragons, to represent the four directions, and the various colors of the dragons indicated various figures from the Three Kingdoms. Each dragon followed a pearl (held at the end of a pole by a dancer, and called, like the Buddhist prayer beads, *fozhu* 佛珠) symbolizing wisdom. At that time *barongsay* would often have been performed by lantern light and torchlight, which enhanced the supernatural atmosphere. The older generation reports that there was once more respect for the *barongsay* because it was felt to be an effective guarantee of good fortune.

72. The attentive reader may wonder how the writer could simultaneously visit the same

festival on two different islands in the same year. The Bandung Chinese community, aware that it does not have the same prominence to compete with more famous Cap Go Meh festivals, chose to hold its celebrations a week after the calendrical Lantern Festival date. This deliberate staggering allowed more temples to attend the Bandung procession.

73. The Chinese characters for Singkawang.

74. Liu, a member of the National Committee of the Chinese People's Political Consultative Conference, is something akin to a Chinese Communist "court painter" (Cong 1997, 16) and has won renown for his kitschy works of Chinese mythology and CCP canonical figures.

75. The star deities represent *fu* (good fortune), *lu* (emolument), and *shou* (long life), and are the personifications of three aspects of an ideal life in Chinese iconography.

76. The presence of Tzu Chi in the Cap Go Meh festivities of Singkawang as well as in those of VDR is one way in which these highly disparate events are linked to international organizations. Tzu Chi, founded in Taiwan, controls large funds and is active in disaster relief and charity projects in over eighty-five countries (Glaser and Vitello 2015, 28). Among the largest social groups active in Taiwan today, it is wildly praised in academic circles and commercial presses. However, its profile in its home territory of Taiwan is more mixed, since its religious agenda is controversial and its activities can also be read in political or economic terms.

77. The plastic blossoms were a telling evocation of a Chinese "cultural homeland," and apparently, even the plastic plum trees had to be imported from the PRC. Northern hemisphere diasporic communities can typically identify with the change in seasons that occurs around the Spring Festival (i.e., the Chinese New Year), since it is in some way reflected in their own climate. But Singkawang's climate is equatorial, and so all of the spring symbolism of Chinese New Year is meteorologically fictitious. The *Taman Meihwa* (plum-flower garden), which might seem to claim universality when deployed in Asia, North America, or Europe, is as distant from reality as the reproductions of karst landscapes.

78. Most obviously a dragon statue in a principal intersection of the city (Tanasaldy 2013, 102; Hertzman 2017, 58–66). Ethnic tensions surrounding this statue were dramatized by Singkawang Hakka author Hanna Fransisca in her 2012 play *Kawan Tidur* (The friend is sleeping).

79. Indeed, there are few regions of the world where such a large population of nonethnic Chinese have acquired some competency in a Chinese language. See Heidhues (1997, 202) and Stenberg (2015).

80. Like many other archipelagic groups, Dayak identities have been formed in response to colonial and postcolonial state analyses of ethnicity. Although in "historical practice Dayak identity has always been fluid and relational" as well as internally diverse, increasingly "an understanding of Dayaks as one large, pan-ethnic entity" has developed (König 2016, 121). These boundaries are further hardened by a sense of religious difference, with Dayaks being Christian and animist as opposed to the Muslim Malay (or, as was evident during the Sampit and Sambas conflicts of 1999 and 2001, the Madurese).

81. Particularly in Indonesian texts, this group is known as *Khe* or *Khek* more often than as *Hakka*. See, for example, Hari Poerwanto's book *Orang Cina Khek dari Singkawang* (Hakka Chinese people from Singkawang).

82. Some histories, especially in Chinese, sometimes claim that it is the "first republic in Asia," which somewhat exaggerates *kongsi* history, given that the federations never gave themselves the title of republic and existed by virtue of a series of special understandings with the Dutch. Nevertheless, no other entity in Chinese history looks quite like the Borneo *kongsi*.

83. The 2000 census counting of Chinese was problematic for numerous reasons, and it seems that North Sumatra severely undercounted its Chinese residents. Also noteworthy is

that the Province of Riau had not separated into the Province of the Riau Archipelago and a province that retains the old name. According to the authors, Riau Archipelago's numbers in the census, if separated out, would also represent a proportionately larger Chinese population than in West Kalimantan.

84. The context of the violence and expulsions, in which thousands died at the hands of mostly Dayak commandos, was the association by the government and the military of all Chinese people with sympathy for the banned PKI.

85. During my visit to Singkawang over Chinese New Year and Lantern Festival 2013, I spoke to Chinese people from Singkawang who had worked in Taiwan (with Taoyuan, Taipei, and Taichung being major centers), Malaysia (Sarawak as well as peninsular Malaysia), Mainland China, Singapore, Java (overwhelmingly Jakarta, but also Surabaya and Bandung), Korea, Japan, the United States, United Kingdom, and Australia. Because migrants return at this time, the population swells over Chinese New Year and Cap Go Meh. Hertzman finds Singkawang Chinese three times likelier to leave the city and sojourn elsewhere compared to other Singkawang people (2017, 23). There is an older, distinct, émigré community, many of whom were evacuated to Mainland China by boat in 1967. One eighty-two-year-old respondent noted with sadness that many others had prepared to leave—but the boats never came back (see also Davidson 2008, 58–62).

86. The Chineseness of the area also has linguistic particularities. According to Matthew Isaac Cohen, in 1920, "more than 99% of the west coast's Chinese spoke a Chinese language rather than Malay; Hakka effectively functioned as interethnic lingua franca" (2006, 317). An American missionary (pers. comm., 2014; prefers anonymity) wrote that in 1974 urban Singkawang was almost entirely Hakka-speaking, and that older Chinese had difficulty expressing themselves in Indonesian unless they ran a store. Those who were then in their thirties (i.e., born in the 1930s and 1940s) could speak Indonesian, although generally they used Hakka except when in government offices and would bring along a translator if it was necessary to conduct affairs there. A decade later, Indonesianist Denys Lombard wrote of the "general use" of Indonesian among young Chinese in West Kalimantan and among those with relatively high levels of schooling (Lombard 1984, 88). Even today, one finds that only older, more rural, and poorer populations have difficulty with Indonesian. Young respondents I interviewed in Singkawang reported speaking Indonesian only in school; similarly, respondents of sociologist Aimée Dawis remarked that "we still spoke *Hakka* to one another during [school] breaks... those who spoke *Bahasa Indonesia* were seen as arrogant" (Dawis 2009a, 115).

87. Historically, the term was in use also among Taiwanese and Malaysian Hakka (Leo 2015, 73) and among Hokkien and Teochew people throughout Southeast Asia as "a generic reference to their ancestral origin on the mainland [of China]" (Chang 2015, 8).

88. Although knowledge of Hakka assists migrants, especially those who migrate to Hakka-speaking areas of Taiwan, the national or transnational Hakka identity is not the core allegiance. Indeed, Singkawang Hakka reported considerable obstacles to mutual intelligibility with PRC, Taiwanese, Bangka, Jakarta, or Malaysian Hakka.

89. See also Judith Nagata's observation that, a generation ago, Chinese Indonesian congregations in Toronto tended to form and separate as much or more by preferred language as by ethnic or theological distinctions (1988, 130).

90. The "Chinese population consists primarily of working class and lower middle class petty merchants, farmers, and primary producers" (Hertzman 2014, 150), and since the city lacks "a functioning port, airport, or a university[,] it has limited economic prospects" (149). Singkawang's relative poverty acts as a foil to stereotypes of Chinese Indonesian wealth and materialism (Dawis 2009a, 89; Hoon 2011a, 4).

91. The respondent goes on to remark that the equal poverty between Singkawang Chinese and *pribumi* engenders a feeling of solidarity. Singkawang Hakka, he says, "are much friendlier to the other ethnic groups and don't look down on *pribumi*... because they are all the same" (Dawis 2009a, 89). This assessment resembles official visions of ethnic harmony, although also, I would argue, elides the complexity of local ethnic relations.

92. For instance, Chinese mediums may channel particular Dayak or Malay spirits (Chan 2009, 132–133).

93. There is, for instance, no contact between Kalimantan temples and VDR, but extensive contacts between VDR and temples on Bali and Sumatra.

94. A case in point was the awarding to Singkawang, in 2012, of the "Gong Perdamaian Nusantara" (Gong of the nation's peace), one of five cities chosen as being representative of ethnic harmony under the ideology of Pancasila.

95. Unsurprisingly, it also becomes the principal concern of Singkawang's best-known author, Hanna Fransisca, who in her poetry, drama, and fiction has repeatedly treated issues of interethnic conflict, stereotyping, and romance. Like many other Singkawangers, she lives in Jakarta.

96. Questioned specifically on the subject of racism, one Singkawang Hakka respondent commented that he felt relations had improved compared to the period of his childhood in the 1980s. In his view, non-Chinese people in Singkawang in recent years had absorbed the idea that racism was undesirable, a concept that he credited to the recent influence of television and the Internet.

97. The ethnic dynamic also has a political expression. Though it is certainly far from absolute, more than one respondent speaking about the then recent 2012 elections remarked that "Chinese vote for Chinese, Malays for Malays"; while another Chinese respondent remarked that the Malay mayor "Awang Ishak doesn't hate us on the surface, but hates us in his heart." On the other hand, the Dayak governor Cornelis M.H. might seem "quite even-handed on the surface, but in his heart he looks after us." Surveys have shown that slightly less than half of West Kalimantan residents would be willing to accept a Chinese governor, and it is widely acknowledged that religion and ethnicity are major electoral divides. Political scientist Karolina Prasad remarks that surveys only confirm what has been "commonsensically known for decades" (2015, 121).

98. One respondent, a Singkawang Chinese who had long resided on Java, said jokingly that "Singkawang is like its own country," but later commented seriously that he felt Kalimantan should be independent or at least autonomous. His rationale for this position, neither uncommon nor politically imaginable, was that Kalimantan resources were going to the central government with little return for people in Singkawang. He added that independence would require "much support from China."

99. According to Chai (2017, 47), the preferred local term is *phan tung* 邦童, though the etymology remains obscure. Chinese characters for *tatung* are not established.

100. This is a vegetable basket covered in a cloth. Since it is possessed, those holding it cannot control it (see also Hui 2011, 286; Chai 2017, 80–84). Though two dozen or more baskets featured in the parade, carried by "a single spirit-channeller... or by sashes between two people, swung and bobbed wildly, dragging those who lead them hither and thither" (Chan 2006, 141), *choi lam sin* are not limited to Cap Go Meh. For use in divination, a writing brush is affixed to the basket that spells out messages from the divinity, a practice comparable also to the "chair writing" known among Singapore Hokkien (Chan 2006, 116). It seems probable that *choi lam sin*, using the alternate name of *choi lam gong*, is at the origin of Javanese practices called *jailangkung*, *jalangkung*, or *jelangkung*. These are puppets, with half a coconut shell for a head

and crossed sticks for the body, that are also used for divination purposes, especially by children. For many younger Indonesians, however, the primary association may be with a successful 2001 horror film. Various ritual practices of the West Kalimantan Hakka, including the "basket god," are also described in Robert L. Peterson's *Roaring Lion* (1968) and *The Demon Gods of Thorny River* (1974), where "Ocean Harbour" presumably corresponds to Singkawang. Needless to say, this work from a missionary press, and based on a missionary's account, regards the practices as "terrible satanic bondage" (vii), and the narrative misses no opportunity to cast them in the worst possible light. Peterson, some of whose works were translated into Dutch and Chinese (in Hong Kong), considers Cap Go Meh as "several days [devoted] to the worship of evil spirits" (Peterson 1968, 15), who drive them to "perform acts of self-laceration under the influence of evil spirits" (16). Sylvia Houliston, also of the Overseas Missonary Fellowship, provides a less dogmatic (and dramatic) account of Singkawang religious practices in her *The Broken Dagger* (1967, 47ff.), which also has material on the view of World War II and on the foundation of the People's Republic of China among the Chinese of Singkawang.

101. There is no certain derivation of the local term for spirit medium, *tatung*, although several etymologies have been suggested. In many ways, the *tatung* in Singkawang are similar to the *tang-ki* of the Hokkien world, for which see Chan 2006. In contrast with the *tang-ki*, one might argue, the characteristics of Singkawang *tatung* when possessed do not seem to include childishness (see also Chan 2006, 56–59). The practice of the *tatung* may be connected to the experiences of the first Chinese settlers. One local Hakka respondent explained their role by suggesting that for Chinese settlers in the perilous area, the jungle was a landscape full of evil spirits. The *tatung* constitute a show of spiritual force in order to demonstrate to the local spirits that the new settlers are stronger and more terrible than they. Indeed, many *tatung* have general roles as shamans or medicine men and are asked to intervene throughout the year to help with health problems, remove evil spirits, and bring good luck. *Tatung* are largely but not exclusively male, and newspapers also paid particular attention to the small number of child *tatung*. The practice can be passed on in a family, but need not be. Most *tatung* otherwise have ordinary employment as small traders, serving largely family and neighbors, but some make their living by offering divination and ritual assistance (see Hui 2011, 221). The organization of Cap Go Meh does pay *tatung* to participate in the festival, though I was told that the payment could not cover the cost of the costumes and the assistants engaged. Only a few *tatung* live off their earnings. Similarly, Chan found that *tang-ki* in Singapore, though paid, mostly cannot make a living off their practice as ritual performers (Chan 2006, 124–125). Depending on the elaborateness of their spirit chairs, *choi lam sin*, and/or lion and dragon dancers, the 2013 *tatung* compensation scale ranged from three million to 300,000 rupiah (*Kal Bar Times*, February 8, 2013).

102. See also Margaret Chan's account of *tang-ki* performers in Singapore who "attest that their trance performances—what they do, what costumes they wear and what props they use—are choices the gods made without any cognitive decisions on the part of the human medium" (Chan 2006, 45).

103. The easier availability of costumes from China means that most now are dressed in new garb, not dissimilar to the martial apparel of popular *xiqu* or television costume drama. Unlike in Singapore (see Chan 2006, 63) it is not at present popular to wear *xiqu* makeup for the procession. Among other possible reasons, this may reflect the absence of *xiqu* familiarity in present-day Singkawang.

104. Locally, it is also common for Malay or Dayak spirits called *datuks* to be venerated. Hui considers it possible that "the Datuk is a fetishization of the ethnic other" (Hui 2011, 220) and that "the antagonistic spirit is made familiar by assimilating it within the Chinese religious pantheon" (213–215). In the past, *tatung* had also killed puppies and carried the corpses in their

mouths, though in 2013 that practice was forbidden. Likely this was at variance with a public image that municipal authorities wanted to project, especially to outside tourists. Ann David notes, similarly, that "piercing or hooks in the back" (David 2012, 461–462) are not allowed in Tamil Hindu processions in London, likely out of concern for the public image the community wishes to project.

105. Instead, they attributed real efficacy to the events of the preceding day, when the various *tatung* visited the principal temple to "ask for permission" for the next day's procession.

106. It is noteworthy, however, that in 2013 *tatung* were not being permitted in the smaller Cap Go Meh celebrations in the provincial capital of Pontianak. It is clear from the work of other scholars that public procession of *tatung* has been a contentious issue in the provincial capital for some years (Chan 2009, 133–137; Tanasaldy 2013, 102).

107. Among VDR members in Bandung also, there was a frequent appeal to authenticity, which could be expressed, paradoxically, by both presence and absence of the "same thing" in China. Some respondents felt that this was like "in China" and therefore authentic; others felt that the practice in China "was gone" (*yijing meiyou le*) and that consequently Sino-Indonesian Cap Go Meh practice was more "authentic" than in China.

108. It is true that in Mao's China all manner of religious observances were suppressed, though it is also true that they were never completely extinguished and many are now being successfully revived. Furthermore, the identification of Singkawang's Cap Go Meh practices with any historic practices in Hakka areas of China is difficult to establish. As already noted, even the Chinese characters for *tatung* cannot be established with any certainty. Finally, it is, among other things, the marks of syncretism with Malay and Dayak practices that make West Kalimantan's Chinese observances, including Cap Go Meh, remarkable.

109. The same claim is often made, erroneously, by scholarship on *wayang potehi*, who state that the genre is "extinct" in its place of origin, a dire result of the restrictions imposed on it during the Cultural Revolution in China (Mastuti 2014, xvi). Without wishing to diminish the harm done to puppet troupes by the Cultural Revolution, *potehi* genres are alive in southern Fujian, not to mention in Taiwan, Malaysia, and Singapore.

110. It is clear that Cap Go Meh was already a major part of West Borneo communal life during the early twentieth century; Christian missionaries tried to prevent their converts from watching the procession (Heidhues 1997, 203). Despite the prohibition of public displays of Chinese culture from the 1960s, the festival did not wholly disappear. An American missionary (who prefers to remain anonymous) remembers visiting from the countryside, where he worked among Dayaks: "The Cap Go Meh celebration was a big deal in 1974. Basically the city of Singkawang shut down for the day. The parade started at the temple by the river and went for about 1/8 mile through town to an empty lot on what was then the far end of town by the big banyan tree." Singkawang Hakka respondents concurred with this account, reporting instead that curtailments of public display began to be more strongly enforced during the 1980s. One older man recalled that public dragon dances for the Lantern Festival were banned in the early 1980s; lion dances were continued, however, as they could be considered more "Indonesian." Everyone agreed that during New Order the celebrations were smaller, but also more sacred, "authentic," and community-oriented. When asked how it was possible that Cap Go Meh performances went on despite the interdiction of expressions of Chinese culture, one respondent rubbed his thumb and forefinger and said "You can't get around this in Indonesia," meaning bribes. It seems likely that even though there was no official involvement or approbation, arrangements must have been made to allow for the festival to continue. Even today, it is widely presumed that payments must be made (not only in Singkawang) to relevant authorities to prevent the disruption of Chinese festivals.

111. According to one committee member quoted in a recent article, Cap Go Meh celebrations in the late 1980s were permitted as part of a local quid pro quo, with the condition being that local Chinese support Suharto's Golkar party in local elections (Ong et al. 2017, 46).

112. Founded in 1878, this temple is generally called, whether in Indonesian or Hakka, *tuapekong* and, like all central temples of West Singkawang towns of any size, is devoted to that deity. Officially, however, it is known as a Vihara Tri Dharma Bumi Raya. Temple-produced Chinese-language materials refer to it as Central *pekong* 中央伯公.

113. The records were for the largest *kue keranjang* (lit.: basket cake, a form of *niangao*), at 99 centimeters thick, almost 3 meters long, and over 8 tonnes heavy; for the largest lantern (23 m high, diameter 32 m), and for largest number of *tatung* (*KalBar Times*, January 22, 2013).

114. The spells are written charms. As in Margaret Chan's observations among Hokkien populations in Singapore, these are often "indecipherable scrawls made in crimson ink on yellow paper strips. The illegible writing reaffirms status difference since mortals naturally cannot read the writing of a god" (Chan 2006, 74).

115. Indeed, Tanasaldy's analysis of the 2008 and 2012 municipal elections supports the view that, in the former, Chinese electors were united behind one candidate and Malay electors divided between several; and, in the latter, the reverse was true (2015, 459–460, 462). See also Prasad (2015, 181). In 2017, Singkawang returned its first woman mayor, Tjhai Chui Mie, who also became the first Chinese woman elected mayor of an Indonesian city. Chinese, she and her Malay running mate Irwan defeated Ishak's Hakka wife and the Madurese deputy mayor (both with Malay running mates). Hui considers that their success "depended on their subtle navigation of ethnoreligious politics, support from the Singkawang Chinese elite in Jakarta, and their ability to fend off smear campaigns that reveal deep-seated divisions in Indonesia" (Hui 2017, 1).

116. *Da'i* is the term for a Muslim proselytizer, often translated as "missionary."

117. There are, of course, a variety of views among Indonesian religious authorities about the attitude to be taken towards non-Muslim cultural, religious, or ritual activities. The Islamic Defenders' Front (FPI), perhaps best known abroad for its successful campaign to cancel a 2012 Jakarta concert by Lady Gaga, is on the radically uncompromising edge of this discourse. The FPI has been associated with harassment of public Chinese festivities in other parts of Indonesia as well (Tanasaldy 2013, 102).

118. A few years earlier, a Malay respondent of Margaret Chan's reported an "attack" for the same reason (Chan 2013, 148). Respondents widely acknowledged that Malays participated more widely as assistants to *tatung* by carrying the spirit chairs of musicians and dancers. Since the celebration is regarded as idolatry by some devout Muslims, the municipal support for it has caused some resentment, perhaps particularly under the previous, ethnic Chinese, mayor (La Ode 2012, 262–266). La Ode, who uses the contested term *Cina* in his title, and who opposes the involvement of Sino-Indonesians in politics (385–396), also claims that some non-Chinese may have felt obliged to participate in Cap Go Meh under the Hasan Karman government, either because they wanted to garner Chinese support or because they otherwise deemed it prudent to support the events for career or financial reasons (315–316).

119. I thus found in Singkawang a Chinese Protestant church sporting "Happy New Year" greetings in Chinese with zodiac animals. Another banner showed that Cap Go Meh could be integrated into a worldwide commercial festivity by highlighting the calendrical proximity that year of Cap Go Meh and Valentine's Day.

120. Recent reports, however, suggest that waning government interest and funding has decreased the number of *tatung* participating and shortened the parade route (Chai 2017, 114).

121. Indeed, the attractiveness of *tatung* performance as an exotic expression of Chineseness

for Cap Go Meh was shown by its inclusion as part of Cap Go Meh celebrations at Jakarta Fairground (*The Jakarta Post*, February 25, 2013). The movement of such performance from the streets of Singkawang into the amusement parks of Jakarta perfectly illustrates its transition from ritual necessity to exotic and ethnic minority performance.

Conclusions

1. In fact, my father is not Jewish, and my surname is of Swedish origin, though I often am addressed or introduced as "Sternberg" or "Steinberg" as a result of mistaken assumptions. Of course, I might claim "half-Jew," but many interlocutors will appeal to the traditional (and legal) Jewish tradition of membership by matrilineal descent. Therefore, the claim is apt to be rejected or questioned, resulting in another round of justification or explanation. An Indonesian might likewise find it tiring to insist on "half-Chinese" and end up adopting or rejecting the identity wholesale. Except for those who are particularly fond of discussing themselves, there is an incentive to the adoption of false binaries.

2. I acknowledge that being a white person in East and Southeast Asia (as in many other places) generates privilege and elicits forbearance. Certainly, an African or an Indian or a nonwhite Westerner would not have been treated, at least by some respondents, with the same respect or amity. However, the general stereotype of, say, the *laowai* man—frank, liberated, drunken, smelly, promiscuous, wealthy but spendthrift, loud, Christian, grossly physical, and not smart or studious enough to learn Asian languages—is not an especially positive one.

3. For instance, a senior Chinese Indonesian scholar, Myra Sidharta, writes that a 2006 temple festival in Gresik involved "an auction of the jewelry donated by some sponsors." They had been "hung around Mazu's effigy's neck and are supposed to bring luck to the owner" (Sidharta 2015, 10). The elements of visible and perhaps competitive wealth, often with a large non-Chinese (and largely less affluent) public, may reinforce images of Sino-Indonesians as a closed and wealthy group.

4. The dance form *cokek* and the orchestral music *gambang kromong* are both part of a distinctly Batavian culture that was highly influenced by the local Chinese population. The popular song style *keroncong* also has Chinese elements. See Kartomi 2000; Yampolsky 2013a, 2013b.

5. I refer to the visits of the twenty-member Long Tack Sam revue to Batavia, Bandung, and Malang in August and September 1935 (*NDNI*, August 2, 1935; *De Indische Courant*, September 10, 1935).

6. For instance, the visit of the May Hua Cabaret, also described as an "operetta troupe" to Batavia, Surabaya, and Malang in September–December 1935. Numbers included tap dancing and imitations of animal calls (*NDNI*, September 20, 1935; *De Indische Courant*, November 21 and December 24, 1935). This is almost surely the Meihua Gewu jutuan 梅花歌舞劇團 (Plum Flower Dance Troupe), founded by Wei Yingbo 魏縈波, given that name in 1929, and active on Shanghai radio and stages in the 1920s and 1930s.

7. I refer to *Siddharta* 釋迦摩尼, a Mandarin-language musical that in May 2007 was performed twice in the Jakarta International Exhibition Center, with the assistance of Jakarta Chinese groups and individuals, and with a largely Sino-Indonesian audience. He Linghui, the producer, director, and playwright, noted considerable difficulties, due to the fact that the Chinese Indonesians spoke no Chinese, and the Malaysian Chinese "terrible Indonesian" (He and Gan 2009, 45–47).

8. For instance, Koko Liem and Tan Mei Hwa (Hew 2010).

REFERENCES

Books, Articles, and Audiovisual Materials

Abeyasekere, Susan. 1983. "Women as Cultural Intermediaries in Nineteenth-Century Batavia." In *Women's Work and Women's Roles: Economics and Everyday Life in Indonesia, Malaysia and Singapore,* edited by Lenore Manderson, 15–29. Canberra: ANU Press.

Acciaioli, Greg. 1985. "Culture as Art: From Practice to Spectacle in Indonesia." *Canberra Anthropology* 8 (1–2): 148–172.

Adam, Ahmat. 1995. *The Vernacular Press and the Emergence of Modern Indonesian Consciousness (1855–1913).* Ithaca, NY: Southeast Asia Program, Cornell University.

Aguilar, Filomeno. 2001. "Citizenship, Inheritance, and the Indigenizing of 'Orang Chinese' in Indonesia." *positions: east asia cultures critique* 9 (3): 501–533.

Ahlquist, Karen. 2006. "Introduction." *Chorus and Community,* edited by Karen Ahlquist, 1–15. Urbana: University of Illinois Press.

Aizawa, Nobuhiro. 2010. "Assimilation, Differentiation, and Depoliticization: Chinese Indonesians and the Ministry of Home Affairs in Suharto's Indonesia." In *Chinese Indonesians and Regime Change,* edited by Marleen Dieleman, Juliette Koning, and Peter Post, 47–64. Leiden: Brill.

Alexander, Jeffrey C. 2004. "Cultural Pragmatics: Social Performance between Ritual and Strategy." *Sociological Theory* 22 (4): 527–573.

Altenburger, Roland. 2005. "Is It Clothes That Make the Man? Cross-Dressing, Gender and Sex in Pre-Twentieth Century Zhu Yingtai Lore." *Asian Folklore Studies* 64:165–205.

Ananta, Aris, Evi Nurvidya Arifin, and Bakhtiar Kusnadi. 2008. "Chinese Indonesians in Indonesia and in the Province of Riau Archipelago: A Demographic Analysis." In *Ethnic Chinese in Contemporary Indonesia,* edited by Leo Suryadinata, 17–47. Singapore: ISEAS.

Ang, Ien. 2001. *On Not Speaking Chinese: Living between Asia and the West.* New York: Routledge.

———. 2004. "Beyond Transnational Nationalism: Questioning the Borders of the Chinese

Diaspora in the Global City." In *State/Nation/Transnation: Perspectives on Transnationalism in the Asia-Pacific,* edited by Brenda S. A. Yeoh and Katie Willis, 179–198. New York: Routledge.

———. 2013. "No Longer Chinese? Residual Chineseness after the Rise of China." In *Diasporic Chineseness after the Rise of China: Communities and Cultural Production,* edited by Kam Louie, David M. Pomfret, and Julia Kuehn, 17–31. Vancouver: UBC Press.

Arifin, Evi Nurvidya, M. Sairi Hasbullah, and Agus Pramono. 2016. "Chinese Indonesians: How Many, Who and Where?" *Asian Ethnicity,* 1–20.

Arifin, Evi Nurvidya, Agus Pramono, Nur Budi Handayani, and M. Sairi Hasbullah. 2015. *Demography of Indonesia's Ethnicity.* Singapore: ISEAS Publishing.

ASA. 1990. "Prakata" (Preface). In *San Pek Eng Tay,* retold by OKT, vii–xxv. Jakarta: Yayasan Obor Indonesia.

Asia Watch. 1990. *Injustice, Persecution, Eviction: A Human Rights Update on Indonesia and East Timor.* New York: Asia Watch.

Asmara, Cobina Gillitt. 1995. "*Tradisi Baru:* A 'New Tradition' of Indonesian Theatre." *Asian Theatre Journal* 12 (1): 164–174.

Bachmid, Talha. 2011. "Celebrating the Right to be Hybrid: *Sie Jin Kwie:* A Play by Indonesian Group, Teater Koma." *SPAFA Journal* 21 (3): 29–41.

Bandem, I Madé, and Fredrik Eugene deBoer. 1981. *Kaja and Kelod: Balinese Dance in Transition.* Kuala Lumpur: Oxford University Press.

———. 1983. "Notes on the Development of Arja Dance Drama." *Indonesia Circle* 11 (30): 28–32.

Baren. 1986. *Wu zu miao* (Five ancestor temple), edited by Wang Keping. Guangzhou: Huacheng chubanshe.

———. 1996. *Baren wenji: Xiju juan* (Collection of Baren's writings: Drama). Edited by Zhejiang Sheng Shehui Kexueyuan. Ningbo: Ningbo chubanshe.

Bertrand, Jacques. 2004. *Nationalism and Ethnic Conflict in Indonesia.* Cambridge: Cambridge University Press.

Blussé, Leonard. 1981. "Batavia, 1619–1740: The Rise and Fall of a Chinese Colonial Town." *Journal of Southeast Asian Studies* 12 (1): 159–178.

———. 1986. *Strange Company: Chinese Settlers, Mestizo Women, and the Dutch in VOC Batavia.* Dordrecht: Foris.

———. 1991. "The Role of Indonesian Chinese in Shaping Modern Indonesian Life: A Conference in Retrospect." *Indonesia,* 1–11.

———. 2004. "Wayang." In *The World of Jan Brandes, 1743–1808: Drawings of a Dutch Traveller in Batavia, Ceylon and Southern Africa,* edited by Max de Bruijn, R. Raben, and An Duits, 207–209. Zwolle: Waanders.

Blussé, Leonard, and Chen Menghong. 2003. *The Archives of the Kong Koan of Batavia.* Leiden: Brill.

Boachi, Aquasie. 1856. "Mededeelingen over de Chinezen op het eiland Java" (Information regarding the Chinese on the island of Java). *Bijdragen tot de Taal-, Land- en Volkenkunde van Nederlandsch-Indië* 4 (4): 278–301.

Bodden, Michael. 2007. "Languages of Traumas, Bodies, and Myths: Learning to Speak again in Post-1998 Indonesian Theatre." In *Arts, Popular Culture and Social Change in the New Indonesia,* edited by Michael Leaf, 119–151. Vancouver: UBC Institute of Asian Research.

———. 2010. *Resistance on the National Stage: Modern Theater and Politics in Late New Order Indonesia*. Athens: Ohio University Press.

Boretz, Avron A. 2003. "*Righteous Brothers and Demon Slayers:* Subjectivities and Collective Identities in Taiwanese Temple Processions." In *Religion and the Formation of Taiwanese Identities*, edited by Paul R. Katz and Murray Rubenstein, 219–251. New York: Palgrave.

Bougainville, Louis-Antoine de. 1771 (1982). *Voyage autour du monde: Par la frégate du Roi la Boudeuse et la flûte L'Étoile* (Voyage around the world: By the frigate *Boudeuse* and the fluyt *Étoile*). Paris: Gallimard.

Brand, Manny, and Wai-Chung Ho. 1999. "China Recaptures Hong Kong: A Study of Change for Music Education." *British Journal of Music Education* 16 (3): 227–236.

Brandon, James. 1967. *Theatre in Southeast Asia*. Cambridge, MA: Harvard University Press.

Brown, Colin. 2006. "Playing the Game: Ethnicity and Politics in Indonesian Badminton." *Indonesia* 81:71–93.

Brown, Ian Jarvis. 2001. "Developments in Modern Theatre of Indonesia: Generation, Degeneration, and Regeneration of a Cultural Medium." PhD diss., Northern Territory University.

Brown, Iem. 1987. "Contemporary Indonesian Buddhism and Monotheism." *Journal of Southeast Asian Studies* 18 (1): 108–117.

Bruyn, Cornelis de. 1714. *Cornelis de Bruins reizen over Moskovië, door Persië en Indië.* (Cornelis de Bruin's travels over Muscovy, through Persia and India). Amsterdam: Rudolf en Gerard Wetstein. http://objects.library.uu.nl/reader/index.php?obj=1874-186812&lan=en#page//15/28/46/152846428680107201890163930095066670280.jpg/mode/1up (accessed January 29, 2018).

———. 1737. *Travels into Muscovy, Persia, and Part of the East-Indies*, vol. 2. London: Eighteenth Century Collections Online. Gale. ESTC: T110676 (accessed September 25, 2018). http://find.galegroup.com.ezproxy1.library.usyd.edu.au/ecco/infomark.do?&source=gale&prodId=ECCO&userGroupName=usyd&tabID=T001&docId=CW100770062&type=multipage&contentSet=ECCOArticles&version=1.0&docLevel=FASCIMILE (accessed January 29, 2018).

Budianta, Melani. 2007. "The Dragon Dance: Shifting Meanings of Chineseness in Indonesia." In *Asian and Pacific Cosmopolitans: Self and Subject in Motion*, edited by Kathryn Robinson, 169–189. Basingstoke: Palgrave Macmillan.

———. 2012. "*Malang Mignon:* Cultural Expressions of the Chinese, 1940–1960." In *Heirs to World Culture: Being Indonesian 1950–1965*, edited by Jennifer Lindsay and Maya H. T. Liem, 255–281. Leiden: KITLV Press.

Budiman, Arief. 1990. "Introduction: From a Conference to a Book." In *State and Civil Society in Indonesia*, edited by Arief Budiman, 1–14. Clayton, Victoria: Centre of Southeast Asian Studies, Monash University.

Budiman, Hikmat. 2013. "Renegotiating Unity and Diversity: Multiculturalism in Post-Suharto Indonesia." In *Nations, National Narratives and Communities in the Asia-Pacific*, edited by Norman Vasu, Yolanda Chin, and Kam-yee Law, 189–209. New York: Routledge.

Buys, M. 1892. *Twee Maanden op Borneo's Westkust: Herinneringen* (Two months on Borneo's West Coast: Memories). Leiden: S. C. van Doesburgh.

Cai Shupeng (= Chua Soo Pong). 2011a. *Cai Shupeng wenji* (A collection of writings by Chua Soo Pong). Singapore: Xinjiapo wenyi xiehui.

———. 2011b. "Xinjiapo *yueju* ban *Handan meng* zai Yinni huanggong zhong de yanju" (Performance of a Singaporean *yueju* version of *Dream of Handan* at an Indonesian palace). *Wenhua yichan* 4:26–32.

Cao Guanghui. 2007. "*Buguniao you jiao le* yu *Caoyuan zhi ge*" (The cuckoo cries again and Song of the grasslands). In *Guanghui suiye, suiyue haoge: Yijiusiwunian zhanhou Subei Yinhua wenyi huodong gaikuang* (Glorious years, years of great song: An overview of Sino-Indonesian cultural activities in Northern Sumatra during the afterwar post-1945 period), edited by Liao Zhangran, 63–64. Medan: Lingnan meishu.

Carey, Peter. 1976. "The Origins of the Java War (1825–30)." *The English Historical Review* 91 (358): 52–78.

———. 1984. "Changing Javanese Perceptions of the Chinese Communities in Central Java, 1755–1825." *Indonesia* 37:1–47.

Chaffee, John. 2008. "Muslim Merchants and Quanzhou in the Late Yuan–Early Ming: Conjectures on the Ending of the Medieval Muslim Trade Diaspora." In *The East Asian "Mediterranean": Maritime Crossroads of Culture, Commerce and Human Migration*, edited by Angela Schlottenhammer, 115–132. Wiesbaden: Harassowitz Verlag.

Chai Chin Fern, Elena Gregoria. 2013. "Ancestor Power: Marriage Rituals of a Hakka Community in Sarawak, Malaysia." *Malaysian Journal of Chinese Studies* 2 (1): 35–47.

———. 2017. *Of Temple and Tatung Tradition in Singkawang*. Samarahan: Universiti Malaysia Sarawak.

Chan, Margaret. 2006. *Ritual Is Theatre, Theatre Is Ritual: Tang-ki, Chinese Spirit Medium Worship*. Singapore: Wee Kim Wee Centre, Singapore Management University.

———. 2009. "Chinese New Year in West Kalimantan: Ritual Theatre and Political Circus." *Chinese Southern Diaspora Studies* 3:106–142.

———. 2010. "Celebrating Community." *Inside Indonesia* 99. http://www.insideindonesia.org/celebrating-community?highlight=WyJjZWxlYnJhdGluZyIsImNvbW11bml0eSIsImNlbGVicmF0aW5nIGNvbW11bml0eSJd. (accessed October 10, 2018).

———. 2013. "The Spirit-Mediums of Singkawang: Performing 'Peoplehood'." In *Chinese Indonesians Reassessed: History, Religion and Belonging*, edited by Siew-Min Sai and Chang-Yau Hoon, 138–158. London: Routledge.

Chandavij, Natthapatra, and Promporn Pramualratana. 1998. *Thai Puppets and Khon Masks*. Bangkok: River Books.

Chang, Bi-yu. 2015. *Place, Identity, and National Imagination in Post-war Taiwan*. London: Routledge.

Chang, Pin-tsun. 1991. "The First Chinese Diaspora in Southeast Asia in the Fifteenth Century." In *Emporia, Commodities and Entrepreneurs in Asian Maritime Trade, c. 1400–1750*, edited by Roderich Ptak and Dietmar Rothermund, 13–28. Stuttgart: Steiner Verlag.

Chen, Fan Pen. 2003. "Shadow Theatres of the World." *Asian Folklore Studies* 62:25–64.

———. 2007. *Chinese Shadow Theatre: History, Popular Religion, and Women Warriors*. Montreal: McGill-Queen's University Press.

Chen Fusheng. 2010. "Xianci" (Congratulatory message). In *Yinni Wanlong Keshu Lianyihui chengli shizhounian jinian tekan 2000 nian-2010 nian*, edited by Yinni Wanlong Keshu Lianyihui. Bandung: Yinni Wanlong Keshu Lianyihui.

Chen Lei, Liu Xiangru, and Lin Ruiwu. 1997. *Fujian difang xiju* (Fujian regional theatre). Fuzhou: Fujian renmin chubanshe.

Chen Menghong. 2009. *De Chinese gemeenschap van Batavia, 1843–1865* (The Chinese community of Batavia, 1843–1865). PhD diss., University of Leiden.

Chen Yiling. 1954. *Yinni xianzhuang yu Huaqiao* (The current situation of Indonesia and the resident Chinese). Taipei: Zhongyang wenwu.

Chia, Caroline. 2016. "*Potehi* in Singapore: Survival and Change." In *Potehi: Glove Puppet Theatre in Southeast Asia in Taiwan*, edited by Kaori Fushiki and Robin Ruizendaal, 65–80. Taipei: Taiyuan Publishing.

Chia, Jack Meng-Tat. 2013. "A Recent Quest for Religious Roots: The Revival of the Guangze Zunwang Cult and Its Sino-Southeast Asian Networks, 1978–2009." *Journal of Chinese Religions* 41 (2): 91–123.

Chia, Lucille. 2011. "Chinese Books in the Philippines." In *Chinese Circulations: Capital, Commodities, and Networks in Southeast Asia*, edited by Eric Tagliacozzo and Wen-Chin Chang, 259–282. Durham, NC: Duke University Press.

Chin Woo Ping. 1991. Review of *Literary Migrations: Traditional Chinese Fiction in Asia, 17–20th Centuries*. *Journal of Southeast Asian Studies* 22 (1): 137–141.

"Chinese poppenkast te Solok op Sumatra's Westkust" (Chinese puppet-box in Solok on Sumatra's West Coast). 1891. Image code 3666, KITLV Digital Image Library.

Cho, Sookja. 2014. "Within and between Cultures: The Liang-Zhu Narrative in Local Korean Cultures." *Harvard Journal of Asiatic Studies* 74 (2): 207–248.

Chou Hui-ling. 1997. "Striking Their Own Poses: The History of Cross-Dressing on the Chinese Stage." *The Drama Review* 41 (2): 130–152.

Christie, Jan Wisseman. 1999. "Asian Sea Trade between the Tenth and Thirteenth Centuries and Its Impact on the States of Java and Bali." In *The Archaeology of Seafaring*, edited by Himanshu Prabha Ray, 271–290. Delhi: Pragati Publications.

Claus-Bachmann, Martina. 2006. "Portative dreifache Zuflucht im urbanen Alptraum: Wayang Potehi in Jakarta" (A portative triple refuge in the urban nightmare: *Wayang potehi* in Jakarta). In *Musik verbindet uns. Festschrift für Marianne Bröcker*, edited by Heidi Christ, 65–76. Uffenheim: Forschungsstelle für Fränkische Volksmusik.

Clendinning, Elizabeth. 2017. Review of *Bali 1928*. *Ethnomusicology* 61 (1): 166–178.

Cohen, Matthew Isaac. 2001. "On the Origin of the Komedie Stamboel: Popular Culture, Colonial Society, and the Parsi Theatre Movement." *Bijdragen tot de Taal-, Land- en Volkenkunde* 157 (2): 313–357.

———. 2002. "Border Crossings: Bangsawan in the Netherlands Indies in the Nineteenth and Early Twentieth Centuries." *Indonesia and the Malay World* 30 (87): 101–115.

———. 2003. "Look at the Clouds: Migration and West Sumatran 'Popular Theatre'." *New Theatre Quarterly* 19 (3): 214–229.

———. 2006. *The Komedie Stamboel: Popular Theater in Colonial Indonesia, 1891–1903*. Athens: Ohio University Press.

———. 2007. "Puppet Theatre: Indonesia." In *Encyclopedia of Asian Theatre*, edited by Samuel L. Leiter, 1:571–577. London: Greenwood Press.

———. 2016. *Inventing the Performing Arts: Modernity and Tradition in Colonial Indonesia*. Honolulu: University of Hawai'i Press.

———. 2018. "The Dr. Walter Angst and Sir Henry Angest Collection of Indonesian Puppets: The Structure of the Conjuncture." *Asian Theatre Journal* 35 (2): 300–328.

Cohen, Myron L. 1991. "Being Chinese: The Peripheralization of Traditional Identity." *Daedalus* 120 (2): 113–134.

Cong, Dachang. 1997. *When Heroes Pass Away: The Invention of a Chinese Communist Pantheon*. Lanham, MD: University Press of America.

Cooper, Thomas L. 2007. "Matjong, a Master Painter of Late Colonial Bali." *Archipel* 73 (1): 33–58.

Coppel, Charles A. 1983. *Indonesian Chinese in Crisis*. Oxford: Oxford University Press.

Couperus, Louis, 1924. *Eastward*. Translated by J. Menzies Wilson and C. C. Crispin. New York: George H. Doran Co.

Crouch, Harold A. 2007. *The Army and Politics in Indonesia*. Jakarta: Equinox.

Da Ai TV Mandarin. 2013. "*Sampek Engtay* Teater Koma 2013" (Teater Koma's *Sampek Engtay* 2013). www.youtube.com/watch?v=watch?v=xG3NzctSAWc (accessed February 16, 2017).

David, Ann R. 2012. "Sacralising the City: Sound, Space and Performance in Hindu Ritual Practices in London." *Culture and Religion* 13 (4): 449–467.

Davidson, Jamie Seth. 2008. *From Rebellion to Riots: Collective Violence on Indonesian Borneo*. Madison: University of Wisconsin Press.

Davidson, Jamie S., and Douglas Kammen. 2002. "Indonesia's Unknown War and the Lineages of Violence in West Kalimantan." *Indonesia* 73:53–87.

Davies, Stephen. 2008. "The Origins of Balinese Legong." *Bijdragen tot de Taal-, Land- en Volkenkunde* 164 (2/3): 194–211.

Dawis, Aimee. 2009a. *The Chinese of Indonesia and Their Search for Identity: The Relationship between Collective Memory and the Media*. Amherst, NY: Cambria.

———. 2009b. "China and the Cultural Identity of the Chinese of Indonesia." In *Connecting and Distancing: Southeast Asia and China*, edited by Ho Khai Leong, 153–184. Singapore: Institute of Southeast Asian Studies.

de Wit, Augusta. *Java: Facts and Fancies*. The Hague: W. P. Van Stockum & Son.

Dean, Kenneth. 1993. *Taoist Ritual and Popular Cults of Southeast China*. Princeton, NJ: Princeton University Press.

———. 1998. *Lord of the Three in One: The Spread of a Cult in Southeast China*. Princeton, NJ: Princeton University Press.

Delgado, Maria M., Dominic Johnson, Aofie Monks, and Lara Shalson. 2013. "Editorial." *Contemporary Theatre Review* 23 (1): 1–2.

DeMare, Brian James. 2015. *Mao's Cultural Army: Drama Troupes in China's Rural Revolution*. Cambridge: Cambridge University Press.

Deng Niudun, ed. 2002. "Wenxie xuanji" (Selected works from the Association of Writers). *Nanjing shifan daxue wenxueyuan xuebao* 3:179–188.

Dibia, I. Wayan. 2012. "Revitalizing Arja in Globalized Bali." *Asian Theatre Journal*, 466–494.

Didik Nini Thowok. 2011. "Sepatah Kata dari Seniman Tari Didik Nini Thowok" (Foreword by the dance artist Didik Nini Thowok). In Hirwan Kuardhani, *Maecenas Potehi dari Gudo: Toni Harsono*, 8–9. Yogyakarta: ISACBOOK.

Dieleman, Marleen, Juliette Koning, and Peter Post. 2010. "Chinese Indonesians and Regime Change: Alternative Perspectives." In *Chinese Indonesians and Regime Change*, edited by Marleen Dieleman, Juliette Koning, and Peter Post, 65–90. Leiden: Brill.

Ding Lixing. 2009a. "Shilun Suhatuo shidai Yinni Huaren shetuan yu Yinni duoyuan

hexie shehui de goujian" (On post-Suharto Sino-Indonesian associations and the building of pluralistic harmonious society in Indonesia). *Dongnanya yanjiu* 5:65–70.
———. 2009b. "Cong beidong shiying dao zhudong rongru: Yindunixiya Huaqiao Huaren shetuan de lishi yanjin" (From passive adaptation to active integration: The historical evolution of Sino-Indonesian associations). *Dongnanya zongheng* 8:24–27.
Dongrui. 2006. *Liujinjijie xubian* (A golden season: Part two). Hong Kong: Huoyi chuban shiye youxian gongsi.
Duara, Prasenjit. 2004. "Nationalists among Transnationalists: Overseas Chinese and the Idea of China, 1900–1911." In *Ungrounded Empires: The Cultural Politics of Modern Chinese Transnationalism,* edited by Aihwa Ong and Donald M. Nonini, 39–60. New York: Routledge.
———. 2009. *The Global and Regional in China's Nation-Formation.* London: Routledge.
Elson, R. E. 2008. *The Idea of Indonesia: A History.* Cambridge: Cambridge University Press.
Faruk, H. T. 2004. "Memanusiakan Stereotipe Orang Tionghao di Indonesia (Menyamput Pentas *Sampek Engtay* Teater Koma di Yogya" (Humanizing the stereotype of Chinese people in Indonesia—to welcome Teater Koma's *Sampek Engtay* to Yogya). Initially published in *Cybersastra* (January 25), it is now available on Faruk H. T.'s Facebook page: https://www.facebook.com/notes/faruk-tripoli/memanusiakan-streotipe-orang-tionghoa-di-indonesia-menyambut-pentas-sampek-engta/10150144286063335?comment_id=23800253.
Faucher, Carole. 2007. "Contesting Boundaries in the Riau Archipelago." In *Renegotiating Boundaries: Local Politics in Post-colonial Indonesia,* edited by Henk Schulte Nordholt and Gerry van Klinken, 443–458. Leiden: KITLV Press.
Fei Na. 1947. *Niliu* (Countercurrent). Batavia: Bacheng Zhonghua xiju xiehui chubanshe.
FJSWSYJG = Fujian Sheng wenshi yanjiuguan (Fujian Province cultural history research institute). N.d. "Dong Yifang.1902–1965.7." http://www.fjwsg.com/mechanism/biography/successive/256.html (accessed January 20, 2017).
Fogel, Joshua A. 1995. *The Cultural Dimension of Sino-Japanese Relations: Essays on the Nineteenth and Twentieth Centuries.* Armonk, NY: M. E. Sharpe.
Foulcher, Keith. 1990. "The Construction of an Indonesian National Culture: Patterns of Hegemony and Resistance." In *State and Civil Society in Indonesia,* edited by Arief Budiman: 301–320. Clayton, Victoria: Monash University.
Fu Shuyin. 2012. "Dingyi guan Chaoju yougan" (The emotions of watching *Chaoju* in Tebing Tinggi). *Siantar People* (February 23). http://siantarpeople.org/portal.php?mod=view&aid=1306 (accessed January 20, 2017).
"Fujian liyuanxi Chen San Wuniang" (The Fujian *liyuanxi* play *Chen San and Wuniang*). 1957. *Nanyang Post* 112 (February): unpaginated.
Gao, James Zheng. 2004. *The Communist Takeover of Hangzhou: The Transformation of City and Cadre, 1949–1954.* Honolulu: University of Hawai'i Press.
Ghulam-Sarwar Yousof. 1994. *Dictionary of Traditional South-East Asian Theatre.* Kuala Lumpur: Oxford University Press.
Giblin, Susan. 2003. "Civil Society Groups Overcoming Stereotypes? Chinese Indonesian Civil Society Groups in Post-Suharto Indonesia." *Asian Ethnicity* 4 (3): 353–368.
Gillitt, Cobina (= Asmara, Cobina Gillitt). 2010. "Introduction." *The Lontar Anthology of*

Indonesian Drama, Vol. 3: *New Directions, 1965–1998*, edited by Cobina Gillitt and John McGlynn, vii–xiv. Jakarta: Lontar Foundation.

Glaser, Bonnie S., and Jacqueline A. Vitello. 2015. *Taiwan's Marginalized Role in International Security: Paying a Price.* Lanham, MD: Rowman & Littlefield.

Godley, Michael R., and Charles A. Coppel. 1990. "The Pied Piper and the Prodigal Children: A Report on the Indonesian-Chinese Students Who Went to Mao's China." *Archipel* 39 (1): 179–198.

Goenawan Mohamad. 2015. *In Other Words: Forty Years of Essays.* Translated by Jennifer Lindsay. Sydney, NSW: NewSouth Publishing. Ebook.

Goffman, Erving. 1956. *The Presentation of Self in Everyday Life.* Edinburgh: University of Edinburgh, Social Sciences Research Centre.

Goodman, Bryna. 1995. *Native Place, City, and Nation: Regional Networks and Identities in Shanghai, 1853–1937.* Berkeley: University of California Press.

Goodrich-Hedrick, Karen, and John D. Hedrick. 1972. "Cruise of the United States Frigate *Potomac.*" *Expedition* 14 (2): 27–33.

Gunew, Sneja. 2004. *Haunted Nations: The Colonial Dimensions of Multiculturalisms.* London: Routledge.

Guritno, Pandam. 1988. *Wayang, Kebudayaan Indonesia dan Pancasila* (Wayang, Indonesian culture and Pancasila). Jakarta:Penerbit Universitas Indonesia.

Haan, Fonger de. 1922. *Oud Batavia* (Old Batavia). Batavia: G. Kolff & Co.

Hamonic, Gilbert, and Claudine Salmon. 2013. "Translations of Chinese Fiction into Makassarese." In *Literary Migrations: Traditional Chinese Fiction in Asia, 17–20th Centuries,* edited by Claudine Salmon, 359–374. Singapore: Singapore Institute of Asian Studies.

Han Ping. 2007a. "Tonghua ju *Malan hua*" (Children's theatre: *The Iris*). In *Guanghui suiye, suiyue haoge: Yijiusiwunian zhanhou Subei Yinhua wenyi huodong gaikuang* (Glorious years, years of great song: An overview of Sino-Indonesian cultural activities in Northern Sumatra during the afterwar post-1945 period), edited by Liao Zhangran, 63–64. Medan: Lingnan meishu.

———. 2007b. "Hongdong Subei de guanzhong" (A sensation for the North Sumatra audiences). In *Guanghui suiye, suiyue haoge: Yijiusiwunian zhanhou Subei Yinhua wenyi huodong gaikuang* (Glorious years, years of great song: An overview of Sino-Indonesian cultural activities in Northern Sumatra during the afterwar post-1945 period), edited by Liao Zhangran, 67. Medan: Lingnan meishu.

Hansson, Anders. 1996. *Chinese Outcasts: Discrimination and Emancipation in Late Imperial China.* Leiden: Brill.

Harsono, Andreas. 1989. "A Star Is Banned." *Inside Indonesia* 21 (December): 14–15.

Hauser-Schäublin, Brigitta. 2014. "From *Subandar* to Tridharma: Transformations and Interactions between Chinese Communities in Bali." In *Between Harmony and Discrimination: Negotiating Religious Identities within Majority-Minority Relationships in Bali and Lombok,* edited by Brigitta Hauser-Schäublin and David D. Harnish, 84–111. Leiden: Brill.

Hazeu, Godard Arend Johannes. 1897. *Bijdrage tot de kennis van het Javaansche tooneel* (Contribution to the knowledge of the Javanese stage). Leiden: Brill.

He Linghui and Gan Lulu. 2009. *Zizai 10 nian: Shinian xiangju—huanxiao yanlei hanshui jiaozhierchengde yinyueju shi wo rensheng zhong zuimeide shipian* (10 tears unrestrained: Ten years together—a musical woven from laughter, tears, and sweat is the most beautiful poem of my life). Puchong: Musical On Stage Productions.

Heidhues, Mary Somers. 1988. "Citizenship and Identity. Ethnic Chinese and the Indonesian Revolution." In *Changing Identities of the Southeast Asian Chinese since World War II,* edited by Jennifer Cushman and Wang Gungwu, 115–138. Hong Kong: Hong Kong University Press.

———. 1992. *Bangka Tin and Mentok Pepper: Chinese Settlement on an Indonesian Island.* Singapore: Institute of Southeast Asian Studies.

———. 1996. "Identity and the Minority: Ethnic Chinese on the Indonesian Periphery." *Indonesia Circle. School of Oriental and African Studies. Newsletter* 24 (70): 181–192.

———. 1997. "Chinese Identity in the Diaspora: Religion and Language in West Kalimantan, Indonesia." In *Nationalism and Cultural Revival in Southeast Asia: Perspectives from the Centre and the Region,* edited by Volker Grabowsky and Martin Grossheim, 201–210. Wiesbaden: Harrassowitz.

———. 2003. *Golddiggers, Farmers, and Traders in the "Chinese Districts" of West Kalimantan, Indonesia.* Ithaca, NY: Southeast Asia Program Publications, Southeast Asia Program, Cornell University.

———. 2006. "Chinese Voluntary and Involuntary Associations in Indonesia."In *Voluntary Organizations in the Chinese Diaspora,* edited by Khun Eng Kuah-Pearce and Evelyn Hu-Dehart, 77–97. Hong Kong: Hong Kong University Press.

———. 2012. "Anti-Chinese Violence in Java during the Indonesian Revolution, 1945–49." *Journal of Genocide Research* 14 (3–4): 381–401.

———. 2017. "Violent, Political, and Administrative Repression of the Chinese Minority in Indonesia, 1945–1998." *Wacana* 18 (1): 94–105.

Hellman, Jörgen. 2003. *Performing the Nation: Cultural Politics in New Order Indonesia.* Copenhagen: NIAS.

Hering, Bob, ed. 1982. *Siauw Giok Tjhan Remembers: A Peranakan-Chinese and the Quest for Indonesian Nation-hood.* Townsville: James Cook University of North Queensland.

Herlijanto, Johanes. 2016. "What Does Indonesia's Pribumi Elite Think of Ethnic Chinese Today?" *Perspective* 32:1–9.

———. 2017. "'Search for Knowledge as Far as China!': Indonesian Responses to the Rise of China." In *Chinese Encounters in Southeast Asia: How People, Money, and Ideas from China Are Changing a Region,* edited by Pál Nyíri and Danielle Tan, 195–213. Seattle: University of Washington Press.

Hermawan, Iwan. 2014. "Pendidikan bagi pendatang di tengah mayoritas masyarakat pribumi" (Education for immigrants among the majority *pribumi* population). *SOSIO-DIDAKTIKA: Social Science Education Journal* 1 (1): 79–88.

Hertzman, Emily. 2014. "Returning to the *Kampung Halaman:* Limitations of Cosmopolitan Transnational Aspirations among Hakka Chinese Indonesians Overseas." *Austrian Journal of South-East Asian Studies* 7 (2): 147–164.

———. 2017. "*Pulang Kampung* (Returning home): Circuits of Mobility from a Chinese Town in Indonesia." PhD diss., University of Toronto.

Heryanto, Ariel. 1998. "Ethnic Identities and Erasure: Chinese Indonesians in Public Culture." In *Southeast Asian Identities: Culture and the Politics of Representation in Indonesia, Malaysia, Singapore, and Thailand,* edited by Joel S. Kahn, 95–114. Singapore: ISEAS.

———. 1999. "Identity Politics of Indonesia's New Rich." In *Culture and Privilege in Capitalist Asia,* edited by Michael Pinches, 159–187. London: Routledge.

———. 2008. "Citizenship and Indonesian Ethnic Chinese in Post-1998 Films." In *Popular Culture in Indonesia: Fluid Identities in Post-Authoritarian Politics,* edited by Ariel Heryanto, 70–93. London: Routledge.

Hew, Wai Weng. 2010. "Marketing the Chinese Face of Islam." *Inside Indonesia* 99. http://www.insideindonesia.org/marketing-the-chinese-face-of-islam (accessed October 10, 2018).

———. 2017. "Translocal Pious Entrepreneuralism: Hui Business and Religious Activities in Malaysia and Indonesia." In *Chinese Encounters in Southeast Asia: How People, Money and Ideas from China Are Changing a Region,* edited by Pál Nyiri and Danielle Tan, 58–78. Seattle: University of Washington Press.

Hindman, Heather. 2013. *Mediating the Global: Expatria's Forms and Consequences in Kathmandu.* Stanford, CA: Stanford University Press.

Hitchcock, Michael. 1998. "Tourism, *Taman Mini,* and National Identity." *Indonesia and the Malay World* 26 (75): 124–135.

Holm Pedersen, Marianne. 2014. *Iraqi Women in Denmark: Ritual Performance and Belonging in Everyday Life.* Manchester: Manchester University Press.

Hoon, Chang-Yau. 2006a. "Assimilation, Multiculturalism, Hybridity: The Dilemmas of the Ethnic Chinese in Post-Suharto Indonesia." *Asian Ethnicity* 7 (2): 149–166.

———. 2006b. "The Re-Emergence of the Chinese Press in Post-Suharto Indonesia." In *Media and the Chinese Diaspora: Community, Communications and Commerce,* edited by Wanning Sun, 91–118. London: Routledge.

———. 2009a. "More Than a Cultural Celebration: The Politics of Chinese New Year in Post-Suharto Indonesia." *Chinese Southern Diaspora Studies* 3:90–105.

———. 2009b. "The Politics of Imlek." *Inside Indonesia* 95 (January–March). http://www.insideindonesia.org/the-politics-of-imlek (accessed September 25, 2018).

———. 2011a. *Chinese Identity in Post-Suharto Indonesia: Culture, Politics and Media.* Brighton: Sussex Academic Press.

———. 2011b. "Mapping 'Chinese'Christian Schools in Indonesia: Ethnicity, Class and Religion." *Asia Pacific Education Review* 12 (3): 403–411.

Hooykaas, C. 1963. "Books Made in Bali." *Bijdragen tot de Taal-, Land- en Volkenkunde* 119 (4): 371–386.

Hou Qiangzhao. 2011. "Chengji feiran, qianjing huihuang" (Striking achievements, glorious future). In *Yinni Wanlong Boliangan Fuli Jijinhui chengli sanshiwuzhounian jinian tekan,* edited by Yinni Wanlong Boliangan Fuli Jijinhui. Bandung: Yinni Wanlong Boliangan Fuli Jijinghui.

Hu Xuntao. 1947. "Xu" (Preface). In *Niliu,* by Fei Na, ii. Batavia: Bacheng Zhonghua xiju xiehui chubanshe.

Huaiying. 2015. "Mianlan 'Wuzu miao' he 'Wuye ci' lishi." (The history of Medan's Five Ancestors Temple and Five Patriarchs Hall). In *Yinni Subei Huaqiao Huaren cangsang suiyu,* vol. 1, edited by Zheng Guanghuang, 94–96. Hong Kong: Yinni Subei Huaqiao Huaren lishishe.

Huang, Alexander C. Y. 2009. *Chinese Shakespeares: Two Centuries of Cultural Exchange.* New York: Columbia University Press.

Huang Changping. 2003. "Jushe shenru Yinni kongzhiqu yanchu" (The Theatre Society goes deeply into the Indonesian-controlled territory for performance). In *Wangbuliao de suiyue,* edited by Huang Shuhai, 304–306. Beijing: Shijie zhishi chubanshe.

Huang Jianjin. 2015. "Cong 'Xueyou geyong dui' dao 'Minhua juyishe'" (From "Classmates Song Troupe" to "Chinese People's Perfoming Arts Society"). In *Yinni Subei Huaqiao Huaren cangsang suiyu,* vol. 1, edited by Zheng Guanghuang, 438–442. Hong Kong: Yinni Subei Huaqiao Huaren lishishe.

Huang Kunzhang. 1991. "Sishi nian lai Yinni Huaqiao Huaren wenjiao shiye de xingshuai" (The rise and fall of Sino-Indonesian cultural and educational enterprises over the last forty years). *Huaqiao Huaren lishi yanjiu* 4:28–34.

———. 2005. *Yinni Huaqiao Huarenshi: 1950 zhi 2004 nian* (History of Indonesian Chinese and their descendants from 1950 to 2004). Guangzhou: Guangdong gaodeng jiaoyu chubanshe.

Huang Shuhai. 2008. *Xianda zhaopian: Gaoyuan xiaocheng de gushi* (Siantar photos: Stories of a small town on the plateau). Beijing: Hongwenquan jijinhui.

Huang Yinggu. 2010. " 'Liedui ge' langsongci' " ("Line-up song" recitation). In *Yinni Wanlong Keshu Lianyihui chengli shizhounian jinian tekan 2000 nian-2010 nian,* edited by Yinni Wanlong Keshu Lianyihui, 70. Bandung: Yinni Wanlong Keshu Lianyihui.

Huang Zhenkun. 2010. "Yi wei Xianda ren de 'guofan riji'—yi Huang Zhongcheng xiansheng" (A Siantar person's diary of "going abroad"—in Memory of Mr. Huang Zhongcheng). *Siantar People* (May 20). http://www.siantarpeople.org/portal.php?mod=view&aid=10 (accessed 20 January 2017).

Huaqiao lishi dang'an guan (Overseas Chinese archive). "Huaqiao yu kangzhan" (Overseas Chinese and the [anti-Japanese] resistance war). http://www.zghqwx.com/zjxs.asp?whichpage=328 (accessed February 9, 2017).

Hue, Guan Thye, and Kenneth Dean. 2016. "Chinese Religious Traditions in Singapore: Buddhism, Taoism and Christianity." In *Fifty Years of the Chinese Community in Singapore,* edited by Pang Cheng Lian, 169–190. Hong Kong: World Scientific.

Hui, Yew-Foong. 2011. *Strangers at Home: History and Subjectivity among the Chinese Communities of West Kalimantan, Indonesia.* Leiden: Brill.

———. 2017. "Decentralization and Chinese Indonesian Politics: The Case of Singkawang, West Kalimantan." *Perspective* 19:1–9.

Idema, W. L. 1989. Review of *Literary Migrations: Traditional Chinese Fiction in Asia (17th–20th Centuries). Bijdragen tot de Taal-, Land- en Volkenkunde* 145 (4): 582–584.

———. 2010. *The Butterfly Lovers: The Legend of Liang Shanbo and Zhu Yingtai; Four Versions, with Related Texts.* Indianapolis: Hackett Publishing Company.

Idema, Wilt, and Lloyd Haft. 1997. *A Guide to Chinese Literature.* Ann Arbor: Center for Chinese Studies, University of Michigan.

Irving, D. R. M. 2010. *Colonial Counterpoint: Music in Early Modern Manila.* Oxford: Oxford University Press.

Janarto, Herry Gendut. 1997. *Teater Koma: Potret Tragedi dan Komedi Manusi [Indonesia]* (Teater Koma: Portrait of the [Indonesian] human tragedy and comedy). Jakarta: Grasindo.

Jay, Sain. 1989. "The Basir and Tukang Sangiang: Two Kinds of Shaman among the Ngaju Dayak." *Indonesia Circle* 17 (49): 31–44.

Jedamski, Doris. 2008. " '. . . And Then the Lights Went Out and It Was Pitch-Dark': From

Stamboel to *Tonil*—Theatre and the Transformation of Perceptions." *South East Asia Research* 16 (3): 481–511.

Jiang, Jin. 2009. *Women Playing Men: Yue Opera and Social Change in Twentieth-Century Shanghai.* Seattle: University of Washington Press.

Jones, Tod. 2013. *Culture, Power, and Authoritarianism in the Indonesian State: Cultural Policy across the Twentieth Century to the Reform Era.* Leiden: Brill.

Jugang Zhonghua Xuexiao. 1938. *Jugang Zhonghua Xuexiao sazhounian jiniankan* (Palembang Chinese School thirty-year anniversary commemorative volume). Palembang: Jugang Zhonghua Xuexiao.

Jurriëns, Edwin. 2004. *Cultural Travel and Migrancy: The Artistic Representation of Globalization in the Electronic Media of West Java.* Leiden: Brill.

Kagan, Alan Lloyd. 1978. "Cantonese Puppet Theater: An Operatic Tradition and Its Role in the Chinese Religious Belief System." PhD diss., Indiana University.

Kartomi, Margaret J. 2000. "Indonesian-Chinese Oppression and the Musical Outcomes in the Netherlands East Indies." In *Music and the Racial Imagination,* edited by Ronald M. Radano and Philip V. Bohlman, 271–317. Chicago: University of Chicago Press.

———. 2012. *Musical Journeys in Sumatra.* Urbana: University of Illinois Press.

Katritzky, M. A. 2007. *Women, Medicine and Theatre, 1500–1750: Literary Mountebanks and Performing Quacks.* Aldershot, UK: Ashgate.

Kell, Tim. 1995. *The Roots of Acehnese Rebellion, 1989–1992.* Ithaca, NY: Cornell University Press.

Kelley, Liam. 1998. "Batavia through the Eyes of Vietnamese Envoys." *Explorations in Southeast Asian Studies* 2 (1). https://scholarspace.manoa.hawaii.edu/bitstream/10125/2522/1/Batavia%20Through%20the%20Eyes%20of%20Vietnamese%20Envoys.pdf (accessed January 20, 2017).

KGPH TA Sinuhun Tedjowulan ("Sri Susuhan Pakubuwono XIII"). 2011. "Sambutan Sri Susuhunan Pakubuwono XII Sinuhun Tedjowulan Surakarta" (Welcome by Susuhunan Pakubuwono XII Sinuhun Tedjowulan Surakarta). In Hirwan Kuardhani, *Maecenas Potehi dari Gudo: Toni Harsono,* 6–7. Yogyakarta: ISACBOOK.

Khor, Neil. 2014. "Lady White: The Literary Migration of a Chinese Tale." *Indonesia and the Malay World* 42 (123): 286–303.

Knaap, Gerrit J. 1991. "A City of Migrants: Kota Ambon at the End of the Seventeenth Century." *Indonesia,* no. 51, 105–128.

König, Anika. 2016. "Identity Constructions and Dayak Ethnic Strife in West Kalimantan, Indonesia." *The Asia Pacific Journal of Anthropology* 17 (2): 121–137.

Koning, Juliette. 2007. "Chineseness and Chinese Indonesian Business Practices: A Generational and Discursive Enquiry." *East Asia* 24 (2): 129–152.

———. 2011. "Business, Belief and Belonging: Small Business Owners and Conversion to Charismatic Christianity." In *Chinese Indonesians Reassessed: History, Religion and Belonging,* edited by Siew Min Sai and Chang-Yau Hoon, 23–46. Abingdon-on-Thames: Routledge.

Kuardhani, Hirwan. 2011. *Maecenas Potehi dari Gudo: Toni Harsono* (A *potehi* patron from Gudo: Toni Harsono). Yogyakarta: ISACBOOK.

———. 2012. *Mengenal Wayang Potehi di Jawa* (Concerning *wayang potehi* in Java). Mojokerto: Yensen Project Network.

Kuhn, Philip A. 2008. *Chinese among Others: Emigration in Modern Times.* Lanham, MD: Rowman & Littlefield.

Kumar, Ann. 1987. "Islam, the Chinese, and Indonesian Historiography—A Review Article." *The Journal of Asian Studies* 46 (3): 603–616.

———. 1989. "A Swedish View of Batavia in 1783–4: Hornstedt's Letters." *Archipel* 37: 247–262.

Kunst, Jaap. 1973. *Music in Java: Its History, Its Theory, and Its Technique*. The Hague: Martinus Nijhoff.

Kuppers, Petra. 2007. *Community Performance: An Introduction*. London: Routledge.

Kwartanada, Didi. 2010a. "The Road to Resinification: Education for the Chinese during the Japanese Occupation." In *The Encyclopedia of Indonesia in the Pacific War*, edited by Peter Post et al., 327–334. Leiden: Brill.

———. 2010b. "Chinese Socio-cultural Life in Java during the Occupation." In *The Encyclopedia of Indonesia in the Pacific War*, edited by Peter Post et al., 397–402. Leiden: Brill.

———. 2013. "The Tiong Hoa Hwee Koan School: A Transborder Project of Modernity in Batavia, c. 1900s." In *Chinese Indonesians Reassessed: History, Religion and Belonging*, edited by Siew Min Sai and Chang-Yau Hoon, 27–44. Abingdon-on-Thames: Routledge.

———. 2014. Untitled Promotional *Obi* Attached to *Wayang Potehi of Java*, by Ardian Purwoseputro. Translated by Hermanto Lim. Jakarta: Afterhours Books.

Kwee, John B. 1978. "Chinese Malay Literature of the Peranakan Chinese in Indonesia 1880–1942." PhD diss., University of Auckland.

———. 1980. "Kwee Tek Hoay: A Productive Chinese Writer of Java (1880–1952)." *Archipel* 19: 81–92.

———. 1996. "A Study of *Potehi*, the Chinese Puppet Theatre in Indonesia." *Asian Culture* 20: 45–54.

Kwee Kek Beng. 1936. "Het cultureele leven der Chineezen in Nederlandsch-Indië" (The cultural life of the Dutch Indies). *Koloniale Studien*, nos. 5/6, 78–96.

———. 1951. "Toneel en muziek der Chinezen in Indonesie" (Theatre and music of the Chinese in Indonesia). *Java Bode* (February 10).

Kwee Tek Hoay. 1969. *The Origins of the Modern Chinese Movement in Indonesia*. Ithaca, NY: Modern Indonesia Project, Southeast Asia Program, Cornell University.

La Ode, M. D. 2012. *Etnis Cina Indonesia dalam Politik: Politik Etnis Cina Pontianak dan Singkawang di Era Reformasi, 1998–2008* (Indonesian ethnic Chinese in politics: The politics of ethnic Chinese of Pontianak and Singkawang in the Reformasi Era, 1998–2008). Jakarta: Yayasan Pustaka Obor Indonesia.

Labrousse, Pierre. 2002."La traversée des années 90 par les calembours (plesetan)" (Across the nineties with *plesatan* punning). *Archipel* 64 (1): 39–58.

Lai Bojiang. 1993. *Dongnanya Huawen xiju gaiguan* (General survey of Southeast Asian Chinese-language drama). Beijing: Zhongguo xiju chubanshe.

———. 1995. "Dong nanya Huawen xiju de lishi he xianzhuang" (History and contemporary state of Chinese-language drama in Southeast Asia). *Xiju yishu* 3:45–56.

———. 2007. "Youjiu er duocai de Yinni Huaren waiwen wenxue" (Long-standing and colorful Sino-Indonesian literature in foreign languages). *Yishu yanjiu* 1:136–140.

Lai Dengming. 2014. "Mintai Kejia kuileixi de chuancheng yubianqian" (Hakka marionette transmission and change in Fujian and Taiwan). *Zhongguo yinyue* 1:83–87, 105.

Lai, Him Mark. 2010. *Chinese American Transnational Politics*. Urbana: University of Illinois Press.

Lai Suchun. 2007. "Xinjiapo Huayu Xiqu de fazhan (1920 nian–1945 nian" (Chinese-language *xiqu*'s development in Singapore [1920–1945]). In *Dongnanya Huayu xijushi,* edited by Zhou Ning, 468–518. Xiamen: Xiamen daxue chubanshe.

Lam, Joseph S. C. 1997. "Ming Music and Music History." *Ming Studies* 38:21–62.

Lao Pan. 2007. "Mianlan wushiniandai wenyi bibo gungunbuxi" (The waves of literature and culture in 1950s Medan were surging). In *Guanghui suiye, suiyue haoge: Yijiusiwu-nian zhanhou Subei Yinhua wenyi huodong gaikuang* (Glorious years, years of great song: An overview of Sino-Indonesian cultural activities in Northern Sumatra during the afterwar post-1945 period), edited by Liao Zhangran, 279–280. Medan: Lingnan meishu.

Lau, Frederick. 2005. "Morphing Chineseness: The Changing Image of Chinese Music Clubs in Singapore." In *Diasporas and Interculturalism in Asian Performing Arts: Translating Traditions,* edited by Hae-Kyung Um, 30–42. London: Routledge.

Lee Tong Soon. 2009. *Chinese Street Opera in Singapore.* Urbana: University of Illinois Press.

Leo, Jessieca. 2015. *Global Hakka: Hakka Identity in the Remaking.* Leiden: Brill.

Lev, Daniel S. 1985. "Colonial Law and the Genesis of the Indonesian State." *Indonesia* 40:57–74.

Lev, Daniel S., and Arlene O. Lev. 2011. *No Concessions: The Life of Yap Thiam Hien, Indonesian Human Rights Lawyer.* Seattle: University of Washington Press.

Li Jing (= Shalihong). 2015. "Rili yanyuan Huaren qiyue laogong de xinsuan" (The bitterness of Deli tobacco field laborers). In *Yinni Subei Huaqiao Huaren cangsang suiyu,* vol. 1, edited by Zheng Guanghuang, 46–48. Hong Kong: Yinni Subei Huaqiao Huaren lishishe.

Li Ying and Zhang Gui. 2012. "Guangdong *Hanju* zaoqi *waijiang* ban bentuhua licheng (On the process of indigenization of early *waijiang* troupes of Cantonese *Hanju*). *Jiaying xueyuan xuebao* 3:5–9.

Liao Jianyu [= Suryadinata, Leo]. 2002. *Xian jieduan de Yinni Huaren zuqun* (Present-day Indonesian Chinese). Singapore: Xinjiapo Guoli Daxue zhongwenxi.

Liao Zhangran, ed. 2007. *Guanghui suiye, suiyue haoge: Yijiusiwunian zhanhou Subei Yinhua wenyi huodong gaikuang* (Glorious years, years of great song: An overview of Sino-Indonesian cultural activities in Northern Sumatra during the afterwar post-1945 period). Medan: Lingnan meishu.

Liaw Yock Fang. 2013. *A History of Classical Malay Literature.* Translated by Razif Bahari and Harry Aveling. Singapore: ISEAS.

Liem Thian Joe. 1933. *Riwajat Semarang* (History of Semarang). Semarang: Ho Kim Yoe.

Lim, Wah Guan. 2016. "The Changing Landscape of Politics and Language Use in Singaporean Theatre: Towards a Multilingual Practice." In *Singapore: Negotiating State and Society, 1965–2015,* edited by Jason Lim and Terence Lee, 76–93. New York: Routledge.

Linbai [Lin Lairong]. 2011. "Xiang dangnian . . . *Huoshao Linjianglou*" (Remembering . . . *The Burning of Linjiang Temple*). *Mian Zhong wang.* http://mianzhong.org.hk/theme_detail.php?theme_id=1057 (accessed January 20, 2017).

Lin Jia. 2009. "Xinjiapo kuileixi de xianzai yu weilai" (The present and future of Singapore marionettes). In *Change and Innovation in Chinese Opera: A Post Conference Publication,* edited by Chua Soo Pong, 134–143. Singapore: National Heritage Board.

Lin Jinzhi. 1989. "Fujian wenhua zai Dongnanya de chuanbo jiqi yingxiang" (The transmission and influence of Fujian culture in Southeast Asia). *Fujian luntan: Renwen shehuikexue* 6:40–44, 58.

Lin Longfei. 2007. "Wo genzhe Kunlun zouchu xiangyata" (Following Kunlun, I left the ivory tower). In *Guanghui suiye, suiyue haoge: Yijiusiwunian zhanhou Subei Yinhua wenyi huodong gaikuang* (Glorious years, years of great song: An overview of Sino-Indonesian cultural activities in Northern Sumatra during the afterwar post-1945 period), edited by Liao Zhangran, 279–280. Medan: Lingnan meishu.

Lin Miansi. 2011. "Zhanqian Yinni Huren zuojia Guo Dehuai zhi shehui guanhuai" (The social concerns of prewar Sino-Indonesian writer Kwee Tek Hoay). MA thesis, National Central University (Zhongli, Taiwan).

Lin Xuehua. 2009. *Fengyu Nanyang* (Trials of Nanyang). Bali Scan: Medan.

Liu, Hong. 2010. "The Historicity of China's Soft Power: The PRC and the Cultural Politics of Indonesia, 1945–1965." In *The Cold War in Asia: The Battle for Hearts and Minds*, edited by Zheng Yanwen, Hong Liu, and Michael Szonyi, 147–182. Leiden: Brill.

Liu Jiesheng. 2010. "Keshu: Mingtian hui geng hao!" (Hakka Association: Tomorrow will be better!). In *Yinni Wanlong Keshu Lianyihui chengli shizhounian jinian tekan 2000 nian–2010 nian*, edited by Yinni Wanlong Keshu Lianyihui, 117. Bandung: Yinni Wanlong Keshu Lianyihui.

Loh, Wai-fong. 1984. "From Romantic Love to Class Struggle: Reflections on the Film *Liu Sanjie*." In *Popular Chinese Literature and Performing Arts in the People's Republic of China 1949–1979*, edited by Bonnie S. McDougall, 165–176. Berkeley: University of California Press.

Lombard, Denys. 1984. "Guide *Archipel* IV: Pontianak et son arrière-pays." (*Archipel* Guide IV: Pontianak and surroundings) *Archipel* 28 (1): 77–97.

———. 1990. *Le carrefour javanais: Essai d'histoire globale* (The Javanese crossroads: Towards a global history), vol. 2: *Les réseaux asiatiques* (Asian networks). Paris: Éditions de l'École des hautes études en sciences sociales.

Lombard-Salmon, Claudine. 1974. "Aux origines de la littérature sino-malaise: Un *sjair* publicitaire de 1886." (At the origin of Sino-Malay literature: An advertising *sjair* from 1886). *Archipel* 8 (1): 155–186.

Loo Fung Ying and Loo Fung Chiat. 2012. "Innovation for Survival? Dama Orchestra's *Butterfly Lovers*—The Musical on a Contemporary Multiracial Malaysian Stage." *Asian Theatre Journal* 29 (2): 339–356.

Loon, Piet van der. 1992. *The Classical Song and Art Song of South Fukien: A Study of Three Ming Anthologies.* Taipei: SMC.

Louw Eng Hoeij. 1934. *Pi Pa Chi* (The Story of the Lute). Tan's Drukkerij: Soerabaia.

Lu Yongjie. 2003. "Xianda Xinmin Gejushe de zhengrong suiyue" (The lofty years of Siantar's New People's Musical Theatre Society). In *Wangbuliao de suiyue*, edited by Huang Shuhai, 313–315. Beijing: Shijie zhishi chubanshe.

Lyons, Lenore, and Michele Ford. 2013. "The Chinese of Karimun: Citizenship and Belonging at Indonesia's Margins." In *Chinese Indonesians Reassessed: History, Religion and Belonging*, edited by Siew Min Sai and Chang-Yau Hoon, 121–137. Abingdon-on-Thames: Routledge.

Ma Jianhua. 2012. "Minnan muouxi shiji gouchen" (Review of historical materials on Southern Fujian wood puppetry). *Fujian yishu* 2:32–35.

Mackie, J. A. C. 1976. *The Chinese in Indonesia: Five Essays.* Honolulu: University of Hawai'i Press.

Maier, Henk. 2006. "Explosions in Semarang: Reading Malay Tales in 1895." *Bijdragen tot de Taal-, Land- en Volkenkunde* 162 (1): 1–34.

Marrison, Geoffrey E. 1987. "Modern Balinese—A Regional Literature of Indonesia." *Bijdragen tot de Taal-, Land- en Volkenkunde/Journal of the Humanities and Social Sciences of Southeast Asia* 143 (4): 468–498.

Martowijoyo, Sumantoro. 2004. "Indonesia's Microfinance and the Bri Unit System." In *Priorities and Strategies in Rural Poverty Reduction,* edited by Diana Alarcón, 237–261. Washington, DC: Inter-American Development Bank.

Maskurin, Sunariyadi, and Septina Alrianingrum. 2014. "Perkembengan Wayang Potehi di Surabaya Tahun 1967–2001" (Development of *wayang potehi* in Surabaya during the years 1967–2001). *Jurnal Mahasiswa Teknologi Pendidikan* 2 (3): 169–182.

Mastuti, Dwi Woro R. 2004. "Wayang Cina di Jawa sebagai wujud akulturasi budaya dan perekat negara kesatuan Republik Indonesia" (Chinese *wayang* on Java as a feature of acculturation and adhesion to the unity of the Republic of Indonesia). Paper presented at the Seminar Naskah Kuno Nusantara dengan tema Naskah Kuno Sebagai Perekat Negara Kesatuan Republik Indonesia, Jakarta, October 12.

———. 2011. "Menjadi Jawa: Naskah Cina-Jawa" (Becoming Javanese: Sino-Javanese scripts). *Jurnal Manassa* 1 (1): 47–77.

———. 2014. *Wayang potehi Gudo: Seni pertunjukan Peranakan Tionghoa di Indonesia* (*Wayang potehi* of Gudo: A performing art of Indonesian Chinese *Peranakan*). Jakarta: Sinar Harapan.

McDougall, Bonnie S., and Kam Louie. 1997. *The Literature of China in the Twentieth Century.* New York: Columbia University Press.

McGlynn, John H. 1998. *Language and Literature.* Singapore: Archipelago Press.

McMillan, Richard. 2005. *The British Occupation of Indonesia 1945–1946.* London: Routledge.

Meijer, Am. 1840. "Dagboek gehouden gedurende eene reis naar China (in het jaar 1827)" (Diary kept during a journey to China [in the year 1827]). *Tijdschrift voor Neêrland's Indie* 3 (2): 181–221.

Melvin, Jess. 2018. *The Army and the Indonesian Genocide : Mechanics of Mass Murder.* New York: Routledge.

Melvin, Jess, and Annie Pohlman. 2018. "A Case for Genocide: Indonesia, 1965–1966." In *The Indonesian Genocide of 1965*, edited by Katherine McGregor, Jess Melvin, and Annie Pohlman, 27–47. Cham: Palgrave Macmillan.

Melvin, Sheila, and Jindong Cai. 2004. *Rhapsody in Red: How Western Classical Music Became Chinese.* New York: Algora Publishing.

Moens, J. L. 1949. "Een Chineesche poppenkast en het spel van den linen zak" (A Chinese puppet theatre and the linen bag show). *Jade* 12 (3): 1–9.

Mrázek, Jan. 2005a. *Phenomenology of a Puppet Theatre: Contemplations of the Art of Javanese Wayang Kulit.* Leiden: KITLV Press.

———. 2005b. "Masks and Selves in Contemporary Java: The Dances of Didik Nini Thowok." *Journal of Southeast Asian Studies* 36 (2): 249–279.

Munoz, Paul Michel. 2006. *Early Kingdoms: Indonesian Archipelago and the Malay Peninsula.* Singapore: Editions Didier Millet.

Myutel, Maria. 2017. "Ethnicity and Social Relations in Indonesian Television Production Houses." *Journal of Southeast Asian Studies* 48 (2): 219–236.

Myutel, Maria, and Evamaria Sandkühler. 2015. "(In)visibility Ethnicity: Celebrating Chinese and Indian Descent in Indonesia." *Occasional Paper Series: Southeast Asian Studies at the University of Freiburg* 36:1–18.

Nagata, Judith. 1988. "Religion, Ethnicity and Language: Indonesian Chinese Immigrants in Toronto." *Southeast Asian Journal of Social Science,* 116–131.

———. 2003. "Local and Transnational Initiatives towards Improving Chinese-Indigenous Relations in Post-Suharto Indonesia: The Role of the Voluntary Sector." *Asian Ethnicity* 4 (3): 369–381.

Nanhua zhongxue, ed. 1956. *Yinni Sumendala Jugang Keshu Gonghui Nanhua Zhongxue chengli nianwu zhounian jinian lianhe tekan* (Joint special issue for the twenty-fifth anniversary of the Nanhua Middle School of the Hakka Association in Palembang, Sumatra, Indonesia). Palembang: Nanhua Zhongxue.

National Archives [of Singapore]. 1988. *Wayang: A History of Chinese Opera in Singapore.* Singapore: National Archives.

Nio Joe Lan. 1935. "Chinese Songs and Plays in Batavia." *The China Journal* 23 (4): 198–200.

———. 1943. "Maleische Bewerking van Chineesche Literatuur" (Malay-language adaptations of Chinese literature). *Cultureel Indië* 5:170–177, 260–269.

———. 1947. "Chineesche Literatuur in Indonesië" (Chinese literature in Indonesia). *Oriëntatie* 1 (2): 14–15.

———. 1948. "Het Chinese Toneel" (The Chinese stage). *Oriëntatie* 6:24–27.

———. 1962. *Sastera Indonesia-Tionghoa* (Sino-Indonesian literature). Jakarta: Gunung Agung.

Noor, Agus, and Indra Tranggano. 2003. "Teater Gandrik: Non-Confrontational Critique." *Seagull Theatre Quarterly* 36/37:100–106.

Oetomo, Dede. 1987. *Chinese of Pasuruan: Their Language and Identity.* Canberra: Australian National University.

———. 2013. "*Sam Pek Eng Tay:* A Chinese Love Story in Madurese." In *Literary Migrations: Traditional Chinese Fiction in Asia, 17–20th Centuries,* edited by Claudine Salmon, 375–392. Singapore: Singapore Institute of Asian Studies.

Ong, Chin Ee, Meghann Ormond, and Dian Sulianti. 2017. "Performing 'Chinese-ness' in Singkawang: Diasporic Moorings, Festivals and Tourism." *Asia Pacific Viewpoint* 58 (1): 41–56.

Ong, Eng-Die. 1943. "Chineezen en Nederlandsch-Indie: Sociografie van een Indonesische Bevolkingsgroep" (Chinese in the Netherlands Indies: Sociography of an Indonesian population group). PhD diss., Amsterdam University.

Ong, Susy. 2008. "Ethnic Chinese Religions: Some Recent Developments." In *Ethnic Chinese in Contemporary Indonesia,* edited by Leo Suryadinata, 97–116. Singapore: ISEAS.

Ontoro, Ons. 2014. "Wayang Kulit Cina-Jawa Silang Identitas Antara Cina dan Jawa" (Chinese-Javanese shadow puppet: A cross-identity between China and Java). In *Wacinwa: Silang Budaya Cina-Jawa: Koleksi Museum Negeri Sonobudoyo,* edited by Museum Negeri Sunobudoyo, 17–25. Yogyakarta: Museum Negeri Sunobudoyo.

Ooi, Keat Gin. 2011. *The Japanese Occupation of Borneo, 1941–45.* New York: Routledge.

Paramita, Viriya. 2015. "50 Kencan Pertama Bersama Tragedi 1965" (50 first dates with the 1965 tragedy). *Indoprogress* (November 21). http://indoprogress.com/2015/11/50-kencan-pertama-bersama-tragedi-1965/ (accessed February 5, 2017).

Parker, Lyn. 2010. "Teaching Religious Tolerance." *Inside Indonesia* 102. http://www.insideindonesia.org/teaching-religious-tolerance?highlight=WyJ0ZWFjaGluZyIsInRlYWNoIiwiJ3RlYWNoIiwiJ3RlYWNoJyIsInJlbGlnaW91cyIsInRvbGVyYW5jZSIsInRlYWNoaW5nIHJlbGlnaW91cyIsInRlYWNoaW5nIHJlbGlnaW91cyB0b2xlcmFuY2UiLCJyZWxpZ2lvdXMgdG9sZXJhbmNlIl0%3D (accessed October 10, 2018).

Pätzold, Uwe U. 2011. "Self-Defense and Music in Muslim Contexts in West Java." In *Divine Inspiration: Music and Islam in Indonesia,* edited by David D. Harnish and Anne K. Rasmussen, 161–193. New York: Oxford University Press.

Pausacker, Helen. 2004. "Presidents as *Punakawan:* Portrayal of National Leaders as Clown-Servants in Central Javanese *Wayang.*" *Journal of Southeast Asian Studies* 35 (2): 213–233.

———. 2005. "*Peranakan* Chinese and *Wayang* in Java." In *Chinese Indonesians: Remembering, Distorting, Forgetting,* edited by Tim Lindsey and Helen Pausacker, 185–208. Singapore: ISEAS.

———. 2007. "The Sixth Religion." *Inside Indonesia* 89. http://www.insideindonesia.org/the-sixth-religion (accessed October 10, 2018).

Pepinsky, Thomas B. 2009. *Economic Crises and the Breakdown of Authoritarian Regimes: Indonesia and Malaysia in Comparative Perspective.* New York: Cambridge University Press.

PERTIP (Persatuan Tionghoa Peranakan). 1953. *Buku Peringatan "PERTIP" 1946–53* (Commemorative book for PERTIP 1946–53). Makassar: PERTIP.

Petersen, Robert. 1991. "The Role of the Raksasa: An Interview with Pak Asep Sunanda, Dalang of Wayang Golek Purwa." *The Drama Review* 35 (2): 129–137.

Peterson, Robert L. 1975. *The Demon Gods of Thorny River: A True-to-life Story of a Chinese Family in West Kalimantan, Indonesian Borneo.* London: OMF Books.

Pfeiffer, Ida. 1856. *Meine zweite Weltreise* (My second trip around the world). Vienna: Gerold.

Phoa Kian Sioe. 1949. "Orkest Gambang, Hasil Kesenian Tionghoa Peranakan di Djakarta" (The Gambang Orchestra, an artistic product of the Peranakan Chinese of Jakarta). *Pantja Warna* 1 (9): 37–39.

Pigeaud, Theodore G. T. 1938. *Javaanse Volksvertoningen* (Javanese popular performances). Batavia: Volkslectuur.

———. 1975. *Javanese and Balinese Manuscripts and Some Codices Written in Related Idioms Spoken in Java and Bali: Descriptive Catalogue, with Examples of Javanese Script, Introductory Chapters, a General Index of Names and Subjects.* Wiesbaden: Steiner.

———. 2003. "The Present State of Theatre, Dance, and Music in Java." In *The Kraton: Selected Essays on Javanese Courts,* translated by Rosemary Robson-McKillop, edited by Stuart Robson, 295–310. Leiden: KITLV Press.

Pramoedya Ananta Toer. 2007. *The Chinese in Indonesia: An English Translation of Hoakiau Di Indonesia (First Published in 1960).* Translated by Max Lane, edited by Mary Redway. Singapore: Select Publishing.

Prasad, Karolina. 2016. *Identity Politics and Elections in Malaysia and Indonesia: Ethnic Engineering in Borneo.* London: Routledge.

Prasetya, Hanggar Budi. 2014a. "Wacinwa: Silang Budaya Cina-Jawa di Yogyakarta"

(Wacinwa: Chinese-Javanese acculturation in Yogyakarta). In *Wacinwa: Silang Budaya Cina-Jawa: Koleksi Museum Negeri Sonobudoyo,* edited by Museum Negeri Sunobudoyo, 9–16. Yogyakarta: Museum Negeri Sunobudoyo.

———. 2014b. "Reconstruction of Chinese-Javanese Shadow Puppet Theatre." In *10th International Conference on Southeast Asian Cultural Values: Community of Destiny,* edited by the Royal Academy of Cambodia, 126–133. Phnom Penh: Royal Academy of Cambodia, Asia Research Center.

Prasetyo, Frans Ari. 2016. "City Performance: Chinese New Year in West Kalimantan." *PORTAL Journal of Multidisciplinary International Studies* 13 (1): 1–12.

Pregadio, Fabrizio. 2008. *The Encyclopedia of Taoism.* London: Routledge.

Ptak, Roderich. 1993. "China and the Trade in Cloves, circa 960–1435." *Journal of the American Oriental Society* 113:1–13.

———. 2007. *Die maritime Seidenstrasse: Küstenräume, Seefahrt und Handel in vorkolonialer Zeit* (The maritime Silk Road: Coastal areas, seafaring, and trade in the precolonial period). Munich: Beck.

Purchas, Samuel. 1625. *Purchase His Pilgrimes,* vol. 1. London: William Stanby. Available on Google Books. https://books.google.com.au/books?id=0jSN5RNaVNkC&source=gbs_navlinks_s (accessed September 25, 2018).

Purdey, Jemma. 2006. *Anti-Chinese Violence in Indonesia, 1996–1999.* Honolulu: University of Hawai'i Press in association with the Asian Studies Association of Australia.

Purwoseputro, Ardian. 2014. *Wayang Potehi of Java.* Translated by Hermanto Lim. Jakarta: Afterhours Books.

Putra, I. Nyoman Darma. 2008. "Modern Performing Arts as a Reflection of Changing Balinese Identity." *Indonesia and the Malay World* 36 (104): 87–114.

———. 2009. "*Kidung interaktif:* Vocalising and Interpreting Traditional Literature through Electronic Mass Media in Bali." *Indonesia and the Malay World* 37 (109): 249–276.

Qian Guoliang. 2015. "Chuangli 'Haifeng xueyishe' de guocheng" (The process of establishing the Ocean Wave Artistic Study Society). In *Yinni Subei Huaqiao Huaren cangsang suiyu,* vol. 1, edited by Zheng Guanghuang, 435–437. Hong Kong: Yinni Subei Huaqiao Huaren lishishe.

Qin, Dashu, and Kunpeng Xiang. 2011. "Sri Vijaya as the Entrepôt for Circum-Indian Ocean Trade." *Études Océan Indien* 46–47:308–336.

"Qin Xianglian" (Qin Xianglian). 1957. *Nanyang Post* 114 (April): unpaginated.

Quinn, George. 2013. "*Liang Shanbo yu Zhu Yingtai:* A Chinese Folk Romance in Java and Bali." In *Literary Migrations: Traditional Chinese Fiction in Asia, 17–20th Centuries,* edited by Claudine Salmon, 336–358. Singapore: Singapore Institute of Asian Studies.

Ramage, Douglas E. 1995. *Politics in Indonesia: Democracy, Islam, and the Ideology of Tolerance.* New York: Routledge.

Rees, W. A. 1858. *Montrado: Geschied- En Krijgskundige Bijdrage Betreffende de Onderwerping der Chinezen op Borneo: Naar het Dagboek van een Indisch Officier over 1854–1856* (Montrado: Historical and military contribution concerning the subjugation of the Chinese on Borneo: After the diary of an Indies officer from 1854 to 1856). 's Hertogenbosch: Muller.

Reid, Anthony. 1996. "*Flows and Seepages* in the Long-term Chinese Interaction with Southeast Asia." In *Sojourners and Settlers: Histories of Southeast Asia and the Chinese in Honour of Jennifer Cushman*, edited by Anthony Reid, 15–50. St Leonards, NSW: Asian Studies Association of Australia.

———. 1997. "Entrepreneurial Minorities, Nationalism, and the State." In *Essential Outsiders: Chinese and Jews in the Modern Transformation of Southeast Asia and Central Europe*, edited by Daniel Chirot and Anthony Reid, 33–71. Seattle: University of Washington Press.

———. 2014. *The Blood of the People: Revolution and the End of Traditional Rule in Northern Sumatra*. Singapore: NUS Press.

Reynolds, Craig J. 2001. "Tycoons and Warlords: Modern Thai Social Formations and Chinese Historical Romance." In *Sojourners and Settlers: Histories of Southeast Asia and the Chinese*, edited by Anthony Reid, 115–147. Honolulu: University of Hawai'i Press.

Reynolds, J. N. 1835. *Voyage of the United States Frigate Potomac*. New York: Harper & Brothers.

Riantiarno, Nano. 1999. *Sampek Engtay*. Jakarta: Pustaka Jaya.

———. 2003. "An Urban Folk Theatre?" *Seagull Theatre Quarterly* 36/37:116–123.

———. 2011. *Kitab Teater: Tanya Jawab Seputar Seni Pertunjukan* (The Book of Theatre: Questions and answers about the performing arts). Jakarta: Gramedia Widiasarana Indonesia.

Ricklefs, M. C. 1983. "The Crisis of 1740–1 in Java: The Javanese, Chinese, Madurese and Dutch, and the Fall of the Court of Kartasura," *Bijdragen tot de Taal-, Land- en Volkenkunde van Nederlandsch-Indië* 139 (2/3): 268–290.

Ridwan, Indra. 2014. "The Art of the Arranger in Pop Sunda, Sundanese Popular Music of West Java, Indonesia." PhD diss., University of Pittsburgh.

Riharyani. 2014. "Sambutan" (Foreword). In *Wacinwa: Silang Budaya Cina-Jawa: Koleksi Museum Negeri Sonobudoyo*, edited by Museum Negeri Sunobudoyo, 6–8. Yogyakarta: Museum Negeri Sunobudoyo.

Riharyani, ed. 2015. *Kajian Wacinwa: Silang Budaya Cina-Jawa* (Research on Wacinwa: Sino-Javanese interculture). Yogyakarta: Museum Sonobudoyo Yogyakarta.

Roadnight, Andrew. 2002. *United States Policy towards Indonesia in the Truman and Eisenhower Years*. Basingstoke: Palgrave Macmillan.

Robison, Richard. 2009. *Indonesia: The Rise of Capital*. Singapore: Equinox Publishing.

Roosa, John. 2006. *Pretext for Mass Murder: The September 30th Movement and Suharto's Coup d'État in Indonesia*. Madison: University of Wisconsin Press.

Rosidi, Ajip, ed. 2000. *Ensiklopedi Sunda: Alam, Budaya, dan Manusia* (Sundanese Encyclopedia: Nature, culture, and humans). Jakarta: Pustaka Jaya.

———. 2003. *Apa siapa orang Sunda* (Sundanese who's who). Bandung: PT Kiblat Buku in cooperation with Yayasan Kebudayaan Rancage.

Ross, Laurie Margot. 2013. "Performing Piety from the Inside Out: Fashioning Gender and Public Space in a Mask 'Tradition' from Java's Northwest Coast." In *Performance, Popular Culture, and Piety in Muslim Southeast Asia*, edited by Timothy P. Daniels, 13–43. New York: Palgrave Macmillan.

Ruizendaal, Robin. 2006. *Marionette Theatre in Quanzhou*. Leiden: Brill.

———. 2016. "*Potehi* in Taiwan: Chinese Roots and Taiwanese Innovation." In *Potehi: Glove Puppet Theatre in Southeast Asia in Taiwan*, edited by Kaori Fushiki and Robin Ruizendaal, 7–22. Taipei: Taiyuan Publishing.

Ruizendaal, Robin, and Ma Si-yuan. 2016. "The Last *Potehi* Performer of Yangon, Myanmar." In *Potehi: Glove Puppet Theatre in Southeast Asia in Taiwan*, edited by Kaori Fushiki and Robin Ruizendaal, 37–42. Taipei: Taiyuan Publishing.

Rusconi, Jan. 1935. *Sja'ir Kompeni Welanda berperang dengan Tjina* (Syair of the Dutch Company fighting a Chinese uprising). Wageningen: H. Veenman & Zonen.

Sai, Siew Min. 2006. "Representing the Past of Chinese Language Education: Language, History and Chinese Identities in Indonesia." PhD diss., University of Michigan.

———. 2016. "Mandarin Lessons: Modernity, Colonialism and Chinese Cultural Nationalism in the Dutch East Indies, c. 1900s." *Inter-Asia Cultural Studies* 17 (3): 375–394.

Sai, Siew-Min, and Chang-Yau Hoon. 2013. "Introduction." In *Chinese Indonesians Reassessed: History, Religion and Belonging*, edited by Siew-Min Sai and Chang-Yau Hoon, 1–26. London: Routledge.

Said, Salim. 1992. "The Rise of the Indonesian Film Industry." *East-West Film Journal* 6 (2): 99–115.

Saidi, Ridwan. 1991. "Gadis WNI bernama Engtay" (A [Chinese] Indonesian citizen girl named Engtay). In *Nonpri dimata Pribumi*, edited by H. Junus Jahja, 17–21. Jakarta: Yayasan Tunas Bangsa.

Salmon, Claudine, ed. 1981. *Literature in Malay by the Chinese of Indonesia*. Paris: Éditions de la Maison des sciences de l'homme.

———. 2013a. "Introduction." In *Literary Migrations: Traditional Chinese Fiction in Asia, 17–20th Centuries*, edited by Claudine Salmon, 1–36. Singapore: Singapore Institute of Asian Studies.

———. 2013b. "A Note on Javanese Works Derived from Chinese Fiction." In *Literary Migrations: Traditional Chinese Fiction in Asia, 17–20th Centuries*, edited by Claudine Salmon, 235–247. Singapore: Singapore Institute of Asian Studies.

———. 2013c. "Malay Translations of Chinese Fictions in Indonesia." In *Literary Migrations: Traditional Chinese Fiction in Asia, 17–20th Centuries*, edited by Claudine Salmon, 248–276. Singapore: Singapore Institute of Asian Studies.

———. 2013d. "Writings in Romanized Malay by the Chinese of Malaya: A Preliminary Inquiry." In *Literary Migrations: Traditional Chinese Fiction in Asia, 17–20th Centuries*, edited by Claudine Salmon, 277–314. Singapore: Singapore Institute of Asian Studies.

Salmon, Claudine, and Denys Lombard. 1975. "À propos de quelques stèles chinoises récemment retrouvées à Banten (Java ouest)" (On a few Chinese steles recently found at Banten [West Java]). *Archipel* 9 (1): 99–127.

———. 1980. *Les Chinois de Jakarta: Temples et vie collective* (The Chinese of Jakarta: Temples and communal life). Paris: Éditions de la maison des sciences de l'homme.

———. 1981. "Le poème en malais d'un Peranakan sur la visite du Roi Chulalongkorn à Batavia en 1871." (The Malay poem of a Peranakan on the visit of King Chulalongkorn to Batavia in 1871). *Archipel* 22 (1): 133–166.

Salmon, Claudine, and Myra Sidharta. 2000. "The Hainanese of Bali: A Little Known Community." *Archipel* 60 (4): 87–124.

Sato, Shigeru. 1994. *War, Nationalism and Peasants: Java under the Japanese Occupation 1942–1945*. St Leonards, NSW: Allen & Unwin.

Schipper, Kristofer. 1979. *Une collection de manuscrits de pièces de théâtre d'ombres chinoises* (A collection of dramatic manuscripts for Chinese shadow puppets), edited by Piet van der Loon. Paris: European Association of Chinese Studies.

Schlegel, G[ustaaf]. 1891. "Chinese-Malay and Javanese Literature in Java." *T'oung Pao* 2 (2): 148–151.

Schlottenhammer, Angelika. 1999. "The Maritime Trade of Quanzhou (Zaitun) from the Ninth through the Thirteenth Century." In *The Archaeology of Seafaring,* edited by Himanshu Prabha Ray, 271–290. Delhi: Pragati Publications.

Schulze, L. F. M. 1890. *Führer auf Java: Ein Handbuch für Reisende* (Java Guide: A handbook for travelers). Leipzig: Th. Grieben's Verlag.

Schwarz, Adam. 1999. *A Nation in Waiting: Indonesia's Search for Stability.* St Leonards, NSW: Allen & Unwin.

Scidmore, Eliza Ruhamah. 1984. *Java, the Garden of the East.* Singapore: Oxford University Press.

Scott, Edmund. 1606. *An exact discourse of the subtilties, fashishions* [sic], *pollicies, religion, and ceremonies of the East Indians as well Chyneses as Iauans, there abyding and dweling. Together with the manner of trading with those people, as well by vs English, as by the Hollanders: as also what hath happened to the English nation at Bantan in the East Indies, since the 2. of February 1602. vntil the 6. of October 1605. Whereunto is added a briefe discription of Iaua Maior. Written by Edmund Scott, resident there, and in other places neere adioyng* [sic], *the space of three yeeres and a halfe.* London: Printed by W. W[hite] for Walter Burre. British Library copy digitized at Early English Books Online (www.eebo.chadwyck.com) Bib Name/Number: STC (2nd ed.) / 22061 (accessed January 27, 2017).

Seltmann, Friedrich. 1976. "Wajang Titi—Chinesisches Schattenspiel in Jogjakarta" (*Wayang titi*—Chinese shadow puppets in Yogyakarta). *RIMA* 10 (1): 51–75.

Semedi, Pujo. 2011. "Padvinders, Pandu, Pramuka: Youth and State in the 20th Century Indonesia." *Africa Development* 36 (3–4): 19–38.

Sen, Krishna. 2006. "'Chinese' Indonesians in National Cinema." *Inter-Asia Cultural Studies* 7 (1): 171–184.

Serrurier, Lindor. 1896. *De wajang poerwa, eene ethnologische studie* (*Wayang purwa,* an ethnological study). Leiden: Brill.

Setianto, Benny D. 2010. "In Search of Protection: Facing Janus Faces in Protecting Chinese-Ethnic in Indonesia." In *State Power and the Legal Regulation of Evil,* edited by Francesca Dominello, 79–88. Oxford: Inter-Disciplinary Press.

Setijadi, Charlotte. 2015. "Being Chinese Again." In *Multilingualism in the Chinese Diaspora Worldwide: Transnational Connections and Local Social Realities,* edited by Li Wei, 141–157. London: Routledge.

———. 2016a. "Ethnic Chinese in Contemporary Indonesia: Changing Identity Politics and the Paradox of Sinification." *Perspective* 12:1–10.

———. 2016b. "'A Beautiful Bridge': Chinese Indonesian Associations, Social Capital and Strategic Identification in a New Era of China–Indonesia Relations." *Journal of Contemporary China* 25 (102): 822–835.

Setyautama, Sam, ed. 2008. *Tokoh-tokoh etnis Tionghoa di Indonesia* (Ethnic Chinese figures in Indonesia). Jakarta: Kepustakaan Populer Gramedia.

Shalihong. 2017. *Wuzu miao* (Temple of the Five Ancestors). Serialized in *Lüdao* 2, November 2, November 8, December 3, and December 5, and on two other dates unmarked in the photocopies provided by the author.

Sheng, Kai. 2013. "The Different Faces of Nezha in Modern Taiwanese Culture." *Archiv Orientální* 81 (3): 391–410.

Sidharta, Myra. 2011. "The Dragon's Tail in Chinese Indonesian Foodways." *Chinese Food and Foodways in Southeast Asia*, edited by Tan Chee Beng, 107–123. Singapore: NUS Press.

———. 2015. "The Mazu Worship on the Island of Java." In *After Migration and Religious Affiliation: Religions, Chinese Identities, and Transnational Networks*, edited by Tan Chee-Beng, 3–17. Singapore: World Scientific.

Skinner, G. William. 1963. "The Chinese Minority." In *Indonesia*, edited by Ruth T. McVey, 97–117. New Haven, CT: Southeast Asia Studies, Yale University, by arrangement with HRAF Press.

Smail, John R. W. 1964. *Bandung in the Early Revolution, 1945–1946: A Study in the Social History of the Indonesian Revolution*. Ithaca, NY: Southeast Asia Program, Department of Asian Studies, Cornell University.

Soedarsono. 1969. "Classical Javanese Dance: History and Characterization." *Ethnomusicology* 13 (3): 498–506.

Soelarto, B., and S. Ilmi Albiladiyah. *Wayang Cina-Jawa Yogykarta*. Jakarta: Depdikbud, 1980/1981.

Somers, Mary F. [= Mary Somers Heidhues]. 1964. *Peranakan Chinese Politics in Indonesia*. Ithaca, NY: Southeast Asia Program, Department of Asian Studies, Cornell University.

Spiller, Henry. 2010. *Erotic Triangles: Sundanese Dance and Masculinity in West Java*. Chicago: University of Chicago Press.

Stenberg, Josh. 2015. "Multilingualism and the West Kalimantan Hakka." In *Multilingualism in the Chinese Diaspora Worldwide: Transnational Connections and Local Social Realities*, edited by Li Wei, 123–140. London: Routledge.

———. 2017. "The Lost Keychain? Contemporary Sinophone Writing in Indonesia." Under review at *Sojourn: Journal of Southeast Asian Studies*.

———. 2018. "A Showcase of Harmony." *Inside Indonesia* 131. http://www.insideindonesia.org/a-showcase-of-harmony (accessed October 10, 2018).

Stoler, Ann Laura. 1995. *Capitalism and Confrontation in Sumatra's Plantation Belt, 1870–1979*. Ann Arbor: University of Michigan Press.

Strassler, Karen. 2008. "Cosmopolitan Visions: Ethnic Chinese and the Photographic Imagining of Indonesia in the Late Colonial and Early Postcolonial Periods." *Journal of Asian Studies* 67 (2): 395–432.

———. 2010. *Refracted Visions: Popular Photography and National Modernity in Java*. Durham, NC: Duke University Press. Print.

Sturler, W. L., de. 1841. "Aanhangsel" (Appendix). In Eduard Selberg, *Over den verledenen en tegenwoordigen toestand van het eiland Java* (Regarding the past and present condition of the island of Java), translated by W. L. de Sturler, 129–144. Groningen: Omkens.

Su Wen. 2007. "Huaqiao wei Yinni duli jiefang fuwu de diandi huiyi" (Jotted recollections of the services rendered by Overseas Chinese for the independence and liberation of Indonesia). In *Guanghui suiye, suiyue haoge: Yijiusiwunian zhanhou Subei Yinhua wenyi huodong gaikuang* (Glorious years, years of great song: An overview of Sino-Indonesian cultural activities in Northern Sumatra during the afterwar post-1945 period), edited by Liao Zhangran, 17–19. Medan: Lingnan meishu.

Suaedy, Ahmad. 2014. "The Role of Volunteers and Political Participation in the 2012 Gubernatorial Election." *Journal of Current Southeast Asian Affairs* 33 (1): 111–138.

Sumardjo, Jakob. 1992. *Perkembengan Teater Modern dan Sastra Drama Indonesia* (The development of Indonesian modern theatre and dramatic literature). Bandung: Citra Aditya Bakti.

———. 2001. *Seni Pertunjukan Indonesia: Suatu Pendekatan Sejarah* (Indonesian performing arts: A short history). Bandung: STSI Press Bandung.

Sumari, ed. 2016. *Almanak Wayang Indonesia* (Almanac of Indonesian *wayang*). Jakarta: Direktorat Jenderal Kebudayaan, Kementerian Pendidikan dan Kebudayaan.

Sumarsam. 1995. *Gamelan: Cultural Interaction and Musical Development in Central Java.* Chicago: University of Chicago Press.

———. 2013. "Past and Present Issues of Javanese–European Musical Hybridity: *Gendhing mares* and Other Hybrid Genres." In *Recollecting Resonances: Indonesian-Dutch Musical Encounters,* edited by B. Barendregt and E. Bogaerts, 87–110. Leiden: Brill/KITLV.

Suryadinata, Leo. 1978. *The Chinese Minority in Indonesia: Seven Papers.* Singapore: Chopmen Enterprises.

———. 1993. "The State and Chinese Minority in Indonesia." In *Chinese Adaptations and Diversity: Essays on Society and Literature in Indonesia, Malaysia and Singapore,* edited by Leo Suryadinata, 77–100. Singapore: Singapore University Press.

———. 2004. *The Culture of the Chinese Minority in Indonesia.* Singapore: Marshall Cavendish.

———. 2005a. "Zheng He, Semarang and the Islamization of Java: Between History and Legend." In *Admiral Zheng He and Southeast Asia,* edited by Leo Suryadinata, 72–93. Singapore: ISEAS–Yusof Ishak Institute.

———. 2005b. "Buddhism and Confucianism in Contemporary Indonesia: Recent Developments." In *Chinese Indonesians: Remembering, Distorting, Forgetting,* edited by Tim Lindsey and Helen Pausacker, 77–94. Singapore: ISEAS.

———. 2014. "State and 'Chinese Religions' in Indonesia: Confucianism, Tridharma and Buddhism during the Suharto Rule and After." In *After Migration and Religious Affiliation: Religions, Chinese Identities, and Transnational Networks,* edited by Tan Chee-Beng, 19–42. Singapore: World Scientific.

Susanto, Andreas. 2010. "Diversity in Compliance: Yogyakarta Chinese and the New Order Assimilation Policy." In *Chinese Indonesians and Regime Change,* edited by Marleen Dieleman, Juliette Koning, and Peter Post, 65–90. Leiden: Brill.

Sutherland, Heather. 2011. "*A Sino-Indonesian Commodity Chain*: The Trade in Tortoiseshell in the Late Seventeenth and Eighteenth Centuries." In *Chinese Circulations: Capital, Commodities, and Networks in Southeast Asia,* edited by Eric Tagliacozzo and Wen-Chin Chang, 172–199. Durham, NC: Duke University Press.

Szonyi, Michael. 2002. *Practicing Kinship: Lineage and Descent in Late Imperial China.* Stanford, CA: Stanford University Press.

Taal, Sandra. 2002. "Cultural Expressions, Collective Memory, and the Urban Landscape in Palembang." In *The Indonesian Town Revisited,* edited by Peter J. M. Nas, 172–200. Münster: Lit Verlag.

Tagliacozzo, Eric, and Wen-Chin Chang. 2011. "Introduction." In *Chinese Circulations: Capital, Commodities, and Networks in Southeast Asia,* edited by Eric Tagliacozzo and Wen-Chin-Chang, 1–17. Durham, NC: Duke University Press.

Tan, Chee-Beng. 2001. "Chinese in Southeast Asia and Identities in a Changing Global

Context." In *Chinese Populations in Contemporary Southeast Asian Societies*, edited by M. Jocelyn Armstrong, R. Warwick Armstrong, and Kent Mulliner, 210–236. New York: Routledge.

———. 2004. *Chinese Overseas: Comparative Cultural Issues.* Hong Kong: Hong Kong University Press.

———. 2015. "Ancestral God, Locality God, and Chinese Transnational Pilgrimage." In *After Migration and Religious Affiliation: Religions, Chinese Identities, and Transnational Networks*, edited by Tan Chee-Beng, 351–376. Singapore: World Scientific.

Tan Deseng, Mohamad. 1989. "Perkembangan musik pop daerah yang bertanggungjawab menyangkut pencipta dan pembawa lagu, instrument, warna dan komposisi" (The development of a responsible regional pop music as concerns the creators and transmitters of song, instrument, color, and composition). In *Apa itu lagu pop daerah* (What are regional pop songs?), edited by Gunawan Subagio, 42–44. Bandung: Citra Aditya Bakti.

Tan, Giok-lan [= Mély G. Tan]. 1963. *The Chinese of Sukabumi: A Study of Social and Cultural Accommodation.* Ithaca, NY: Modern Indonesia Project, Southeast Asia Program, Department of Asian Studies, Cornell University.

Tan, Mély G. 1991. "The Social and Cultural Dimensions of the Role of Ethnic Chinese in Indonesian Society." *Indonesia*, 113–125.

Tan, Sooi-Beng. 1981."The Glove Puppet Theatre (*po te hi*) in Malaysia." *Asian Music* 13 (1): 53–72.

———. 1989. "From Popular to "Traditional" Theater: The Dynamics of Change in Bangsawan of Malaysia." *Ethnomusicology* 33 (2): 229–274.

———. 1993. *Bangsawan: A Social and Stylistic History of Popular Malay Opera.* Singapore: Oxford University Press.

———. 2007. "The Lion Dances to the Fore: Articulating Chinese Identities in Penang and Medan." *Senri Ethnological Reports* 65:63–78.

———. 2016. "*Potehi* of Penang, Malaysia: Adapting to the Times." In *Potehi: Glove Puppet Theatre in Southeast Asia in Taiwan*, edited by Kaori Fushiki and Robin Ruizendaal, 23–36. Taipei: Taiyuan Publishing.

Tanasaldy, Taufiq. 2012. *Regime Change and Ethnic Politics in Indonesia: Dayak Politics of West Kalimantan.* Leiden: KITLV.

———. 2013. "Opportunities and Challenges: Social and Political Activism of the Indonesian Chinese in Post-Reform Indonesia." *Review of Indonesian and Malaysian Affairs* 47 (2): 91–116.

———. 2015. "A Decade after the Reform: Political Activism of the Chinese of West Kalimantan, Indonesia." *Asian Ethnicity* 16 (4): 446–479.

Tang Xiaobing. 2016. "Street Theater and Subject Formation in Wartime China: Toward a New Form of Public Art." *Cross-Currents: East Asian History and Culture Review* 5 (1): 85–114.

Taylor, Jeremy E. 2011. *Rethinking Transnational Chinese Cinemas: The Amoy-Dialect Film Industry in Cold War Asia.* New York: Routledge.

———. 2018. "Lychees and Mirrors: Local Opera, Cinema, and Diaspora in the Chinese Cultural Cold War." *Twentieth-Century China* 43 (2): 163–180.

Teater Koma. 2005. "Forum Teater Koma." Teater Koma archives.

Terrence, John Thomas. 1997. "The Psychocultural Significance of the Balinese Shadow

Theatre from the Perspective of Its Master Practitioners." PhD diss., UCLA (University of California Los Angeles).

Thio Tjin Boen. 2002. *Cerita Oey Se* (Story of Oey Se). In *Kesastraan Melayu Tionghoa dan Kebangsaan Indonesia*, vol. 1, edited by Marcus A.S. and Pax Benedanto, 175–250. Jakarta: Kepustakaan Populer Gramedia.

Thorn, William. 1815. *Memoir of the Conquest of Java: With the Subsequent Operations of the British Forces, in the Oriental Archipelago.* London: T. Egerton.

Tjan Tjoe Som. 1947/1948. "De culturele positie der chinezen in Indonesië" (The cultural position of the Chinese in Indonesia). *Indonesië: Tweemandeliks tidscrhift gewijd van her Indonesisch cultuurgebied* 1:53–61.

Tjoa Tjin Mo. 1941. "Tiauw Sian" (Diaochan). *Mededeelingen van het China Instituut* 2:161–185.

Tong, Chee Kiong. 2010. *Identity, Cultural Contact and Ethnic Relations in Southeast Asia: Racializing Chineseness.* Dordrecht: Springer.

Tonnet, Martine. 1902. "De gele kapelletjes: Maleisch-chinesisch sprookje" (The yellow butterflies: Malay-Chinese fairy tale). *Woord en beeld* 7 (2): 165–182.

Triandafyllidou, Anna. 1998. "National Identity and the 'Other'." *Ethnic and Racial Studies* 21 (4): 593–612.

Tripathy, Jyotirmaya, and Sudarsan Padmanabhan. 2014a. "Preface." In *Becoming Minority: How Discourses and Policies Produce Minorities in Europe and Asia*, edited by Jyotirmaya Tripathy and Sudarsan Padmanabhan, xi–xv. New Delhi: SAGE.

———. 2014b. "Becoming a Minority Category." In *Becoming Minority: How Discourses and Policies Produce Minorities in Europe and Asia*, edited by Jyotirmaya Tripathy and Sudarsan Padmanabhan, 3–23. New Delhi: SAGE.

Tsai Tsung-te (Cai Zongde). 2015. "Yindunixiya Huaren budaixi de lishi, yanchu xingtai yu yinyue" (The history, performance type, and music of Sino-Indonesian *potehi*). *Zhongyang Yinyue Xueyuan xuebao* 2:69–88, 108.

———. 2017. "Moluo yu zaisheng: Yindunixiya Zhuawa Huaren piyingxi de fazhan zhuangkuang" (Decline and rebirth: The developmental situation of Indonesian Sino-Javanese shadow puppets). *Zhongyang Yinyue Xueyuan xuebao* 1:47–64, 89.

Tsai, Yen-ling. 2008. "Strangers Who Are Not Foreign: Intimate Exclusion and Racialized Boundary in Urban Indonesia." PhD diss., University of California Santa Cruz.

———. 2013. "Materializing Racial Formation: The Social Lives of Confiscated Chinese Properties in North Sumatra." In *Chinese Indonesians Reassessed: History, Religion and Belonging*, edited by Siew-Min Sai and Chang-Yau Hoon, 83–102. London: Routledge.

Tseng Yong-yih (Zeng Yongyi). 2010. "Zhongguo lidai ouxi kaoshu (xia)" (Investigation into Chinese historical puppet theatre [final section]). *Xiqu xuebao* 7:21–62.

Tsuda Koji. 2012. "The Legal and Cultural Status of Chinese Temples in Contemporary Java." *Asian Ethnicity* 13 (4): 389–398.

Tunas, Devisanthi. 2007. "The Chinese Settlement of Bandung at the Turn of the Twentieth Century." MA thesis, National University of Singapore.

Twang, Peck Yang. 1998. *The Chinese Business Elite in Indonesia and the Transition to Independence, 1940–1950.* Kuala Lumpur: Oxford University Press.

UNESCO. 2009. "Indonesian Angklung." http://www.unesco.org/culture/ich/en/RL/indonesian-angklung-00393 (accessed February 12, 2017).

Valentijn, François. (1724–1726) 1858. *Oud en Nieuw Oost-Indien* (Old and New East Indies). 's Gravenhage [The Hague]: H. C. Susan. https://archive.org/stream/franoisvalentij00valegoog#page/n6/mode/2up (accessed January 20, 2017).
van der Chijs, Jacobus Anne. 1889. *Nederlandsch-Indisch Plakaatboek, 1602–1811* (Book of edicts for the Dutch Indies 1602–1811), vol. 6. Batavia: Bataviaasch Genootschap van Kunsten en Wetenschappen. https://archive.org/details/nederlandschind00chijgoog (accessed January 20, 2017).
van der Loon, Piet. 1992. *The Classical Theatre and Art Song of South Fukien: A Study of Three Ming Anthologies.* Taipei: Oriental Book Store.
van der Putten, Jan, and Al Azhar, eds. 2007. *Dalam berkekalan persahabatan: Surat-surat Raja Ali Haji kepada Von de Wall* (In lasting friendship: Correspondence of Raja Ali Haji to Von de Wall). Jakarta: Kepustakaan Populer Gramedia.
van der Veer, Anne. 2013. "The Pao An Tui in Medan: A Chinese Security Force in Dutch Occupied Indonesia, 1945–1948." MA thesis, Utrecht University.
van Groenendael, Victoria M. Clara. 1993. "Potéhi, the Chinese Glove-Puppet Theatre in East Java." In *Performance in Java and Bali: Studies of Narrative, Theatre, Music and Dance,* edited by Ben Arps. London: School of Oriental and African Studies.
van Hasselt, Arend Ludolf. 1882. *Volksbeschrijving van Midden-Sumatra* (Description of the people of Central Sumatra). Leiden: Brill.
van Langenberg, Michael. 1985. "East Sumatra: Accommodating an Indonesian Nation within a Sumatran Residency." In *Regional Dynamics of the Indonesian Revolution: Unity from Diversity,* edited by Audrey R. Kahin, 113–143. Honolulu: University of Hawai'i Press.
Vickers, Adrian. 2005. *A History of Modern Indonesia.* Cambridge: Cambridge University Press.
———. 2009. "When Did *legong* Start? A Reply to Stephen Davies." *Bijdragen tot de Taal-, Land- en Volkenkunde/Journal of the Humanities and Social Sciences of Southeast Asia* 165 (1): 1–7.
———. 2012. *Bali: A Paradise Created.* North Clarendon, VT: Tuttle Publishing.
Vihara Tri Dharma Bumi Raya. 2013 (?). *Vihara Tri Dharma Bumi Raya, Pusat Kota Singkawang. Zhongyang bogong dan Profil Kota Singkawang* (Tri Dharma Bumi Raya Temple, Singkawang City Center, Zhongyang Bogong, and profile of Singkawang City). Singkawang (?): Vihara Tri Dharma Bumi Raya (?).
Wade, Geoff. 2009a. "General Introduction" In *China and Southeast Asia,* edited by Geoff Wade, 1:1–28. London: Routledge.
———. 2009b. "An Early Age of Commerce in Southeast Asia, 900–1300 CE." *Journal of Southeast Asian Studies* 40 (2): 221–265.
Wagner, Rudolf G. 1990. *The Contemporary Chinese Historical Drama: Four Studies.* Berkeley: University of California Press.
Walravens, Hartmut, ed. 2000. *Vincenz Hundhausen (1878–1955): Nachdichtungen chinesischer Lyrik, die Pekinger Bühnenspiele und die zeitgenössische Kritik* (Vincenz Hundhausen 1878–1955: Adaptations of Chinese poetry, the Peking Stage Society and the contemporary reception). Wiesbaden: Otto Harrassowitz Verlag.
Wang, Cangbai, and Wong Siu-Lun. 2007. "Home as a Circular Process: The Indonesian-Chinese in Hong Kong." In *Beyond Chinatown: New Chinese Migration and the Global Expansion of China,* edited by Mette Thunø, 183–209. Copenhagen: NIAS Press.

Wang, Gungwu. 1991. *The Chineseness of China: Selected Essays.* Hong Kong: Oxford University Press.

Wang Hanmin. 2011. *Fujian xiqu haiwai chuanbo yanjiu.* Beijing: Zhongguo shehui kexue chubanshe.

Wang Jiyuan. 1947. "Xu" (Preface). In *Niliu,* by Fei Na, i. Batavia: Bacheng Zhonghua xiju xiehui chubanshe.

Wang Qianyu. 2012. "Baren xiansheng yu 'Gongxueshe—Xianda wangshi" (Mister Baren and the Joint Study Society—Siantar's bygone days). *Xianda tongxun* 134. http://www.siantarpeople.org/portal.php?mod=view&aid=1581 (accessed February 8, 2017).

Wang Yilin. 2006. "Zhangzhou zhangzhong muouxi jiqi dui Taiwan chuanbo" (Zhangzhou *zhangzhong* glove puppet theatre and its spread to Taiwan). *Fujian luntan* 1:225–226.

———. 2009. "Zai shuai san jie haishi zunshi yanghui—Zhangzhou mu'ou jutuan fazhan licheng chuyi" (Dying out or biding its time—Humble remarks on the developmental process of the Zhangzhou puppet troupe). *Fujian jiaoyu xueyuan xuebao* 10 (4): 110–113.

Warriner, Francis. 1835. *Cruise of the United States Frigate Potomac.* New York: Leavitt, Lord and Co.

Weeratne, Suranjan. 2009. "Degrees of 'Scapegoatability': Assessing Spatial Variations in Collective Violence against the Ethnic Chinese in Indonesia." PhD diss., McGill University.

Weintraub, Andrew N. 2004. *Power Plays: Wayang Golek Puppet Theater of West Java.* Athens: Ohio University Press.

Weitzel, A. W. P. 1860. *Batavia in 1858: Of Schetsen en Beelden uit de Hoofdstad van Neèrlandsch Indië* (Batavia in 1858: Or sketches and pictures from the capital of the Dutch East Indies). Gorinchem: J. Noorduijn en Zoon.

Wen Xinqiang. 2007. "Shankouyang minzhong yingjie 2007 nian difang shouzhang minzhu xuanju" (The Singkawang population welcomes the 2007 democratic election of local leadership). *Buletin PERMASIS,* special ed., 52–53.

Wiles, David. 2003. *A Short History of Western Performance Space.* New York: Cambridge University Press.

Williams, Lea E. 1960. *Overseas Chinese Nationalism; The Genesis of the Pan-Chinese Movement in Indonesia, 1900–1916.* Glencoe, IL: Free Press.

Williams, Sean. 1989. "Current Developments in Sundanese Popular Music." *Asian Music* 21 (1): 105–136.

———. 1990. "The Urbanization of Tembang Sunda: An Aristocratic Musical Genre of West Java, Indonesia." PhD diss., University of Washington.

Willmott, Donald Earl. 1961. *The National Status of the Chinese in Indonesia, 1900–1958.* Ithaca, NY: Modern Indonesia Project, Southeast Asia Program, Department of Far Eastern Studies, Cornell University.

Wimmer, Andreas, and Nina Glick Schiller. 2002. "Methodological Nationalism and Beyond: Nation-State Building, Migration and the Social Sciences." *Global Networks: A Journal of Transnational Affairs* 2 (4): 301–334.

Winarnita, Monika Swasti. 2014. "Chinese-Indonesian Belonging: Diasporic, Transnational and Local." *New Scholar* 3 (1): 85–98.

Winarnita, Monika, and Natalie Araujo. 2016. "The Cosmopolitan Performers: Chinese-

Indonesian Migrants in Perth Australia." *Sites: A Journal of Social Anthropology and Cultural Studies* 13 (1): 134–155.

Winet, Evan Darwin. 2010. *Indonesian Postcolonial Theatre: Spectral Genealogies and Absent Faces*. Basingstoke: Palgrave Macmillan.

Winkelmann, Christine. 2008. *Kulturelle Identitätskonstruktionen in der post-Suharto Zeit: chinesischstämmige Indonesier zwischen Assimilation und Besinnung auf ihre Wurzeln* (Cultural identity constructions in the post-Suharto period: Indonesians of Chinese origin between assimilation and reflections on their roots). Wiesbaden: Otto Harrassowitz Verlag.

Wirawan, Yerry. 2013. *Sejarah Masyarakat Tionghoa Makassar* (History of the Makassar Chinese). Jakarta: KPG.

Wong, Isabel K. F. 1984. "*Geming gequ:* Songs for the Education of the Masses." In *Popular Chinese Literature and Performing Arts in the People's Republic of China 1949–1979*, edited by Bonnie S. McDougall, 112–143. Berkeley: University of California Press.

Wong, Yoon-wah. 1988. *Essays on Chinese Literature: A Comparative Approach*. Singapore: Singapore University Press, National University of Singapore.

Wu Yuanchang. 2010. "Xianci" (Congratulatory message). In *Yinni Wanlong Keshu Lianyihui chengli shizhounian jinian tekan 2000 nian–2010 nian*, edited by Yinni Wanlong Keshu Lianyihui, 8. Bandung: Yinni Wanlong Keshu Lianyihui.

Wulandari, Benedikta Juliatri Widi. 2009. *Wayang Gantung*. Departeman Kebudayaan dan Parawisata, Pontianak: Balai Pelestarian Sejarah dan Nilai Tradisional Pontianak.

Xiao Bangjie. 2015. "Zhonglou fengyun" (The Clocktower issue). *Siantar People* (November 13). http://www.siantarpeople.org/portal.php?mod=view&aid=4103&page=2 (accessed January 20, 2017).

Xiao Feifei. 2010. "Yinni Sishui de 'Fengdexuan' miaoyu budaixituan fazhan shi" (Historical development of *potehi* at Hong Tiek Hian Temple in Surabaya, Indonesia). *Minsu quyi* 170 (12): 233–281.

Xie Chongguang. 2012. "Cankui zushi shenshi, fahao, tahao, xinyang xingzhi zhu wenti jiqi zai Taiwan chuanbo de tedian shixi" (Analysis of the Ashamed Patriarch's life experience, ritual names, tower names, and faith characteristics as well as the particularities of his cult's transmission to Taiwan). *Shijie zongjiao yanjiu* 4:64–71.

Xie Zhongxian. 2009. *Taiwan budaixi fazhan zhi yanjiu* (Research into the development of Taiwanese *potehi*). Taipei: Daoxiang chubanshe.

"Xinchuan xiqu huiyan" (*Xiqu* transmission performance). 2004. Theatre Program, May 28–30. Chinese Opera Institute. National Library (of Singapore) ephemeral materials: EPHE 01267 V1.16

Xu Anru 2001. "Wang Renshu jiqi 'Wuzumiao' " (Wang Renshu and his "Temple of Five Ancestors"). In *Baren yu Indunixiya*, edited by Zhou Nanjing, 484–492. Xianggang: Nandao chubanshe.

Xu Mingfang. 2011. "Qunxian chengsong meimingyang" (Singing the praises of the virtuous people). In *Yinni Wanlong Boliangan Fuli Jijinhui chengli sanshiwuzhounian jinian tekan*, edited by Yinni Wanlong Boliangan Fuli Jijinhui, 79–82. Bandung: Yinni Wanlong Boliangan Fuli Jijinghui.

Yampolsky, Philip Bradford. 2013a. "Music and Media in the Dutch East Indies: Gramophone Records and Radio in the Late Colonial Era, 1903–1942." PhD diss., University of Washington.

———. 2013b. "Three Genres of Indonesian Popular Music: Genre, Hybridity, and Globalization, 1960–2012." *Asian Music* 44 (2): 24–80.

Yang, Hon-Lun. 2005. "The Making of a National Music Icon: Xian Xinghai and His Yellow River Cantata." In *Music, Power, and Politics*, edited by Annie Randall, 87–111. New York: Routledge.

Yao Xiangying. 2007. "Xianda Xinmin gejushe xunhui ge chengshi yanchu" (The Siantar New People's Musical Theatre Society touring performances in various cities). In *Guanghui suiye, suiyue haoge: Yijiusiwunian zhanhou Subei Yinhua wenyi huodong gaikuang* (Glorious years, years of great song: An overview of Sino-Indonesian cultural activities in Northern Sumatra during the afterwar post-1945 period), edited by Liao Zhangran, 244. Medan: Lingnan meishu.

Ye Mingsheng. 2009. *Fujian kuileixi shilun* (On the history of Fujian puppet theatre). Beijing: Zhongguo xiju chubanshe.

———. 2010. "Fujian minjian kuileixi de jiyi wenhua tezhi" (Special characteristics of the ritual culture of popular Fujian puppet theatre). *Wenhua yichan* 3:36–40.

Yeh, Diana. 2014. *The Happy Hsiungs: Performing China and the Struggle for Modernity.* Hong Kong: Hong Kong University Press.

Yeung, Tuen Wai Mary. 2007. "To Entertain and Renew: Operas, Puppet Plays, and Ritual in South China." PhD diss., University of British Columbia.

Yinni Guiqiao Xiehui (Indonesian Overseas Chinese Association). 2009. Yinni Guiqiao Xiehui chengli wushi zhounian jinian tekan (Special commemorative issue for the fiftieth anniversary of the establishment of the Indonesian Overseas Chinese Association). Taipei County: Zhonghua Minguo Yinni Guiqiao Xiehui.

Yinni Subei Keshu Lianyihui. 2011. *Yinni Subei Keshu Lianyihui Shizhounian Jinian Tekan* (Special commemorative publication for the tenth anniversary of the Indonesian North Sumatra Hakka Friendship Society). Medan: Yinni Subei Keshu lianyihui.

Yinni Wanlong Boliangan Fuli Jijinhui (Yayasan Dana Sosial Priangan). 2011. Yinni Wanlong Boliangan Fuli Jijinhui chengli sanshiwuzhounian jinian tekan (Special commemorative issue for the third anniversary of Yayasan Dana Sosial Priangan). Bandung: Yinni Wanlong Boliangan Fuli Jijinghui.

Yinni Wanlong Keshu Lianyihui. 2010. *Yinni Wanlong Keshu Lianyihui chengli shizhounian jinian tekan 2000 nian–2010 nian* (Special commemorative issue for the tenth anniversary of the Bandung Indonesia Hakka Association, 2000–2010). Bandung: Yinni Wanlong Keshu Lianyihui.

Yuan Bingling. 2000. *Chinese Democracies: A Study of the Kongsis of West Borneo (1776–1884).* Leiden: Research School of Asian, African, and Amerindian Studies, Leiden University.

Yudaningrat, GBPH. 2014. "Sambutan" (Foreword). In *Wacinwa: Silang Budaya Cina-Jawa: Koleksi Museum Negeri Sonobudoyo*, edited by Museum Negeri Sunobudoyo, 4–5. Yogyakarta: Museum Negeri Sunobudoyo.

Yulianto, Herfin. 2013. *Landscape Musik Tionghoa Pontianak* (Musical landscape of the Pontianak Chinese). Pontianak: Borneo Culture Indonesia.

ZGXQZ = Zhongguo xiqu zhi bianji weiyuanhui (Editorial committee of the Chinese *xiqu* gazetteer), ed. 1993. *Zhongguo Xiqu zhi: Fujian juan* (Chinese *Xiqu* Gazetteer: Fujian volume). Beijing: Wenhua yishu chubanshe.

Zhang Jian. 2013. "Ershi shiji 90 niandai qian Liu Sanjie wenhua pinpai haiwai chuanbo guocheng jiqi guojihua celüe yanjiu" (Cursory research on the strategies of the process of overseas transmission and the internationalization of *Liu Sanjie* as a cultural brand before the 1990s). *Hezhou xueyuan xuebao* 29 (1): 19–27, 51.

Zhang Minhua. 2003. "Huainian Kunlun juyishe" (Remembering the Kunlun Dramatic Arts Company). In *Wangbuliao de suiyue,* edited by Huang Shuhai, 307–312. Beijing: Shijie zhishi chubanshe.

———. 2007. "Ji 'Silian' de zuhe he yanchu" (Remembering the combination and performances of the "League of Four"). In *Guanghui suiye, suiyue haoge: Yijiusiwunian zhanhou Subei Yinhua wenyi huodong gaikuang* (Glorious years, years of great song: An overview of Sino-Indonesian cultural activities in Northern Sumatra during the afterwar post-1945 period), edited by Liao Zhangran, 201. Medan: Lingnan meishu.

———. 2015. " 'Kunlun juyishe' chuchuang diandi" (Beginnings of the Kunlun Dramatic Arts Company). In *Yinni Subei Huaqiao Huaren cangsang suiyu,* vol. 1, edited by Zheng Guanghuang, 433–434. Hong Kong: Yinni Subei Huaqiao Huaren lishishe.

Zhang Rui, ed. 2012. "Saving Traditional Chinese Opera in Indonesia." *CNTV.* Video report by Andy Saputra. January 26. http://english.cntv.cn/program/newsupdate/20120126/103188.shtml (accessed January 21, 2017).

Zhang Tao. 2007. "Yindunixiya Huayu Xiju" (Chinese-language drama in Indonesia). In *Dongnanya Huayu xijushi,* edited by Zhou Ning, 726–797. Xiamen: Xiamen daxue chubanshe.

———. 2008. "Zhenxing yu fanrong: Kangzhan ji zhanhou chuqi de Yinni Huawen xiju" (Development and flourishing: Indonesian sinophone theatre during the War of Resistance and early postwar). *Huawen wenxue* 4:98–105.

Zhang, Yingjin. 1995. "The Texture of the Metropolis: Modernist Inscriptions of Shanghai in the 1930s." *Modern Chinese Literature* 9 (1): 11–30.

Zheng Yuanxin. 2007. "Mianlan Haifengshe de dansheng" (The birth of Medan's Sea Breeze Society). In *Guanghui suiye, suiyue haoge: Yijiusiwunian zhanhou Subei Yinhua wenyi huodong gaikuang* (Glorious years, years of great song: An overview of Sino-Indonesian cultural activities in Northern Sumatra during the afterwar post-1945 period), edited by Liao Zhangran, 244. Medan: Lingnan meishu.

Zheng Zhaoxian. 2008. "Fang Wanlong Basunta Huaren yishu xiehui" (Visiting Bandung's Pasundan Asih Chinese Arts Association). *Dongnanya Huaren: Zheng Zhaoxian buluoge.* http://southeastasiachinese.blogspot.fr/2008/12/blog-post.html (accessed February 9, 2017).

Zhou Aili. 1999. "Haiwai Chaoju zongheng tan" (Wide-ranging discussion on *Chaoju* Overseas"). In *Chaoju yanjiu [3]: Chaoju wushi nian wenlunxian* 3, edited by Shantou shi yishu yanjiu shi, 176–191. Beijing: Zhongguo xiju chubanshe.

Zhou Erfu. 1986. "Meng de zhuiqiu—Yi Renshu" (Pursuit of the dream—Remembering Renshu). In Baren,*Wuzu miao,* edited by Wang Keping, 1–11. Guangzhou: Huacheng chubanshe.

Zhou Nanjing. 1987. "Lishi shang Zhongguo he Yindunixiya de wenhua jiaoliu" (Historical cultural exchange between China and Indonesia). In *Zhongwai wenhua jiaoliu shi,* edited by Zhou Yiliang, 190–238. Zhengzhou: Henan renmin chubanshe.

———, ed. 1993. *Shijie Huaqiao Huaren cidian* (World dictionary of Overseas Chinese). Peking: Beijing daxue chubanshe.

———, ed. 2001. *Baren yu Yindunixiya* (Baren and Indonesia). Xianggang: Nandao chubanshe.

Zhou Ning. 2007. "Dongnanya Huayu xiju yanjiu: Wenti he lingyu" (Southeast Asian Chinese-language drama research: Issues and the field). *Xiju* 123:44–59.
Zhu Lin. "Huiyi Yafei huiyi" (Remembering the Asian-African Conference). 1985. *Waijiao xueyuan yuebao* 1:8–11.
Zimmer, Thomas. 2002. *Der chinesische Roman der ausgehenden Kaiserzeit* (The Chinese novel at the end of the Imperial Period). Munich: Saur.
Zoete, Beryl, de, and Walter Spies. 1938. *Dance and Drama in Bali*. London: Faber & Faber.

Newspapers and Magazines

Algemeen Indisch dagblad: De Preangerbode
Antara Kalbar
Bataviaasch Handelsblad
Bataviaasch Nieuwsblad
BeritAnda
Dagblad, Het: Uitgave van de Nederlandsche Dagbladpers te Batavia
Detik
Equator News
Flying Inkpot, The
Galamedia
Goulburn Evening Post
Guoji ribao
Haobao
Harian Analisa
Harian Indonesia
Indische Courant, De
IndoPos
InfoPublik
Jakarta Post, The
Java-bode
Jia Xiang
Jugang xingbao
Kabar Independen
Kal Bar Times
Kompas
Kompasiana
Lianhe wanbao
Lianhe zaobao
LIFE
Locomotief, De: Samarangsch handels- en advertentie-blad
New York Times, The
Nieuwe courant
Nieuwsblad voor Sumatra, Het
Nieuws van den Dag voor Nederlandsch-Indië, Het (= NDNI)
Pikiran Rakyat
Pontianak Post
Preangerbode, De

Qiandao ribao
Rakyat Kalbar
Shangbao Indonesia
Shenghuo bao
Shijie ribao
Soerabaijasch Handelsblad
Straits Times, The
SuakaOnline
Sumatra Post, De
Tempo
Xinbao
Yinhua ribao
Yinni Shangbao
Yinni Xingzhou ribao

Audiovisual Examples

Chapter 1:
Temple *gezaixi* in Palembang, 2016.
https://www.youtube.com/watch?v=lFORgMUNgqU

Chapter 2:
The *wayang gantung* puppets of Singkawang in 2007.
https://www.youtube.com/watch?v=sOwzto6uxTo&t=2s
A scene from *Sie Djin Kwie* by the *wayang potehi* group Fu He An in 2015.
https://www.youtube.com/watch?v=BI-iSHpGbeE

Chapter 4:
Teater Koma's 2004 revival of *Sampek Engtay*.
https://www.youtube.com/watch?v=tATqXmHtjTk
Sampek Engtay–themed *campursari*.
https://www.youtube.com/watch?v=wDrCWWUgS3Q

Chapter 5:
Sino-Sundanese *jaipong* by Pasundan Asih, 2012.
https://www.youtube.com/watch?v=cai8krGjvo0
Tan Deseng playing the *kacapi* at home in 2016.
https://www.youtube.com/watch?v=UFKBeRRCs5A
The Indonesian national anthem played by 100 *guzheng*, principally by Sino-Indonesians, in Jakarta, 2008. https://www.youtube.com/watch?v=O4IYSiFrIn4
Yensen dragon dance team, 2017. https://www.youtube.com/watch?v=qQ-CakjJFqo

Chapter 6:
Cap Go Meh procession in Bandung, 2016.
https://www.youtube.com/watch?v=UWFfg1xfDCo.
Cap Go Meh in Singkawang, 2017. https://www.youtube.com/watch?v=Kej1yrkS32k

INDEX

Page numbers in **boldface** type refer to figures and maps.

ABOUT THE AUTHOR

Josh Stenberg is a lecturer in the Department of Chinese Studies, School of Languages and Cultures, Faculty of Arts and Social Sciences, the University of Sydney. Educated at Harvard College, the University of British Columbia, and Nanjing University, he has published widely on Chinese performance and on Overseas Chinese communities, including articles in *Asian Theatre Journal, Theatre Journal, Theatre Research International, The Journal of Southeast Asian Studies, China Information, Nan Nü, Theatre Topics,* and *The Journal of Chinese Overseas.*